Memoirs of Extraordinary Popular Delusions

and the

Madness of Crowds.

Volume II

Charles MacKay

First published in 1852

Ockham Classics

contents

N'en déplaise à ces fous nommés sages de Grèce,
En ce monde il n'est point de parfaite sagesse;
Tous les hommes sont fous, et malgré tous leurs soîns
Ne diffèrent entre eux que du plus ou du moins.

Boileau.

Chapter 1.

The Crusades.

They heard, and up they sprang upon the wing
Innumerable. As when the potent rod
Of Amram's son, in Egypt's evil day,
Waved round the coast, up call'd a pitchy cloud
Of locusts, warping on the eastern wind
That o'er the realm of impious Pharaoh hung
Like night, and darken'd all the realm of Nile,
*So numberless were they. * * * ***
All in a moment through the gloom were seen
Ten thousand banners rise into the air,
With orient colours waving. With them rose
A forest huge of spears; and thronging helms
Appear'd, and serried shields, in thick array,
Of depth immeasurable.

Paradise Lost.

Every age has its peculiar folly; some scheme, project, or phanta-sy into which it plunges, spurred on either by the love of gain, the necessity of excitement, or the mere force of imitation. Failing in these, it has some madness, to which it is goaded by political or religious causes, or both combined. Every one of these causes influenced the Crusades, and conspired to render them the most extraordinary instance upon record of the extent to which popular enthusiasm can be carried. History in her solemn page informs us, that the Crusaders were but ignorant and savage men, that their motives were those of bigotry unmitigated, and that their pathway was one of blood and tears. Romance, on the other hand, dilates upon their piety and heroism, and portrays, in her most glowing and impassioned hues, their virtue and magnanimity, the imperishable honour they acquired for themselves, and the great services they rendered to Christianity. In the following pages we shall ransack the stores of both, to discover the true spirit that animated the motley multitude who took up arms in the service of the cross, leaving history to vouch for facts, but not disdaining the aid of contemporary poetry and romance, to throw light upon feelings, motives, and opinions.

In order to understand thoroughly the state of public feeling in Europe at the time when Peter the Hermit preached the holy war, it will be necessary to go back for many years anterior to that event. We must make acquaintance with the pilgrims of the eighth, ninth, and tenth centuries, and learn the tales they told of the dangers they had passed and the wonders they had seen. Pilgrimages to the Holy Land seem at first to have been undertaken by converted Jews, and by Christian devotees of lively imagination, pining with a natural curiosity to visit the scenes which of all others were most interesting in their eyes. The pious and the impious alike flocked to Jerusalem,—the one class to feast their sight on the scenes hallowed by the life and sufferings of their Lord, and the other, because it soon became a generally received opinion, that such a pilgrimage was sufficient to rub off the long score of sins, however atrocious. Another and very numerous class of pilgrims were the idle and roving, who visited Palestine then as the moderns visit Italy or Switzerland now, because it was the fashion, and because they might please their vanity by retailing, on their return, the adventures they had met with. But the really pious formed the great majority. Every year their numbers increased, until at last they became so numerous as to be called the "armies of the Lord." Full of enthusiasm, they set the dangers and difficulties of the way at defiance, and lingered with holy rapture on every scene described by the Evangelists. To them it was bliss indeed to drink the clear waters of the Jordan, or be baptised in the same stream where John had baptised the Saviour. They wandered with awe and pleasure in the purlieus of the Temple, on the solemn Mount of Olives, or the awful Calvary, where a God had bled for sinful men. To these pilgrims every object was precious. Relics were eagerly sought after; flagons of water from Jordan, or panniers of mould from the hill of the Crucifixion, were brought home, and sold at extravagant prices to churches and monasteries. More apocryphal relics, such as the wood of the true cross, the tears of the Virgin Mary, the hems of her garments, the toe-nails and hair of the Apostles—even the tents that Paul had helped to manufacture—were exhibited for sale by the knavish in Palestine, and brought back to Europe "with wondrous cost and care." A grove of a hundred oaks would not have furnished all the wood sold in little morsels as remnants of the true cross; and the tears of Mary, if collected together, would have filled a cistern.

For upwards of two hundred years the pilgrims met with no impediment in Palestine. The enlightened Haroun Al Reschid, and his more immediate successors, encouraged the stream which brought so much wealth into Syria, and treated the wayfarers with the utmost courtesy. The race of Fatemite caliphs, — who, although in other respects as tolerant, were more distressed for money, or more unscrupulous in obtaining it, than their predecessors of the house of Abbas, — imposed a tax of a bezant for each pilgrim that entered Jerusalem. This was a serious hardship upon the poorer sort, who had begged their weary way across Europe, and arrived at the bourne of all their hopes without a coin. A great outcry was immediately raised, but still the tax was rigorously levied. The pilgrims unable to pay were compelled to remain at the gate of the holy city until some rich devotee arriving with his train, paid the tax and let them in. Robert of Normandy, father of William the Conqueror, who, in common with many other nobles of the highest rank, undertook the pilgrimage, found on his arrival scores of pilgrims at the gate, anxiously expecting his coming to pay the tax for them. Upon no occasion was such a boon refused.

The sums drawn from this source were a mine of wealth to the Moslem governors of Palestine, imposed as the tax had been at a time when pilgrimages had become more numerous than ever. A strange idea had taken possession of the popular mind at the close of the tenth and commencement of the eleventh century. It was universally believed that the end of the world was at hand; that the thousand years of the Apocalypse were near completion, and that Jesus Christ would descend upon Jerusalem to judge mankind. All Christendom was in commotion. A panic terror seized upon the weak, the credulous, and the guilty, who in those days formed more than nineteen-twentieths of the population. Forsaking their homes, kindred, and occupation, they crowded to Jerusalem to await the coming of the Lord, lightened, as they imagined, of a load of sin by their weary pilgrimage. To increase the panic, the stars were observed to fall from heaven, earthquakes to shake the land, and violent hurricanes to blow down the forests. All these, and more especially the meteoric phenomena, were looked upon as the forerunners of the approaching judgments. Not a meteor shot athwart the horizon that did not fill a district with alarm, and send away to Jerusalem a score of pilgrims, with staff in hand and wallet on their back, praying as they went for the remission of their sins. Men, women, and even children, trudged in droves to the holy city, in expectation of the day when the heavens would open, and the Son of God descend in his glory. This extraordinary delusion, while it augmented the numbers, increased also the hardships of the pilgrims. Beggars became so numerous on all the highways between the west of Europe and Constantinople, that the monks, the great almsgivers upon these occasions, would have brought starvation within sight of their own doors, if they had not economised their resources, and left the devotees to shift for themselves as they could. Hundreds of them were glad to subsist upon the berries that ripened by the road, who, before this great flux, might have shared the bread and flesh of the monasteries. But this was not the greatest of their difficulties. On their arrival in Jerusalem they found that a sterner race had obtained possession of the Holy Land. The caliphs of Bagdad had been succeeded by the harsh Turks of the race of Seljook, who looked upon the pilgrims with contempt and aversion. The Turks of the eleventh century were more ferocious and less scrupulous than the Saracens of the tenth. They were annoyed at the immense number of pilgrims who overran the country, and still more so because they shewed no intention of quitting it. The hourly expectation of the last judgment kept them waiting; and the Turks, apprehensive of being at last driven from the soil by the swarms that were still arriving, heaped up difficulties in their way. Persecution of every kind awaited them. They were plundered, and beaten with stripes, and kept in suspense for months at the gates of Jerusalem, unable to pay the golden bezant that was to procure them admission.

When the first epidemic terror of the day of judgment began to subside, a few pilgrims ventured to return to Europe, their hearts big with indignation at the insults they had suffered. Every where as they passed they related to a sympathising auditory the wrongs of Christendom. Strange to say, even these recitals increased the mania for pilgrimage. The greater the dangers of the way, the fairer chance that sins of deep dye would be atoned for. Difficulty and suffering only heightened the merit, and fresh hordes issued from every town and village, to win favour in the sight of heaven by a visit to the holy sepulchre. Thus did things continue during the whole of the eleventh century.

The train that was to explode so fearfully was now laid, and there wanted but the hand to apply the torch. At last the man appeared upon the scene. Like all who have ever achieved so great an end, Peter the Hermit was exactly suited to the age; neither behind it nor in advance of it; but acute enough to penetrate its mystery ere it was discovered by any other. Enthusiastic, chivalrous, bigoted, and, if not insane, not far removed from insanity, he was the very prototype of the time. True enthusiasm is always persevering and always eloquent, and these two qualities were united in no common degree in the person of this extraordinary preacher. He was a monk of Amiens, and ere he assumed the hood had served as a soldier. He is represented as having been ill favoured and low in stature, but with an eye of surpassing brightness and intelligence. Having been seized with the mania of the age, he visited Jerusalem, and remained there till his blood boiled to see the cruel persecution heaped upon the devotees. On his return home he shook the world by the eloquent story of their wrongs.

Before entering into any further details of the marvellous results of his preaching, it will be advisable to cast a glance at the state of the mind of Europe, that we may understand all the better the causes of his success. First of all, there was the priesthood, which, exercising as it did the most conspicuous influence upon the fortunes of society, claims the largest share of attention. Religion was the ruling idea of that day, and the only civiliser capable of taming such wolves as then constituted the flock of the faithful.

The clergy were all in all; and though they kept the popular mind in the most slavish subjection with regard to religious matters, they furnished it with the means of defence against all other oppression except their own. In the ecclesiastical ranks were concentrated all the true piety, all the learning, all the wisdom of the time; and, as a natural consequence, a great portion of power, which their very wisdom perpetually incited them to extend. The people knew nothing of kings and nobles, except in the way of injuries inflicted. The first ruled for, or more properly speaking against, the barons, and the barons only existed to brave the power of the kings, or to trample with their iron heels upon the neck of prostrate democracy. The latter had no friend but the clergy, and these, though they necessarily instilled the superstition from which they themselves were not exempt, yet taught the cheering doctrine that all men were equal in the sight of heaven. Thus, while Feudalism told them they had no rights in this world, Religion told them they had every right in the next. With this consolation they were for the time content, for political ideas had as yet taken no root. When the clergy, for other reasons, recommended the Crusade, the people joined in it with enthusiasm. The subject of Palestine filled all minds; the pilgrims' tales of two centuries warmed every imagination; and when their friends, their guides, and their instructors preached a war so much in accordance with their own prejudices and modes of thinking, the enthusiasm rose into a frenzy.

But while religion inspired the masses, another agent was at work upon the nobility. These were fierce and lawless; tainted with every vice, endowed with no virtue, and redeemed by one good quality alone, that of courage. The only religion they felt was the religion of fear. That and their overboiling turbulence alike combined to guide them to the Holy Land. Most of them had sins enough to answer for. They lived with their hand against every man, and with no law but their own passions. They set at defiance the secular power of the clergy; but their hearts quailed at the awful denunciations of the pulpit with regard to the life to come. War was the business and the delight of their existence; and when they were promised remission of all their sins upon the easy condition of following their favourite bent, it is not to be wondered at that they rushed with enthusiasm to the onslaught, and became as zealous in the service of the cross as the great majority of the people, who were swayed by more purely religious motives. Fanaticism and the love of battle alike impelled them to the war, while the kings and princes of Europe had still another motive for encouraging their zeal. Policy opened their eyes to the great advantages which would accrue to themselves by the absence of so many restless, intriguing, and bloodthirsty men, whose insolence it required more than the small power of royalty to restrain within due bounds. Thus every motive was favourable to the Crusades. Every class of society was alike incited to join or encourage the war: kings and the clergy by policy, the nobles by turbulence and the love of dominion, and the people by religious zeal and the concentrated enthusiasm of two centuries, skilfully directed by their only instructors.

It was in Palestine itself that Peter the Hermit first conceived the grand idea of rousing the powers of Christendom to rescue the Christians of the East from the thraldom of the Mussulmans, and the sepulchre of Jesus from the rude hands of the infidel. The subject engrossed his whole mind. Even in the visions of the night he was full of it. One dream made such an impression upon him, that he devoutly believed the Saviour of the world himself appeared before him, and promised him aid and protection in his holy undertaking. If his zeal had ever wavered before, this was sufficient to fix it for ever.

Peter, after he had performed all the penances and duties of his pilgrimage, demanded an interview with Simeon, the Patriarch of the Greek Church at Jerusalem. Though the latter was a heretic in Peter's eyes, yet he was still a Christian, and felt as acutely as himself for the persecutions heaped by the Turks upon the followers of Jesus. The good prelate entered fully into his views, and, at his suggestion, wrote letters to the Pope, and to the most influential monarchs of Christendom, detailing the sorrows of the faithful, and urging them to take up arms in their defence. Peter was not a laggard in the work. Taking an affectionate farewell of the Patriarch, he returned in all haste to Italy. Pope Urban II. occupied the apostolic chair. It was at that time far from being an easy seat. His predecessor Gregory had bequeathed him a host of disputes with the Emperor Henry IV. of Germany, and he had converted Philip I. of France into an enemy by his strenuous opposition to an adulterous connexion formed by that monarch. So many dangers encompassed him, that the Vatican was no secure abode, and he had taken refuge in Apulia, under the protection of the renowned Robert Guiscard. Thither Peter appears to have followed him, though in what spot their meeting took place is not stated with any precision by ancient chroniclers or modern historians. Urban received him most kindly; read, with tears in his eyes, the epistle from the Patriarch Simeon, and listened to the eloquent story of the Hermit with an attention which shewed how deeply he sympathised with the woes of the Christian Church. Enthusiasm is contagious; and the Pope appears to have caught it instantly from one whose zeal was so unbounded. Giving the Hermit full powers, he sent him abroad to preach the holy war to all the nations and potentates of Christendom. The Hermit preached, and countless thousands answered to his call. France, Germany, and Italy started at his voice, and prepared for the deliverance of Zion. One of the early historians of the Crusade, who was himself an eye-witness of the rapture of Europe,[1] describes the personal appearance of the Hermit at this time. He says, that there appeared to be something of divine in every thing which he said or did. The people so highly reverenced him, that they plucked hairs from the mane of his mule that they might keep them as relics. While preaching, he wore in general a woollen tunic, with a dark-coloured mantle, which fell down to his heels. His arms and feet were bare; and he ate neither flesh nor bread, supporting himself chiefly upon fish and wine. "He set out," says the chronicler, "from whence I know not; but we saw him passing through the towns and villages, preaching every where, and the people surrounding him in crowds, loading him with offerings, and celebrating his sanctity with such great praises, that I never remember to have seen such honours bestowed upon any one." Thus he went on, untired, inflexible, and full of devotion, communicating his own madness to his hearers, until Europe was stirred from its very depths.

While the Hermit was appealing with such signal success to the people, the Pope appealed with as much success to those who were to become the chiefs and leaders of the expedition. His first step was to call a council at Placentia, in the autumn of the year 1095. Here, in the assembly of the clergy, the Pope debated the grand scheme, and gave audience to emissaries who had been sent from Constantinople by the Emperor of the East, to detail the progress made by the Turks in their design of establishing themselves in Europe. The clergy were of course unanimous in support of the Crusade; and the council separated, each individual member of it being empowered to preach it to his people.

But Italy could not be expected to furnish all the aid required; and the Pope crossed the Alps to inspire the fierce and powerful nobility and chivalrous population of Gaul. His boldness in entering the territory, and placing himself in the power of his foe, King Philip of France, is not the least surprising feature of his mission. Some have imagined that cool policy alone actuated him; while others assert that it was mere zeal, as warm and as blind as that of Peter the Hermit. The latter opinion seems to be the true one. Society did not calculate the consequences of what it was doing. Every man seemed to act from impulse only; and the Pope, in throwing himself into the heart of France, acted as much from impulse as the thousands who responded to his call. A council was eventually summoned to meet him at Clermont, in Auvergne, to consider the state of the Church, reform abuses, and, above all, make preparations for the war. It was in the midst of an extremely cold winter, and the ground was covered with snow. During seven days the council sat with closed doors, while immense crowds from all parts of France flocked into the town, in expectation that the Pope himself would address the people. All the towns and villages for miles around were filled with the multitude; even the fields were encumbered with people, who, unable to procure lodging, pitched their tents under the trees and by the way-side. All the neighbourhood presented the appearance of a vast camp.

The Cathedral of Clermont.

During the seven days' deliberation, a sentence of excommunication was passed upon King Philip for adultery with Bertrade de Montfort, Countess of Anjou, and for disobedience to the supreme authority of the apostolic see. This bold step impressed the people with reverence for so stern a Church, which in the discharge of its duty shewed itself no respecter of persons. Their love and their fear were alike increased, and they were prepared to listen with more intense devotion to the preaching of so righteous and inflexible a pastor. The great square before the cathedral church of Clermont became every instant more densely crowded as the hour drew nigh when the Pope was to address the populace. Issuing from the church in his full canonicals, surrounded by his cardinals and bishops in all the splendour of Romish ecclesiastical costume, the Pope stood before the populace on a high scaffolding erected for the occasion, and covered with scarlet cloth. A brilliant array of bishops and cardinals surrounded him; and among them, humbler in rank, but more important in the world's eye, the Hermit Peter, dressed in his simple and austere habiliments. Historians differ as to whether or not Peter addressed the crowd, but as all agree that he was present, it seems reasonable to suppose that he spoke. But it was the oration of the Pope that was most important. As he lifted up his hands to ensure attention, every voice immediately became still. He began by detailing the miseries endured by their brethren in the Holy Land; how the plains of Palestine were desolated by the outrageous heathen, who with the sword and the firebrand carried wailing into the dwellings and flames into the possessions of the faithful; how Christian wives and daughters were defiled by pagan lust; how the altars of the true God were desecrated, and the relics of the saints trodden under foot. "You," continued the eloquent pontiff (and Urban II. was one of the most eloquent men of the day), "you, who hear me, and who have received the true faith, and been endowed by God with power, and strength, and greatness of soul, — whose ancestors have been the prop of Christendom, and whose kings have put a barrier against the progress of the infidel, — I call upon you to wipe off these impurities from the face of the earth, and lift your oppressed fellow-Christians from the depths into which they have been trampled. The sepulchre of Christ is possessed by the heathen, the sacred places dishonoured by their vileness. Oh, brave knights and faithful people! offspring of invincible fathers! ye will not degenerate from your ancient renown. Ye will not be restrained from embarking in this great cause by the tender ties of wife or little ones, but will remember the words of the Saviour of the world himself, 'Whosoever loves father and mother more than me is not worthy of me. Whosoever shall abandon for my name's sake his house, or his brethren, or his sisters, or his father, or his mother, or his wife, or his children, or his lands, shall receive a hundredfold, and shall inherit eternal life.'"

The warmth of the Pontiff communicated itself to the crowd, and the enthusiasm of the people broke out several times ere he concluded his address. He went on to portray, not only the spiritual but the temporal advantages that would accrue to those who took up arms in the service of the cross. Palestine was, he said, a land flowing with milk and honey, and precious in the sight of God, as the scene of the grand events which had saved mankind. That land, he promised, should be divided among them. Moreover, they should have full pardon for all their offences, either against God or man. "Go, then," he added, "in expiation of your sins; and go assured, that after this world shall have passed away, imperishable glory shall be yours in the world which is to come." The enthusiasm was no longer to be restrained, and loud shouts interrupted the speaker; the people exclaiming as if with one voice, "*Dieu le veult! Dieu le veult!*" With great presence of mind Urban took advantage of the outburst, and as soon as silence was obtained, continued: "Dear brethren, to-day is shewn forth in you that which the Lord has said by his Evangelist, 'When two or three are gathered together in my name, there will I be in the midst of them to bless them.' If the Lord God had not been in your souls, you would not all have pronounced the same words; or rather God himself pronounced them by your lips, for it was he that put them in your hearts. Be they, then, your war-cry in the combat, for those words came forth from God. Let the army of the Lord, when it rushes upon his enemies, shout but that one cry, '*Dieu le veult! Dieu le veult!*' Let whoever is inclined to devote himself to this holy cause make it a solemn engagement, and bear the cross of the Lord either on his breast or his brow till he set out; and let him who is ready to begin his march place the holy emblem on his shoulders, in memory of that precept of our Saviour, 'He who does not take up his cross and follow me is not worthy of me.'"

The news of this council spread to the remotest parts of Europe in an incredibly short space of time. Long before the fleetest horseman could have brought the intelligence, it was known by the people in distant provinces; a fact which was considered as nothing less than supernatural. But the subject was in every body's mouth, and the minds of men were prepared for the result. The enthusiastic merely asserted what they wished, and the event tallied with their prediction. This was, however, quite enough in those days for a miracle, and as a miracle every one regarded it.

For several months after the Council of Clermont, France and Germany presented a singular spectacle. The pious, the fanatic, the needy, the dissolute, the young and the old, even women and children, and the halt and lame, enrolled themselves by hundreds. In every village the clergy were busied in keeping up the excitement, promising eternal rewards to those who assumed the red cross, and fulminating the most awful denunciations against all the worldly-minded who refused or even hesitated. Every debtor who joined the Crusade was freed by the papal edict from the claims of his creditors; outlaws of every grade were made equal with the honest upon the same conditions. The property of those who went was placed under the protection of the Church, and St. Paul and St. Peter themselves were believed to descend from their high abode, to watch over the chattels of the absent pilgrims. Signs and portents were seen in the air, to increase the fervour of the multitude. An aurora-borealis of unusual brilliancy appeared, and thousands of the Crusaders came out to gaze upon it, prostrating themselves upon the earth in adoration. It was thought to be a sure prognostic of the interposition of the Most High; and a representation of his armies fighting with and overthrowing the infidels. Reports of wonders were every where rife. A monk had seen two gigantic warriors on horseback, the one representing a Christian and the other a Turk, fighting in the sky with flaming swords, the Christian of course overcoming the Paynim. Myriads of stars were said to have fallen from heaven, each representing the fall of a Pagan foe. It was believed at the same time that the Emperor Charlemagne would rise from the grave, and lead on to victory the embattled armies of the Lord. A singular feature of the popular madness was the enthusiasm of the women. Every where they encouraged their lovers and husbands to forsake all things for the holy war. Many of them burned the sign of the cross upon their breasts and arms, and coloured the wound with a red dye, as a lasting memorial of their zeal. Others, still more zealous, impressed the mark by the same means upon the tender limbs of young children and infants at the breast.

Guibert de Nogent tells of a monk who made a large incision upon his forehead in the form of a cross, which he coloured with some powerful ingredient, telling the people that an angel had done it when he was asleep. This monk appears to have been more of a rogue than a fool, for he contrived to fare more sumptuously than any of his brother pilgrims, upon the strength of his sanctity. The Crusaders every where gave him presents of food and money, and he became quite fat ere he arrived at Jerusalem, notwithstanding the fatigues of the way. If he had acknowledged in the first place that he had made the wound himself, he would not have been thought more holy than his fellows; but the story of the angel was a clincher.

All those who had property of any description rushed to the mart to change it into hard cash. Lands and houses could be had for a quarter of their value, while arms and accoutrements of war rose in the same proportion. Corn, which had been excessively dear in anticipation of a year of scarcity, suddenly became plentiful; and such was the diminution in the value of provisions, that seven sheep were sold for five *deniers*.[2] The nobles mortgaged their estates for mere trifles to Jews and unbelievers, or conferred charters of immunity upon the towns and communes within their fiefs, for sums which, a few years previously, they would have rejected with disdain. The farmer endeavoured to sell his plough, and the artisan his tools, to purchase a sword for the deliverance of Jerusalem. Women disposed of their trinkets for the same purpose. During the spring and summer of this year (1096) the roads teemed with crusaders, all hastening to the towns and villages appointed as the rendezvous of the district. Some were on horseback, some in carts, and some came down the rivers in boats and rafts, bringing their wives and children, all eager to go to Jerusalem. Very few knew where Jerusalem was. Some thought it fifty thousand miles away, and others imagined that it was but a month's journey; while at sight of every town or castle the children exclaimed, "Is that Jerusalem? Is that the city?"[3] Parties of knights and nobles might be seen travelling eastward, and amusing themselves as they went with the knightly diversion of hawking, to lighten the fatigues of the way.

Guibert de Nogent, who did not write from hearsay, but from actual observation, says the enthusiasm was so contagious, that when any one heard the orders of the Pontiff, he went instantly to solicit his neighbours and friends to join with him in "the way of God," for so they called the proposed expedition. The Counts Palatine were full of the desire to undertake the journey, and all the inferior knights were animated with the same zeal. Even the poor caught the flame so ardently, that no one paused to think of the inadequacy of his means, or to consider whether he ought to yield up his farm, his vineyard, or his fields. Each one set about selling his property at as low a price as if he had been held in some horrible captivity, and sought to pay his ransom without loss of time. Those who had not determined upon the journey joked and laughed at those who were thus disposing of their goods at such ruinous prices, prophesying that the expedition would be miserable and their return worse. But they held this language only for a day; the next they were suddenly seized with the same frenzy as the rest. Those who had been loudest in their jeers gave up all their property for a few crowns, and set out with those they had so laughed at a few hours before. In most cases the laugh was turned against them; for when it became known that a man was hesitating, his more zealous neighbours sent him a present of a knitting-needle or a distaff, to shew their contempt of him. There was no resisting this; so that the fear of ridicule contributed its fair contingent to the armies of the Lord.

Another effect of the Crusade was, the religious obedience with which it inspired the people and the nobility for that singular institution "The Truce of God." At the commencement of the eleventh century, the clergy of France, sympathising for the woes of the people, but unable to diminish them, by repressing the rapacity and insolence of the feudal chiefs, endeavoured to promote universal good-will by the promulgation of the famous "Peace of God." All who conformed to it bound themselves by oath not to take revenge for any injury, not to enjoy the fruits of property usurped from others, nor to use deadly weapons; in reward of which they would receive remission of all their sins. However benevolent the intention of this "Peace," it led to nothing but perjury, and violence reigned as uncontrolled as before. In the year 1041, another attempt was made to soften the angry passions of the semi-barbarous chiefs, and the "Truce of God" was solemnly proclaimed. The *truce* lasted from the Wednesday evening to the Monday morning of every week, in which interval it was strictly forbidden to recur to violence on any pretext, or to seek revenge for any injury. It was impossible to civilise men by these means. Few even promised to become peaceable for so unconscionable a period as five days a-week; or if they did, they made ample amends on the two days left open to them. The truce was afterwards shortened from the Saturday evening to the Monday morning; but little or no diminution of violence and bloodshed was the consequence. At the Council of Clermont, Urban II. again solemnly proclaimed the truce. So strong was the religious feeling, that every one hastened to obey. All minor passions disappeared before the grand passion of crusading. The feudal chief ceased to oppress, the robber to plunder, the people to complain; but one idea was in all hearts, and there seemed to be no room for any other.

The encampments of these heterogeneous multitudes offered a singular aspect. Those vassals who ranged themselves under the banners of their lord erected tents around his castle; while those who undertook the war on their own account constructed booths and huts in the neighbourhood of the towns or villages, preparatory to their joining some popular leader of the expedition. The meadows of France were covered with tents. As the belligerents were to have remission of all their sins on their arrival in Palestine, hundreds of them gave themselves up to the most unbounded licentiousness. The courtesan, with the red cross upon her shoulders, plied her shameless trade with sensual pilgrims without scruple on either side; the lover of good cheer gave loose rein to his appetite, and drunkenness and debauchery flourished. Their zeal in the service of the Lord was to wipe out all faults and follies, and they had the same surety of salvation as the rigid anchorite. This reasoning had charms for the ignorant, and the sounds of lewd revelry and the voice of prayer rose at the same instant from the camp.

It is now time to speak of the leaders of the expedition. Great multitudes ranged themselves under the command of Peter the Hermit, whom, as the originator, they considered the most appropriate leader of the war. Others joined the banner of a bold adventurer, whom history has dignified with no other name than that of Gautier sans Avoir, or Walter the Pennyless, but who is represented as having been of noble family, and well skilled in the art of war. A third multitude from Germany flocked around the standard of a monk named Gottschalk, of whom nothing is known except that he was a fanatic of the deepest dye. All these bands, which together are said to have amounted to three hundred thousand men, women, and children, were composed of the vilest rascality of Europe. Without discipline, principle, or true courage, they rushed through the nations like a pestilence, spreading terror and death wherever they went. The first multitude that set forth was led by Walter the Pennyless early in the spring of 1096, within a very few months after the Council of Clermont. Each man of that irregular host aspired to be his own master. Like their nominal leader, each was poor to penury, and trusted for subsistence on his journey to the chances of the road. Rolling through Germany like a tide, they entered Hungary, where, at first, they were received with some degree of kindness by the people. The latter had not yet caught sufficient of the fire of enthusiasm to join the Crusade themselves, but were willing enough to forward the cause by aiding those embarked in it. Unfortunately this good understanding did not last long. The swarm were not contented with food for their necessities, but craved for luxuries also. They attacked and plundered the dwellings of the country people, and thought nothing of murder where resistance was offered. On their arrival before Semlin, the outraged Hungarians collected in large numbers, and, attacking the rear of the crusading host, slew a great many of the strag-glers, and, taking away their arms and crosses, affixed them as trophies to the walls of the city. Walter appears to have been in no mood or condition to make reprisals; for his army, destructive as a plague of locusts when plunder urged them on, were useless against any regular attack from a determined enemy. Their rear continued to be thus harassed by the wrathful Hungarians until they were fairly out of their territory. On his entrance into Bulgaria, Walter met with no better fate. The cities and towns refused to let him pass; the villages denied him provisions; and the citizens and country people uniting, slaughtered his followers by hundreds. The progress of the army was more like a retreat than an advance; but as it was impossible to stand still, Walter continued his course till he arrived at Constantinople with a force which famine and the sword had diminished to one-third of its original number.

The greater multitude, led by the enthusiastic Hermit, followed close upon his heels, with a bulky train of baggage, and women and children sufficient to form a host of themselves. If it were possible to find a rabble more vile than the army of Walter the Pennyless, it was that led by Peter the Hermit. Being better provided with means, they were not reduced to the necessity of pillage in their progress through Hungary; and had they taken any other route than that which led through Semlin, might perhaps have traversed the country without molestation. On their arrival before that city, their fury was raised at seeing the arms and red crosses of their predecessors hanging as trophies over the gates. Their pent-up ferocity exploded at the sight. The city was tumultuously attacked, and the besiegers entering, not by dint of bravery, but of superior numbers, it was given up to all the horrors which follow when victory, brutality, and licentiousness are linked together. Every evil passion was allowed to revel with impunity, and revenge, lust, and avarice, — each had its hundreds of victims in unhappy Semlin. Any maniac can kindle a conflagration, but it may require many wise men to put it out. Peter the Hermit had blown the popular fury into a flame, but to cool it again was beyond his power. His followers rioted unrestrained, until the fear of retaliation warned them to desist. When the king of Hungary was informed of the disasters of Semlin, he marched with a sufficient force to chastise the Hermit, who, at the news, broke up his camp and retreated towards the Morava, a broad and rapid stream that joins the Danube a few miles to the eastward of Belgrade. Here a party of indignant Bulgarians awaited him, and so harassed him, as to make the passage of the river a task both of difficulty and danger. Great numbers of his infatuated followers perished in the waters, and many fell under the swords of the Bulgarians. The ancient chronicles do not mention the amount of the Hermit's loss at this passage, but represent it in general terms as very great.

At Nissa, the Duke of Bulgaria fortified himself, in fear of an assault; but Peter, having learned a little wisdom from experience, thought it best to avoid hostilities. He passed three nights in quietness under the walls, and the duke, not wishing to exasperate unnecessarily so fierce and rapacious a host, allowed the townspeople to supply them with provisions. Peter took his departure peaceably on the following morning; but some German vagabonds, falling behind the main body of the army, set fire to the mills and house of a Bulgarian, with whom, it appears, they had had some dispute on the previous evening. The citizens of Nissa, who had throughout mistrusted the Crusaders, and were prepared for the worst, sallied out immediately, and took signal vengeance. The spoilers were cut to pieces, and the townspeople pursuing the Hermit, captured all the women and children who had lagged in the rear, and a great quantity of baggage. Peter hereupon turned round and marched back to Nissa, to demand explanation of the Duke of Bulgaria. The latter fairly stated the provocation given, and the Hermit could urge nothing in palliation of so gross an outrage. A negotiation was entered into, which promised to be successful, and the Bulgarians were about to deliver up the women and children, when a party of undisciplined Crusaders, acting solely upon their own suggestion, endeavoured to scale the walls and seize upon the town. Peter in vain exerted his authority; the confusion became general, and after a short but desperate battle, the Crusaders threw down their arms, and fled in all directions. Their vast host was completely routed, the slaughter being so great among them, as to be counted, not by hundreds, but by thousands.

It is said that the Hermit fled from this fatal field to a forest a few miles from Nissa, abandoned by every human creature. It would be curious to know whether, after so dire a reverse,

"His enpierced breast
Sharp sorrow did in thousand pieces rive,"

or whether his fiery zeal still rose superior to calamity, and pictured the eventual triumph of his cause. He, so lately the leader of a hundred thousand men, was now a solitary skulker in the forests, liable at every instant to be discovered by some pursuing Bulgarian, and cut off in mid career. Chance at last brought him within sight of an eminence, where two or three of his bravest knights had collected five hundred of the stragglers. These gladly received the Hermit, and a consultation having taken place, it was resolved to gather together the scattered remnants of the army. Fires were lighted on the hill, and scouts sent out in all directions for the fugitives. Horns were sounded at intervals, to make known that friends were near, and before nightfall the Hermit saw himself at the head of seven thousand men. During the succeeding day, he was joined by twenty thousand more, and with this miserable remnant of his force, he pursued his route towards Constantinople. The bones of the rest mouldered in the forests of Bulgaria.

On his arrival at Constantinople, where he found Walter the Pennyless awaiting him, he was hospitably received by the Emperor Alexius. It might have been expected that the sad reverses they had undergone would have taught his followers common prudence; but, unhappily for them, their turbulence and love of plunder was not to be restrained. Although they were surrounded by friends, by whom all their wants were liberally supplied, they could not refrain from rapine. In vain the Hermit exhorted them to tranquillity; he possessed no more power over them, in subduing their passions, than the obscurest soldier of the host. They set fire to several public buildings in Constantinople out of pure mischief, and stripped the lead from the roofs of the churches, which they afterwards sold for old metal in the purlieus of the city. From this time may be dated the aversion which the Emperor Alexius entertained for the Crusaders, and which was afterwards manifested in all his actions, even when he had to deal with the chivalrous and more honourable armies which arrived after the Hermit. He seems to have imagined that the Turks themselves were enemies less formidable to his power than these outpourings of the refuse of Europe: he soon found a pretext to hurry them into Asia Minor. Peter crossed the Bosphorus with Walter, but the excesses of his followers were such, that, despairing of accomplishing any good end by remaining at their head, he left them to themselves, and returned to Constantinople, on the pretext of making arrangements with the government of Alexius for a proper supply of provisions. The Crusaders, forgetting that they were in the enemy's country, and that union, above all things, was desirable, gave themselves up to dissensions. Violent disputes arose between the Lombards and Normans commanded by Walter the Pennyless, and the Franks and Germans led out by Peter. The latter separated themselves from the former, and, choosing for their leader one Reinaldo, or Reinhold, marched forward, and took possession of the fortress of Exorogorgon. The Sultan Solimaun was on the alert, with a superior force. A party of Crusaders, which had been detached from the fort, and stationed at a little distance as an ambuscade, were surprised and cut to pieces, and Exorogorgon invested on all sides. The siege was protracted for eight days, during which the Christians suffered the most acute agony from the want of water. It is hard to say how long the hope of succour or the energy of despair would have enabled them to hold out: their treacherous leader cut the matter short by renouncing the Christian faith, and delivering up the fort into the hands of the sultan. He was followed by two or three of his officers; all the rest, refusing to become Mahometans, were ruthlessly put to the sword. Thus perished the last wretched remnant of the vast multitude which had traversed Europe with Peter the Hermit.

Walter the Pennyless and his multitude met as miserable a fate. On the news of the disasters of Exorogorgon, they demanded to be led instantly against the Turks. Walter, who only wanted good soldiers to have made a good general, was cooler of head, and saw all the dangers of such a step. His force was wholly insufficient to make any decisive movement in a country where the enemy was so much superior, and where, in case of defeat, he had no secure position to fall back upon; and he therefore expressed his opinion against advancing until the arrival of reinforcements. This prudent counsel found no favour: the army loudly expressed their dissatisfaction at their chief, and prepared to march forward without him. Upon this, the brave Walter put himself at their head, and rushed to destruction. Proceeding towards Nice, the modern Isnik, he was intercepted by the army of the sultan: a fierce battle ensued, in which the Turks made fearful havoc; out of twenty-five thousand Christians, twenty-two thousand were slain, and among them Gautier himself, who fell pierced by seven mortal wounds. The remaining three thousand retreated upon Civitot, where they entrenched themselves.

Isnik.

Disgusted as was Peter the Hermit at the excesses of the multitude, who, at his call, had forsaken Europe, his heart was moved with grief and pity at their misfortunes. All his former zeal revived: casting himself at the feet of the Emperor Alexius, he implored him, with tears in his eyes, to send relief to the few survivors at Civitot. The emperor consented, and a force was sent, which arrived just in time to save them from destruction. The Turks had beleaguered the place, and the Crusaders were reduced to the last extremity. Negotiations were entered into, and the last three thousand were conducted in safety to Constantinople. Alexius had suffered too much by their former excesses to be very desirous of retaining them in his capital: he therefore caused them all to be disarmed, and, furnishing each with a sum of money, he sent them back to their own country.

While these events were taking place, fresh hordes were issuing from the woods and wilds of Germany, all bent for the Holy Land. They were commanded by a fanatical priest, named Gottschalk, who, like Gautier and Peter the Hermit, took his way through Hungary. History is extremely meagre in her details of the conduct and fate of this host, which amounted to at least one hundred thousand men. Robbery and murder seem to have journeyed with them, and the poor Hungarians were rendered almost desperate by their numbers and rapacity. Karloman, the king of the country, made a bold effort to get rid of them; for the resentment of his people had arrived at such a height, that nothing short of the total extermination of the Crusaders would satisfy them. Gottschalk had to pay the penalty, not only for the ravages of his own bands, but for those of the swarms that had come before him. He and his army were induced, by some means or other, to lay down their arms: the savage Hungarians, seeing them thus defenceless, set upon them, and slaughtered them in great numbers. How many escaped their arrows we are not informed; but not one of them reached Palestine.

Other swarms, under nameless leaders, issued from Germany and France, more brutal and more frantic than any that had preceded them. Their fanaticism surpassed by far the wildest freaks of the followers of the Hermit. In bands, varying in numbers from one to five thousand, they traversed the country in all directions, bent upon plunder and massacre. They wore the symbol of the Crusade upon their shoulders, but inveighed against the folly of proceeding to the Holy Land to destroy the

Turks, while they left behind them so many Jews, the still more inveterate enemies of Christ. They swore fierce vengeance against this unhappy race, and murdered all the Hebrews they could lay their hands on, first subjecting them to the most horrible mutilation. According to the testimony of Albert Aquensis, they lived among each other in the most shameless profligacy, and their vice was only exceeded by their superstition. Whenever they were in search of Jews, they were preceded by a goose and goat, which they believed to be holy, and animated with divine power to discover the retreats of the unbelievers. In Germany alone they slaughtered more than a thousand Jews, notwithstanding all the efforts of the clergy to save them. So dreadful was the cruelty of their tormentors, that great numbers of Jews committed self-destruction to avoid falling into their hands.

Again it fell to the lot of the Hungarians to deliver Europe from these pests. When there were no more Jews to murder, the bands collected in one body, and took the old route to the Holy Land, a route stained with the blood of three hundred thousand who had gone before, and destined also to receive theirs. The number of these swarms has never been stated; but so many of them perished in Hungary, that contemporary writers, despairing of giving any adequate idea of their multitudes, state that the fields were actually heaped with their corpses, and that for miles in its course the waters of the Danube were dyed with their blood. It was at Mersburg, on the Danube, that the greatest slaughter took place,—a slaughter so great as to amount almost to extermination. The Hungarians for a while disputed the passage of the river, but the Crusaders forced their way across, and attacking the city with the blind courage of madness, succeeded in making a breach in the walls. At this moment of victory an unaccountable fear came over them. Throwing down their arms, they fled panic-stricken, no one knew why, and no one knew whither. The Hungarians followed, sword in hand, and cut them down without remorse, and in such numbers, that the stream of the Danube is said to have been choked up by their unburied bodies.

This was the worst paroxysm of the madness of Europe; and this passed, her chivalry stepped upon the scene. Men of cool heads, mature plans, and invincible courage stood forward to lead and direct the grand movement of Europe upon Asia. It is upon these men that romance has lavished her most admiring epithets, leaving to the condemnation of history the vileness and brutality of those who went before. Of these leaders the most distinguished were Godfrey of Bouillon duke of Lorraine, and Raymond count of Toulouse. Four other chiefs of the royal blood of Europe also assumed the cross, and led each his army to the Holy Land; Hugh count of Vermandois, brother of the king of France; Robert duke of Normandy, the elder brother of William Rufus; Robert count of Flanders, and Bohemund prince of Tarentum, eldest son of the celebrated Robert Guiscard. These men were all tinged with the fanaticism of the age, but none of them acted entirely from religious motives. They were neither utterly reckless like Gautier sans Avoir, crazy like Peter the Hermit, nor brutal like Gottschalk the Monk, but possessed each of these qualities in a milder form; their valour being tempered by caution, their religious zeal by worldly views, and their ferocity by the spirit of chivalry. They saw whither led the torrent of the public will; and it being neither their wish nor their interest to stem it, they allowed themselves to be carried with it, in the hope that it would lead them at last to a haven of aggrandisement. Around them congregated many minor chiefs, the flower of the nobility of France and Italy, with some few from Germany, England, and Spain. It was wisely conjectured that armies so numerous would find a difficulty in procuring provisions if they all journeyed by the same road. They therefore resolved to separate; Godfrey de Bouillon proceeding through Hungary and Bulgaria, the Count of Toulouse through Lombardy and Dalmatia, and the other leaders through Apulia to Constantinople, where the several divisions were to reunite. The forces under these leaders have been variously estimated. The Princess Anna Comnena talks of them as having been as numerous as the sands on the sea-shore, or the stars in the firmament. Fulcher of Chartres is more satisfactory, and exaggerates less magnificently, when he states, that all the divisions, when they had sat down before Nice in Bithynia, amounted to one hundred thousand horsemen, and six hundred thousand men on foot, exclusive of the priests, women, and children. Gibbon is of opinion that this amount is exaggerated; but thinks the actual numbers did not fall very far short of the calculation. The Princess Anna afterwards gives the number of those under Godfrey of Bouillon as eighty thousand foot and horse; and supposing that each of the other chiefs led an army as numerous, the total would be near half a million. This must be over rather than under the mark, as the army of Godfrey of Bouillon was confessedly the largest when it set out, and suffered less by the way than any other.

Godfrey de Bouillon.

The Count of Vermandois was the first who set foot on the Grecian territory. On his arrival at Durazzo he was received with every mark of respect and courtesy by the agents of the emperor, and his followers were abundantly supplied with provisions. Suddenly, however, and without cause assigned, the count was arrested by order of the Emperor Alexius, and conveyed a close prisoner to Constantinople. Various motives have been assigned by different authors as having induced the emperor to this treacherous and imprudent proceeding. By every writer he has been condemned for so flagrant a breach of hospitality and justice. The most probable reason for his conduct appears to be that suggested by Guibert of Nogent, who states that Alexius, fearful of the designs of the Crusaders upon his throne, resorted to this extremity in order afterwards to force the count to take the oath of allegiance to him, as the price of his liberation. The example of a prince so eminent as the brother of the king of France, would, he thought, be readily followed by the other chiefs of the Crusade. In the result he was wofully disappointed, as every man deserves to be who commits positive evil that doubtful good may ensue. But this line of policy accorded well enough with the narrowmindedness of the emperor, who, in the enervating atmosphere of his highly civilised and luxurious court, dreaded the influx of the hardy and ambitious warriors of the West, and strove to nibble away by unworthy means the power which he had not energy enough to confront. If danger to himself had existed from the residence of the chiefs in his dominions, he might easily have averted it, by the simple means of placing himself at the head of the European movement, and directing its energies to their avowed object, the conquest of the Holy Land. But the emperor, instead of being, as he might have been, the lord and leader of the Crusades, which he had himself aided in no inconsiderable degree to suscitate by his embassies to the Pope, became the slave of men who hated and despised him. No doubt the barbarous excesses of the followers of Gautier and Peter the Hermit made him look upon the whole body of them with disgust, but it was the disgust of a little mind, which is glad of any excuse to palliate or justify its own irresolution and love of ease.

Godfrey of Bouillon traversed Hungary in the most quiet and orderly manner. On his arrival at Mersburg he found the country strewed with the mangled corpses of the Jew-killers, and demanded of the king of Hungary for what reason his people had set upon them. The latter detailed the atrocities they had committed, and made it so evident to Godfrey that the Hungarians had only acted in self-defence, that the high-minded leader declared himself satisfied, and passed on without giving or receiving molestation. On his arrival at Philippopoli he was informed for the first time of the imprisonment of the count of Vermandois. He immediately sent messengers to the emperor, demanding the count's release, and threatening, in case of refusal, to lay waste the country with fire and sword. After waiting a day at Philippopoli, he marched on to Adrianople, where he was met by his messengers returning with the emperor's refusal. Godfrey, the bravest and most determined of the leaders of the Crusade, was not a man to swerve from his word, and the country was given up to pillage. Alexius here committed another blunder. No sooner did he learn from dire experience that the Crusader was not an utterer of idle threats, than he consented to the release of the prisoner. As he had been unjust in the first instance, he became cowardly in the second, and taught his enemies (for so the Crusaders were forced to consider themselves) a lesson which they took care to remember to his cost, that they could hope nothing from his sense of justice, but every thing from his fears. Godfrey remained encamped for several weeks in the neighbourhood of Constantinople, to the great annoyance of Alexius, who sought by every means to extort from him the homage he had extorted from Vermandois. Sometimes he acted as if at open and declared war with the Crusaders, and sent his troops against them. Sometimes he refused to supply them with food, and ordered the markets to be shut against them, while at other times he was all for peace and good-will, and sent costly presents to Godfrey. The honest, straightforward Crusader was at last so wearied by his false kindness, and so pestered by his attacks, that, allowing his indignation to get the better of his judgment, he gave up the country around Constantinople to be plundered by his soldiers. For six days the flames of the farm-houses around struck terror into the heart of Alexius; but, as Godfrey anticipated, they convinced him of his error. Fearing that Constantinople itself would be the next object of attack, he sent messengers to demand an interview with Godfrey, offering at the same time to leave his son as a hostage for his good faith. Godfrey agreed to meet him; and, whether to put an end to these useless dissensions, or for some other unexplained reason, he rendered homage to Alexius as his liege lord. He was thereupon loaded with honours, and, according to a singular custom of that age, underwent the ceremony of the "adoption of honour" as son to the emperor. Godfrey and his brother Baudouin de Bouillon conducted themselves with proper courtesy on this occasion, but were not able to restrain the insolence of their followers, who did not conceive themselves bound to keep any terms with a man so insincere as he had shewn himself. One barbarous chieftain, Count Robert of Paris, carried his insolence so far as to seat himself upon the throne; an insult which Alexius merely resented with a sneer, but which did not induce him to look with less mistrust upon the hordes that were still advancing. It is impossible, notwithstanding his treachery, to avoid feeling some compassion for the emperor, whose life at this time was rendered one long scene of misery by the presumption of the Crusaders, and his not altogether groundless fears of the evil they might inflict upon him, should any untoward circumstance force the current of their ambition to the conquest of his empire. His daughter Anna Comnena feelingly deplores his state of life at this time, and a learned German[4], in a recent work, describes it, on the authority of the princess, in the following manner:

"To avoid all occasion of offence to the Crusaders, Alexius complied with all their whims and their (on many occasions) unreasonable demands, even at the expense of great bodily exertion, at a time when he was suffering severely under the gout, which eventually brought him to his grave. No Crusader who desired an interview with him was refused access; he listened with the utmost patience to the long-winded harangues which their loquacity or zeal continually wearied him with; he endured, without expressing any impatience, the unbecoming and haughty language which they permitted themselves to employ towards him, and severely reprimanded his officers when they undertook to defend the dignity of the imperial station from these rude assaults, for he trembled with apprehension at the slightest disputes, lest they might become the occasion of greater evil. Though the counts often appeared before him with trains altogether unsuitable to their dignity and to his – sometimes with an entire troop, which completely filled the royal

apartment – the emperor held his peace. He listened to them at all hours; he often seated himself on his throne at day-break to attend to their wishes and requests, and the evening twilight saw him still in the same place. Very frequently he could not snatch time to refresh himself with meat and drink. During many nights he could not obtain any repose, and was obliged to indulge in an unrefreshing sleep upon his throne, with his head resting on his hands. Even this slumber was continually disturbed by the appearance and harangues of some newly-arrived rude knights. When all the courtiers, wearied out by the efforts of the day and by night-watching, could no longer keep themselves on their feet, and sank down exhausted – some upon benches and others on the floor – Alexius still rallied his strength to listen with seeming attention to the wearisome chatter of the Latins, that they might have no occasion or pretext for discontent. In such a state of fear and anxiety, how could Alexius comport himself with dignity and like an emperor?"

Alexius, however, had himself to blame, in a great measure, for the indignities he suffered: owing to his insincerity, the Crusaders mistrusted him so much, that it became at last a common saying, that the Turks and Saracens were not such inveterate foes to the Western or Latin Christians as the Emperor Alexius and the Greeks[5]. It would be needless in this sketch, which does not profess to be so much a history of the Crusades, as of the madness of Europe, from which they sprang, to detail the various acts of bribery and intimidation, cajolery and hostility, by which Alexius contrived to make each of the leaders in succession, as they arrived, take the oath of allegiance to him as their suzerain. One way or another he exacted from each the barren homage on which he had set his heart, and they were then allowed to proceed into Asia Minor. One only, Raymond de St. Gilles count of Toulouse, obstinately refused the homage.

Their residence in Constantinople was productive of no good to the armies of the cross. Bickerings and contentions on the one hand, and the influence of a depraved and luxurious court on the other, destroyed the elasticity of their spirits, and cooled the first ardour of their enthusiasm. At one time the army of the Count of Toulouse was on the point of disbanding itself; and, had not their leader energetically removed them across the Bosphorus, this would have been the result. Once in Asia, their spirits in some degree revived, and the presence of danger and difficulty nerved them to the work they had undertaken. The first operation of the war was the siege of Nice, to gain possession of which all their efforts were directed.

Godfrey of Bouillon and the Count of Vermandois were joined under its walls by each host in succession as it left Constantinople. Among the celebrated Crusaders who fought at this siege we find, besides the leaders already mentioned, the brave and generous Tancred, whose name and fame have been immortalised in the *Gerusalemme Liberata*, the valorous Bishop of Puy, Baldwin, afterwards king of Jerusalem, and Peter the Hermit, now an almost solitary soldier, shorn of all the power and influence he had formerly possessed. Kilij Aslaun the sultan of Roum and chief of the Seljukian Turks, whose deeds, surrounded by the false halo of romance, are familiar to the readers of Tasso, under the name of Soliman, marched to defend this city, but was defeated after several obstinate engagements, in which the Christians shewed a degree of heroism that quite astonished him. The Turkish chief had expected to find a wild undisciplined multitude, like that under Peter the Hermit, without leaders capable of enforcing obedience; instead of which, he found the most experienced leaders of the age at the head of armies that had just fanaticism enough to be ferocious, but not enough to render them ungovernable. In these engagements, many hundreds fell on both sides; and on both sides the most revolting barbarity was practised: the Crusaders cut off the heads of the fallen Mussulmans, and sent them in panniers to Constantinople, as trophies of their victory. After the temporary defeat of Kilij Aslaun, the siege of Nice was carried on with redoubled vigour. The Turks defended themselves with the greatest obstinacy, and discharged showers of poisoned arrows upon the Crusaders. When any unfortunate wretch was killed under the walls, they let down iron hooks from above, and drew the body up, which, after stripping and mutilating, they threw back again at the besiegers. The latter were well supplied with provisions, and for six-and-thirty days the siege continued without any relaxation of the efforts on either side. Many tales are told of the almost superhuman heroism of the Christian leaders — how one man put a thousand to flight; and how the arrows of the faithful never missed their mark. One anecdote of Godfrey of Bouillon, related by Albert of Aix, is worth recording, not only as shewing the high opinion entertained of his valour, but as shewing the contagious credulity of the armies — a credulity which as often led them to the very verge of defeat, as it incited them to victory. One Turk, of gigantic stature, took his station day by day on the battlements of Nice, and, bearing an enormous bow, committed great havoc among the Christian host. Not a shaft he sped but bore death upon its point; and although the Crusaders aimed repeatedly at his breast, and he stood in the most exposed position, their arrows fell harmless at his feet. He seemed to be invulnerable to attack; and a report was soon spread abroad, that he was no other than the Arch Fiend himself, and that mortal hand could not prevail against him. Godfrey of Bouillon, who had no faith in the supernatural character of the Mussulman, determined, if possible, to put an end to the dismay which was rapidly paralysing the exertions of his best soldiers. Taking a huge cross-bow, he stood forward in front of the army, to try the steadiness of his hand against the much-dreaded archer: the shaft was aimed directly at his heart, and took fatal effect. The Moslem fell amid the groans of the besieged, and the shouts of *Deus adjuva! Deus adjuva!* the war-cry of the besiegers.

At last the Crusaders imagined that they had overcome all obstacles, and were preparing to take possession of the city, when, to their great astonishment, they saw the flag of the Emperor Alexius flying from the battlements. An emissary of the emperor, named Faticius or Tatin, had contrived to gain admission, with a body of Greek troops, at a point which the Crusaders had left unprotected, and had persuaded the Turks to surrender to him rather than to the crusading forces. The greatest indignation prevailed in the army when this stratagem was discovered, and the soldiers were, with the utmost difficulty, prevented from renewing the attack and besieging the Greek emissary.

The army, however, continued its march, and, by some means or other, was broken into two divisions; some historians say accidentally,[6] while others affirm by mutual consent, and for the convenience of obtaining provisions on the way.[7] The one division was composed of the forces under Bohemund, Tancred, and the Duke of Normandy; while the other, which took a route at some distance on the right, was commanded by Godfrey of Bouillon and the other chiefs. The Sultan of Roum, who, after his losses at Nice, had been silently making great efforts to crush the Crusaders at one blow, collected in a very short time all the multitudinous tribes that owed him allegiance, and with an army which, according to a moderate calculation, amounted to two hundred thousand men, chiefly cavalry, he fell upon the first division of the Christian host in the valley of Dorylæum. It was early in the morning of the 1st of July 1097, when the Crusaders saw the first companies of the Turkish horsemen pouring down upon them from the hills. Bohemund had hardly time to set himself in order, and transport his sick and helpless to the rear, when the overwhelming force of the Orientals was upon him. The Christian army, composed principally of men on foot, gave way on all sides, and the hoofs of the Turkish steeds, and the poisoned arrows of their bowmen, mowed them down by hundreds. After having lost the flower of their chivalry, the Christians retreated upon their baggage, when a dreadful slaughter took place. Neither women nor children, nor the sick, were spared. Just as they were reduced to the last extremity, Godfrey of Bouillon and the Count of Toulouse made their appearance on the field, and turned the tide of battle. After an obstinate engagement the Turks fled, and their rich camp fell into the hands of the enemy. The loss of the Crusaders amounted to about four thousand men, with several chiefs of renown, among whom were Count Robert of Paris and William the brother of Tancred. The loss of the Turks, which did not exceed this number, taught them to pursue a different mode of warfare. The sultan was far from being defeated. With his still gigantic army, he laid waste all the country on either side of the Crusaders. The latter, who were unaware of the tactics of the enemy, found plenty of provisions in the Turkish camp; but so far from economising these resources, they gave themselves up for several days to the most unbounded extravagance. They soon paid dearly for their heedlessness. In the ravaged country of Phrygia, through which they advanced towards Antiochetta, they suffered dreadfully for want of food for themselves and pasture for their cattle. Above them was a scorching sun, almost sufficient of itself to dry up the freshness of the land, a task which the firebrands of the sultan had but too surely effected, and water was not to be had after the first day of their march. The pilgrims died at the rate of five hundred a day. The horses of the knights perished on the road, and the baggage which they had aided to transport was either placed upon dogs, sheep, and swine, or abandoned altogether. In some of the calamities that afterwards befell them, the Christians gave themselves up to the most reckless profligacy; but upon this occasion, the dissensions which prosperity had engendered were all forgotten. Religion, often disregarded, arose in the stern presence of misfortune, and cheered them as they died by the promises of eternal felicity.

At length they reached Antiochetta, where they found water in abundance, and pastures for their expiring cattle. Plenty once more surrounded them, and here they pitched their tents. Untaught by the bitter experience of famine, they again gave themselves up to luxury and waste.

On the 18th of October they sat down before the strong city of Antioch, the siege of which, and the events to which it gave rise, are among the most extraordinary incidents of the Crusade. The city, which is situated on an eminence, and washed by the river Orontes, is naturally a very strong position, and the Turkish garrison were well supplied with provisions to endure a long siege. In this respect the Christians were also fortunate, but unluckily for themselves, unwise. Their force amounted to three hundred thousand fighting men; and we are informed by Raymond d'Argilles, that they had so much provision, that they threw away the greater part of every animal they killed, being so dainty, that they would only eat particular parts of the beast. So insane was their extravagance, that in less than ten days famine began to stare them in the face. After making a fruitless attempt to gain possession of the city by a *coup de main*, they, starving themselves, sat down to starve out the enemy. But with want came a cooling of enthusiasm. The chiefs began to grow weary of the expedition. Baldwin had previously detached himself from the main body of the army, and, proceeding to Edessa, had intrigued himself into the supreme power in that little principality. The other leaders were animated with less zeal than heretofore. Stephen of Chartres and Hugh of Vermandois began to waver, unable to endure the privations which their own folly and profusion had brought upon them. Even Peter the Hermit became sick at heart ere all was over. When the famine had become so urgent that they were reduced to eat human flesh in the extremity of their hunger, Bohemund and Robert of Flanders set forth on an expedition to procure a supply. They were in a slight degree successful; but the relief they brought was not economised, and in two days they were as destitute as before. Faticius, the Greek commander and representative of Alexius, deserted with his division under pretence of seeking for food, and his example was followed by various bodies of Crusaders. Misery was rife among those who remained, and they strove to alleviate it by a diligent attention to signs and omens. These, with extraordinary visions seen by the enthusiastic, alternately cheered and depressed them according as they foretold the triumph or pictured the reverses of the cross. At one time a violent hurricane arose, levelling great trees with the ground, and blowing down the tents of the Christian leaders. At another time an earthquake shook the camp, and was thought to prognosticate some great impending evil to the cause of Christendom. But a comet which appeared shortly afterwards raised them from the despondency into which they had fallen; their lively imaginations making it assume the form of a flaming cross leading them on to victory. Famine was not the least of the evils they endured. Unwholesome food, and the impure air from the neighbouring marshes, engendered pestilential diseases, which carried them off more rapidly than the arrows of the enemy. A thousand of them died in a day, and it became at last a matter of extreme difficulty to afford them burial. To add to their misery, each man grew suspicious of his neighbour; for the camp was infested by

Turkish spies, who conveyed daily to the besieged intelligence of the movements and distresses of the enemy. With a ferocity, engendered by despair, Bohemund caused two spies, whom he had detected, to be roasted alive in presence of the army, and within sight of the battlements of Antioch. But even this example failed to reduce their numbers, and the Turks continued to be as well informed as the Christians themselves of all that was passing in the camp.

The news of the arrival of a reinforcement of soldiers from Europe, with an abundant stock of provisions, came to cheer them when reduced to the last extremity. The welcome succour landed at St. Simeon, the port of Antioch, and about six miles from that city. Thitherwards the famishing Crusaders proceeded in tumultuous bands, followed by Bohemund and the Count of Toulouse, with strong detachments of their retainers and vassals, to escort the supplies in safety to the camp. The garrison of Antioch, forewarned of this arrival, was on the alert, and a corps of Turkish archers was despatched to lie in ambuscade among the mountains and intercept their return. Bohemund, laden with provisions, was encountered in the rocky passes by the Turkish host. Great numbers of his followers were slain, and he himself had just time to escape to the camp with the news of his defeat. Godfrey of Bouillon, the Duke of Normandy, and the other leaders had heard the rumour of this battle, and were at that instant preparing for the rescue. The army was immediately in motion, animated both by zeal and by hunger, and marched so rapidly as to intercept the victorious Turks before they had time to reach Antioch with their spoil. A fierce battle ensued, which lasted from noon till the going down of the sun. The Christians gained and maintained the advantage, each man fighting as if upon himself alone had depended the fortune of the day. Hundreds of Turks perished in the Orontes, and more than two thousand were left dead upon the field of battle. All the provision was recaptured and brought in safety to the camp, whither the Crusaders returned singing *Alleluia!* or shouting *Deus adjuva! Deus adjuva!*

This relief lasted for some days, and, had it been duly econo-mised, would have lasted much longer; but the chiefs had no authority, and were unable to exercise any control over its distribution. Famine again approached with rapid strides, and Stephen count of Blois, not liking the prospect, withdrew from the camp with four thousand of his retainers, and established himself at Alexandretta. The moral influence of this desertion was highly prejudicial upon those who remained; and Bohe-mund, the most impatient and ambitious of the chiefs, foresaw that, unless speedily checked, it would lead to the utter failure of the expedition. It was necessary to act decisively; the army murmured at the length of the siege, and the sultan was collect-ing his forces to crush them. Against the efforts of the Crusad-ers Antioch might have held out for months; but treason within effected that which courage without might have striven for in vain.

Baghasihan, the Turkish prince or emir of Antioch, had under his command an Armenian of the name of Phirouz, whom he had entrusted with the defence of a tower on that part of the city wall which overlooked the passes of the mountains. Bohemund, by means of a spy who had embraced the Christian religion, and to whom he had given his own name at baptism, kept up a daily communication with this captain, and made him the most magnificent promises of reward, if he would deliver up his post to the Crusaders. Whether the proposal was first made by Bohemund or by the Armenian is uncertain, but that a good understanding soon existed between them is undoubted; and a night was fixed for the execution of the project. Bohemund communicated the scheme to Godfrey and the Count of Tou-louse, with the stipulation that, if the city were won, he, as the soul of the enterprise, should enjoy the dignity of Prince of Antioch. The other leaders hesitated: ambition and jealousy prompted them to refuse their aid in furthering the views of the intriguer. More mature consideration decided them to acquiesce, and seven hundred of the bravest knights were chosen for the expedition, the real object of which, for fear of spies, was kept a profound secret from the rest of the army. When all was ready, a report was promulgated that the seven hundred were intended to form an ambuscade for a division of the sultan's army, which was stated to be approaching.

Every thing favoured the treacherous project of the Armenian captain, who, on his solitary watch-tower, received due intimation of the approach of the Crusaders. The night was dark and stormy; not a star was visible above, and the wind howled so furiously as to overpower all other sounds: the rain fell in torrents, and the watchers on the towers adjoining to that of Phirouz could not hear the tramp of the armed knights for the wind, nor see them for the obscurity of the night and the dismalness of the weather. When within shot of the walls, Bohemund sent forward an interpreter to confer with the Armenian. The latter urged them to make haste, and seize the favourable interval, as armed men, with lighted torches, patrolled the battlements every half hour, and at that instant they had just passed. The chiefs were instantly at the foot of the wall: Phirouz let down a rope; Bohemund attached it to the end of a ladder of hides, which was then raised by the Armenian, and held while the knights mounted. A momentary fear came over the spirits of the adventurers, and every one hesitated. At last Bohemund,[8] encouraged by Phirouz from above, ascended a few steps on the ladder, and was followed by Godfrey, Count Robert of Flanders, and a number of other knights. As they advanced, others pressed forward, until their weight became too great for the ladder, which, breaking, precipitated about a dozen of them to the ground, where they fell one upon the other, making a great clatter with their heavy coats of mail. For a moment they thought that all was lost; but the wind made so loud a howling as it swept in fierce gusts through the mountain gorges — and the Orontes, swollen by the rain, rushed so noisily along — that the guards heard nothing. The ladder was easily repaired, and the knights ascended two at a time, and reached the platform in safety. When sixty of them had thus ascended, the torch of the coming patrol was seen to gleam at the angle of the wall. Hiding themselves behind a buttress, they awaited his coming in breathless silence. As soon as he arrived at arm's length, he was suddenly seized, and, before he could open his lips to raise an alarm, the silence of death closed them up for ever. They next descended rapidly the spiral staircase of the tower, and opening the portal, admitted the whole of their companions. Raymond of Toulouse, who, cognisant of the whole plan, had been left behind with the main body of the army, heard at this instant the signal horn, which announced that an entry had been effected, and, leading on his legions, the town was attacked from within and without.

Imagination cannot conceive a scene more dreadful than that presented by the devoted city of Antioch on that night of horror. The Crusaders fought with a blind fury, which fanaticism and suffering alike incited. Men, women, and children were indiscriminately slaughtered, till the streets ran with blood. Darkness increased the destruction, for when morning dawned the Crusaders found themselves with their swords at the breasts of their fellow-soldiers, whom they had mistaken for foes. The Turkish commander fled, first to the citadel, and that becoming insecure, to the mountains, whither he was pursued and slain, and his grey head brought back to Antioch as a trophy. At daylight the massacre ceased, and the Crusaders gave themselves up to plunder. They found gold, and jewels, and silks, and velvets in abundance, but of provisions, which were of more importance to them, they found but little of any kind. Corn was excessively scarce, and they discovered to their sorrow that in this respect the besieged had been but little better off than the besiegers.

Siege of Antioch.

Before they had time to instal themselves in their new position, and take the necessary measures for procuring a supply, the city was invested by the Turks. The sultan of Persia had raised an immense army, which he entrusted to the command of Kerbogha, the emir of Mosul, with instructions to sweep the Christian locusts from the face of the land. The emir effected a junction with Kilij Aslaun, and the two armies surrounded the city. Discouragement took complete possession of the Christian host, and numbers of them contrived to elude the vigilance of the besiegers, and escape to Count Stephen of Blois at Alexandretta, to whom they related the most exaggerated tales of the misery they had endured, and the utter hopelessness of continuing the war. Stephen forthwith broke up his camp and retreated towards Constantinople. On his way he was met by the Emperor Alexius, at the head of a considerable force, hastening to take possession of the conquests made by the Christians in Asia. As soon as he heard of their woful plight, he turned back, and proceeded with the Count of Blois to Constantinople, leaving the remnant of the Crusaders to shift for themselves.

The news of this defection increased the discouragement at Antioch. All the useless horses of the army had been slain and eaten, and dogs, cats, and rats were sold at enormous prices. Even vermin were becoming scarce. With increasing famine came a pestilence, so that in a short time but sixty thousand remained of the three hundred thousand that had originally invested Antioch. But this bitter extremity, while it annihilated the energy of the host, only served to knit the leaders more firmly together; and Bohemund, Godfrey, and Tancred swore never to desert the cause as long as life lasted. The former strove in vain to reanimate the courage of his followers. They were weary and sick at heart, and his menaces and promises were alike thrown away. Some of them had shut themselves up in the houses, and refused to come forth. Bohemund, to drive them to their duty, set fire to the whole quarter, and many of them perished in the flames, while the rest of the army looked on with the utmost indifference. Bohemund, animated himself by a worldly spirit, did not know the true character of the Crusaders, nor understand the religious madness which had brought them in such shoals from Europe. A priest, more clear-sighted, devised a scheme which restored all their confidence, and inspired them with a courage so wonderful as to make the poor sixty thousand emaciated, sick, and starving zealots put to flight the well-fed and six times as numerous legions of the Sultan of Persia.

This priest, a native of Provence, was named Peter Barthelemy, and whether he were a knave or an enthusiast, or both; a principal, or a tool in the hands of others, will ever remain a matter of doubt. Certain it is, however, that he was the means of raising the siege of Antioch, and causing the eventual triumph of the armies of the cross. When the strength of the Crusaders was completely broken by their sufferings, and hope had fled from every bosom, Peter came to Count Raymond of Toulouse, and demanded an interview on matters of serious moment. He was immediately admitted. He said that, some weeks previously, at the time the Christians were besieging Antioch, he was reposing alone in his tent, when he was startled by the shock of the earthquake, which had so alarmed the whole host. Through violent terror of the shock he could only ejaculate, God help me! when turning round he saw two men standing before him, whom he at once recognised by the halo of glory around them as beings of another world. One of them appeared to be an aged man, with reddish hair sprinkled with grey, black eyes, and a long flowing grey beard. The other was younger, larger, and handsomer, and had something more divine in his aspect. The elderly man alone spoke, and informed him that he was the holy apostle St. Andrew, and desired him to seek out the Count Raymond, the Bishop of Puy, and Raymond of Altopulto, and ask them why the bishop did not exhort the people, and sign them with the cross which he bore. The apostle then took him, naked in his shirt as he was, and transported him through the air into the heart of the city of Antioch, where he led him into the church of St. Peter, at that time a Saracen mosque. The apostle made him stop by the pillar close to the steps by which they ascend on the south side to the altar, where hung two lamps, which gave out a light brighter than that of the noonday sun; the younger man, whom he did not at that time know, standing afar off, near the steps of the altar. The apostle then descended into the ground and brought up a lance, which he gave into his hand, telling him that it was the very lance that had opened the side whence had flowed the salvation of the world. With tears of joy he held the holy lance, and implored the apostle to allow him to take it away and deliver it into the hands of Count Raymond. The apostle refused, and buried the lance again in the ground, commanding him, when the city was won from the infidels, to go with twelve chosen men, and dig it up again in the same place. The apostle then transported him back to his tent, and the two vanished from his sight. He had neglected, he said, to deliver this message, afraid that his wonderful tale would not obtain credence from men of such high rank. After some days he again saw the holy vision, as he was gone out of the camp to look for food.

This time the divine eyes of the younger looked reproachfully upon him. He implored the apostle to choose some one else more fitted for the mission, but the apostle refused, and smote him with a disorder of the eyes, as a punishment for his disobedience. With an obstinacy unaccountable even to himself, he had still delayed. A third time the apostle and his companion had appeared to him, as he was in a tent with his master William at St. Simeon. On that occasion St. Andrew told him to bear his command to the Count of Toulouse not to bathe in the waters of the Jordan when he came to it, but to cross over in a boat, clad in a shirt and breeches of linen, which he should sprinkle with the sacred waters of the river. These clothes he was afterwards to preserve along with the holy lance. His master William, although he could not see the saint, distinctly heard the voice giving orders to that effect. Again he neglected to execute the commission, and again the saints appeared to him, when he was at the port of Mamistra, about to sail for Cyprus, and St. Andrew threatened him with eternal perdition if he refused longer. Upon this he made up his mind to divulge all that had been revealed to him.

The Count of Toulouse, who, in all probability, concocted this tale with the priest, appeared struck with the recital, and sent immediately for the Bishop of Puy and Raymond of Altapulto. The bishop at once expressed his disbelief of the whole story, and refused to have any thing to do in the matter. The Count of Toulouse, on the contrary, saw abundant motives, if not for believing, for pretending to believe; and, in the end, he so impressed upon the mind of the bishop the advantage that might be derived from it, in working up the popular mind to its former excitement, that the latter reluctantly agreed to make search in due form for the holy weapon. The day after the morrow was fixed upon for the ceremony; and, in the mean time, Peter was consigned to the care of Raymond, the count's chaplain, in order that no profane curiosity might have an opportunity of cross-examining him, and putting him to a nonplus.

Twelve devout men were forthwith chosen for the undertaking, among whom were the Count of Toulouse and his chaplain.

They began digging at sunrise, and continued unwearied till near sunset, without finding the lance; they might have dug till this day with no better success, had not Peter himself sprung into the pit, praying to God to bring the lance to light, for the strengthening and victory of his people. Those who hide know where to find; and so it was with Peter, for both he and the lance found their way into the hole at the same time. On a sudden, he and Raymond the chaplain beheld its point in the earth, and Raymond, drawing it forth, kissed it with tears of joy, in sight of the multitude which had assembled in the church. It was immediately enveloped in a rich purple cloth, already prepared to receive it, and exhibited in this state to the faithful, who made the building resound with their shouts of gladness.

The Holy Lance.

Peter had another vision the same night, and became from that day forth "dreamer of dreams" in general to the army. He stated on the following day, that the Apostle Andrew and "the youth with the divine aspect" appeared to him again, and directed that the Count of Toulouse, as a reward for his persevering piety, should carry the Holy Lance at the head of the army, and that the day on which it was found should be observed as a solemn festival throughout Christendom. St. Andrew shewed him at the same time the holes in the feet and hands of his benign companion; and he became convinced that he stood in the awful presence of the Redeemer.

Peter gained so much credit by his visions that dreaming became contagious. Other monks beside himself were visited by the saints, who promised victory to the host if it would valiantly hold out to the last, and crowns of eternal glory to those who fell in the fight. Two deserters, wearied of the fatigues and privations of the war, who had stealthily left the camp, suddenly returned, and seeking Bohemund, told him that they had been met by two apparitions, who, with great anger, had commanded them to return. The one of them said, that he recognised his brother, who had been killed in battle some months before, and that he had a halo of glory around his head. The other, still more hardy, asserted that the apparition which had spoken to him was the Saviour himself, who had promised eternal happiness as his reward if he returned to his duty, but the pains of eternal fire if he rejected the cross. No one thought of disbelieving these men. The courage of the army immediately revived; despondency gave way to hope; every arm grew strong again, and the pangs of hunger were for a time disregarded. The enthusiasm which had led them from Europe, burned forth once more as brightly as ever, and they demanded, with loud cries, to be led against the enemy. The leaders were not unwilling. In a battle lay their only chance of salvation; and although Godfrey, Bohemund, and Tancred received the story of the lance with much suspicion, they were too wise to throw discredit upon an imposture which bade fair to open the gates of victory.

Peter the Hermit was previously sent to the camp of Kerbogha to propose that the quarrel between the two religions should be decided by a chosen number of the bravest soldiers of each army. Kerbogha turned from him with a look of contempt, and said he could agree to no proposals from a set of such miserable beggars and robbers. With this uncourteous answer Peter returned to Antioch. Preparations were immediately commenced for an attack upon the enemy: the latter continued to be perfectly well informed of all the proceedings of the Christian camp. The citadel of Antioch, which remained in their possession, over-looked the town, and the commander of the fortress could distinctly see all that was passing within. On the morning of the 28th of June, 1098, a black flag, hoisted from its highest tower, announced to the besieging army that the Christians were about to sally forth.

The Moslem leaders knew the sad inroads that famine and disease had made upon the numbers of the foe; they knew that not above two hundred of the knights had horses to ride upon, and that the foot soldiers were sick and emaciated; but they did not know the almost incredible valour which superstition had infused into their hearts. The story of the lance they treated with the most supreme contempt, and, secure of an easy victory, they gave themselves no trouble in preparing for the onslaught. It is related that Kerbogha was playing a game at chess, when the black flag on the citadel gave warning of the enemy's approach, and that, with true oriental coolness, he insisted upon finishing the game ere he bestowed any of his attention upon a foe so unworthy. The defeat of his advanced post of two thousand men aroused him from his apathy.

The Crusaders, after this first victory, advanced joyfully towards the mountains, hoping to draw the Turks to a place where their cavalry would be unable to manœuvre. Their spirits were light and their courage high, as, led on by the Duke of Normandy, Count Robert of Flanders, and Hugh of Vermandois, they came within sight of the splendid camp of the enemy. Godfrey of Bouillon and Adhemar Bishop of Puy, followed immediately after these leaders, the latter clad in complete armour, and bearing the Holy Lance within sight of the whole army: Bohemund and Tancred brought up the rear.

Kerbogha, aware at last that his enemy was not so despicable, took vigorous measures to remedy his mistake, and, preparing himself to meet the Christians in front, he despatched the Sultan Soliman of Roum to attack them in the rear. To conceal this movement, he set fire to the dried weeds and grass with which the ground was covered, and Soliman, taking a wide circuit with his cavalry, succeeded, under cover of the smoke, in making good his position in the rear. The battle raged furiously in front; the arrows of the Turks fell thick as hail, and their well-trained squadrons trod the Crusaders under their hoofs like stubble. Still the affray was doubtful; for the Christians had the advantage of the ground, and were rapidly gaining upon the enemy, when the overwhelming forces of Soliman arrived in the rear. Godfrey and Tancred flew to the rescue of Bohemund, spreading dismay in the Turkish ranks by their fierce impetuosity. The Bishop of Puy was left almost alone with the Provençals to oppose the legions commanded by Kerbogha in person; but the presence of the Holy Lance made a hero of the meanest soldier in his train. Still, however, the numbers of the enemy seemed interminable. The Christians, attacked on every side, began at last to give way, and the Turks made sure of victory.

At this moment a cry was raised in the Christian host that the saints were fighting on their side. The battle-field was clear of the smoke from the burning weeds, which had curled away, and hung in white clouds of fantastic shape on the brow of the distant mountains. Some imaginative zealot, seeing this dimly through the dust of the battle, called out to his fellows, to look at the army of saints, clothed in white, and riding upon white horses, that were pouring over the hills to the rescue. All eyes were immediately turned to the distant smoke; faith was in every heart; and the old battle-cry, *God wills it! God wills it!* resounded through the field, as every soldier, believing that God was visibly sending his armies to his aid, fought with an energy unfelt before. A panic seized the Persian and Turkish hosts, and they gave way in all directions. In vain Kerbogha tried to rally them. Fear is more contagious than enthusiasm, and they fled over the mountains like deer pursued by the hounds. The two leaders, seeing the uselessness of further efforts, fled with the rest; and that immense army was scattered over Palestine, leaving nearly seventy thousand of its dead upon the field of battle.

Their magnificent camp fell into the hands of the enemy, with its rich stores of corn, and its droves of sheep and oxen. Jewels, gold, and rich velvets in abundance were distributed among the army. Tancred followed the fugitives over the hills, and reaped as much plunder as those who had remained in the camp. The way, as they fled, was covered with valuables, and horses of the finest breed of Arabia became so plentiful that every knight of the Christians was provided with a steed. The Crusaders, in this battle, acknowledge to have lost nearly ten thousand men.

Their return to Antioch was one of joy indeed: the citadel was surrendered at once, and many of the Turkish garrison embraced the Christian faith, and the rest were suffered to depart. A solemn thanksgiving was offered up by the Bishop of Puy, in which the whole army joined, and the Holy Lance was visited by every soldier.

The enthusiasm lasted for some days, and the army loudly demanded to be led forward to Jerusalem, the grand goal of all their wishes: but none of their leaders was anxious to move; — the more prudent among them, such as Godfrey and Tancred, for reasons of expediency; and the more ambitious, such as the Count of Toulouse and Bohemund, for reasons of self-interest. Violent dissensions sprang up again between all the chiefs. Raymond of Toulouse, who was left at Antioch to guard the town, had summoned the citadel to surrender, as soon as he saw that there was no fear of any attack upon the part of the Persians; and the other chiefs found, upon their return, his banner waving on its walls. This had given great offence to Bohemund, who had stipulated the principality of Antioch as his reward for winning the town in the first instance. Godfrey and Tancred supported his claim, and, after a great deal of bickering, the flag of Raymond was lowered from the tower, and that of Bohemund hoisted in its stead, who assumed from that time the title of Prince of Antioch. Raymond, however, persisted in retaining possession of one of the city gates and its adjacent towers, which he held for several months, to the great annoyance of Bohemund and the scandal of the army. The count became in consequence extremely unpopular, although his ambition was not a whit more unreasonable than that of Bohemund himself, nor of Baldwin, who had taken up his quarters at Edessa, where he exercised the functions of a petty sovereign.

The fate of Peter Barthelemy deserves to be recorded. Honours and consideration had come thick upon him after the affair of the lance, and he consequently felt bound in conscience to continue the dreams which had made him a personage of so much importance. The mischief of it was, that, like many other liars, he had a very bad memory, and he contrived to make his dreams contradict each other in the most palpable manner. St. John one night appeared to him, and told one tale; while, a week after, St. Paul told a totally different story, and held out hopes quite incompatible with those of his apostolic brother. The credulity of that age had a wide maw, and Peter's visions must have been absurd and outrageous indeed, when the very men who had believed in the lance refused to swallow any more of his wonders. Bohemund at last, for the purpose of annoying the Count of Toulouse, challenged poor Peter to prove the truth of his story of the lance by the fiery ordeal. Peter could not refuse a trial so common in that age, and being besides encouraged by the count and his chaplain Raymond, an early day was appointed for the ceremony. The previous night was spent in prayer and fasting, according to custom, and Peter came forth in the morning bearing the lance in his hand, and walked boldly up to the fire. The whole army gathered round, impatient for the result, many thousands still believing that the lance was genuine, and Peter a holy man. Prayers having been said by Raymond d'Agilles, Peter walked into the flames, and had got nearly through, when pain caused him to lose his presence of mind: the heat too affected his eyes, and, in his anguish, he turned round unwittingly, and passed through the fire again, instead of stepping out of it, as he should have done. The result was, that he was burned so severely that he never recovered, and, after lingering for some days, he expired in great agony.

Most of the soldiers were suffering either from wounds, disease, or weariness; and it was resolved by Godfrey, — the tacitly acknowledged chief of the enterprise, — that the army should have time to refresh itself ere they advanced upon Jerusalem. It was now July, and he proposed that they should pass the hot months of August and September within the walls of Antioch, and march forward in October with renewed vigour, and numbers increased by fresh arrivals from Europe. This advice was finally adopted, although the enthusiasts of the army continued to murmur at the delay. In the mean time the Count of Vermandois was sent upon an embassy to the Emperor Alexius at Constantinople, to reproach him for his base desertion of the cause, and urge him to send the reinforcements he had promised. The count faithfully executed his mission (of which, by the way, Alexius took no notice whatever), and remained for some time at Constantinople, till his zeal, never very violent, totally evaporated. He then returned to France, sick of the Crusade, and determined to intermeddle with it no more.

The chiefs, though they had determined to stay at Antioch for two months, could not remain quiet for so long a time. They would, in all probability, have fallen upon each other, had there been no Turks in Palestine upon whom they might vent their impetuosity. Godfrey proceeded to Edessa, to aid his brother Baldwin in expelling the Saracens from his principality, and the other leaders carried on separate hostilities against them as caprice or ambition dictated. At length the impatience of the army to be led against Jerusalem became so great that the chiefs could no longer delay, and Raymond, Tancred, and Robert of Normandy marched forward with their divisions, and laid siege to the small but strong town of Marah. With their usual improvidence, they had not food enough to last a beleaguering army for a week. They suffered great privations in consequence, till Bohemund came to their aid and took the town by storm. In connexion with this siege, the chronicler, Raymond d'Agilles (the same Raymond the chaplain who figured in the affair of the Holy Lance), relates a legend, in the truth of which he devoutly believed, and upon which Tasso has founded one of the most beautiful passages of his poem. It is worth preserving, as shewing the spirit of the age and the source of the extraordinary courage manifested by the Crusaders on occasions of extreme difficulty. "One day," says Raymond, "Anselme de Ribeaumont beheld young Engelram, the son of the Count de St. Paul, who had been killed at Marah, enter his tent. 'How is it,' said Anselme to him, 'that you, whom I saw lying dead on the field of battle, are full or life?' — 'You must know,' replied Engelram, 'that those who fight for Jesus Christ never die.' 'But whence,' resumed Anselme, 'comes that strange brightness that surrounds you?' Upon this Engelram pointed to the sky, where Anselme saw a palace of diamond and crystal. 'It is thence,' said he, 'that I derive the beauty which surprises you. My dwelling is there; a still finer one is prepared for you, and you shall soon come to inhabit it. Farewell! we shall meet again to-morrow.' With these words Engelram returned to heaven. Anselme, struck by the vision, sent the next morning for the priests, received the sacrament, and although full of health, took a last farewell of all his friends, telling them that he was about to leave this world. A few hours afterwards, the enemy having made a sortie, Anselme went out against them sword in hand, and was struck on the forehead by a stone from a Turkish sling, which sent him to heaven, to the beautiful palace that was prepared for him."

Shrine of the Nativity.

New disputes arose between the Prince of Antioch and the Count of Toulouse with regard to the capture of this town, which were with the utmost difficulty appeased by the other chiefs. Delays also took place in the progress of the army, especially before Archas, and the soldiery were so exasperated that they were on the point of choosing new leaders to conduct them to Jerusalem.

Godfrey, upon this, set fire to his camp at Archas, and marched forward. He was immediately joined by hundreds of the Provençals of the Count of Toulouse. The latter, seeing the turn affairs were taking, hastened after them, and the whole host proceeded towards the holy city, so long desired amid sorrow, and suffering, and danger. At Emmaus they were met by a deputation from the Christians of Bethlehem, praying for immediate aid against the oppression of the infidels. The very name of Bethlehem, the birthplace of the Saviour, was music to their ears, and many of them wept with joy to think they were approaching a spot so hallowed. Albert of Aix informs us that their hearts were so touched that sleep was banished from the camp, and that, instead of waiting till the morning's dawn to recommence their march, they set out shortly after midnight, full of hope and enthusiasm. For upwards of four hours the mail-clad legions tramped stedfastly forward in the dark, and when the sun arose in unclouded splendour, the towers and pinnacles of Jerusalem gleamed upon their sight. All the tender feelings of their nature were touched; no longer brutal fanatics, but meek and humble pilgrims, they knelt down upon the sod, and with tears in their eyes, exclaimed to one another "*Jerusalem! Jerusalem!*" Some of them kissed the holy ground, others stretched themselves at full length upon it, in order that their bodies might come in contact with the greatest possible extent of it, and others prayed aloud. The women and children who had followed the camp from Europe, and shared in all its dangers, fatigues, and privations, were more boisterous in their joy; the former from long-nourished enthusiasm, and the latter from mere imitation,[9] and prayed, and wept, and laughed till they almost put the more sober to the blush.

The Pilgrims at the first sight of Jerusalem.

The first ebullition of their gladness having subsided, the army marched forward, and invested the city on all sides. The assault was almost immediately begun; but after the Christians had lost some of their bravest knights, that mode of attack was abandoned, and the army commenced its preparations for a regular siege. Mangonels, moveable towers, and battering-rams, together with a machine called a sow, made of wood, and covered with raw hides, inside of which miners worked to undermine the walls, were forthwith constructed; and to restore the courage and discipline of the army, which had suffered from the unworthy dissensions of the chiefs, the latter held out the hand of friendship to each other, and Tancred and the Count of Toulouse embraced in sight of the whole camp. The clergy aided the cause with their powerful voice, and preached union and goodwill to the highest and the lowest. A solemn procession was also ordered round the city, in which the entire army joined, prayers being offered up at every spot which gospel records had taught them to consider as peculiarly sacred.

The Saracens upon the ramparts beheld all these manifestations without alarm. To incense the Christians, whom they despised, they constructed rude crosses, and fixed them upon the walls, and spat upon and pelted them with dirt and stones. This insult to the symbol of their faith raised the wrath of the Crusaders to that height that bravery became ferocity, and enthusiasm madness. When all the engines of war were completed, the attack was recommenced, and every soldier of the Christian army fought with a vigour which the sense of private wrong invariably inspires. Every man had been personally outraged, and the knights worked at the battering-rams with as much readiness as the meanest soldiers. The Saracen arrows and balls of fire fell thick and fast among them, but the tremendous rams still heaved against the walls, while the best marksmen of the host were busily employed in the several floors of the moveable towers in dealing death among the Turks upon the battlements. Godfrey, Raymond, Tancred, and Robert of Normandy, each upon his tower, fought for hours with unwearied energy, often repulsed, but ever ready to renew the struggle. The Turks, no longer despising the enemy, defended themselves with the utmost skill and bravery till darkness brought a cessation of hostilities. Short was the sleep that night in the Christian camp. The priests offered up solemn prayers in the midst of the attentive soldiery for the triumph of the cross in this last great struggle; and as soon as morning dawned, every one was in readiness for the affray. The women and children lent their aid, the latter running unconcerned to and fro while the arrows fell fast around them, bearing water to the thirsty combatants. The saints were believed to be aiding their efforts, and the army, impressed with this idea, surmounted difficulties under which a force thrice as numerous, but without their faith, would have quailed and been defeated. Raymond of Toulouse at last forced his way into the city by escalade, while at the very same moment Tancred and Robert of Normandy succeeded in bursting open one of the gates. The Turks flew to repair the mischief, and Godfrey of Bouillon, seeing the battlements comparatively deserted, let down the drawbridge of his moveable tower, and sprang forward, followed by all the knights of his train. In an instant after, the banner of the cross floated upon the walls of Jerusalem. The Crusaders, raising once more their redoubtable war-cry, rushed on from every side, and the city was taken. The battle raged in the streets for several hours, and the Christians, remembering their insulted faith, gave no quarter to young or old, male or female, sick or strong. Not one of the leaders thought himself at liberty to issue orders for staying the carnage, and if he had, he would not have been obeyed. The Saracens fled in great numbers to the mosque of Soliman, but they had not time to fortify themselves within it ere the Christians were upon them. Ten thousand persons are said to have perished in that building alone.

Peter the Hermit, who had remained so long under the veil of neglect, was repaid that day for all his zeal and all his sufferings. As soon as the battle was over, the Christians of Jerusalem issued forth from their hiding-places to welcome their deliverers. They instantly recognised the Hermit as the pilgrim who, years before, had spoken to them so eloquently of the wrongs and insults they had endured, and promised to stir up the princes and people of Europe in their behalf. They clung to the skirts of his garments in the fervour of their gratitude, and vowed to remember him for ever in their prayers. Many of them shed tears about his neck, and attributed the deliverance of Jerusalem solely to his courage and perseverance. Peter afterwards held some ecclesiastical office in the holy city, but what it was, or what was his ultimate fate, history has forgotten to inform us. Some say that he returned to France and founded a monastery, but the story does not rest upon sufficient authority.

Siege of Jerusalem.

The grand object for which the popular swarms of Europe had forsaken their homes was now accomplished. The Moslem mosques of Jerusalem were converted into churches for a purer faith, and the mount of Calvary and the sepulchre of Christ were profaned no longer by the presence or the power of the infidel. Popular frenzy had fulfilled its mission, and, as a natural consequence, it began to subside from that time forth. The news of the capture of Jerusalem brought numbers of pilgrims from Europe, and, among others, Stephen count of Chartres and Hugh of Vermandois, to atone for their desertion; but nothing like the former enthusiasm existed among the nations.

Thus then ends the history of the first Crusade. For the better understanding of the second, it will be necessary to describe the interval between them, and to enter into a slight sketch of the history of Jerusalem under its Latin kings, the long and fruitless wars they continued to wage with the unvanquished Saracens, and the poor and miserable results which sprang from so vast an expenditure of zeal, and so deplorable a waste of human life.

Jerusalem.

The necessity of having some recognised chief was soon felt by the Crusaders, and Godfrey de Bouillon, less ambitious than Bohemund or Raymond of Toulouse, gave his cold consent to wield a sceptre which the latter chiefs would have clutched with eagerness. He was hardly invested with the royal mantle before the Saracens menaced his capital. With much vigour and judgment he exerted himself to follow up the advantages he had gained, and marching out to meet the enemy before they had time to besiege him in Jerusalem, he gave them battle at Ascalon, and defeated them with great loss. He did not, however, live long to enjoy his new dignity, being seized with a fatal illness when he had only reigned nine months. To him succeeded his brother, Baldwin of Edessa. The latter monarch did much to improve the condition of Jerusalem and to extend its territory, but was not able to make a firm footing for his successors. For fifty years, in which the history of Jerusalem is full of interest to the historical student, the Crusaders were exposed to fierce and constant hostilities, often gaining battles and territory, and as often losing them, but becoming every day weaker and more divided, while the Saracens became stronger and more united to harass and root them out. The battles of this period were of the most chivalrous character, and deeds of heroism were done by the handful of brave knights that remained in Syria, which have hardly their parallel in the annals of war. In the course of time, however, the Christians could not avoid feeling some respect for the courage, and admiration for the polished manners and advanced civilisation of the Saracens, so much superior to the rudeness and semi-barbarism of Europe at that day. Difference of faith did not prevent them from forming alliances with the dark-eyed maidens of the East. One of the first to set the example of taking a Paynim spouse was King Baldwin himself, and these connexions in time became not only frequent, but almost universal, among such of the knights as had resolved to spend their lives in Palestine. These Eastern ladies were obliged, however, to submit to the ceremony of baptism before they could be received to the arms of a Christian lord. These, and their offspring, naturally looked upon the Saracens with less hatred than did the zealots who conquered Jerusalem, and who thought it a sin deserving the wrath of God to spare an unbeliever. We find, in consequence, that the most obstinate battles waged during the reigns of the later kings of Jerusalem were fought by the new and raw levies who from time to time arrived from Europe, lured by the hope of glory or spurred by fanaticism. The latter broke without scruple the truces established between the original settlers and the Saracens, and drew down severe retaliation upon many thousands of their brethren in the faith, whose prudence was stronger than their zeal, and whose chief desire was to live in peace.

Bible of Baldwin's Queen.

Things remained in this unsatisfactory state till the close of the year 1145, when Edessa, the strong frontier town of the Christian kingdom, fell into the hands of the Saracens. The latter were commanded by Zenghi, a powerful and enterprising monarch, and, after his death, by his son Nourheddin, as powerful and enterprising as his father. An unsuccessful attempt was made by the Count of Edessa to regain the fortress, but Nourheddin with a large army came to the rescue, and after defeating the count with great slaughter, marched into Edessa and caused its fortifications to be razed to the ground, that the town might never more be a bulwark of defence for the kingdom of Jerusalem. The road to the capital was now open, and consternation seized the hearts of the Christians. Nourheddin, it was known, was only waiting for a favourable opportunity to advance upon Jerusalem, and the armies of the cross, weakened and divided, were not in a condition to make any available resistance. The clergy were filled with grief and alarm, and wrote repeated letters to the Pope and the sovereigns of Europe, urging the expediency of a new Crusade for the relief of Jerusalem. By far the greater number of the priests of Palestine were natives of France, and these naturally looked first to their own country. The solicitations they sent to Louis VII. were urgent and oft repeated, and the chivalry of France began to talk once more of arming in defence of the birthplace of Jesus. The kings of Europe, whose interest it had not been to take any part in the first Crusade, began to bestir themselves in this; and a man appeared, eloquent as Peter the Hermit, to arouse the people as that preacher had done.

We find, however, that the enthusiasm of the second did not equal that of the first Crusade; in fact, the mania had reached its climax in the time of Peter the Hermit, and decreased regularly from that period. The third Crusade was less general than the second, and the fourth than the third, and so on, until the public enthusiasm was quite extinct, and Jerusalem returned at last to the dominion of its old masters without a convulsion in Christendom. Various reasons have been assigned for this; and one very generally put forward is, that Europe was wearied with continued struggles, and had become sick of "precipitating itself upon Asia." M. Guizot, in his admirable lectures upon European civilisation, successfully combats this opinion, and offers one of his own, which is far more satisfactory. He says, in his eighth lecture, "It has been often repeated that Europe was tired of continually invading Asia. This expression appears to me exceedingly incorrect. It is not possible that human beings can be wearied with what they have not done — that the labours of their forefathers can fatigue them. Weariness is a personal, not an inherited feeling. The men of the thirteenth century were not fatigued by the Crusades of the twelfth. They were influenced by another cause. A great change had taken place in ideas, sentiments, and social conditions. The same desires and the same wants were no longer felt. The same things were no longer believed. The people refused to believe what their ancestors were persuaded of."

This is, in fact, the secret of the change; and its truth becomes more apparent as we advance in the history of the Crusades, and compare the state of the public mind at the different periods when Godfrey of Bouillon, Louis VII., and Richard I., were chiefs and leaders of the movement. The Crusades themselves were the means of operating a great change in national ideas, and advancing the civilisation of Europe. In the time of Godfrey, the nobles were all-powerful and all-oppressive, and equally obnoxious to kings and people. During their absence along with that portion of the community the deepest sunk in ignorance and superstition, both kings and people fortified themselves against the renewal of aristocratic tyranny, and in proportion as they became free became civilised. It was during this period that in France, the grand centre of the crusading madness, the *communes* began to acquire strength, and the monarch to possess a practical and not a merely theoretic authority. Order and comfort began to take root, and, when the second Crusade was preached, men were in consequence much less willing to abandon their homes than they had been during the first. Such pilgrims as had returned from the Holy Land came back with minds more liberal and expanded than when they set out. They had come in contact with a people more civilised than themselves; they had seen something more of the world, and had lost some portion, however small, of the prejudice and bigotry of ignorance. The institution of chivalry had also exercised its humanising influence, and coming bright and fresh through the ordeal of the Crusades, had softened the character and improved the hearts of the aristocratic order. The *Trouvères* and *Troubadours*, singing of love and war in strains pleasing to every class of society, helped to root out the gloomy superstitions which, at the first Crusade, filled the minds of all those who were able to think. Men became in consequence less exclusively under the mental thraldom of the priesthood, and lost much of the credulity which formerly distinguished them.

The Crusades appear never to have excited so much attention in England as on the continent of Europe; not because the people were less fanatical than their neighbours, but because they were occupied in matters of graver interest. The English were suffering too severely from the recent successful invasion of their soil, to have much sympathy to bestow upon the distresses of people so far away as the Christians of Palestine; and we find that they took no part in the first Crusade, and very little in the second. Even then those who engaged in it were chiefly Norman knights and their vassals, and not the Saxon franklins and population, who no doubt thought, in their sorrow, as many wise men have thought since, that charity should begin at home.

Germany was productive of more zeal in the cause, and her raw uncivilised hordes continued to issue forth under the banners of the cross in numbers apparently undiminished, when the enthusiasm had long been on the wane in other countries. They were sunk at that time in a deeper slough of barbarism than the livelier nations around them, and took, in consequence, a longer period to free themselves from their prejudices. In fact the second Crusade drew its chief supplies of men from that quarter, where alone the expedition can be said to have retained any portion of popularity.

Such was the state of mind of Europe when Pope Eugenius, moved by the reiterated entreaties of the Christians of Syria, commissioned St. Bernard to preach a new Crusade. St. Bernard was a man eminently qualified for the mission. He was endowed with an eloquence of the highest order, could move an auditory to tears, or laughter, or fury, as it pleased him, and had led a life of such rigid and self-denying virtue, that not even calumny could lift her finger and point it at him. He had renounced high prospects in the Church, and contented himself with the simple abbacy of Clairvaux, in order that he might have the leisure he desired, to raise his powerful voice against abuses wherever he found them. Vice met in him an austere and uncompromising reprover; no man was too high for his reproach, and none too low for his sympathy. He was just as well suited for his age as Peter the Hermit had been for the age preceding. He appealed more to the reason, his predecessor to the passions; Peter the Hermit collected a mob, while St. Bernard collected an army. Both were endowed with equal zeal and perseverance, springing in the one from impulse, and in the other from conviction, and a desire to increase the influence of the Church, that great body of which he was a pillar and an ornament.

Cathedral of Vezelai.

One of the first converts he made was in himself a host. Louis VII. was both superstitious and tyrannical, and, in a fit of remorse for the infamous slaughter he had authorised at the sacking of Vitry, he made a vow to undertake the journey to the Holy Land.[10] He was in this disposition when St. Bernard began to preach, and wanted but little persuasion to embark in the cause. His example had great influence upon the nobility, who, impoverished as many of them were by the sacrifices made by their fathers in the holy wars, were anxious to repair their ruined fortunes by conquests on a foreign shore. These took the field with such vassals as they could command, and in a very short time an army was raised amounting to two hundred thousand men. At Vezelai the monarch received the cross from the hands of St. Bernard, on a platform elevated in sight of all the people. Several nobles, three bishops, and his queen, Eleanor of Aquitaine, were present at this ceremony, and enrolled themselves under the banner of the cross, St. Bernard cutting up his red sacerdotal vestments, and making crosses of them, to be sewn on the shoulders of the people. An exhortation from the Pope was read to the multitude, granting remission of their sins to all who should join the Crusade, and directing that no man on that holy pilgrimage should encumber himself with heavy baggage and vain superfluities, and that the nobles should not travel with dogs or falcons, to lead them from the direct road, as had happened to so many during the first Crusade.

The command of the army was offered to St. Bernard; but he wisely refused to accept a station for which his habits had unqualified him. After consecrating Louis with great solemnity, at St. Denis, as chief of the expedition, he continued his course through the country, stirring up the people wherever he went. So high an opinion was entertained of his sanctity, that he was thought to be animated by the spirit of prophecy, and to be gifted with the power of working miracles. Many women, excited by his eloquence, and encouraged by his predictions, forsook their husbands and children, and, clothing themselves in male attire, hastened to the war. St. Bernard himself wrote a letter to the Pope detailing his success, and stating, that in several towns there did not remain a single male inhabitant capable of bearing arms, and that every where castles and towns were to be seen filled with women weeping for their absent husbands. But in spite of this apparent enthusiasm, the numbers who really took up arms were inconsiderable, and not to be compared to the swarms of the first Crusade. A levy of no more than two hundred thousand men, which was the utmost the number amounted to, could hardly have depopulated a country like France, to the extent mentioned by St. Bernard. His description of the state of the country appears, therefore, to have been much more poetical than true.

Suger, the able minister of Louis, endeavoured to dissuade him from undertaking so long a journey at a time when his own dominions so much needed his presence. But the king was pricked in his conscience by the cruelties of Vitry, and was anxious to make the only reparation which the religion of that day considered sufficient. He was desirous, moreover, of testifying to the world, that though he could brave the temporal power of the Church when it encroached upon his prerogatives, he could render all due obedience to its spiritual decrees whenever it suited his interest or tallied with his prejudices to do so. Suger, therefore, implored in vain, and Louis received the pilgrim's staff at St. Denis, and made all preparations for his pilgrimage.

In the mean time St. Bernard passed into Germany, where similar success attended his preaching. The renown of his sanctity had gone before him, and he found every where an admiring audience. Thousands of people, who could not understand a word he said, flocked around him to catch a glimpse of so holy a man; and the knights enrolled themselves in great numbers in the service of the cross, each receiving from his hands the symbol of the cause. But the people were not led away as in the days of Gottschalk. We do not find that they rose in such tremendous masses of two and three hundred thousand men, swarming over the country like a plague of locusts. Still the enthusiasm was very great. The extraordinary tales that were told and believed of the miracles worked by the preacher brought the country people from far and near. Devils were said to vanish at his sight, and diseases of the most malignant nature to be cured by his touch.[11] The Emperor Conrad caught at last the contagion from his subjects, and declared his intention to follow the cross.

The preparations were carried on so vigorously under the orders of Conrad, that in less than three months he found himself at the head of an army containing at least one hundred and fifty thousand effective men, besides a great number of women who followed their husbands and lovers to the war. One troop of them rode in the attitude and armour of men: their chief wore gilt spurs and buskins, and thence acquired the epithet of the golden-footed lady. Conrad was ready to set out long before the French monarch, and in the month of June 1147, he arrived before Constantinople, having passed through Hungary and Bulgaria without offence to the inhabitants.

Pilgrim's staff.

Manuel Comnenus, the Greek emperor, successor not only to the throne but to the policy of Alexius, looked with alarm upon the new levies who had come to eat up his capital and imperil its tranquillity. Too weak to refuse them a passage through his dominions, too distrustful of them to make them welcome when they came, and too little assured of the advantages likely to result to himself from the war, to feign a friendship which he did not feel, the Greek emperor gave offence at the very outset. His subjects, in the pride of superior civilisation, called the Germans barbarians; while the latter, who, if semi-barbarous, were at least honest and straightforward, retorted upon the Greeks by calling them double-faced knaves and traitors. Disputes continually arose between them, and Conrad, who had preserved so much good order among his followers during their passage, was unable to restrain their indignation when they arrived at Constantinople. For some offence or other which the Greeks had given them, but which is rather hinted at than stated by the scanty historians of the day, the Germans broke into the magnificent pleasure-garden of the emperor, where he had a valuable collection of tame animals, for which the grounds had been laid out in woods, caverns, groves, and streams, that each might follow in captivity his natural habits. The enraged Germans, meriting the name of barbarians that had been bestowed upon them, laid waste this pleasant retreat, and killed or let loose the valuable animals it contained. Manuel, who is said to have beheld the devastation from his palace windows without power or courage to prevent it, was completely disgusted with his guests, and resolved, like his predecessor Alexius, to get rid of them on the first opportunity. He sent a message to Conrad respectfully desiring an interview, but the German refused to trust himself within the walls of Constantinople. The Greek emperor, on his part, thought it compatible neither with his dignity nor his safety to seek the German, and several days were spent in insincere negotiations. Manuel at length agreed to furnish the crusading army with guides to conduct it through Asia Minor; and Conrad passed over the Hellespont with his forces, the advanced guard being commanded by himself, and the rear by the warlike Bishop of Freysinghen.

Historians are almost unanimous in their belief that the wily Greek gave instructions to his guides to lead the army of the German emperor into dangers and difficulties. It is certain that, instead of guiding them through such districts of Asia Minor as afforded water and provisions, they led them into the wilds of Cappadocia, where neither was to be procured, and where they were suddenly attacked by the sultan of the Seljukian Turks, at the head of an immense force. The guides, whose treachery is apparent from this fact alone, fled at the first sight of the Turkish army, and the Christians were left to wage unequal warfare with their enemy, entangled and bewildered in desert wilds. Toiling in their heavy mail, the Germans could make but little effective resistance to the attacks of the Turkish light horse, who were down upon them one instant, and out of sight the next. Now in the front and now in the rear, the agile foe showered his arrows upon them, enticing them into swamps and hollows, from which they could only extricate themselves after long struggles and great losses. The Germans, confounded by this mode of warfare, lost all conception of the direction they were pursuing, and went back instead of forward. Suffering at the same time for want of provisions, they fell an easy prey to their pursuers. Count Bernhard, one of the bravest leaders of the German expedition, was surrounded, with his whole division, not one of whom escaped the Turkish arrows. The emperor himself had nearly fallen a victim, and was twice severely wounded. So persevering was the enemy, and so little able were the Germans to make even a shew of resistance, that when Conrad at last reached the city of Nice, he found that, instead of being at the head of an imposing force of one hundred thousand foot and seventy thousand horse, he had but fifty or sixty thousand men, and these in the most worn and wearied condition.

Totally ignorant of the treachery of the Greek emperor, although he had been warned to beware of it, Louis VII. proceeded, at the head of his army, through Worms and Ratisbon, towards Constantinople. At Ratisbon he was met by a deputation from Manuel, bearing letters so full of hyperbole and flattery, that Louis is reported to have blushed when they were read to him by the Bishop of Langres. The object of the deputation was to obtain from the French king a promise to pass through the Grecian territories in a peaceable and friendly manner, and to yield to the Greek emperor any conquest he might make in Asia Minor. The first part of the proposition was immediately acceded to, but no notice was taken of the second and more unreasonable. Louis marched on, and, passing through Hungary, pitched his tents in the outskirts of Constantinople.

On his arrival, Manuel sent him a friendly invitation to enter the city at the head of a small train. Louis at once accepted it, and was met by the emperor at the porch of his palace. The fairest promises were made; every art that flattery could suggest was resorted to, and every argument employed, to induce him to yield his future conquests to the Greek. Louis obstinately refused to pledge himself, and returned to his army convinced that the emperor was a man not to be trusted. Negotiations were, however, continued for several days, to the great dissatisfaction of the French army. The news that arrived of a treaty entered into between Manuel and the Turkish sultan changed their dissatisfaction into fury, and the leaders demanded to be led against Constantinople, swearing that they would raze the treacherous city to the ground. Louis did not feel inclined to accede to this proposal, and, breaking up his camp, he crossed over into Asia. Here he heard, for the first time, of the mishaps of the German emperor, whom he found in a woful plight under the walls of Nice. The two monarchs united their forces, and marched together along the sea-coast to Ephesus; but Conrad, jealous, it would appear, of the superior numbers of the French, and not liking to sink into a vassal, for the time being, of his rival, withdrew abruptly with the remnant of his legions, and returned to Constantinople. Manuel was all smiles and courtesy. He condoled with the German so feelingly upon his losses, and cursed the stupidity or treachery of the guides with such apparent heartiness, that Conrad was half inclined to believe in his sincerity.

Louis, marching onward in the direction of Jerusalem, came up with the enemy on the banks of the Meander. The Turks contested the passage of the river, but the French bribed a peasant to point out a ford lower down: crossing the river without difficulty, they attacked the Turks with much vigour, and put them to flight. Whether the Turks were really defeated, or merely pretended to be so, is doubtful; but the latter supposition seems to be the true one. It is probable that it was part of a concerted plan to draw the invaders onwards to more unfavourable ground, where their destruction might be more certain. If such were the scheme, it succeeded to the heart's wish of its projectors. The Crusaders, on the third day after their victory, arrived at a steep mountain-pass, on the summit of which the Turkish host lay concealed so artfully, that not the slightest vestige of their presence could be perceived. "With labouring steps and slow," they toiled up the steep ascent, when suddenly a tremendous fragment of rock came bounding down the precipices with an awful crash, bearing dismay and death before it. At the same instant the Turkish archers started from their hiding-places, and discharged a shower of arrows upon the foot-soldiers, who fell by hundreds at a time. The arrows rebounded harmlessly against the iron mail of the knights, which the Turks observing, took aim at their steeds, and horse and rider fell down the steep into the rapid torrent which rushed below. Louis, who commanded the rear-guard, received the first intimation of the onslaught from the sight of the wounded and flying soldiers, and, not knowing the numbers of the enemy, he pushed vigorously forward to stay, by his presence, the panic which had taken possession of his army. All his efforts were in vain. Immense stones continued to be hurled upon them as they advanced, bearing men and horse before them; and those who succeeded in forcing their way to the top were met hand-to-hand by the Turks, and cast down headlong upon their companions. Louis himself fought with the energy of desperation, but had great difficulty to avoid falling into the enemy's hands. He escaped at last under cover of the night, with the remnant of his forces, and took up his position before Attalia. Here he restored the discipline and the courage of his disorganised and disheartened followers, and debated with his captains the plan that was to be pursued. After suffering severely both from disease and famine, it was resolved that they should march to Antioch, which still remained an independent principality under the successors of Bohemund of Tarentum. At this time the sovereignty was vested in the person of Raymond, the uncle of Eleanor of Aquitaine. This prince, presuming upon his relationship to the French queen, endeavoured to withdraw Louis from the grand object of the Crusade — the defence of the kingdom of Jerusalem, and secure his co-operation in extending the limits and the power of his principality of Antioch. The Prince of Tripoli formed a similar design; but Louis rejected the offers of both, and marched, after a short delay, to Jerusalem. The Emperor Conrad was there before him, having left Constantinople with promises of assistance from Manuel Comnenus — assistance which never arrived, and was never intended.

Damascus.

A great council of the Christian princes of Palestine, and the leaders of the Crusade, was then summoned, to discuss the future operations of the war. It was ultimately determined that it would further the cause of the cross in a greater degree if the united armies, instead of proceeding to Edessa, laid siege to the city of Damascus, and drove the Saracens from that strong position. This was a bold scheme, and, had it been boldly followed out, would have insured, in all probability, the success of the war. But the Christian leaders never learned from experience the necessity of union, that very soul of great enterprises. Though they all agreed upon the policy of the plan, yet every one had his own notions as to the means of executing it. The princes of Antioch and Tripoli were jealous of each other, and of the king of Jerusalem. The Emperor Conrad was jealous of the king of France, and the king of France was disgusted with them all. But he had come out to Palestine in accordance with a solemn vow; his religion, though it may be called bigotry, was sincere; and he determined to remain to the very last moment that a chance was left of effecting any good for the cause he had set his heart on.

The siege of Damascus was accordingly commenced, and with so much ability and vigour that the Christians gained a considerable advantage at the very outset. For weeks the siege was pressed, till the shattered fortifications and diminishing resistance of the besieged gave evidence that the city could not hold out much longer. At that moment the insane jealousy of the leaders led to dissensions that soon caused the utter failure, not only of the siege but of the Crusade. A modern cookery-book, in giving a recipe for cooking a hare, says, "first catch your hare, and then kill it" — a maxim of indisputable wisdom. The Christian chiefs, on this occasion, had not so much sagacity, for they began a violent dispute among themselves for the possession of a city which was still unconquered. There being already a prince of Antioch and a prince of Tripoli, twenty claimants started for the principality of Damascus; and a grand council of the leaders was held to determine the individual on whom the honour should devolve. Many valuable days were wasted in this discussion, the enemy in the meanwhile gaining strength from their inactivity. It was at length, after a stormy deliberation, agreed that Count Robert of Flanders, who had twice visited the Holy Land, should be invested with the dignity. The other claimants refused to recognise him or to co-operate in the siege until a more equitable arrangement had been made. Suspicion filled the camp; the most sinister rumours of intrigues and treachery were set afloat; and the discontented candidates withdrew at last to the other side of the city, and commenced operations on their own account without a probability of success. They were soon joined by the rest of the army. The consequence was that the weakest side of the city, and that on which they had already made considerable progress in the work of demolition, was left uncovered. The enemy was prompt to profit by the mistake, and received an abundant supply of provisions, and refortified the walls, before the Crusaders came to their senses again. When this desirable event happened, it was too late. Saph Eddin, the powerful emir of Mousoul, was in the neighbourhood, at the head of a large army, advancing by forced marches to the relief of the city. The siege was abruptly abandoned, and the foolish Crusaders returned to Jerusalem, having done nothing to weaken the enemy, but every thing to weaken themselves.

The freshness of enthusiasm had now completely subsided; even the meanest soldiers were sick at heart. Conrad, from whose fierce zeal at the outset so much might have been expected, was wearied with reverses, and returned to Europe with the poor remnant of his host. Louis lingered a short time longer, for very shame, but the pressing solicitations of his minister Suger induced him to return to France. Thus ended the second Crusade. Its history is but a chronicle of defeats. It left the kingdom of Jerusalem in a worse state than when it quitted Europe, and gained nothing but disgrace for its leaders, and discouragement for all concerned.

St. Bernard, who had prophesied a result so different, fell after this into some disrepute, and experienced, like many other prophets, the fate of being without honour in his own country. What made the matter worse, he could not obtain it in any other. Still, however, there were not wanting zealous advocates to stand forward in his behalf, and stem the tide of incredulity, which, unopposed, would have carried away his reputation. The Bishop of Freysinghen declared that prophets were not always able to prophesy, and that the vices of the Crusaders drew down the wrath of heaven upon them. But the most ingenious excuse ever made for St. Bernard is to be found in his life by Geoffroi de Clairvaux, where he pertinaciously insists that the Crusade was not unfortunate. St. Bernard, he says, had prophesied a happy result, and that result could not be considered other than happy which had peopled heaven with so glorious an army of martyrs. Geoffroi was a cunning pleader, and, no doubt, convinced a few of the zealous; but plain people, who were not wanting even in those days, retained their own opinion, or, what amounts to the same thing, "were convinced against their will."

We now come to the consideration of the third Crusade, and of the causes which rendered it necessary. The epidemic frenzy, which had been cooling ever since the issue of the first expedition, was now extinct, or very nearly so, and the nations of Europe looked with cold indifference upon the armaments of their princes. But chivalry had flourished in its natural element of war, and was now in all its glory. It continued to supply armies for the Holy Land when the popular ranks refused to deliver up their able-bodied swarms. Poetry, which, more than religion, inspired the third Crusade, was then but "*caviare* to the million,*" who had other matters, of sterner import, to claim all their attention. But the knights and their retainers listened with delight to the martial and amatory strains of the minstrels, minnesängers, trouvères, and troubadours, and burned to win favour in ladies' eyes by shewing prowess in the Holy Land. The third was truly the romantic era of the Crusades. Men fought then, not so much for the sepulchre of Jesus, and the maintenance of a Christian kingdom in the East, as to gain glory for themselves in the best and almost only field where glory could be obtained. They fought, not as zealots, but as soldiers; not for religion, but for honour; not for the crown of martyrdom, but for the favour of the lovely.

Seal of Barbarossa.

It is not necessary to enter into a detail of the events by which Saladin attained the sovereignty of the East, or how, after a succession of engagements, he planted the Moslem banner once more upon the battlements of Jerusalem. The Christian knights and population, including the grand orders of St. John, the Hospitallers, and the Templars, were sunk in an abyss of vice, and, torn by unworthy jealousies and dissensions, were unable to resist the well-trained armies which the wise and mighty Saladin brought forward to crush them. But the news of their fall created a painful sensation among the chivalry of Europe, whose noblest members were linked to the dwellers in Palestine by many ties, both of blood and friendship. The news of the great battle of Tiberias, in which Saladin defeated the Christian host with terrible slaughter, arrived first in Europe, and was followed in quick succession by that of the capture of Jerusalem, Antioch, Tripoli, and other cities. Dismay seized upon the clergy. The Pope (Urban III.) was so affected by the news that he pined away for grief, and was scarcely seen to smile again, until he sank into the sleep of death.[12] His successor, Gregory VIII., felt the loss as acutely, but had better strength to bear it, and instructed all the clergy of the Christian world to stir up the people to arms for the recovery of the Holy Sepulchre. William Archbishop of Tyre, a humble follower in the path of Peter the Hermit, left Palestine to preach to the kings of Europe the miseries he had witnessed, and to incite them to the rescue. The renowned Frederick Barbarossa, the emperor of Germany, speedily collected an army, and passing over into Syria with less delay than had ever before awaited a crusading force, defeated the Saracens, and took possession of the city of Iconium. He was unfortunately cut off in the middle of his successful career, by imprudently bathing in the Cydnus[13] while he was overheated, and the Duke of Suabia took the command of the expedition. The latter did not prove so able a general, and met with nothing but reverses, although he was enabled to maintain a footing at Antioch until assistance arrived from Europe.

Henry II. of England.

Henry II. of England and Philip Augustus of France, at the head of their chivalry, supported the Crusade with all their influence, until wars and dissensions nearer home estranged them from it for a time. The two kings met at Gisors in Normandy in the month of January, 1188, accompanied by a brilliant train of knights and warriors. William of Tyre was present, and expounded the cause of the cross with considerable eloquence, and the whole assembly bound themselves by oath to proceed to Jerusalem. It was agreed at the same time that a tax, called Saladin's tithe, and consisting of the tenth part of all possessions, whether landed or personal, should be enforced over Christendom, upon every one who was either unable or unwilling to assume the cross. The lord of every feof, whether lay or ecclesiastical, was charged to raise the tithe within his own jurisdiction; and any one who refused to pay his quota, became by that act the bondsman and absolute property of his lord. At the same time the greatest indulgence was shewn to those who assumed the cross; no man was at liberty to stay them by process of any kind, whether for debt, or robbery, or murder. The king of France, at the breaking up of the conference, summoned a parliament at Paris, where these resolutions were solemnly confirmed, while Henry II. did the same for his Norman possessions at Rouen, and for England at Geddington, in Northamptonshire. To use the words of an ancient chronicler,[14] "he held a parliament about the voyage into the Holy Land, and troubled the whole land with the paying of tithes towards it."

Chateau of Gisors.

Philip Augustus.

But it was not England alone that was "*troubled*" by the tax. The people of France also looked upon it with no pleasant feelings, and appear from that time forth to have changed their indifference for the Crusade into aversion. Even the clergy, who were exceedingly willing that other people should contribute half, or even all their goods in furtherance of their favourite scheme, were not at all anxious to contribute a single sous themselves. Millot[15][15] relates that several of them cried out against the impost. Among the rest, the clergy of Rheims were called upon to pay their quota, but sent a deputation to the king, begging him to be contented with the aid of their prayers, as they were too poor to contribute in any other shape. Philip Augustus knew better, and by way of giving them a lesson, employed three nobles of the vicinity to lay waste the Church lands. The clergy, informed of the outrage, applied to the king for redress. "I will aid you with my prayers," said the monarch condescendingly, "and will entreat those gentlemen to let the Church alone." He did as he had promised, but in such a manner that the nobles, who appreciated the joke, continued their devastations as before. Again the clergy applied to the king. "What would you have of me?" he replied, in answer to their remonstrances: "you gave me your prayers in my necessity, and I have given you mine in yours." The clergy understood the argument, and thought it the wiser course to pay their quota of Saladin's tithe without further parley.

This anecdote shews the unpopularity of the Crusade. If the clergy disliked to contribute, it is no wonder that the people felt still greater antipathy. But the chivalry of Europe was eager for the affray: the tithe was rigorously collected, and armies from England, France, Burgundy, Italy, Flanders, and Germany, were soon in the field. The two kings who were to have led it were, however, drawn into broils by an aggression of Richard duke of Guienne, better known as Richard Cœur de Lion, upon the territory of the Count of Toulouse, and the proposed journey to Palestine was delayed. War continued to rage between France and England, and with so little probability of a speedy termination, that many of the nobles, bound to the Crusade, left the two monarchs to settle the differences at their leisure, and proceeded to Palestine without them.

Death at last stepped in and removed Henry II. from the hostility of his foes, and the treachery and ingratitude of his children. His son Richard immediately concluded an alliance with Philip Augustus; and the two young, valiant, and impetuous monarchs united all their energies to forward the Crusade. They met with a numerous and brilliant retinue at Nonancourt in Normandy, where, in sight of their assembled chivalry, they embraced as brothers, and swore to live as friends and true allies, until a period of forty days after their return from the Holy Land. With a view of purging their camp from the follies and vices which had proved so ruinous to preceding expeditions, they drew up a code of laws for the government of the army. Gambling had been carried to a great extent, and proved the fruitful source of quarrels and bloodshed; and one of their laws prohibited any person in the army, beneath the degree of a knight, from playing at any game for money.[16] Knights and clergymen might play for money, but no one was permitted to lose or gain more than twenty shillings in a day, under a penalty of one hundred shillings. The personal attendants of the monarchs were also allowed to play to the same extent. The penalty in their case for infraction was that they should be whipped naked through the army for the space of three days. Any Crusader, who struck another and drew blood, was ordered to have his hand cut off; and whoever slew a brother Crusader was condemned to be tied alive to the corpse of his victim, and buried with him. No young women were allowed to follow the army, to the great sorrow of many vicious and of many virtuous dames, who had not courage to elude the decree by dressing in male attire. But many high-minded and affectionate maidens and matrons, bearing the sword or the spear, followed their husbands and lovers to the war in spite of King Richard, and in defiance of danger. The only women allowed to accompany the army in their own habiliments were washerwomen of fifty years complete, and any others of the fair sex who had reached the same age.

These rules having been promulgated, the two monarchs marched together to Lyons, where they separated, agreeing to meet again at Messina. Philip proceeded across the Alps to Genoa, where he took ship, and was conveyed in safety to the place of rendezvous. Richard turned in the direction of Marseilles, where he also took ship for Messina. His impetuous disposition hurried him into many squabbles by the way, and his knights and followers, for the most part as brave and as foolish as himself, imitated him very zealously in this particular. At Messina the Sicilians charged the most exorbitant prices for every necessary of life. Richard's army in vain remonstrated. From words they came to blows, and, as a last resource, plundered the Sicilians, since they could not trade with them. Continual battles were the consequence, in one of which Lebrun, the favourite attendant of Richard, lost his life. The peasantry from far and near came flocking to the aid of the townspeople, and the battle soon became general. Richard, irritated at the loss of his favourite, and incited by report that Tancred, the king of Sicily, was fighting at the head of his own people, joined the *mêlée* with his boldest knights, and, beating back the Sicilians, attacked the city sword in hand, stormed the battlements, tore down the flag of Sicily, and planted his own in its stead. This collision gave great offence to the king of France, who became from that time jealous of Richard, and apprehensive that his design was not so much to re-establish the Christian kingdom of Jerusalem, as to make conquests for himself. He, however, exerted his influence to restore peace between the English and Sicilians, and shortly afterwards set sail for Acre, with distrust of his ally germinating in his heart.

The Island of Rhodes.

Richard remained behind for some weeks in a state of inactivity quite unaccountable in one of his temperament. He appears to have had no more squabbles with the Sicilians, but to have lived an easy, luxurious life, forgetting, in the lap of pleasure, the objects for which he had quitted his own dominions and the dangerous laxity he was introducing into his army. The superstition of his soldiers recalled him at length to a sense of his duty: a comet was seen for several successive nights, which was thought to menace them with the vengeance of Heaven for their delay. Shooting stars gave them similar warning; and a fanatic, of the name of Joachim, with his drawn sword in his hand, and his long hair streaming wildly over his shoulders, went through the camp, howling all night long, and predicting plague, famine, and every other calamity, if they did not set out immediately. Richard did not deem it prudent to neglect the intimations; and, after doing humble penance for his remissness, he set sail for Acre.

A violent storm dispersed his fleet, but he arrived safely at Rhodes with the principal part of the armament. Here he learned that three of his ships had been stranded on the rocky coasts of Cyprus, and that the ruler of the island, Isaac Comnenus, had permitted his people to pillage the unfortunate crews, and had refused shelter to his betrothed bride, the Princess Berengaria, and his sister, who, in one of the vessels, had been driven by stress of weather into the port of Limisso. The fiery monarch swore to be revenged, and, collecting all his vessels, sailed back to Limisso. Isaac Comnenus refused to apologise or explain, and Richard, in no mood to be trifled with, landed on the island, routed with great loss the forces sent to oppose him, and laid the whole country under contribution.

Richard I. and Berengaria.

On his arrival at Acre he found the whole of the chivalry of Europe there before him. Guy of Lusignan, the king of Jerusalem, had long before collected the bold Knights of the Temple, the Hospital, and St. John, and had laid siege to Acre, which was resolutely defended by the Sultan Saladin, with an army magnificent both for its numbers and its discipline. For nearly two years the Crusaders had pushed the siege, and made efforts almost superhuman to dislodge the enemy. Various battles had taken place in the open fields with no decisive advantage to either party, and Guy of Lusignan had begun to despair of taking that strong position without aid from Europe. His joy was extreme on the arrival of Philip with all his chivalry, and he only awaited the coming of Cœur de Lion to make one last decisive attack upon the town. When the fleet of England was first seen approaching the shores of Syria, a universal shout arose from the Christian camp; and when Richard landed with his train, one louder still pierced to the very mountains of the south, where Saladin lay with all his army.

It may be remarked as characteristic of this Crusade, that the Christians and the Moslems no longer looked upon each other as barbarians, to whom mercy was a crime. Each host entertained the highest admiration for the bravery and magnanimity of the other, and, in their occasional truces, met upon the most friendly terms. The Moslem warriors were full of courtesy to the Christian knights, and had no other regret than to think that such fine fellows were not Mahomedans. The Christians, with a feeling precisely similar, extolled to the skies the nobleness of the Saracens, and sighed to think that such generosity and valour should be sullied by disbelief in the Gospel of Jesus. But when the strife began, all these feelings disappeared, and the struggle became mortal.

The jealousy excited in the mind of Philip by the events of Messina still rankled, and the two monarchs refused to act in concert. Instead of making a joint attack upon the town, the French monarch assailed it alone, and was repulsed. Richard did the same, and with the same result. Philip tried to seduce the soldiers of Richard from their allegiance by the offer of three gold pieces per month to every knight who would forsake the banners of England for those of France. Richard endeavoured to neutralise the offer by a larger one, and promised four pieces to every French knight who should join the Lion of England. In this unworthy rivalry their time was wasted, to the great detriment of the discipline and efficiency of their followers. Some good was nevertheless effected; for the mere presence of two such armies prevented the besieged city from receiving supplies, and the inhabitants were reduced by famine to the most woful straits. Saladin did not deem it prudent to risk a general engagement by coming to their relief, but preferred to wait till dissension had weakened his enemy, and made him an easy prey. Perhaps if he had been aware of the real extent of the extremity in Acre, he would have changed his plan; but, cut off from the town, he did not know its misery till it was too late. After a short truce the city capitulated upon terms so severe that Saladin afterwards refused to ratify them. The chief conditions were, that the precious wood of the true cross, captured by the Moslems in Jerusalem, should be restored; that a sum of two hundred thousand gold pieces should be paid; and that all the Christian prisoners in Acre should be released, together with two hundred knights and a thousand soldiers detained in captivity by Saladin. The eastern monarch, as may be well conceived, did not set much store on the wood of the cross, but was nevertheless anxious to keep it, as he knew its possession by the Christians would do more than a victory to restore their courage. He refused, therefore, to deliver it up, or to accede to any of the conditions; and Richard, as he had previously threatened, barbarously ordered all the Saracen prisoners in his power to be put to death.

The possession of the city only caused new and unhappy dissensions between the Christian leaders. The Archduke of Austria unjustifiably hoisted his flag on one of the towers of Acre, which Richard no sooner saw than he tore it down with his own hands, and trampled it under his feet. Philip, though he did not sympathise with the archduke, was piqued at the assumption of Richard, and the breach between the two monarchs became wider than ever. A foolish dispute arose at the same time between Guy of Lusignan and Conrad of Montferrat for the crown of Jerusalem. The inferior knights were not slow to imitate the pernicious example, and jealousy, distrust, and ill-will reigned in the Christian camp. In the midst of this confusion the king of France suddenly announced his intention to return to his own country. Richard was filled with indignation, and exclaimed, "Eternal shame light on him, and on all France, if, for any cause, he leave this work unfinished!" But Philip was not to be stayed. His health had suffered by his residence in the East; and, ambitious of playing a first part, he preferred to play none at all than to play second to King Richard. Leaving a small detachment of Burgundians behind, he returned to France with the remainder of his army; and Cœur de Lion, without feeling, in the multitude of his rivals, that he had lost the greatest, became painfully convinced that the right arm of the enterprise was lopped off.

After his departure, Richard re-fortified Acre, restored the Christian worship in the churches, and, leaving a Christian garrison to protect it, marched along the sea-coast towards Ascalon. Saladin was on the alert, and sent his light horse to attack the rear of the Christian army, while he himself, miscalculating their weakness since the defection of Philip, endeavoured to force them to a general engagement. The rival armies met near Azotus. A fierce battle ensued, in which Saladin was defeated and put to flight, and the road to Jerusalem left free for the Crusaders.

Again discord exerted its baleful influence, and prevented Richard from following up his victory. His opinion was constantly opposed by the other leaders, all jealous of his bravery and influence; and the army, instead of marching to Jerusalem, or even to Ascalon, as was first intended, proceeded to Jaffa, and remained in idleness until Saladin was again in a condition to wage war against them.

Bethlehem.

Many months were spent in fruitless hostilities and as fruitless negotiations. Richard's wish was to recapture Jerusalem; but there were difficulties in the way, which even his bold spirit could not conquer. His own intolerable pride was not the least cause of the evil; for it estranged many a generous spirit, who would have been willing to co-operate with him in all cordiality. At length it was agreed to march to the Holy City; but the progress made was so slow and painful, that the soldiers murmured, and the leaders meditated retreat. The weather was hot and dry, and there was little water to be procured. Saladin had choked up the wells and cisterns on the route, and the army had not zeal enough to push forward amid such privation. At Bethlehem a council was held, to debate whether they should retreat or advance. Retreat was decided upon, and immediately commenced. It is said, that Richard was first led to a hill, whence he could obtain a sight of the towers of Jerusalem, and that he was so affected at being so near it, and so unable to relieve it, that he hid his face behind his shield, and sobbed aloud.

The army separated into two divisions, the smaller falling back upon Jaffa, and the larger, commanded by Richard and the Duke of Burgundy, returning to Acre. Before the English monarch had made all his preparations for his return to Europe, a messenger reached Acre with the intelligence that Jaffa was besieged by Saladin, and that, unless relieved immediately, the city would be taken. The French, under the Duke of Burgundy, were so wearied with the war, that they refused to aid their brethren in Jaffa. Richard, blushing with shame at their pusillanimity, called his English to the rescue, and arrived just in time to save the city. His very name put the Saracens to flight, so great was their dread of his prowess. Saladin regarded him with the warmest admiration, and when Richard, after his victory, demanded peace, willingly acceded. A truce was concluded for three years and eight months, during which Christian pilgrims were to enjoy the liberty of visiting Jerusalem without hindrance or payment of any tax. The Crusaders were allowed to retain the cities of Tyre and Jaffa, with the country intervening. Saladin, with a princely generosity, invited many of the Christians to visit Jerusalem; and several of the leaders took advantage of his offer to feast their eyes upon a spot which all considered so sacred. Many of them were entertained for days in the sultan's own palace, from which they returned with their tongues laden with the praises of the noble infidel. Richard and Saladin never met, though the impression that they did will remain on many minds, who have been dazzled by the glorious fiction of Sir Walter Scott. But each admired the prowess and nobleness of soul of his rival, and agreed to terms far less onerous than either would have accepted, had this mutual admiration not existed. [17]

The king of England no longer delayed his departure, for messengers from his own country brought imperative news that his presence was required to defeat the intrigues that were fomenting against his crown. His long imprisonment in the Austrian dominions and final ransom are too well known to be dwelt upon. And thus ended the third Crusade, less destructive of human life than the two first, but quite as useless.

The flame of popular enthusiasm now burned pale indeed, and all the efforts of popes and potentates were insufficient to rekindle it. At last, after flickering unsteadily, like a lamp expiring in the socket, it burned up brightly for one final instant, and was extinguished for ever.

The fourth Crusade, as connected with popular feeling, requires little or no notice. At the death of Saladin, which happened a year after the conclusion of his truce with Richard of England, his vast empire fell to pieces. His brother Saif Eddin, or Saphaddin, seized upon Syria, in the possession of which he was troubled by the sons of Saladin. When this intelligence reached Europe, the Pope, Celestine III., judged the moment favourable for preaching a new Crusade. But every nation in Europe was unwilling and cold towards it. The people had no ardour, and kings were occupied with more weighty matters at home. The only monarch of Europe who encouraged it was the Emperor Henry of Germany, under whose auspices the Dukes of Saxony and Bavaria took the field at the head of a considerable force. They landed in Palestine, and found any thing but a welcome from the Christian inhabitants. Under the mild sway of Saladin, they had enjoyed repose and toleration, and both were endangered by the arrival of the Germans. They looked upon them in consequence as over-officious intruders, and gave them no encouragement in the warfare against Saphaddin. The result of this Crusade was even more disastrous than the last; for the Germans contrived not only to embitter the Saracens against the Christians of Judea, but to lose the strong city of Jaffa, and cause the destruction of nine-tenths of the army with which they had quitted Europe. And so ended the fourth Crusade.

The fifth was more important, and had a result which its projectors never dreamed of — no less than the sacking of Constantinople, and the placing of a French dynasty upon the imperial throne of the eastern Cæsars. Each succeeding pope, however much he may have differed from his predecessors on other points, zealously agreed in one, that of maintaining by every possible means the papal ascendency. No scheme was so likely to aid in this endeavour as the Crusades. As long as they could persuade the kings and nobles of Europe to fight and die in Syria, their own sway was secured over the minds of men at home. Such being their object, they never inquired whether a Crusade was or was not likely to be successful, whether the time were well or ill chosen, or whether men and money could be procured in sufficient abundance. Pope Innocent III. would have been proud if he could have bent the refractory monarchs of

England and France into so much submission. But John and Philip Augustus were both engaged. Both had deeply offended the Church, and had been laid under her ban, and both were occupied in important reforms at home; Philip in bestowing immunities upon his subjects, and John in having them forced from him. The emissaries of the pope therefore plied them in vain; but as in the first and second Crusades, the eloquence of a powerful preacher incited the nobility, and through them a certain portion of the people; Foulque bishop of Neuilly, an ambitious and enterprising prelate, entered fully into the views of the court of Rome, and preached the Crusade wherever he could find an audience. Chance favoured him to a degree he did not himself expect, for he had in general found but few proselytes, and those few but cold in the cause. Theobald count of Champagne had instituted a grand tournament, to which he had invited all the nobles from far and near. Upwards of two thousand knights were present with their retainers, besides a vast concourse of people to witness the sports. In the midst of the festivities Foulque arrived upon the spot, and conceiving the opportunity to be a favourable one, he addressed the multitude in eloquent language, and passionately called upon them to enrol themselves for the new Crusade. The Count de Champagne, young, ardent, and easily excited, received the cross at his hands. The enthusiasm spread rapidly. Charles count of Blois followed the example, and of the two thousand knights present, scarcely one hundred and fifty refused. The popular phrensy seemed on the point of breaking out as in the days of yore. The Count of Flanders, the Count of Bar, the Duke of Burgundy, and the Marquis of Montferrat, brought all their vassals to swell the train, and in a very short space of time an effective army was on foot and ready to march to Palestine.

The dangers of an overland journey were too well understood, and the Crusaders endeavoured to make a contract with some of the Italian states to convey them over in their vessels. Dandolo, the aged doge of Venice, offered them the galleys of the Republic; but the Crusaders, on their arrival in that city, found themselves too poor to pay even half the sum demanded. Every means was tried to raise money; the Crusaders melted down their plate, and ladies gave up their trinkets. Contributions were solicited from the faithful, but came in so slowly as to make it evident to all concerned, that the faithful of Europe were outnumbered by the prudent. As a last resource, Dandolo offered to convey them to Palestine at the expense of the Republic, if they would previously aid in the recapture of the city of Zara, which had been seized from the Venetians a short time previously by the king of Hungary. The Crusaders consented, much to the displeasure of the pope, who threatened excommunication upon all who should be turned aside from the voyage to Jerusalem. But notwithstanding the fulminations of the Church, the expedition never reached Palestine. The siege of Zara was speedily undertaken. After a long and brave defence, the city surrendered at discretion, and the Crusaders were free, if they had so chosen it, to use their swords against the Saracens. But the ambition of the chiefs had been directed, by unforeseen circumstances, elsewhere.

After the death of Manuel Comnenus, the Greek empire had fallen a prey to intestine divisions. His son Alexius II. had succeeded him, but was murdered after a short reign by his uncle Andronicus, who seized upon the throne. His reign also was but of short duration. Isaac Angelus, a member of the same family, took up arms against the usurper, and having defeated and captured him in a pitched battle, had him put to death. He also mounted the throne only to be cast down from it. His brother Alexius deposed him, and to incapacitate him from reigning, put out his eyes, and shut him up in a dungeon. Neither was Alexius III. allowed to remain in peaceable possession of the throne; the son of the unhappy Isaac, whose name also was Alexius, fled from Constantinople, and hearing that the Crusaders had undertaken the siege of Zara, made them the most magnificent offers if they would afterwards aid him in deposing his uncle. His offers were, that if by their means he was re-established in his father's dominions, he would place the Greek Church under the authority of the Pope of Rome, lend the whole force of the Greek empire to the conquest of Palestine, and distribute two hundred thousand marks of silver among the crusading army. The offer was accepted, with a proviso on the part of some of the leaders, that they should be free to abandon the design, if it met with the disapproval of the pope. But this was not to be feared. The submission of the schismatic Greeks to the See of Rome was a greater bribe to the Pontiff than the utter annihilation of the Saracen power in Palestine would have been.

The Crusaders were soon in movement for the imperial city. Their operations were skilfully and courageously directed, and spread such dismay as to paralyse the efforts of the usurper to retain possession of his throne. After a vain resistance, he abandoned the city to its fate, and fled no one knew whither. The aged and blind Isaac was taken from his dungeon by his subjects, and placed upon the throne ere the Crusaders were apprised of the flight of his rival. His son Alexius IV. was afterwards associated with him in the sovereignty.

But the conditions of the treaty gave offence to the Grecian people, whose prelates refused to place themselves under the dominion of the See of Rome. Alexius at first endeavoured to persuade his subjects to admission, and prayed the Crusaders to remain in Constantinople until they had fortified him in the possession of a throne which was yet far from secure. He soon became unpopular with his subjects; and breaking faith with regard to the subsidies, he offended the Crusaders. War was at length declared upon him by both parties; by his people for his tyranny, and by his former friends for his treachery. He was seized in his palace by his own guards and thrown into prison, while the Crusaders were making ready to besiege his capital. The Greeks immediately proceeded to the election of a new monarch; and looking about for a man of courage, energy, and perseverance, they fixed upon Alexius Ducas, who, with almost every bad quality, was possessed of the virtues they needed. He ascended the throne under the name of Murzuphlis. One of his first acts was to rid himself of his youngest predecessor — a broken heart had already removed the blind old Isaac, no longer a stumbling-block in his way — and the young Alexius was soon after put to death in his prison.

Constantinople.

War to the knife was now declared between the Greeks and the Franks; and early in the spring of the year 1204, preparations were commenced for an assault upon Constantinople. The French and Venetians entered into a treaty for the division of the spoils among their soldiery; for so confident were they of success, that failure never once entered into their calculations. This confidence led them on to victory; while the Greeks, cowardly as treacherous people always are, were paralysed by a foreboding of evil. It has been a matter of astonishment to all historians, that Murzuphlis, with the reputation for courage which he had acquired, and the immense resources at his disposal, took no better measures to repel the onset of the Crusaders. Their numbers were as a mere handful in comparison with those which he could have brought against them; and if they had the hopes of plunder to lead them on, the Greeks had their homes to fight for, and their very existence as a nation to protect. After an impetuous assault, repulsed for one day, but renewed with double impetuosity on another, the Crusaders lashed their vessels against the walls, slew every man who opposed them, and, with little loss to themselves, entered the city. Murzuphlis fled, and Constantinople was given over to be pillaged by the victors. The wealth they found was enormous. In money alone there was sufficient to distribute twenty marks of silver to each knight, ten to each squire or servant at arms, and five to each archer. Jewels, velvets, silks, and every luxury of attire, with rare wines and fruits, and valuable merchandise of every description, also fell into their hands, and were bought by the trading Venetians, and the proceeds distributed among the army. Two thousand persons were put to the sword; but had there been less plunder to take up the attention of the victors, the slaughter would in all probability have been much greater.

In many of the bloody wars which defile the page of history, we find that soldiers, utterly reckless of the works of God, will destroy his masterpiece, man, with unsparing brutality, but linger with respect round the beautiful works of art. They will slaughter women and children, but spare a picture; will hew down the sick, the helpless, and the hoary-headed, but refrain from injuring a fine piece of sculpture. The Latins, on their entrance into Constantinople, respected neither the works of God nor man, but vented their brutal ferocity upon the one, and satisfied their avarice upon the other. Many beautiful bronze statues, above all price as works of art, were broken into pieces to be sold as old metal. The finely-chiselled marble, which could be put to no such vile uses, was also destroyed with a recklessness, if possible, still more atrocious.[18]

The carnage being over, and the spoil distributed, six persons were chosen from among the Franks and six from among the Venetians, who were to meet and elect an emperor, previously binding themselves by oath to select the individual best qualified among the candidates. The choice wavered between Baldwin count of Flanders and Boniface marquis of Montferrat, but fell eventually upon the former. He was straightway robed in the imperial purple, and became the founder of a new dynasty. He did not live long to enjoy his power, or to consolidate it for his successors, who, in their turn, were soon swept away. In less than sixty years the rule of the Franks at Constantinople was brought to as sudden and disastrous a termination as the reign of Murzuphlis: and this was the grand result of the fifth Crusade.

Pope Innocent III., although he had looked with no very unfavourable eye upon these proceedings, regretted that nothing had been done for the relief of the Holy Land; still, upon every convenient occasion, he enforced the necessity of a new Crusade.

Until the year 1213, his exhortations had no other effect than to keep the subject in the mind of Europe. Every spring and summer detachments of pilgrims continued to set out for Palestine to the aid of their brethren, but not in sufficient numbers to be of much service. These periodical passages were called the *passagium Martii*, or the passage of March, and the *passagium Johannis*, or the passage of the festival of St. John. These did not consist entirely of soldiers, armed against the Saracen, but of pilgrims led by devotion, and in performance of their vows, bearing nothing with them but their staff and their wallet. Early in the spring of 1213 a more extraordinary body of Crusaders was raised in France and Germany. An immense number of boys and girls, amounting, according to some accounts, to thirty thousand, were incited by the persuasion of two monks to undertake the journey to Palestine. They were no doubt composed of the idle and deserted children who generally swarm in great cities, nurtured in vice and daring, and ready for any thing. The object of the monks seems to have been the atrocious one of inveigling them into slave-ships, on pretence of sending them to Syria, and selling them for slaves on the coast of Africa.[19] Great numbers of these poor victims were shipped at Marseilles; but the vessels, with the exception of two or three, were wrecked on the shores of Italy, and every soul perished. The remainder arrived safely in Africa, and were bought up as slaves, and sent off into the interior of the country. Another detachment arrived at Genoa; but the accomplices in this horrid plot having taken no measures at that port, expecting them all at Marseilles, they were induced to return to their homes by the Genoese.

Fuller, in his quaint history of the *Holy Warre*, says that this Crusade was done by the instinct of the devil; and he adds a reason, which may provoke mirth now, but which was put forth by the worthy historian in all soberness and sincerity. He says, "the devil, being cloyed with the murdering of men, desired a cordial of children's blood to comfort his weak stomach;" as epicures, when tired of mutton, resort to lamb for a change.

It appears from other authors that the preaching of the vile monks had such an effect upon these deluded children that they ran about the country, exclaiming, "O Lord Jesus, restore thy cross to us!" and that neither bolts nor bars, the fear of fathers, nor the love of mothers, was sufficient to restrain them from journeying to Jerusalem.

The details of these strange proceedings are exceedingly meagre and confused, and none of the contemporary writers who mention the subject have thought it worth while to state the names of the monks who originated the scheme, or the fate they met for their wickedness. Two merchants of Marseilles, who were to have shared in the profits, were, it is said, brought to justice for some other crime, and suffered death; but we are not informed whether they divulged any circumstances relating to this matter.

Pope Innocent III. does not seem to have been aware that the causes of this juvenile Crusade were such as have been stated, for, upon being informed that numbers of them had taken the cross, and were marching to the Holy Land, he exclaimed, "These children are awake while we sleep!" He imagined, apparently, that the mind of Europe was still bent on the recovery of Palestine, and that the zeal of these children implied a sort of reproach upon his own lukewarmness. Very soon afterwards, he bestirred himself with more activity, and sent an encyclical letter to the clergy of Christendom, urging them to preach a new Crusade. As usual, a number of adventurous nobles, who had nothing else to do, enrolled themselves with their retainers. At a Council of Lateran, which was held while these bands were collecting, Innocent announced that he himself would take the Cross, and lead the armies of Christ to the defence of his sepulchre. In all probability he would have done so, for he was zealous enough; but death stepped in, and destroyed his project ere it was ripe. His successor encouraged the Crusade, though he refused to accompany it; and the armament continued in France, England, and Germany. No leaders of any importance joined it from the former countries. Andrew king of Hungary was the only monarch who had leisure or inclination to leave his dominions. The Dukes of Austria and Bavaria joined him with a considerable army of Germans, and marching to Spalatro, took ship for Cyprus, and from thence to Acre.

The whole conduct of the king of Hungary was marked by pusillanimity and irresolution. He found himself in the Holy Land at the head of a very efficient army; the Saracens were taken by surprise, and were for some weeks unprepared to offer any resistance to his arms. He defeated the first body sent to oppose him, and marched towards Mount Tabor with the intention of seizing upon an important fortress which the Saracens had recently constructed. He arrived without impediment at the mount, and might have easily taken it; but a sudden fit of cowardice came over him, and he returned to Acre without striking a blow. He very soon afterwards abandoned the enterprise altogether, and returned to his own country.

Tardy reinforcements arrived at intervals from Europe; and the Duke of Austria, now the chief leader of the expedition, had still sufficient forces at his command to trouble the Saracens very seriously. It was resolved by him, in council with the other chiefs, that the whole energy of the Crusade should be directed upon Egypt, the seat of the Saracen power in its relationship to Palestine, and from whence were drawn the continual levies that were brought against them by the sultan. Damietta, which commanded the river Nile, and was one of the most important cities of Egypt, was chosen as the first point of attack. The siege was forthwith commenced, and carried on with considerable energy, until the Crusaders gained possession of a tower, which projected into the middle of the stream, and was looked upon as the very key of the city.

While congratulating themselves upon this success, and wasting in revelry the time which should have been employed in turning it to further advantage, they received the news of the death of the wise Sultan Saphaddin. His two sons, Camhel and Cohreddin, divided his empire between them. Syria and Palestine fell to the share of Cohreddin, while Egypt was consigned to the other brother, who had for some time exercised the functions of lieutenant of that country. Being unpopular among the Egyptians, they revolted against him, giving the Crusaders a finer opportunity for making a conquest than they had ever enjoyed before. But, quarrelsome and licentious as they had been from time immemorial, they did not see that the favourable moment had come; or seeing, could not profit by it. While they were revelling or fighting among themselves, under the walls of Damietta, the revolt was suppressed, and Camhel firmly established on the throne of Egypt. In conjunction with his brother Cohreddin, his next care was to drive the Christians from Damietta, and for upwards of three months they bent all their efforts to throw in supplies to the besieged, or draw on the besiegers to a general engagement. In neither were they successful; and the famine in Damietta became so dreadful that vermin of every description were thought luxuries, and sold for exorbitant prices. A dead dog became more valuable than a live ox in time of prosperity. Unwholesome food brought on disease, and the city could hold out no longer for absolute want of men to defend the walls.

Cohreddin and Camhel were alike interested in the preservation of so important a position, and, convinced of the certain fate of the city, they opened a conference with the crusading chiefs, offering to yield the whole of Palestine to the Christians upon the sole condition of the evacuation of Egypt. With a blindness and wrong-headedness almost incredible, these advantageous terms were refused, chiefly through the persuasion of Cardinal Pelagius, an ignorant and obstinate fanatic, who urged upon the Duke of Austria and the French and English leaders, that infidels never kept their word; that their offers were deceptive, and merely intended to betray. The conferences were brought to an abrupt termination by the Crusaders, and a last attack made upon the walls of Damietta. The besieged made but slight resistance, for they had no hope, and the Christians entered the city, and found, out of seventy thousand people, but three thousand remaining: so fearful had been the ravages of the twin fiends, plague and famine.

Several months were spent in Damietta. The climate either weakened the frames or obscured the understandings of the Christians; for, after their conquest, they lost all energy, and abandoned themselves more unscrupulously than ever to riot and debauchery. John of Brienne, who, by right of his wife, was the nominal sovereign of Jerusalem, was so disgusted with the pusillanimity, arrogance, and dissensions of the chiefs, that he withdrew entirely from them and retired to Acre. Large bodies also returned to Europe, and Cardinal Pelagius was left at liberty to blast the whole enterprise whenever it pleased him. He managed to conciliate John of Brienne, and marched forward with these combined forces to attack Cairo. It was only when he had approached within a few hours' march of that city that he discovered the inadequacy of his army. He turned back immediately; but the Nile had risen since his departure; the sluices were opened, and there was no means of reaching Damietta. In this strait, he sued for the peace he had formerly spurned, and, happily for himself, found the generous brothers Camhel and Cohreddin still willing to grant it. Damietta was soon afterwards given up, and the cardinal returned to Europe. John of Brienne retired to Acre, to mourn the loss of his kingdom, embittered against the folly of his pretended friends, who had ruined where they should have aided him. And thus ended the sixth Crusade. The seventh was more successful. Frederic II., emperor of Germany, had often vowed to lead his armies to the defence of Palestine, but was as often deterred from the journey by matters of more pressing importance. Cohreddin was a mild and enlightened monarch, and the Christians of Syria enjoyed repose and toleration under his rule: but John of Brienne was not willing to lose his kingdom without an effort; and the popes in Europe were ever willing to embroil the nations for the sake of extending their own power. No monarch of that age was capable of rendering more effective assistance than Frederic of Germany. To inspire him with more zeal, it was proposed that he should wed the young Princess Violante, daughter of John of Brienne, and heiress of the kingdom of Jerusalem. Frederic consented with joy and eagerness. The princess was brought from Acre to Rome without delay, and her marriage celebrated on a scale of great magnificence. Her father, John of Brienne, abdicated all his rights in favour of his son-in-law, and Jerusalem had once more a king, who had not only the will, but the power, to enforce his claims. Preparations for the new Crusade were immediately commenced, and in the course of six months the emperor was at the head of a well-disciplined army of sixty thousand men. Matthew Paris informs us, that an army of the same amount was gathered in England; and most of the writers upon the Crusades adopt his statement. When John of Brienne was in England, before his daughter's marriage with the emperor was thought of, praying for the aid of Henry III. and his nobles to recover his lost kingdom, he did not meet with much encouragement. Grafton, in his *Chronicle*, says, "he departed again without any great comfort." But when a man of more influence in European politics appeared upon the scene, the English nobles were as ready to sacrifice themselves in the cause as they had been in the time of Cœur de Lion.

The army of Frederic encamped at Brundusium; but a pestilential disease having made its appearance among them, their departure was delayed for several months. In the mean time the Empress Violante died in childbed. John of Brienne, who had already repented of his abdication, and was besides incensed against Frederic for many acts of neglect and insult, no sooner saw the only tie which bound them severed by the death of his daughter, than he began to bestir himself, and make interest with the pope to undo what he had done, and regain the honorary crown he had renounced. Pope Gregory IX., a man of a proud, unconciliating, and revengeful character, owed the emperor a grudge for many an act of disobedience to his authority, and encouraged the overtures of John of Brienne more than he should have done. Frederic, however, despised them both, and, as soon as his army was convalescent, set sail for Acre. He had not been many days at sea when he was himself attacked with the malady, and obliged to return to Otranto, the nearest port. Gregory, who had by this time decided in the interest of John of Brienne, excommunicated the emperor for returning from so holy an expedition on any pretext whatever. Frederic at first treated the excommunication with supreme contempt; but when he got well, he gave his holiness to understand that he was not to be outraged with impunity, and sent some of his troops to ravage the papal territories. This, however, only made the matter worse, and Gregory despatched messengers to Palestine forbidding the faithful, under severe pains and penalties, to hold any intercourse with the excommunicated emperor. Thus between them both, the scheme which they had so much at heart bade fair to be as effectually ruined as even the Saracens could have wished. Frederic still continued his zeal in the Crusade, for he was now king of Jerusalem, and fought for himself, and not for Christendom, or its representative, Pope Gregory. Hearing that John of Brienne was preparing to leave Europe, he lost no time in taking his own departure, and arrived safely at Acre. It was here that he first experienced the evil effects of excommunication. The Christians of Palestine refused to aid him in any way, and looked with distrust, if not with abhorrence, upon him. The Templars, Hospitallers, and other knights, shared at first the general feeling; but they were not men to yield a blind obedience to a distant potentate, especially when it compromised their own interests. When, therefore, Frederic prepared to march upon Jerusalem without them, they joined his banners to a man.

Templar and Hospitaller.

It is said that, previous to quitting Europe, the German emperor had commenced a negotiation with the Sultan Camhel for the restoration of the Holy Land, and that Camhel, who was jealous of the ambition of his brother Cohreddin, was willing to stipulate to that effect, on condition of being secured by Frederic in the possession of the more important territory of Egypt. But before the Crusaders reached Palestine, Camhel was relieved from all fears by the death of his brother. He nevertheless did not think it worth while to contest with the Crusaders the barren corner of the earth which had already been dyed with so much Christian and Saracen blood, and proposed a truce of three years, only stipulating, in addition, that the Moslems should be allowed to worship freely in the temple of Jerusalem. This happy termination did not satisfy the bigoted Christians of Palestine. The tolerance they sought for themselves, they were not willing to extend to others, and they complained bitterly of the privilege of free worship allowed to their opponents. Unmerited good fortune had made them insolent, and they contested the right of the emperor to become a party to any treaty, as long as he remained under the ecclesiastical ban. Frederic was disgusted with his new subjects; but, as the Templars and Hospitallers remained true to him, he marched to Jerusalem to be crowned. All the churches were shut against him, and he could not even find a priest to officiate at his coronation. He had despised the papal authority too long to quail at it now, when it was so unjustifiably exerted, and, as there was nobody to crown him, he very wisely crowned himself. He took the royal diadem from the altar with his own hands, and boldly and proudly placed it on his brow. No shouts of an applauding populace made the welkin ring; no hymns of praise and triumph resounded from the ministers of religion; but a thousand swords started from their scabbards to testify that their owners would defend the new monarch to the death.

It was hardly to be expected that he would renounce for any long period the dominion of his native land for the uneasy crown and barren soil of Palestine. He had seen quite enough of his new subjects before he was six months among them, and more important interests called him home. John of Brienne, openly leagued with Pope Gregory against him, was actually employed in ravaging his territories at the head of a papal army. This intelligence decided his return. As a preliminary step, he made those who had contemned his authority feel, to their sorrow, that he was their master. He then set sail, loaded with the curses of Palestine. And thus ended the seventh Crusade, which, in spite of every obstacle and disadvantage, had been productive of more real service to the Holy Land than any that had gone before; a result solely attributable to the bravery of Frederic and the generosity of the Sultan Camhel.

Soon after the emperor's departure a new claimant started for the throne of Jerusalem, in the person of Alice queen of Cyprus, and half-sister of the Mary who, by her marriage, had transferred her right to John of Brienne. The grand military orders, however, clung to Frederic, and Alice was obliged to withdraw.

So peaceful a termination to the Crusade did not give unmixed pleasure in Europe. The chivalry of France and England were unable to rest, and long before the conclusion of the truce, were collecting their armies for an eighth expedition. In Palestine also the contentment was far from universal. Many petty Mahomedan states in the immediate vicinity were not parties to the truce, and harassed the frontier towns incessantly. The Templars, ever turbulent, waged bitter war with the sultan of Aleppo, and in the end were almost exterminated. So great was the slaughter among them that Europe resounded with the sad story of their fate, and many a noble knight took arms to prevent the total destruction of an order associated with so many high and inspiring remembrances. Camhel, seeing the preparations that were making, thought that his generosity had been sufficiently shewn, and the very day the truce was at an end assumed the offensive, and marching forward to Jerusalem, took possession of it, after routing the scanty forces of the Christians. Before this intelligence reached Europe a large body of Crusaders was on the march, headed by the king of Navarre, the Duke of Burgundy, the Count de Bretagne, and other leaders. On their arrival, they learned that Jerusalem had been taken, but that the sultan was dead, and his kingdom torn by rival claimants to the supreme power. The dissensions of their foes ought to have made them united, but as in all previous Crusades, each feudal chief was master of his own host, and acted upon his own responsibility, and without reference to any general plan. The consequence was that nothing could be done. A temporary advantage was gained by one leader, who had no means of improving it; while another was defeated, without means of retrieving himself. Thus the war lingered till the battle of Gaza, when the king of Navarre was defeated with great loss, and compelled to save himself from total destruction by entering into a hard and oppressive treaty with the emir of Karac.

At this crisis aid arrived from England, commanded by Richard earl of Cornwall, the namesake of Cœur de Lion, and inheritor of his valour. His army was strong and full of hope. They had confidence in themselves and in their leader, and looked like men accustomed to victory. Their coming changed the aspect of affairs. The new sultan of Egypt was at war with the sultan of Damascus, and had not forces to oppose two enemies so powerful. He therefore sent messengers to meet the English earl, offering an exchange of prisoners and the complete cession of the Holy Land. Richard, who had not come to fight for the mere sake of fighting, agreed at once to terms so advantageous, and became the deliverer of Palestine without striking a blow. The sultan of Egypt then turned his whole force against his Moslem enemies, and the Earl of Cornwall returned to Europe. Thus ended the eighth Crusade, the most beneficial of all. Christendom had no further pretence for sending her fierce levies to the East. To all appearance the holy wars were at an end: the Christians had entire possession of Jerusalem, Tripoli, Antioch, Edessa, Acre, Jaffa, and, in fact, of nearly all Judea; and, could they have been at peace among themselves, they might have overcome, without great difficulty, the jealousy and hostility of their neighbours. A circumstance, as unforeseen as it was disastrous, blasted this fair prospect, and reillumed, for the last time, the fervour and fury of the Crusades.

Gengis Khan and his successors had swept over Asia like a tropical storm, overturning in their progress the landmarks of ages. Kingdom after kingdom was cast down as they issued, innumerable, from the far recesses of the North and East, and, among others, the empire of Korasmin was overrun by these all-conquering hordes. The Korasmins, a fierce, uncivilised race, thus driven from their homes, spread themselves, in their turn, over the south of Asia with fire and sword, in search of a resting-place. In their impetuous course they directed themselves towards Egypt, whose sultan, unable to withstand the swarm that had cast their longing eyes on the fertile valleys of the Nile, endeavoured to turn them from their course. For this purpose, he sent emissaries to Barbaquan, their leader, inviting them to settle in Palestine; and the offer being accepted by the wild horde, they entered the country before the Christians received the slightest intimation of their coming. It was as sudden as it was over-whelming. Onwards, like the simoom, they came, burning and slaying, and were at the walls of Jerusalem before the inhabitants had time to look round them. They spared neither life nor property; they slew women and children, and priests at the altar, and profaned even the graves of those who had slept for ages. They tore down every vestige of the Christian faith, and commit-ted horrors unparalleled in the history of warfare. About seven thousand of the inhabitants of Jerusalem sought safety in retreat; but before they were out of sight, the banner of the cross was hoisted upon the walls by the savage foe to decoy them back. The artifice was but too successful. The poor fugitives imagined that help had arrived from another direction, and turned back to regain their homes. Nearly the whole of them were massacred, and the streets of Jerusalem ran with blood.

Jaffa.

The Templars, Hospitallers, and Teutonic knights forgot their long and bitter animosities, and joined hand in hand to rout out this desolating foe. They entrenched themselves in Jaffa with all the chivalry of Palestine that yet remained, and endeavoured to engage the sultans of Emissa and Damascus to assist them against the common enemy. The aid obtained from the Moslems amounted at first to only four thousand men, but with these reinforcements Walter of Brienne, the lord of Jaffa, resolved to give battle to the Korasmins. The conflict was as deadly as despair on the one side, and unmitigated ferocity on the other, could make it. It lasted with varying fortune for two days, when the sultan of Emissa fled to his fortifications, and Walter of Brienne fell into the enemy's hands. The brave knight was suspended by the arms to a cross in sight of the walls of Jaffa, and the Korasminian leader declared that he should remain in that position until the city surrendered. Walter raised his feeble voice, not to advise surrender, but to command his soldiers to hold out to the last. But his gallantry was unavailing. So great had been the slaughter, that out of the grand array of knights, there now remained but sixteen Hospitallers, thirty-three Templars, and three Teutonic cavaliers. These with the sad remnant of the army fled to Acre, and the Korasmins were masters of Palestine.

The sultans of Syria preferred the Christians to this fierce horde for their neighbours. Even the sultan of Egypt began to regret the aid he had given to such barbarous foes, and united with those of Emissa and Damascus to root them from the land. The Korasmins amounted to but twenty thousand men, and were unable to resist the determined hostility which encompassed them on every side. The sultans defeated them in several engagements, and the peasantry rose up in masses to take vengeance upon them. Gradually their numbers were diminished. No mercy was shewn them in defeat. Barbaquan their leader was slain; and after five years of desperate struggles, they were finally extirpated, and Palestine became once more the territory of the Mussulmans.

William Longsword.

A short time previous to this devastating eruption, Louis IX. fell sick in Paris, and dreamed in the delirium of his fever that he saw the Christian and Moslem host fighting before Jerusalem, and the Christians defeated with great slaughter. The dream made a great impression on his superstitious mind, and he made a solemn vow, that if ever he recovered his health, he would take a pilgrimage to the Holy Land. When the news of the misfortunes of Palestine, and the awful massacres at Jerusalem and Jaffa, arrived in Europe, St. Louis remembered him of his dream. More persuaded than ever that it was an intimation direct from heaven, he prepared to take the cross at the head of his armies, and march to the deliverance of the Holy Sepulchre. From that moment he doffed the royal mantle of purple and ermine, and dressed in the sober serge becoming a pilgrim. All his thoughts were directed to the fulfilment of his design, and although his kingdom could but ill spare him, he made every preparation to leave it. Pope Innocent IV. applauded his zeal and afforded him every assistance. He wrote to Henry III. of England to forward the cause in his dominions, and called upon the clergy and laity all over Europe to contribute towards it. William Longsword, the celebrated Earl of Salisbury, took the cross at the head of a great number of valiant knights and soldiers. But the fanaticism of the people was not to be awakened either in France or England. Great armies were raised, but the masses no longer sympathised. Taxation had been the great cooler of zeal. It was no longer a disgrace even to a knight if he refused to take the cross. Rutebeuf, a French minstrel, who flourished about this time (1250), composed a dialogue between a Crusader and a non-Crusader, which the reader will find translated in Way's *Fabliaux*. The Crusader uses every argument to persuade the non-Crusader to take up arms, and forsake every thing, in the holy cause; but it is evident from the greater force of the arguments used by the non-Crusader, that he was the favourite of the minstrel. To a most urgent solicitation of his friend the Crusader, he replies:

> "I read thee right, thou holdest good
> To this same land I straight should hie,
> And win it back with mickle blood,
> Nor gaine one foot of soil thereby;
> While here dejected and forlorn
> My wife and babes are left to mourn;
> My goodly mansion rudely marred,
> All trusted to my dogs to guard.
> But I, fair comrade, well I wot
> An ancient saw of pregnant wit
> Doth bid us keep what we have got;
> And troth I mean to follow it."

This being the general feeling, it is not to be wondered at that Louis IX. was occupied fully three years in organising his forces, and in making the necessary preparations for his departure. When all was ready he set sail for Cyprus, accompanied by his queen, his two brothers, the Counts d'Anjou and d'Artois, and a long train of the noblest chivalry of France. His third brother, the Count de Poitiers, remained behind to collect another corps of Crusaders, and followed him in a few months afterwards. The army united at Cyprus, and amounted to fifty thousand men, exclusive of the English Crusaders under William Longsword. Again, a pestilential disease made its appearance, to which many hundreds fell victims. It was in consequence found necessary to remain in Cyprus until the spring. Louis then embarked for

Egypt with his whole host; but a violent tempest separated his fleet, and he arrived before Damietta with only a few thousand men. They were, however, impetuous and full of hope; and although the Sultan Melick Shah was drawn up on the shore with a force infinitely superior, it was resolved to attempt a landing without waiting the arrival of the rest of the army. Louis himself, in wild impatience, sprang from his boat, and waded on shore; while his army, inspired by his enthusiastic bravery, followed, shouting the old war-cry of the first Crusaders, *Dieu le veut! Dieu le veut!* A panic seized the Turks. A body of their cavalry attempted to bear down upon the Crusaders, but the knights fixed their large shields deep in the sands of the shore, and rested their lances upon them, so that they projected above, and formed a barrier so imposing, that the Turks, afraid to breast it, turned round and fairly took to flight. At the moment of this panic, a false report was spread in the Saracen host, that the sultan had been slain. The confusion immediately became general — the *deroute* was complete: Damietta itself was abandoned, and the same night the victorious Crusaders fixed their head-quarters in that city. The soldiers who had been separated from their chief by the tempest arrived shortly afterwards; and Louis was in a position to justify the hope, not only of the conquest of Palestine, but of Egypt itself.

But too much confidence proved the bane of his army. They thought, as they had accomplished so much, that nothing more remained to be done, and gave themselves up to ease and luxury. When, by the command of Louis, they marched towards Cairo, they were no longer the same men; success, instead of inspiring, had unnerved them; debauchery had brought on disease, and disease was aggravated by the heat of a climate to which none of them were accustomed. Their progress towards Massoura, on the road to Cairo, was checked by the Thanisian canal, on the banks of which the Saracens were drawn up to dispute the passage. Louis gave orders that a bridge should be thrown across: and the operations commenced under cover of two cat-castles, or high movable towers. The Saracens soon destroyed them by throwing quantities of Greek fire, the artillery of that day, upon them, and

Louis was forced to think of some other means of effecting his design. A peasant agreed, for a considerable bribe, to point out a ford where the army might wade across, and the Count d'Artois was despatched with fourteen hundred men to attempt it, while Louis remained to face the Saracens with the main body of the army. The Count d'Artois got safely over, and defeated the detachment that had been sent to oppose his landing. Flushed with the victory, the brave count forgot the inferiority of his numbers, and pursued the panic-stricken enemy into Massoura. He was now completely cut off from the aid of his brother Crusaders, which the Moslems perceiving, took courage and returned upon him, with a force swollen by the garrison of Massoura, and by reinforcements from the surrounding districts. The battle now became hand to hand. The Christians fought with the energy of desperate men, but the continually increasing numbers of the foe surrounded them completely, and cut off all hope, either of victory or escape. The Count d'Artois was among the foremost of the slain; and when Louis arrived to the rescue, the brave advanced-guard was nearly cut to pieces. Of the fourteen hundred but three hundred remained. The fury of the battle was now increased threefold. The French king and his troops performed prodigies of valour, and the Saracens, under the command of the Emir Ceccidun, fought as if they were determined to exterminate, in one last decisive effort, the new European swarm that had settled upon their coast. At the fall of the evening dews the Christians were masters of the field of Massoura, and flattered themselves that they were the victors. Self-love would not suffer them to confess that the Saracens had withdrawn, and not retreated; but their leaders were too wofully convinced that that fatal field had completed the disorganisation of the Christian army, and that all hopes of future conquest were at an end.

Impressed with this truth, the Crusaders sued for peace. The sultan insisted upon the immediate evacuation of Damietta, and that Louis himself should be delivered as hostage for the fulfilment of the condition. His army at once refused, and the negotiations were broken off. It was now resolved to attempt a retreat;

but the agile Saracens, now in the front and now in the rear, rendered it a matter of extreme difficulty, and cut off the stragglers in great numbers. Hundreds of them were drowned in the Nile; and sickness and famine worked sad ravages upon those who escaped all other casualties. Louis himself was so weakened by disease, fatigue, and discouragement, that he was hardly able to sit upon his horse. In the confusion of the flight he was separated from his attendants, and left a total stranger upon the sands of Egypt, sick, weary, and almost friendless. One knight, Geffry de Sergines, alone attended him, and led him to a miserable hut in a small village, where for several days he lay in the hourly expectation of death. He was at last discovered and taken prisoner by the Saracens, who treated him with all the honour due to his rank and all the pity due to his misfortunes. Under their care his health rapidly improved, and the next consideration was that of his ransom.

The Saracens demanded, besides money, the cession of Acre, Tripoli, and other cities of Palestine. Louis unhesitatingly refused, and conducted himself with so much pride and courage that the sultan declared he was the proudest infidel he had ever beheld. After a good deal of haggling, the sultan agreed to waive these conditions, and a treaty was finally concluded. The city of Damietta was restored; a truce of ten years agreed upon, and ten thousand golden bezants paid for the release of Louis and the liberation of all the captives. Louis then withdrew to Jaffa, and spent two years in putting that city, and Cesarea, with the other possessions of the Christians in Palestine, into a proper state of defence. He then returned to his own country, with great reputation as a saint, but very little as a soldier.

Matthew Paris informs us that, in the year 1250, while Louis was in Egypt, "thousands of the English were resolved to go to the holy war, had not the king strictly guarded his ports and kept his people from running out of doors." When the news arrived of the reverses and captivity of the French king, their ardour cooled; and the Crusade was sung of only, but not spoken of.

In France, a very different feeling was the result. The news of the king's capture spread consternation through the country. A fanatic monk of Citeaux suddenly appeared in the villages, preaching to the people, and announcing that the Holy Virgin, accompanied by a whole army of saints and martyrs, had appeared to him, and commanded him to stir up the shepherds and farm-labourers to the defence of the cross. To them only was his discourse addressed; and his eloquence was such, that thousands flocked around him, ready to follow wherever he should lead. The pastures and the corn-fields were deserted, and the shepherds, or *pastoureaux*, as they were termed, became at last so numerous as to amount to upwards of fifty thousand, — Millot says one hundred thousand men.[20] The Queen Blanche, who governed as regent during the absence of the king, encouraged at first the armies of the *pastoureaux*; but they soon gave way to such vile excesses that the peaceably disposed were driven to resistance. Robbery, murder, and violation marked their path; and all good men, assisted by the government, united in putting them down. They were finally dispersed, but not before three thousand of them had been massacred. Many authors say that the slaughter was still greater.

The ten years' truce concluded in 1264, and St. Louis was urged by two powerful motives to undertake a second expedition for the relief of Palestine. These were, fanaticism on the one hand, and a desire of retrieving his military fame on the other, which had suffered more than his parasites liked to remind him of. The pope, of course, encouraged his design, and once more the chivalry of Europe began to bestir themselves. In 1268, Edward, the heir of the English monarchy, announced his determination to join the Crusade; and the pope (Clement IV.) wrote to the prelates and clergy to aid the cause by their persuasions and their revenues. In England, they agreed to contribute a tenth of their possessions; and by a parliamentary order, a twentieth was taken from the corn and movables of all the laity at Michaelmas. In spite of the remonstrances of the few clear-headed statesmen who surrounded him, urging the ruin that might in consequence fall upon his then prosperous kingdom, Louis made every preparation for his departure. The warlike nobility were nothing loath; and in the spring of 1270, the king set sail with an army of sixty thousand men. He was driven by stress of weather into Sardinia, and while there, a change in his plans took place. Instead of proceeding to Acre, as he originally intended, he shaped his course for Tunis, on the African coast. The king of Tunis had some time previously expressed himself favourably disposed towards the Christians and their religion, and Louis, it appears, had hopes of converting him, and securing his aid against the sultan of Egypt. "What honour would be mine," he used to say, "if I could become godfather to this Mussulman king!" Filled with this idea he landed in Africa, near the site of the city of Carthage, but found that he had reckoned without his host. The king of Tunis had no thoughts of renouncing his religion, nor intention of aiding the Crusaders in any way. On the contrary, he opposed their landing with all the forces that could be collected on so sudden an emergency. The French, however, made good their first position, and defeated the Moslems with considerable loss. They also gained some advantage over the reinforcements that were sent to oppose them; but an infectious flux appeared in the army, and put a stop to all future victories. The soldiers died at the rate of a hundred in a day. The enemy, at the same time, made as great havoc as the plague. St. Louis himself was one of the first attacked by the disease. His constitution had been weakened by fatigues, and even before he left France he was unable to bear the full weight of his armour. It was soon evident to his sorrowing soldiers that their beloved monarch could not long survive. He lingered for some days, and died in Carthage in the fifty-sixth year of his age, deeply regretted by his army and his subjects, and leaving behind him one of the most singular reputations in history. He is the model-king of ecclesiastical writers, in whose eyes his very defects became virtues, because they were manifested in furtherance of their cause. More unprejudiced historians, while they condemn his fanaticism, admit that he was endowed with many high and rare qualities; that he was in no one point behind his age, and in many in advance of it.

His brother, Charles of Anjou, in consequence of a revolution in Sicily, had become king of that country. Before he heard of the death of Louis, he had sailed from Messina with large reinforcements. On his landing near Carthage, he advanced at the head of his army, amid the martial music of drums and trumpets. He was soon informed how inopportune was his rejoicing, and shed tears before his whole army, such as no warrior would have been ashamed to shed. A peace was speedily agreed upon with the king of Tunis, and the armies of France and Sicily returned to their homes.

Seal of Edward I.

So little favour had the Crusade found in England, that even the exertions of the heir to the throne had only collected a small force of fifteen hundred men. With these few Prince Edward sailed from Dover to Bourdeaux, in the expectation that he would find the French king in that city. St. Louis, however, had left a few weeks previously; upon which Edward followed him to Sardinia, and afterwards to Tunis. Before his arrival in Africa, St. Louis was no more, and peace had been concluded between France and Tunis. He determined, however, not to relinquish the Crusade. Returning to Sicily, he passed the winter in that country, and endeavoured to augment his little army. In the spring he set sail for Palestine, and arrived in safety at Acre. The Christians were torn, as usual, by mutual jealousies and animosities. The two great military orders were as virulent and as intractable as ever; opposed to each other, and to all the world. The arrival of Edward had the effect of causing them to lay aside their unworthy contention, and of uniting heart to heart in one last effort for the deliverance of their adopted country. A force of six thousand effective warriors was soon formed to join those of the English prince, and preparations were made for the renewal of hostilities. The Sultan Bibars or Bendocdar,[21] a fierce Mamluke, who had been placed on the throne by a bloody revolution, was at war with all his neighbours, and unable, for that reason, to concentrate his whole strength against them. Edward took advantage of this, and marching boldly forward to Nazareth, defeated the Turks and gained possession of that city. This was the whole amount of his successes. The hot weather engendered disease among his troops, and he himself, the life and soul of the expedition, fell sick among the first. He had been ill for some time, and was slowly recovering, when a messenger desired to speak with him on important matters, and to deliver some despatches into his own hand. While the prince was occupied in examining them, the traitorous messenger drew a dagger from his belt and stabbed him in the breast. The wound fortunately was not deep, and Edward had regained a portion of his strength. He struggled with the assassin, and put him to death with his own dagger, at the same time calling loudly for assistance.[22] His attendants came at his call, and found him bleeding profusely, and ascertained on inspection that the dagger was poisoned. Means were instantly taken to purify the wound, and an antidote was sent by the Grand Master of the Templars which removed all danger from the effects of the poison. Camden, in his history, has adopted the more popular, and certainly more beautiful version of this story, which says that the Princess Eleonora, in her love for her gallant husband, sucked the poison from his wound at the risk of her own life: to use the words of old Fuller, "it is a pity so pretty a story should not be true; and that so sovereign a remedy as a woman's tongue, anointed with the virtue of loving affection," should not have performed the good deed.

Edward suspected, and doubtless not without reason, that the assassin was employed by the sultan of Egypt. But it amounted to suspicion only; and by the sudden death of the assassin the principal clue to the discovery of the truth was lost for ever. Edward, on his recovery, prepared to resume the offensive; but the sultan, embarrassed by the defence of interests which, for the time being, he considered of more importance, made offers of peace to the Crusaders. This proof of weakness on the part of the enemy was calculated to render a man of Edward's temperament more anxious to prosecute the war; but he had also other interests to defend. News arrived in Palestine of the death of his father, King Henry III.; and his presence being necessary in England, he agreed to the terms of the sultan. These were, that the Christians should be allowed to retain their possessions in the Holy Land, and that a truce of ten years should be proclaimed. Edward then set sail for England; and thus ended the last Crusade.

The after-fate of the Holy Land may be told in a few words. The Christians, unmindful of their past sufferings and of the jealous neighbours they had to deal with, first broke the truce by plundering some Egyptian traders near Margat. The sultan immediately revenged the outrage by taking possession of Margat, and war once more raged between the nations. Margat made a gallant defence, but no reinforcements arrived from Europe to prevent its fall. Tripoli was the next, and other cities in succession, until at last Acre was the only city of Palestine that remained in possession of the Christians.

Tomb of Queen Eleanor.

The Grand Master of the Templars collected together his small and devoted band, and, with the trifling aid afforded by the King of Cyprus, prepared to defend to the death the last possession of his order. Europe was deaf to his cry for aid, the numbers of the foe were overwhelming, and devoted bravery was of no avail. In that disastrous siege the Christians were all but exterminated. The king of Cyprus fled when he saw that resistance was vain, and the Grand Master fell at the head of his knights, pierced with a hundred wounds. Seven Templars, and as many Hospitallers, alone escaped from the dreadful carnage. The victorious Moslems then set fire to the city, and the rule of the Christians in Palestine was brought to a close for ever.

This intelligence spread alarm and sorrow among the clergy of Europe, who endeavoured to rouse once more the energy and enthusiasm of the nations in the cause of the Holy Land. But the popular mania had run its career; the spark of zeal had burned its appointed time, and was never again to be re-illumined. Here and there a solitary knight announced his determination to take up arms, and now and then a king gave cold encouragement to the scheme; but it dropped almost as soon as spoken of, to be renewed again, still more feebly, at some longer interval.

Now what was the grand result of all these struggles? Europe expended millions of her treasures, and the blood of two millions of her children; and a handful of quarrelsome knights retained possession of Palestine for about one hundred years! Even had Christendom retained it to this day, the advantage, if confined to that, would have been too dearly purchased. But notwithstanding the fanaticism that originated, and the folly that conducted them, the Crusades were not productive of unmitigated evil. The feudal chiefs became better members of society by coming in contact, in Asia, with a civilisation superior to their own; the people secured some small instalments of their rights; kings, no longer at war with their nobility, had time to pass some good laws; the human mind learned some little wisdom from hard experience, and, casting off the slough of superstition in which the Roman clergy had so long enveloped it, became prepared to receive the seeds of the approaching Reformation. Thus did the all-wise Disposer of events bring good out of evil, and advance the civilisation and ultimate happiness of the nations of the West by means of the very fanaticism that had led them against the East. But the whole subject is one of absorbing interest, and, if carried fully out in all its bearings, would consume more space than the plan of this work will allow. The philosophic student will draw his own conclusions; and he can have no better field for the exercise of his powers than this European madness — its advantages and disadvantages, its causes and results.

Chapter 2.

The Witch Mania.

Arras.

What wrath of gods, or wicked influence
Of tears, conspiring wretched men t' afflict,
Hath pour'd on earth this noyous pestilence
That mortal minds doth inwardly infect
With love of blindness and of ignorance?

Spencer's Tears of the Muses.

Countrymen. Hang her! beat her! kill her!
Justice. How now? Forbear this violence!
Mother Sawyer. A crew of villains — a knot of bloody hangmen! set
to torment me! I know not why.
Justice. Alas, neighbour Banks! are you a ringleader in mischief? Fie!
to abuse an aged woman!
Banks. Woman! a she hell-cat, a witch! To prove her one, we no
sooner set fire on the thatch of her house, but in she came running, as
if the devil had sent her in a barrel of gunpowder.

Ford's Witch of Edmonton.

The belief that disembodied spirits may be permitted to revisit this world has its foundation upon that sublime hope of immortality which is at once the chief solace and greatest triumph of our reason. Even if revelation did not teach us, we feel that we have that within us which shall never die; and all our experience of this life but makes us cling the more fondly to that one repaying hope. But in the early days of "little knowledge" this grand belief became the source of a whole train of superstitions, which, in their turn, became the fount from whence flowed a deluge of blood and horror. Europe, for a period of two centuries and a half, brooded upon the idea, not only that parted spirits walked the earth to meddle in the affairs of men, but that men had power to summon evil spirits to their aid to work woe upon their fellows. An epidemic terror seized upon the nations; no man thought himself secure, either in his person or possessions, from the machinations of the devil and his agents. Every calamity that befell him he attributed to a witch. If a storm arose and blew down his barn, it was witchcraft; if his cattle died of a murrain—if disease fastened upon his limbs, or death entered suddenly and snatched a beloved face from his hearth—they were not visitations of Providence, but the works of some neighbouring hag, whose wretchedness or insanity caused the ignorant to raise their finger and point at her as a witch. The word was upon every body's tongue. France, Italy, Germany, England, Scotland, and the far north successively ran mad upon this subject, and for a long series of years furnished their tribunals with so many trials for witchcraft, that other crimes were seldom or never spoken of. Thousands upon thousands of unhappy persons fell victims to this cruel and absurd delusion. In many cities of Germany, as will be shewn more fully in its due place hereafter, the average number of executions for this pretended crime was six hundred annually, or two every day, if we leave out the Sundays, when it is to be supposed that even this madness refrained from its work.

A misunderstanding of the famous text of the Mosaic law, "Thou shalt not suffer a witch to live," no doubt led many conscientious men astray, whose superstition, warm enough before, wanted but a little corroboration to blaze out with desolating fury. In all ages of the world men have tried to hold converse with superior beings, and to pierce by their means the secrets of futurity. In the time of Moses, it is evident that there were impostors who trafficked upon the credulity of mankind, and insulted the supreme majesty of the true God by pretending to the power of divination. Hence the law which Moses, by Divine command, promulgated against these criminals; but it did not follow, as the superstitious monomaniacs of the middle ages imagined, that the Bible established the existence of the power of divination by its edicts against those who pretended to it. From the best authorities, it appears that the Hebrew word, which has been rendered *venefica* and *witch*, means a poisoner and divineress, a dabbler in spells, or fortune-teller. The modern witch was a very different character, and joined to her pretended power of foretelling future events that of working evil upon the life, limbs, and possessions of mankind. This power was only to be acquired by an express compact, signed in blood, with the devil himself, by which the wizard or witch renounced baptism, and sold his or her immortal soul to the evil one, without any saving clause of redemption.

There are so many wondrous appearances in nature for which science and philosophy cannot even now account, that it is not surprising that, when natural laws were still less understood, men should have attributed to supernatural agency every appearance which they could not otherwise explain. The merest tyro now understands various phenomena which the wisest of old could not fathom. The schoolboy knows why, upon high mountains, there should on certain occasions appear three or four suns in the firmament at once, and why the figure of a traveller upon one eminence should be reproduced, inverted and of a gigantic stature, upon another. We all know the strange pranks which imagination can play in certain diseases; that the hypochondriac can see visions and spectres; and that there have been cases in which men were perfectly persuaded that they were teapots. Science has lifted up the veil, and rolled away all the fantastic horrors in which our forefathers shrouded these and similar cases. The man who now imagines himself a wolf is sent to the hospital instead of to the stake, as in the days of the witch mania; and earth, air, and sea are unpeopled of the grotesque spirits that were once believed to haunt them.

Before entering further into the history of Witchcraft, it may be as well if we consider the absurd impersonation of the evil principle formed by the monks in their legends. We must make acquaintance with the *primum mobile*, and understand what sort of a personage it was who gave the witches, in exchange for their souls, the power to torment their fellow-creatures. The popular notion of the devil was, that he was a large, ill-formed, hairy sprite, with horns, a long tail, cloven feet, and dragon's wings. In this shape he was constantly brought on the stage by the monks in their early "miracles" and "mysteries." In these representations he was an important personage, and answered the purpose of the clown in the modern pantomime. The great fun for the people was to see him well belaboured by the saints with clubs or cudgels, and to hear him howl with pain as he limped off, maimed by the blow of some vigorous anchorite. St. Dunstan generally served him the glorious trick for which he is renowned, catching hold of his nose with a pair of red-hot pincers, till "Rocks and distant dells resounded with his cries."

Some of the saints spat in his face, to his very great annoyance; and others chopped pieces off of his tail, which, however, always grew on again. This was paying him in his own coin, and amused the populace mightily, for they all remembered the scurvy tricks he had played them and their forefathers. It was believed that he endeavoured to trip people up by laying his long invisible tail in their way, and giving it a sudden whisk when their legs were over it; — that he used to get drunk, and swear like a trooper, and be so mischievous in his cups as to raise tempests and earthquakes, to destroy the fruits of the earth, and the barns and homesteads of true believers; — that he used to run invisible spits into people by way of amusing himself in the long winter evenings, and to proceed to taverns and regale himself with the best, offering in payment pieces of gold which, on the dawn of the following morning, invariably turned into slates.

Sometimes, disguised as a large drake, he used to lurk among the bulrushes, and frighten the weary traveller out of his wits by his awful quack. The reader will remember the lines of Burns in his address to the "De'il," which so well express the popular notion on this point:

> "Ae dreary, windy, winter night,
> The stars shot down wi' sklentin light,
> Wi' you mysel, I got a fright
> Ayont the lough;
> Ye, like a rash-bush, stood in sight
> Wi' waving sough.
> The cudgel in my nieve did shake,
> Each bristled hair stood like a stake,
> When wi' an eldritch stour, 'quaick! quaick!'
> Among the springs
> Awa' ye squattered, like a drake,
> On whistling wings."

In all the stories circulated and believed about him, he was represented as an ugly, petty, mischievous spirit, who rejoiced in playing off all manner of fantastic tricks upon poor humanity. Milton seems to have been the first who succeeded in giving any but a ludicrous description of him. The sublime pride, which is the quintessence of evil, was unconceived before his time. All other limners made him merely grotesque, but Milton made him awful. In this the monks shewed themselves but miserable romancers; for their object undoubtedly was to represent the fiend as terrible as possible. But there was nothing grand about their Satan; on the contrary, he was a low, mean devil, whom it was easy to circumvent, and fine fun to play tricks with. But, as is well and eloquently remarked by a modern writer,[23] the subject has also its serious side. An Indian deity, with its wild distorted shape and grotesque attitude, appears merely ridiculous when separated from its accessories and viewed by daylight in a museum; but restore it to the darkness of its own hideous temple, bring back to our recollection the victims that have bled upon its altar or been crushed beneath its car, and our sense of the ridiculous subsides into aversion and horror. So, while the superstitious dreams of former times are regarded as mere speculative insanities, we may be for a moment amused with the wild incoherencies of the patients; but when we reflect that out of these hideous misconceptions of the principle of evil arose the belief in witchcraft—that this was no dead faith, but one operating on the whole being of society, urging on the wisest and the mildest to deeds of murder, or cruelties scarcely less than murder—that the learned and the beautiful, young and old, male and female, were devoted by its influence to the stake and the scaffold—every feeling disappears, except that of astonishment that such things could be, and humiliation at the thought that the delusion was as lasting as it was universal.

Besides this chief personage, there was an infinite number of inferior demons, who played conspicuous parts in the creed of witchcraft. The pages of Bekker, Leloyer, Bodin, Delrio, and De Lancre, abound with descriptions of the qualities of these imps, and the functions which were assigned them. From these authors,—three of whom were commissioners for the trial of witches, and who wrote from the confessions made by the supposed criminals and the evidence delivered against them,—and from the more recent work of M. Jules Garinet, the following summary of the creed has been, with great pains, extracted. The student who is desirous of knowing more is referred to the works in question; he will find enough in every leaf to make his blood curdle with shame and horror: but the purity of these pages shall not be soiled by any thing so ineffably humiliating and disgusting as a complete exposition of them; what is here culled will be a sufficient sample of the popular belief, and the reader would but lose time who should seek in the writings of the demonologists for more ample details. He will gain nothing by lifting the veil which covers their unutterable obscenities, unless, like Sterne, he wishes to gather fresh evidence of "what a beast man is." In that case, he will find plenty there to convince him that the beast would be libelled by the comparison.

It was thought that the earth swarmed with millions of demons of both sexes, many of whom, like the human race, traced their lineage up to Adam, who after the fall was led astray by devils, assuming the forms of beautiful women to deceive him.

These demons "increased and multiplied" among themselves with the most extraordinary rapidity. Their bodies were of the thin air, and they could pass through the hardest substances with the greatest ease. They had no fixed residence or abiding place, but were tossed to and fro in the immensity of space. When thrown together in great multitudes, they excited whirlwinds in the air and tempests in the waters, and took delight in destroying the beauty of nature and the monuments of the industry of man. Although they increased among themselves like ordinary creatures, their numbers were daily augmented by the souls of wicked men, of children still-born, of women who died in childbed, and of persons killed in duels. The whole air was supposed to be full of them, and many unfortunate men and women drew them by thousands into their mouths and nostrils at every inspiration; and the demons, lodging in their bowels or other parts of their bodies, tormented them with pains and diseases of every kind, and sent them frightful dreams. St. Gregory of Nice relates a story of a nun who forgot to say her *benedicite* and make the sign of the cross before she sat down to supper, and who in consequence swallowed a demon concealed among the leaves of a lettuce. Most persons said the number of these demons was so great that they could not be counted, but Wierus asserted that they amounted to no more than seven millions four hundred and five thousand nine hundred and twenty-six; and that they were divided into seventy-two companies or battalions, to each of which there was a prince or captain. They could assume any shape they pleased. When they were male, they were called incubi; and when female, succubi. They sometimes made themselves hideous; and at other times they assumed shapes of such transcendent loveliness, that mortal eyes never saw beauty to compete with theirs.

Although the devil and his legions could appear to mankind at any time, it was generally understood that he preferred the night between Friday and Saturday. If Satan himself appeared in human shape, he was never perfectly and in all respects like a man. He was either too black or too white, too large or too small, or some of his limbs were out of proportion to the rest of his body. Most commonly his feet were deformed, and he was obliged to curl up and conceal his tail in some part of his habiliments; for, take what shape he would, he could not get rid of that encumbrance. He sometimes changed himself into a tree or a river; and upon one occasion he transformed himself into a barrister, as we learn from Wierus, book iv. chapter 9. In the reign of Philippe le Bel, he appeared to a monk in the shape of a dark man riding a tall black horse, then as a friar, afterwards as an ass and finally as a coach-wheel. Instances are not rare in which both he and his inferior demons have taken the form of handsome young men, and, successfully concealing their tails, have married beautiful young women, who have had children by them. Such children were easily recognisable by their continual shrieking, by their requiring five nurses to suckle them, and by their never growing fat.

All these demons were at the command of any individual who would give up his immortal soul to the prince of evil for the privilege of enjoying their services for a stated period. The wizard or witch could send them to execute the most difficult missions: whatever the witch commanded was performed, except it was a good action, in which case the order was disobeyed, and evil worked upon herself instead.

At intervals, according to the pleasure of Satan, there was a general meeting of the demons and all the witches. This meeting was called the Sabbath, from its taking place on the Saturday, or immediately after midnight on Fridays. These sabbaths were sometimes held for one district, sometimes for another, and once at least every year it was held on the Brocken, or among other high mountains, as a general sabbath of the fiends for the whole of Christendom.

The devil generally chose a place where four roads met as the scene of this assembly, or if that was not convenient, the neighbourhood of a lake. Upon this spot nothing would ever afterwards grow, as the hot feet of the demons and witches burnt the principle of fecundity from the earth, and rendered it barren for ever. When orders had been once issued for the meeting of the sabbath, all the wizards and witches who failed to attend it were lashed by demons with a rod made of serpents or scorpions, as a punishment for their inattention or want of punctuality.

In France and England the witches were supposed to ride uniformly upon broomsticks; but in Italy and Spain, the devil himself, in the shape of a goat, used to transport them on his back, which lengthened or shortened according to the number of witches he was desirous of accommodating. No witch, when proceeding to the sabbath, could get out by a door or window, were she to try ever so much. Their general mode of ingress was by the keyhole, and of egress by the chimney, up which they flew, broom and all, with the greatest ease. To prevent the absence of the witches from being noticed by their neighbours, some inferior demon was commanded to assume their shapes and lie in their beds, feigning illness, until the sabbath was over. When all the wizards and witches had arrived at the place of rendezvous, the infernal ceremonies of the sabbath began. Satan, having assumed his favourite shape of a large he-goat, with a face in front and another in his haunches, took his seat upon a throne; and all present, in succession, paid their respects to him, and kissed him in his face behind. This done, he appointed a master of the ceremonies, in company with whom he made a personal examination of all the wizards and witches, to see whether they had the secret mark about them by which they were stamped as the devil's own. This mark was always insensible to pain. Those who had not yet been marked, received the mark from the master of the ceremonies, the devil at the same time bestowing nicknames upon them. This done, they all began to sing and dance in the most furious manner, until some one arrived who was anxious to be admitted into their society. They were then silent for a while, until the new-comer had denied his salvation, kissed the devil, spat upon the Bible, and sworn obedience to him in all things. They then began dancing again with all their might, and singing these words,

"*Alegremos, Alegremos!*
Que gente va tenemos!"

In the course of an hour or two they generally became wearied of this violent exercise, and then they all sat down and recounted the evil deeds they had done since their last meeting. Those who had not been malicious and mischievous enough towards their fellow-creatures, received personal chastisement from Satan himself, who flogged them with thorns or scorpions till they were covered with blood, and unable to sit or stand.

When this ceremony was concluded, they were all amused by a dance of toads. Thousands of these creatures sprang out of the earth, and standing on their hind legs, danced, while the devil played the bagpipes or the trumpet. These toads were all endowed with the faculty of speech, and entreated the witches to reward them with the flesh of unbaptised babes for their exertions to give them pleasure. The witches promised compliance. The devil bade them remember to keep their word; and then stamping his foot, caused all the toads to sink into the earth in an instant. The place being thus cleared, preparation was made for the banquet, where all manner of disgusting things were served up and greedily devoured by the demons and witches; although the latter were sometimes regaled with choice meats and expensive wines from golden plates and crystal goblets; but they were never thus favoured unless they had done an extraordinary number of evil deeds since the last period of meeting.

After the feast, they began dancing again; but such as had no relish for any more exercise in that way, amused themselves by mocking the holy sacrament of baptism. For this purpose, the toads were again called up, and sprinkled with filthy water; the devil making the sign of the cross, and all the witches calling out, "*In nomine Patricâ, Aragueaco Petrica, agora! agora! Valentia, jouando goure gaits goustia!*" which meant, "In the name of Patrick, Petrick of Aragon, now, now, all our ills are over!"

When the devil wished to be particularly amused, he made the witches strip off their clothes and dance before him, each with a cat tied round her neck, and another dangling from her body in form of a tail. When the cock crew, they all disappeared, and the sabbath was ended.

This is a summary of the belief which prevailed for many centuries nearly all over Europe, and which is far from eradicated even at this day. It was varied in some respects in several countries, but the main points were the same in France, Germany, Great Britain, Italy, Spain, and the far North of Europe.

The early annals of France abound with stories of supposed sorcery, but it was not until the time of Charlemagne that the crime acquired any great importance. "This monarch," says M. Jules Garinet,[24] "had several times given orders that all necromancers, astrologers, and witches should be driven from his states; but as the number of criminals augmented daily, he found it necessary at last to resort to severer measures. In consequence, he published several edicts, which may be found at length in the *Capitulaire de Baluse*. By these, every sort of magic, enchantment, and witchcraft was forbidden; and the punishment of death decreed against those who in any way evoked the devil, compounded love-philters, afflicted either man or woman with barrenness, troubled the atmosphere, excited tempests, destroyed the fruits of the earth, dried up the milk of cows, or tormented their fellow-creatures with sores and diseases. All persons found guilty of exercising these execrable arts were to be executed immediately upon conviction, that the earth might be rid of the burden and curse of their presence; and those even who consulted them might also be punished with death."[25]

After this time, prosecutions for witchcraft are continually mentioned, especially by the French historians. It was a crime imputed with so much ease, and repelled with so much difficulty, that the powerful, whenever they wanted to ruin the weak, and could fix no other imputation upon them, had only to accuse them of witchcraft to ensure their destruction. Instances in which this crime was made the pretext for the most violent persecution, both of individuals and of communities, whose real offences were purely political or religious, must be familiar to every reader. The extermination of the Stedinger in 1234, of the Templars from 1307 to 1313, the execution of Joan of Arc in 1429, and the unhappy scenes of Arras in 1459, are the most prominent. The first of these is perhaps the least known, but is not among the least remarkable. The following account, from Dr. Kortüm's interesting history [26] of the republican confederacies of the middle ages, will shew the horrible convenience of imputations of witchcraft when royal or priestly wolves wanted a pretext for a quarrel with the sheep.

The Frieslanders, inhabiting the district from the Weser to the Zuydersee, had long been celebrated for their attachment to freedom, and their successful struggles in its defence. As early as the eleventh century they had formed a general confederacy against the encroachments of the Normans and the Saxons, which was divided into seven *seelands*, holding annually a diet under a large oak-tree at Aurich, near the Upstalboom. Here they managed their own affairs, without the control of the clergy and ambitious nobles who surrounded them, to the great scandal of the latter. They already had true notions of a representative government. The deputies of the people levied the necessary taxes, deliberated on the affairs of the community, and performed, in their simple and patriarchal manner, nearly all the functions of the representative assemblies of the present day. Finally, the Archbishop of Bremen, together with the Count of Oldenburg and other neighbouring potentates, formed a league against that section of the Frieslanders known by the name of the Stedinger, and succeeded, after harassing them and sowing dissensions among them for many years, in bringing them under the yoke. But the Stedinger, devotedly attached to their ancient laws, by which they had attained a degree of civil and religious liberty very uncommon in that age, did not submit without a violent struggle. They arose in insurrection in the year 1204, in defence of the ancient customs of their country, refused to pay taxes to the feudal chiefs or tithes to the clergy — who had forced themselves into their peaceful retreats — and drove out many of their oppressors. For a period of eight-and-twenty years the brave Stedinger continued the struggle single-handed against the forces of the Archbishops of Bremen and the Counts of Oldenburg, and destroyed, in the year 1232, the strong castle of Slutterberg, near Delmenhorst, built by the latter nobleman as a position from which he could send out his marauders to plunder and destroy the possessions of the peasantry.

The invincible courage of these poor people proving too strong for their oppressors to cope with by the ordinary means of warfare, the Archbishop of Bremen applied to Pope Gregory IX. for his spiritual aid against them. That prelate entered cordially into the cause, and launching forth his anathema against the Stedinger as heretics and witches, encouraged all true believers to assist in their extermination. A large body of thieves and fanatics broke into their country in the year 1233, killing and burning wherever they went, and not sparing either women or children, the sick or the aged, in their rage. The Stedinger, however, rallied in great force, routed their invaders, and killed in battle their leader, Count Burckhardt of Oldenburg, with many inferior chieftains.

Again the pope was applied to, and a crusade against the Stedinger was preached in all that part of Germany. The pope wrote to all the bishops and leaders of the faithful an exhortation to arm, to root out from the land those abominable witches and wizards. "The Stedinger," said his holiness, "seduced by the devil, have abjured all the laws of God and man, slandered the Church, insulted the holy sacraments, consulted witches to raise evil spirits, shed blood like water, taken the lives of priests, and concocted an infernal scheme to propagate the worship of the devil, whom they adore under the name of Asmodi. The devil appears to them in different shapes, — sometimes as a goose or a duck, and at others in the figure of a pale black-eyed youth, with a melancholy aspect, whose embrace fills their hearts with eternal hatred against the holy Church of Christ. This devil presides at their sabbaths, when they all kiss him and dance around him. He then envelopes them in total darkness, and they all, male and female, give themselves up to the grossest and most disgusting debauchery."

In consequence of these letters of the pope, the emperor of Germany, Frederic II., also pronounced his ban against them. The Bishops of Ratzebourg, Lubeck, Osnabrück, Munster, and Minden took up arms to exterminate them, aided by the Duke of Brabant, the Counts of Holland, of Clêves, of the Mark, of Oldenburg, of Egmond, of Diest, and many other powerful nobles. An army of forty thousand men was soon collected, which marched, under the command of the Duke of Brabant, into the country of the Stedinger. The latter mustered vigorously in defence of their lives and liberties, but could raise no greater force, including every man capable of bearing arms, than eleven thousand men to cope against the overwhelming numbers of their foe. They fought with the energy of despair, but all in vain. Eight thousand of them were slain on the field of battle; the whole race was exterminated; and the enraged conquerors scoured the country in all directions, slew the women and children and old men, drove away the cattle, fired the woods and cottages, and made a total waste of the land.

Philip IV.

Just as absurd and effectual was the charge brought against the Templars in 1307, when they had rendered themselves obnoxious to the potentates and prelacy of Christendom. Their wealth, their power, their pride, and their insolence had raised up enemies on every side; and every sort of accusation was made against them, but failed to work their overthrow, until the terrible cry of witchcraft was let loose upon them. This effected its object, and the Templars were extirpated. They were accused of having sold their souls to the devil, and of celebrating all the infernal mysteries of the witches' sabbath. It was pretended that, when they admitted a novice into their order, they forced him to renounce his salvation and curse Jesus Christ; that they then made him submit to many unholy and disgusting ceremonies, and forced him to kiss the superior on the cheek, the navel, and the breech, and spit three times upon a crucifix; that all the members were forbidden to have connexion with women, but might give themselves up without restraint to every species of unmentionable debauchery; that when by any mischance a Templar infringed this order, and a child was born, the whole order met, and tossed it about like a shuttlecock from one to the other until it expired; that they then roasted it by a slow fire, and with the fat which trickled from it anointed the hair and beard of a large image of the devil. It was also said that when one of the knights died, his body was burnt into a powder, and then mixed with wine and drunk by every member of the order. Philip IV., who, to exercise his own implacable hatred, invented, in all probability, the greater part of these charges, issued orders for the immediate arrest of all the Templars in his dominions. The pope afterwards took up the cause with almost as much fervour as the king of France; and in every part of Europe the Templars were thrown into prison, and their goods and estates confiscated. Hundreds of them, when put to the rack, confessed even the most preposterous of the charges against them, and by so doing increased the popular clamour and the hopes of their enemies. It is true that, when removed from the rack, they denied all they had previously confessed; but this circumstance only increased the outcry, and was numbered as an additional crime against them. They were considered in a worse light than before, and condemned forthwith to the flames as relapsed heretics. Fifty-nine of these unfortunate victims were all burned together by a slow fire in a field in the suburbs of Paris, protesting to the very last moment of their lives their innocence of the crimes imputed to them, and refusing to accept of pardon upon condition of acknowledging themselves guilty. Similar scenes were enacted in the provinces; and for four years hardly a month passed without witnessing the execution of one or more of these unhappy men. Finally, in 1313, the last scene of this tragedy closed by the burning of the Grand-Master, Jacques de Molay, and his companion Guy, the commander of Normandy. Any thing more atrocious it is impossible to conceive, — disgraceful alike to the monarch who originated, the pope who supported, and the age which tolerated the monstrous iniquity. That the malice of a few could invent such a charge is a humiliating thought for the lover of his species; but that millions of mankind should credit it is still more so.

The execution of Joan of Arc is the next most notorious example which history affords us of the imputation of witchcraft against a political enemy. Instances of similar persecution, in which this crime was made the pretext for the gratification of political or religious hatred, might be multiplied to a great extent. But it is better to proceed at once to the consideration of the bull of Pope Innocent, the torch that set fire to the long-laid train, and caused so fearful an explosion over the Christian world. It will be necessary, however, to go back for some years anterior to that event, the better to understand the motives that influenced the Church in the promulgation of that fearful document.

Towards the close of the fourteenth and beginning of the fifteenth century, many witches were burned in different parts of Europe. As a natural consequence of the severe persecution, the crime, or the pretenders to it, increased. Those who found themselves accused and threatened with the penalties, if they happened to be persons of a bad and malicious disposition, wished they had the power imputed to them, that they might be revenged upon their persecutors. Numerous instances are upon record of half-crazed persons being found muttering the spells which were supposed to raise the evil one. When religion and law alike recognised the crime, it is no wonder that the weak in reason and the strong in imagination, especially when they were of a nervous temperament, fancied themselves endued with the terrible powers of which all the world was speaking. The belief of their neighbours did not lag behind their own, and execution was the speedy consequence.

Joan of Arc.

As the fear of witchcraft increased, the Catholic clergy strove to fix the imputation of it upon those religious sects, the pioneers of the Reformation, who began about this time to be formidable to the Church of Rome. If a charge of heresy could not ensure their destruction, that of sorcery and witchcraft never failed. In the year 1459, a devoted congregation of the Waldenses at Arras, who used to repair at night to worship God in their own manner in solitary places, fell victims to an accusation of sorcery. It was rumoured in Arras that in the desert places to which they retired the devil appeared before them in human form, and read from a large book his laws and ordinances, to which they all promised obedience; that he then distributed money and food among them, to bind them to his service, which done, they gave themselves up to every species of lewdness and debauchery. Upon these rumours several creditable persons in Arras were seized and imprisoned, together with a number of decrepit and idiotic old women. The rack, that convenient instrument for making the accused confess any thing, was of course put in requisition. Monstrelet, in his chronicle, says that they were tortured until some of them admitted the truth of the whole accusations, and said, besides, that they had seen and recognised in their nocturnal assemblies many persons of rank; many prelates, seigneurs, governors of bailliages, and mayors of cities, being such names as the examiners had themselves suggested to the victims. Several who had been thus informed against were thrown into prison, and so horribly tortured, that reason fled, and in their ravings of pain they also confessed their midnight meetings with the devil, and the oaths they had taken to serve him. Upon these confessions judgment was pronounced. The poor old women, as usual in such cases, were hanged and burned in the market-place; the more wealthy delinquents were allowed to escape upon payment of large sums. It was soon after universally recognised that these trials had been conducted in the most odious manner, and that the judges had motives of private vengeance against many of the more influential persons who had been implicated. The parliament of Paris afterwards declared the sentence illegal, and the judges iniquitous; but its *arrêt* was too late to be of service even to those who had paid the fine, or to punish the authorities who had misconducted themselves, for it was not delivered until thirty-two years after the executions had taken place.

In the mean time, accusations of witchcraft spread rapidly in France, Italy, and Germany. Strange to say, that although in the first instance chiefly directed against heretics, the latter were as firm believers in the crime as even the Catholics themselves. In after times we also find that the Lutherans and Calvinists became greater witch-burners than ever the Romanists had been, so deeply was the prejudice rooted. Every other point of belief was in dispute, but that was considered by every sect to be as well established as the authenticity of the Scriptures or the existence of a God.

But at this early period of the epidemic the persecutions were directed by the heads of the Catholic Church. The spread of heresy betokened, it was thought, the coming of Antichrist. Florimond, in his work concerning Antichrist, exposed the secret of these prosecutions. He says: "All who have afforded us some signs of the approach of Antichrist agree that the increase of sorcery and witchcraft is to distinguish the melancholy period of his advent; and was ever age so afflicted as ours? The seats destined for criminals in our courts of justice are blackened with persons accused of this guilt. There are not judges enough to try them. Our dungeons are gorged with them. No day passes that we do not render our tribunals bloody by the dooms which we pronounce, or in which we do not return to our homes discoun-tenanced and terrified at the horrible confessions which we have heard. And the devil is accounted so good a master, that we cannot commit so great a number of his slaves to the flames but what there shall arise from their ashes a sufficient number to supply their place."

Florimond here spoke the general opinion of the Church of Rome; but it never suggested itself to the mind of any person engaged in these trials, that if it were indeed a devil who raised up so many new witches to fill the places of those consumed, it was no other than one in their own employ — the devil of persecution. But so it was. The more they burned, the more they found to burn, until it became a common prayer with women in the humbler walks of life, that they might never live to grow old. It was sufficient to be aged, poor, and half-crazed, to ensure death at the stake or the scaffold.

Gate of Constance.

In the year 1487 there was a severe storm in Switzerland, which laid waste the country for four miles around Constance. Two wretched old women, whom the popular voice had long accused of witchcraft, were arrested on the preposterous charge of having raised the tempest. The rack was displayed, and the two poor creatures were extended upon it. In reply to various questions from their tormentors, they owned in their agony that they were in the constant habit of meeting the devil; that they had sold their souls to him; and that at their command he had raised the tempest. Upon this insane and blasphemous charge they were condemned to die. In the criminal registers of Constance there stands against the name of each the simple but significant phrase, "*convicta et combusta.*"

This case and hundreds of others were duly reported to the ecclesiastical powers. There happened at that time to be a pontiff at the head of the Church who had given much of his attention to the subject of witchcraft, and who, with the intention of rooting out the supposed crime, did more to increase it than any other man that ever lived. John Baptist Cibo, elected to the papacy in 1485, under the designation of Innocent VIII., was sincerely alarmed at the number of witches, and launched forth his terrible manifesto against them. In his celebrated bull of 1488, he called the nations of Europe to the rescue of the Church of Christ upon earth, imperilled by the arts of Satan, and set forth the horrors that had reached his ears; how that numbers of both sexes had intercourse with the infernal fiends; how by their sorceries they afflicted both man and beast; how they blighted the marriage-bed, destroyed the births of women and the increase of cattle; and how they blasted the corn on the ground, the grapes of the vineyard, the fruits of the trees, and the herbs of the field. In order that criminals so atrocious might no longer pollute the earth, he appointed inquisitors in every country, armed with the apostolic power to convict and punish.

It was now that the *Witch Mania*, properly so called, may be said to have fairly commenced. Immediately a class of men sprang up in Europe, who made it the sole business of their lives to discover and burn the witches. Sprenger, in Germany, was the most celebrated of these national scourges. In his notorious work, the *Malleus Maleficarum*, he laid down a regular form of trial, and appointed a course of examination by which the inquisitors in other countries might best discover the guilty. The questions, which were always enforced by torture, were of the most absurd and disgusting nature. The inquisitors were required to ask the suspected whether they had midnight meetings with the devil? whether they attended the witches' sabbath on the Brocken? whether they had their familiar spirits? whether they could raise whirlwinds and call down the lightning? and whether they had had sexual intercourse with Satan?

Straightway the inquisitors set to work: Cumanus, in Italy, burned forty-one poor women in one province alone; and Sprenger, in Germany, burned a number which can never be ascertained correctly, but which, it is agreed on all hands, amounted to more than five hundred in a year. The great resemblance between the confessions of the unhappy victims was regarded as a new proof of the existence of the crime. But this is not astonishing. The same questions from the *Malleus Maleficarum* were put to them all, and torture never failed to educe the answer required by the inquisitor. Numbers of people, whose imaginations were filled with these horrors, went further in the way of confession than even their tormentors anticipated, in the hope that they would thereby be saved from the rack, and put out of their misery at once. Some confessed that they had had children by the devil; but no one who had ever been a mother gave utterance to such a frantic imagining, even in the extremity of her anguish. The childless only confessed it, and were burned instanter as unworthy to live.

For fear the zeal of the enemies of Satan should cool, successive popes appointed new commissions. One was appointed by Alexander VI. in 1494, another by Leo X. in 1521, and a third by Adrian VI. in 1522. They were all armed with the same powers to hunt out and destroy, and executed their fearful functions but too rigidly. In Geneva alone five hundred persons were burned in the years 1515 and 1516, under the title of Protestant witches. It would appear that their chief crime was heresy, and their witchcraft merely an aggravation. Bartolomeo de Spina has a list still more fearful. He informs us that in the year 1524 no less than a thousand persons suffered death for witchcraft in the district of Como, and that for several years afterwards the average number of victims exceeded a hundred annually. One inquisitor, Remigius, took great credit to himself for having, during fifteen years, convicted and burned nine hundred.

In France, about the year 1520, fires for the execution of witches blazed in almost every town. Danæus, in his *Dialogues of Witches*, says they were so numerous that it would be next to impossible to tell the number of them. So deep was the thraldom of the human mind, that the friends and relatives of the accused parties looked on and approved. The wife or sister of a murderer might sympathise in his fate, but the wives and husbands of sorcerers and witches had no pity. The truth is that pity was dangerous, for it was thought no one could have compassion on the sufferings of a witch who was not a dabbler in sorcery: to have wept for a witch would have insured the stake. In some districts, however, the exasperation of the people broke out, in spite of superstition. The inquisitor of a rural township in Piedmont burned the victims so plentifully and so fast, that there was not a family in the place which did not lose a member. The people at last arose, and the inquisitor was but too happy to escape from the country with whole limbs. The archbishop of the diocese proceeded afterwards to the trial of such as the inquisitor had left in prison.

Some of the charges were so utterly preposterous that the poor wretches were at once liberated; others met a harder, but the usual fate. Some of them were accused of having joined the witches' dance at midnight under a blasted oak, where they had been seen by creditable people. The husbands of several of these women (two of whom were young and beautiful) swore positively that at the time stated their wives were comfortably asleep in their arms; but it was all in vain. Their word was taken, but the archbishop told them they had been deceived by the devil and their own senses. It was true they might have had the semblance of their wives in their beds, but the originals were far away at the devil's dance under the oak. The honest fellows were confounded, and their wives burned forthwith.

Charles IX.

In the year 1561, five poor women of Verneuil were accused of transforming themselves into cats, and in that shape attending the sabbath of the fiends — prowling around Satan, who presided over them in the form of a goat, and dancing, to amuse him, upon his back. They were found guilty, and burned.[27]

In 1564, three wizards and a witch appeared before the Presidents Salvert and D'Avanton: they confessed, when extended on the rack, that they anointed the sheep-pens with infernal unguents to kill the sheep; that they attended the sabbath, where they saw a great black goat, which spoke to them, and made them kiss him, each holding a lighted candle in his hand while he performed the ceremony. They were all executed at Poitiers.

In 1571 the celebrated sorcerer Trois Echelles was burned in the Place de Grève in Paris. He confessed, in the presence of Charles IX., and of the Marshals de Montmorency, De Retz, and the Sieur du Mazille, physician to the king, that he could perform the most wonderful things by the aid of a devil to whom he had sold himself. He described at great length the saturnalia of the fiends, the sacrifices which they offered up, the debaucheries they committed with the young and handsome witches, and the various modes of preparing the infernal unguent for blighting cattle. He said he had upwards of twelve hundred accomplices in the crime of witchcraft in various parts of France, whom he named to the king, and many of whom were afterwards arrested and suffered execution.

At Dôle, two years afterwards, Gilles Garnier, a native of Lyons, was indicted for being a *loup-garou*, or man-wolf, and for prowling in that shape about the country at night to devour little children. The indictment against him, as read by Henri Camus, doctor of laws and counsellor of the king, was to the effect that he, Gilles Garnier, had seized upon a little girl, twelve years of age, whom he drew into a vineyard and there killed, partly with his teeth and partly with his hands, seeming like wolf's paws; that from thence he trailed her bleeding body along the ground with his teeth into the wood of La Serre, where he ate the greatest portion of her at one meal, and carried the remainder home to his wife; that upon another occasion, eight days before the festival of All Saints, he was seen to seize another child in his teeth, and would have devoured her had she not been rescued by the country people, and that the said child died a few days afterwards of the injuries he had inflicted; that fifteen days after the same festival of All Saints, being again in the shape of a wolf, he devoured a boy thirteen years of age, having previously torn off his leg and thigh with his teeth, and hid them away for his breakfast on the morrow. He was furthermore indicted for giving way to the same diabolical and unnatural propensities even in his shape of a man; and that he had strangled a boy in a wood with the intention of eating him, which crime he would have effected if he had not been seen by the neighbours and prevented.

Gilles Garnier was put to the rack after fifty witnesses had deposed against him. He confessed every thing that was laid to his charge. He was thereupon brought back into the presence of his judges, when Dr. Camus, in the name of the parliament of Dôle, pronounced the following sentence:

"Seeing that Gilles Garnier has, by the testimony of credible witnesses, and by his own spontaneous confession, been proved guilty of the abominable crimes of lycanthropy and witchcraft, this court condemns him, the said Gilles, to be this day taken in a cart from this spot to the place of execution, accompanied by the executioner (*maître exécuteur de la haute justice*), where he, by the said executioner, shall be tied to a stake and burned alive, and that his ashes be then scattered to the winds. The court further condemns him, the said Gilles, to the costs of this prosecution."

"Given at Dôle, this 18th day of January, 1573."

In 1578, the parliament of Paris was occupied for several days with the trial of a man named Jacques Rollet. He also was found guilty of being a *loup-garou*, and in that shape devouring a little boy. He was burnt alive in the Place de Grève.

In 1579, so much alarm was excited in the neighbourhood of Melun by the increase of witches and *loup-garous*, that a council was held to devise some measures to stay the evil. A decree was passed that all witches and consulters with witches should be punished with death; and not only those, but fortune-tellers and conjurors of every kind. The parliament of Rouen took up the same question in the following year, and decreed that the possession of a *grimoire*, or book of spells, was sufficient evidence of witchcraft, and that all persons on whom such books were found should be burned alive. Three councils were held in different parts of France in the year 1583, all in relation to the same subject. The parliament of Bourdeaux issued strict injunctions to all curates and clergy whatever to use redoubled efforts to root out the crime of witchcraft. The parliament of Tours was equally peremptory, and feared the judgments of an offended God if all these dealers with the devil were not swept from the face of the land. The parliament of Rheims was particularly severe against the *noueurs d'aiguillette*, or "tyers of the knot" — people of both sexes who took pleasure in preventing the consummation of marriage, that they might counteract the command of God to our first parents to increase and multiply. This parliament held it to be sinful to wear amulets to preserve from witchcraft; and that this practice might not be continued within its jurisdiction, drew up a form of exorcism, which would more effectually defeat the agents of the devil, and put them to flight.

A case of witchcraft, which created a great sensation in its day, occurred in 1588, at a village in the mountains of Auvergne, about two leagues from Apchon. A gentleman of that place being at his window, there passed a friend of his who had been out hunting, and who was then returning to his own house. The gentleman asked his friend what sport he had had; upon which the latter informed him that he had been attacked in the plain by a large and savage wolf, which he had shot at without wounding, and that he had then drawn out his hunting-knife and cut off the animal's fore-paw as it sprang upon his neck to devour him. The huntsman upon this put his hand into his bag to pull out the paw, but was shocked to find that it was a woman's hand, with a wedding-ring on the finger. The gentleman immediately recognised his wife's ring, "which," says the indictment against her, "made him begin to suspect some evil of her." He immediately went in search of her, and found her sitting by the fire in the kitchen, with her arm hidden underneath her apron. He tore off her apron with great vehemence, and found that she had no hand, and that the stump was even then bleeding. She was given into custody, and burnt at Riom in presence of some thousands of spectators.[28]

In the midst of these executions, rare were the gleams of mercy. Few instances are upon record of any acquittal taking place when the crime was witchcraft. The discharge of fourteen persons by the parliament of Paris, in the year 1589, is almost a solitary example of a return to reason. Fourteen persons condemned to death for witchcraft appealed against the judgment to the parliament of Paris, which for political reasons had been exiled to Tours. The parliament named four commissioners — Pierre Pigray, the king's surgeon, and Messieurs Leroi, Renard, and Falaiseau, the king's physicians — to visit and examine these witches, and see whether they had the mark of the devil upon them. Pigray, who relates the circumstance in his work on Surgery (book vii. chap. 10), says the visit was made in presence of two counsellors of the court. The witches were all stripped naked, and the physicians examined their bodies very diligently, pricking them in all the marks they could find to see whether they were insensible to pain, which was always considered a certain proof of guilt. They were, however, very sensible of the pricking, and some of them called out very lustily when the pins were driven into them. "We found them," continues Pierre Pigray, "to be very poor, stupid people, and some of them insane. Many of them were quite indifferent about life, and one or two of them desired death as a relief for their sufferings. Our opinion was, that they stood more in need of medicine than of punishment; and so we reported to the parliament. Their case was thereupon taken into further consideration; and the parliament, after mature counsel amongst all the members, ordered the poor creatures to be sent to their homes, without inflicting any punishment upon them."

Such was the dreadful state of Italy, Germany, and France during the sixteenth century, which was far from being the worst crisis of the popular madness with regard to witchcraft. Let us see what was the state of England during the same period. The Reformation, which in its progress had rooted out so many errors, stopped short at this, the greatest error of all. Luther and Calvin were as firm believers in witchcraft as Pope Innocent himself; and their followers shewed themselves more zealous persecutors than the Romanists. Dr. Hutchinson, in his work on Witchcraft, asserts that the mania manifested itself later in England, and raged with less virulence than on the continent. The first assertion only is true; for though the persecution began later both in England and Scotland, its progress was as fearful as elsewhere.

It was not until more than fifty years after the issuing of the bull of Innocent VIII. that the legislature of England thought fit to make any more severe enactments against sorcery than those already in operation. The statute of 1541 was the first that specified the particular crime of witchcraft. At a much earlier period many persons had suffered death for sorcery, in addition to other offences; but no executions took place for attending the witches' sabbath, raising tempests, afflicting cattle with barrenness, and all the fantastic trumpery of the continent. Two statutes were passed in 1551: the first relating to false prophecies, caused mainly, no doubt, by the impositions of Elizabeth Barton, the holy maid of Kent, in 1534; and the second against conjuration, witchcraft, and sorcery. But even this enactment did not consider witchcraft as penal in itself, and only condemned to death those who, by means of spells, incantations, or contracts with the devil, attempted the lives of their neighbours. The statute of Elizabeth, in 1562, at last recognised witchcraft as a crime of the highest magnitude, whether exerted or not to the injury of the lives, limbs, and possessions of the community. From that date the persecution may be fairly said to have commenced in England. It reached its climax in the early part of the seventeenth century, which was the hottest period of the mania all over Europe.

A few cases of witch persecution in the sixteenth century will enable the reader to form a more accurate idea of the progress of this great error than if he plunged at once into that busy period of its history when Matthew Hopkins and his coadjutors exercised their infernal calling. Several instances occur in England during the latter years of the reign of Elizabeth. At this time the public mind had become pretty familiar with the details of the crime. Bishop Jewell, in his sermons before her majesty, used constantly to conclude them by a fervent prayer that she might be preserved from witches. Upon one occasion, in 1598, his words were, "It may please your grace to understand that witches and sorcerers within these last four years are marvellously increased within this your grace's realm. Your grace's subjects pine away even unto the death; their colour fadeth — their flesh rotteth — their speech is benumbed — their senses are bereft! I pray God they may never practise further than upon the *subject*!"

Jewell.

By degrees, an epidemic terror of witchcraft spread into the villages. In proportion as the doctrine of the Puritans took root, this dread increased, and, of course, brought persecution in its train. The Church of England has claimed, and is entitled to the merit, of having been less influenced in these matters than any other sect of Christians; but still they were tainted with the superstition of the age. One of the most flagrant instances of cruelty and delusion upon record was consummated under the authority of the Church, and commemorated till a very late period by an annual lecture at the University of Cambridge.

This is the celebrated case of the witches of Warbois, who were executed about thirty-two years after the passing of the statute of Elizabeth. Although in the interval but few trials are recorded, there is, unfortunately, but too much evidence to shew the extreme length to which the popular prejudice was carried. Many women lost their lives in every part of England without being brought to trial at all, from the injuries received at the hands of the people. The number of these can never be ascertained.

The case of the witches of Warbois merits to be detailed at length, not only from the importance attached to it for so many years by the learned of the University, but from the singular absurdity of the evidence upon which men, sensible in all other respects, could condemn their fellow-creatures to the scaffold.

The principal actors in this strange drama were the families of Sir Samuel Cromwell and a Mr. Throgmorton, both gentlemen of landed property near Warbois in the county of Huntingdon. Mr. Throgmorton had several daughters, the eldest of whom, Mistress Joan, was an imaginative and melancholy girl, whose head was filled with stories of ghosts and witches. Upon one occasion she chanced to pass the cottage of one Mrs., or, as she was called, Mother Samuel, a very aged, a very poor, and a very ugly woman. Mother Samuel was sitting at her door knitting, with a black cap upon her head, when this silly young lady passed, and taking her eyes from her work she looked stedfastly at her. Mistress Joan immediately fancied that she felt sudden pains in all her limbs, and from that day forth never ceased to tell her sisters, and every body about her, that Mother Samuel had bewitched her. The other children took up the cry, and actually frightened themselves into fits whenever they passed within sight of this terrible old woman.

Mr. and Mrs. Throgmorton, not a whit wiser than their children, believed all the absurd tales they had been told; and Lady Cromwell, a gossip of Mrs. Throgmorton, made herself very active in the business, and determined to bring the witch to the ordeal. The sapient Sir Samuel joined in the scheme; and the children, thus encouraged, gave loose reins to their imaginations, which seem to have been of the liveliest. They soon invented a whole host of evil spirits, and names for them besides, which they said were sent by Mother Samuel to torment them continually. Seven spirits especially, they said, were raised from hell by this wicked woman to throw them into fits; and as the children were actually subject to fits, their mother and her commeres gave the more credit to the story. The names of these spirits were, "First Smack," "Second Smack," "Third Smack," "Blue," "Catch," "Hardname," and "Pluck."

Throgmorton, the father, was so pestered by these idle fancies, and yet so well inclined to believe them, that he marched valiantly forth to the hut where Mother Samuel resided with her husband and daughter, and dragged her forcibly into his own grounds. Lady Cromwell, Mrs. Throgmorton, and the girls were in waiting, armed with long pins to prick the witch, and see if they could draw blood from her. Lady Cromwell, who seems to have been the most violent of the party, tore the old woman's cap off her head, and plucking out a handful of her grey hair, gave it to Mrs. Throgmorton to burn, as a charm which would preserve them all from her future machinations. It was no wonder that the poor creature, subjected to this rough usage, should give vent to an involuntary curse upon her tormentors. She did so, and her curse was never forgotten. Her hair, however, was supposed to be a grand specific, and she was allowed to depart, half dead with terror and ill-usage. For more than a year the families of Cromwell and Throgmorton continued to persecute her, and to assert that her imps afflicted them with pains and fits, turned the milk sour in their pans, and prevented their cows and ewes from bearing. In the midst of these fooleries, Lady Cromwell was taken ill and died. It was then remembered that her death had taken place exactly a year and a quarter since she was cursed by Mother Samuel, and that on several occasions she had dreamed of the witch and a black cat, the latter being of course the arch-enemy of mankind himself.

Sir Samuel Cromwell now conceived himself bound to take more energetic measures against the sorceress, since he had lost his wife by her means. The year and a quarter and the black cat were proofs positive. All the neighbours had taken up the cry of witchcraft against Mother Samuel; and her personal appearance, unfortunately for her, the very ideal of what a witch ought to be, increased the popular suspicion. It would appear that at last the poor woman believed, even to her own disadvantage, that she was what every body represented her to be. Being forcibly brought into Mr. Throgmorton's house, when his daughter Joan was in one of her customary fits, she was commanded by him and Sir Samuel Cromwell to expel the devil from the young lady. She was told to repeat her exorcism, and to add, "as I am a witch, and the causer of Lady Cromwell's death, I charge thee, fiend, to come out of her!" She did as was required of her; and moreover confessed that her husband and daughter were leagued with her in witchcraft, and had, like her, sold their souls to the devil. The whole family were immediately arrested, and sent to Hunting-don to prison.

The trial was instituted shortly afterwards before Mr. Justice Fenner, when all the crazy girls of Mr. Throgmorton's family gave evidence against Mother Samuel and her family. They were all three put to the torture. The old woman confessed in her anguish that she was a witch; that she had cast her spells upon the young ladies; and that she had caused the death of Lady Cromwell. The father and daughter, stronger in mind than their unfortunate wife and parent, refused to confess any thing, and asserted their innocence to the last. They were all three con-demned to be hanged, and their bodies burned. The daughter, who was young and good-looking, excited the pity of many persons, and she was advised to plead pregnancy, that she might gain at least a respite from death. The poor girl refused proudly, on the ground that she would not be accounted both a witch and a strumpet. Her half-witted old mother caught at the idea of a few weeks' longer life, and asserted that she was pregnant. The court was convulsed with laughter, in which the wretched victim herself joined; and this was accounted an additional proof that she was a witch. The whole family were executed on the 7th of April, 1593.

Sir Samuel Cromwell, as lord of the manor, received the sum of 40l. out of the confiscated property of the Samuels, which he turned into a rent-charge of 40s. yearly, for the endowment of an annual sermon or lecture upon the enormity of witchcraft, and this case in particular, to be preached by a doctor or bachelor of divinity of Queen's College, Cambridge. I have not been able to ascertain the exact date at which this annual lecture was discontinued; but it appears to have been preached so late as 1718, when Dr. Hutchinson published his work upon witchcraft.

To carry on in proper chronological order the history of the witch delusion in the British isles, it will be necessary to examine into what was taking place in Scotland during all that part of the sixteenth century anterior to the accession of James VI. to the crown of England. We naturally expect that the Scotch—a people renowned from the earliest times for their powers of imagination—should be more deeply imbued with this gloomy superstition than their neighbours of the south. The nature of their soil and climate tended to encourage the dreams of early ignorance. Ghosts, goblins, wraiths, kelpies, and a whole host of spiritual beings, were familiar to the dwellers by the misty glens of the Highlands and the romantic streams of the Lowlands. Their deeds, whether of good or ill, were enshrined in song, and took a greater hold upon the imagination because "verse had sanctified them." But it was not till the religious reformers began the practice of straining Scripture to the severest extremes that the arm of the law was called upon to punish witchcraft as a crime *per se*. What Pope Innocent VIII. had done for Germany and France, the preachers of the Reformation did for the Scottish people. Witchcraft, instead of being a mere article of faith, became enrolled in the statute-book; and all good subjects and true Christians were called upon to take arms against it. The ninth parliament of Queen Mary passed an act in 1563, which decreed the punishment of death against witches and consulters with witches, and immediately the whole bulk of the people were smitten with an epidemic fear of the devil and his mortal agents. Persons in the highest ranks of life shared and encouraged the delusion of the vulgar. Many were themselves accused of witchcraft; and noble ladies were shewn to have dabbled in mystic arts, and proved to the world that if they were not witches, it was not for want of the will.

Among the dames who became notorious for endeavouring to effect their wicked ends by the devil's aid may be mentioned the celebrated Lady Buccleugh of Branxholme (familiar to all the readers of Sir Walter Scott), the Countess of Lothian, the Countess of Angus, the Countess of Athol, Lady Kerr, the Countess of Huntley, Euphemia Macalzean (the daughter of Lord Cliftonhall), and Lady Fowlis. Among the celebrated of the other sex who were accused of wizardism was Sir Lewis Ballantyne, the Lord Justice-Clerk for Scotland, who, if we may believe Scot of Scotstarvet, "dealt by curiosity with a warlock called Richard Grahame," and prayed him to raise the devil. The warlock consented, and raised him *in propriâ personâ* in the yard of his house in the Canongate, "at sight of whom the Lord Justice-Clerk was so terrified, that he took sickness and thereof died." By such idle reports as these did the envious ruin the reputation of those they hated; though it would appear in this case that Sir Lewis had been fool enough to make the attempt of which he was accused, and that the success of the experiment was the only apocryphal part of the story.

John Knox.

The enemies of John Knox invented a similar tale, which found ready credence among the Roman Catholics, glad to attach any stigma to that grand scourge of the vices of their Church. It was reported that he and his secretary went into the churchyard of St. Andrew's with the intent to raise "some sanctes;" but that, by a mistake in their conjurations, they raised the great fiend himself instead of the saints they wished to consult. The popular rumour added, that Knox's secretary was so frightened at the great horns, goggle eyes, and long tail of Satan, that he went mad, and shortly afterwards died. Knox himself was built of sterner stuff, and was not to be frightened.

The first name that occurs in the records of the High Court of Justiciary of persons tried or executed for witchcraft, is that of Janet Bowman in 1572, nine years after the passing of the act of Mary. No particulars of her crimes are given, and against her name there only stands the words, "convict and brynt." It is not, however, to be inferred, that in this interval no trials or executions took place; for it appears, on the authority of documents of unquestioned authenticity in the Advocates' Library at Edinburgh,[29] that the Privy Council made a practice of granting commissions to resident gentlemen and ministers in every part of Scotland to examine, try, and execute witches within their own parishes. No records of those who suffered from the sentence of these tribunals have been preserved; but if popular tradition may be believed even to the amount of one-fourth of its assertions, their number was fearful. After the year 1572, the entries of executions for witchcraft in the records of the High Court become more frequent, but do not average more than one per annum, — another proof that trials for this offence were in general entrusted to the local magistracy. The latter appear to have ordered witches to the stake with as little compunction, and after as summary a mode, as modern justices of the peace order a poacher to the stocks.

As James VI. advanced in manhood, he took great interest in the witch trials. One of them especially — that of Gellie Duncan, Dr. Fian, and their accomplices, in the year 1591 — engrossed his whole attention, and no doubt suggested in some degree the famous work on Demonology, which he wrote shortly afterwards. As these witches had made an attempt upon his own life, it is not surprising, with his habits, that he should have watched the case closely, or become strengthened in his prejudice and superstition by its singular details. No other trial that could be selected would give so fair an idea of the delusions of the Scottish people as this. Whether we consider the number of victims, the absurdity of the evidence, and the real villany of some of the persons implicated, it is equally extraordinary.

Gellie Duncan, the prime witch in these proceedings, was servant to the deputy bailiff of Tranent, a small town in Haddingtonshire, about ten miles from Edinburgh. Though neither old nor ugly (as witches usually were), but young and good-looking, her neighbours, from some suspicious parts of her behaviour, had long considered her a witch. She had, it appears, some pretensions to the healing art. Some cures which she effected were so sudden, that the worthy bailiff, her master, who, like his neighbours, mistrusted her, considered them no less than miraculous. In order to discover the truth, he put her to the torture; but she obstinately refused to confess that she had dealings with the devil. It was the popular belief that no witch would confess as long as the mark which Satan had put upon her remained undiscovered upon her body. Somebody present reminded the torturing bailie of this fact, and on examination, the devil's mark was found upon the throat of poor Gellie. She was put to the torture again, and her fortitude giving way under the extremity of her anguish, she confessed that she was indeed a witch — that she had sold her soul to the devil, and effected all her cures by his aid. This was something new in the witch creed, according to which, the devil delighted more in laying diseases on than in taking them off; but Gellie Duncan fared no better on that account. The torture was still applied, until she had named all her accomplices, among whom were one Cunningham, a reputed wizard, known by the name of Dr. Fian; a grave and matron-like witch, named Agnes Sampson; Euphemia Macalzean, the daughter of Lord Cliftonhall, already mentioned, and nearly forty other persons, some of whom were the wives of respectable individuals in the city of Edinburgh. Every one of these persons was arrested, and the whole realm of Scotland thrown into commotion by the extraordinary nature of the disclosures which were anticipated.

About two years previous to this time, James had suddenly left his kingdom, and proceeded gallantly to Denmark, to fetch over his bride, the Princess of Denmark, who had been detained by contrary weather in the harbour of Upslo. After remaining for some months in Copenhagen, he set sail with his young bride, and arrived safely in Leith, on the 1st of May 1590, having experienced a most boisterous passage, and been nearly wrecked. As soon as the arrest of Gellie Duncan and Fian became known in Scotland, it was reported by every body who pretended to be well-informed, that these witches and their associates had, by the devil's means, raised the storms which had endangered the lives of the king and queen. Gellie, in her torture, had confessed that such was the fact, and the whole kingdom waited aghast and open-mouthed for the corroboration about to be furnished by the trial.

Agnes Sampson, the "grave and matron-like" witch implicated by Gellie Duncan, was put to the horrible torture of the *pilliewinkis*. She laid bare all the secrets of the sisterhood before she had suffered an hour, and confessed that Gellie Duncan, Dr. Fian, Marian Lincup, Euphemia Macalzean, herself, and upwards of two hundred witches and warlocks, used to assemble at midnight in the kirk of North Berwick, where they met the devil; that they had plotted there to attempt the king's life; that they were incited to this by the old fiend himself, who had asserted with a thundering oath that James was the greatest enemy he ever had, and that there would be no peace for the devil's children upon earth until he were got rid of; that the devil upon these occasions always liked to have a little music, and that Gellie Duncan used to play a reel before him on a trump or Jew's harp, to which all the witches danced.

James was highly flattered at the idea that the devil should have said that he was the greatest enemy he ever had. He sent for Gellie Duncan to the palace, and made her play before him the same reel which she had played at the witches' dance in the kirk.

Torture of the Boots.

Dr. Fian, or rather Cunningham, a petty schoolmaster of Tranent, was put to the torture among the rest. He was a man who had led an infamous life, was a compounder of and dealer in poisons, and a pretender to magic. Though not guilty of the preposterous crimes laid to his charge, there is no doubt that he was a sorcerer in will, though not in deed, and that he deserved all the misery he endured. When put on the rack, he would confess nothing, and held out so long unmoved, that the severe torture of the *boots* was resolved upon. He endured this till exhausted nature could bear no longer, when insensibility kindly stepped in to his aid. When it was seen that he was utterly powerless, and that his tongue cleaved to the roof of his mouth, he was released.

Restoratives were administered; and during the first faint gleam of returning consciousness, he was prevailed upon to sign, ere he well knew what he was about, a full confession, in strict accordance with those of Gellie Duncan and Agnes Sampson. He was then remanded to his prison, from which, after two days, he managed, some how or other, to escape. He was soon recaptured, and brought before the Court of Justiciary, James himself being present. Fian now denied all the circumstances of the written confession which he had signed; whereupon the king, enraged at his "stubborn wilfulness," ordered him once more to the torture. His finger nails were riven out with pincers, and long needles thrust up to the eye into the quick; but he did not wince. He was then consigned again to the *boots*, in which, to quote a pamphlet published at the time,[30] he continued "so long, and abode so many blows in them, that his legs were crushed and beaten together as small as might be, and the bones and flesh so bruised, that the blood and marrow spouted forth in great abundance, whereby they were made unserviceable for ever."

The astonishing similarity of the confessions of all the persons implicated in these proceedings has often been remarked. It would appear that they actually endeavoured to cause the king's death by their spells and sorceries. Fian, who was acquainted with all the usual tricks of his profession, deceived them with pretended apparitions, so that many of them were really convinced that they had seen the devil. The sum of their confessions was to the following effect:

Satan, who was, of course, a great foe of the reformed religion, was alarmed that King James should marry a Protestant princess. To avert the consequences to the realms of evil, he had determined to put an end to the king and his bride by raising a storm on their voyage home. Satan, first of all, sent a thick mist over the waters, in the hope that the king's vessel might be stranded on the coast amid the darkness. This failing, Dr. Fian, who, from his superior scholarship, was advanced to the dignity of the devil's secretary, was commanded to summon all the witches to meet their master, each one sailing on a sieve on the high seas.

On All Hallowmas Eve, they assembled to the number of upwards of two hundred, including Gellie Duncan, Agnes Sampson, Euphemia Macalzean, one Barbara Napier, and several warlocks; and each embarking in a riddle or sieve, they sailed "over the ocean very substantially." After cruising about for some time, they met with the fiend, bearing in his claws a cat, which had been previously drawn nine times through the fire. This he delivered to one of the warlocks, telling him to cast it into the sea and cry "Hola!" This was done with all solemnity, and immediately the ocean became convulsed, the waters hissed loudly, and the waves rose mountains high,

"Twisting their arms to the dun-coloured heaven."

The witches sailed gallantly through the tempest they had raised, and landing on the coast of Scotland, took their sieves in their hands and marched on in procession to the haunted kirk of North Berwick, where the devil had resolved to hold a preaching. Gellie Duncan, the musician of the party, tripped on before, playing on her Jew's harp and singing,

"Cummer, go ye before, cummer, go ye;
Gif ye will not go before, cummer, let me!"

Arrived at the kirk, they paced around it *withershins*, that is, in reverse of the apparent motion of the sun. Dr. Fian then blew into the keyhole of the door, which opened immediately, and all the witches entered. As it was pitch dark, Fian blew with his mouth upon the candles, which immediately lighted, and the devil was seen occupying the pulpit. He was attired in a black gown and hat, and the witches saluted him by crying "All hail, master!" His body was hard, like iron; his face terrible; his nose, like the beak of an eagle; he had great burning eyes; his hands and legs were hairy; and he had long claws upon his hands and feet, and spake with an exceedingly gruff voice. Before commencing his sermon he called over the names of his congregation, demanding whether they had been good servants, and what success had attended their operations against the life of the king and his bride.

Gray Meill, a crazy old warlock, who acted as beadle or doorkeeper, was silly enough to answer "that nothing ailed the king yet, God be thanked;" upon which the devil, in a rage, stepped down from the pulpit and boxed his ears for him. He then remounted and commenced the preaching, commanding them to be dutiful servants to him and do all the evil they could. Euphemia Macalzean and Agnes Sampson, bolder than the rest, asked him whether he had brought the image or picture of King James, that they might, by pricking it, cause pains and diseases to fall upon him. "The father of lies" spoke truth for once, and confessed that he had forgotten it; upon which Euphemia Macalzean upbraided him loudly for his carelessness. The devil, however, took it all in good part, although Agnes Sampson and several other women let loose their tongues at him immediately. When they had done scolding, he invited them all to a grand entertainment. A newly buried corpse was dug up and divided among them, which was all they had in the way of edibles. He was more liberal in the matter of drink, and gave them so much excellent wine that they soon became jolly. Gellie Duncan then played the old tune upon her trump, and the devil himself led off the dance with Euphemia Macalzean. Thus they kept up the sport till the cock crew.

James the Demonologist.

Agnes Sampson, the wise woman of Keith, as she was called, added some other particulars in her confession. She stated, that on a previous occasion, she had raised an awful tempest in the sea by throwing a cat into it, with four joints of men tied to its feet. She said also, that on their grand attempt to drown King James, they did not meet with the devil after cruising about, but that he had accompanied them from the first, and that she had seen him dimly in the distance, rolling himself before them over the great waves, in shape and size not unlike a huge haystack. They met with a foreign ship richly laden with wines and other good things, which they boarded, and sunk after they had drunk all the wine and made themselves quite merry.

Some of these disclosures were too much even for the abundant faith of King James, and he more than once exclaimed, that the witches were like their master, "extreme lyars." But they confessed many other things of a less preposterous nature, and of which they were no doubt really guilty. Agnes Sampson said she was to have taken the king's life by anointing his linen with a strong poison. Gellie Duncan used to threaten her neighbours by saying she would send the devil after them; and many persons of weaker minds than usual were frightened into fits by her, and rendered subject to them for the remainder of their lives. Dr. Fian also made no scruple in aiding and abetting murder, and would rid any person of an enemy by means of poison, who could pay him his fee for it. Euphemia Macalzean also was far from being pure. There is no doubt that she meditated the king's death, and used such means to compass it as the superstition of the age directed. She was a devoted partisan of Bothwell, who was accused by many of the witches as having consulted them on the period of the king's death. They were all found guilty, and sentenced to be hanged and burned. Barbara Napier, though found guilty upon other counts, was acquitted upon the charge of having been present at the great witch meeting in Berwick kirk. The king was highly displeased, and threatened to have the jury indicted for a wilful error upon an assize. They accordingly reconsidered their verdict, and threw themselves upon the king's mercy for the fault they had committed. James was satisfied, and Barbara Napier was hanged along with Gellie Duncan, Agnes Sampson, Dr. Fian, and five-and-twenty others. Euphemia Macalzean met a harder fate. Her connexion with the bold and obnoxious Bothwell, and her share in poisoning one or two individuals who had stood in her way, were thought deserving of the severest punishment the law could inflict. Instead of the ordinary sentence, directing the criminal to be first strangled and then burned, the wretched woman was doomed "to be bound to a stake, and burned in ashes, *quick* to the death." This cruel sentence was executed on the 25th of June, 1591.

These trials had the most pernicious consequences all over Scotland. The lairds and ministers in their districts, armed with due power from the privy council, tried and condemned old women after the most summary fashion. Those who still clung to the ancient faith of Rome were the severest sufferers, as it was thought, after the disclosures of the fierce enmity borne by the devil towards a Protestant king and his Protestant wife, that all the Catholics were leagued with the powers of evil to work woe on the realm of Scotland. Upon a very moderate calculation, it is presumed that from the passing of the act of Queen Mary till the accession of James to the throne of England, a period of thirty-nine years, the average number of executions for witchcraft in Scotland was two hundred annually, or upwards of seventeen thousand altogether. For the first nine years the number was not one quarter so great; but towards the years 1590 to 1593, the number must have been more than four hundred. The case last cited was one of an extraordinary character. The general aspect of the trials will be better seen from that of Isabel Gowdie, which, as it would be both wearisome and disgusting to go through them all, is given as a fair specimen, although it took place at a date somewhat later than the reign of James. This woman, wearied of her life by the persecutions of her neighbours, voluntarily gave herself up to justice, and made a confession, embodying the whole witch-creed of the period. She was undoubtedly a monomaniac of the most extraordinary kind. She said that she deserved to be stretched upon an iron rack, and that her crimes could never be atoned for, even if she were to be drawn asunder by wild horses. She named a long list of her associates, including nearly fifty women and a few warlocks. They dug up the graves of unchristened infants, whose limbs were serviceable in their enchantments. When they wanted to destroy the crops of an enemy, they yoked toads to his plough, and on the following night Satan himself ploughed the land with his team, and blasted it for the season. The witches had power to assume almost any shape; but they generally chose either that of a cat or a hare, oftenest the latter. Isabel said, that on one occasion, when she was in this disguise, she was sore pressed by a pack of hounds, and had a very narrow escape with her life. She reached her own door at last, feeling the hot breath of the pursuing dogs at her haunches. She managed, however, to hide herself behind a chest, and got time to pronounce the magic words that could alone restore her to her proper shape. They were:

> "Hare! hare!
> God send thee care!
> I am in a hare's likeness now;
> But I shall be a woman e'en now!
> Hare! hare!
> God send thee care!"

If witches, when in this shape, were bitten by the dogs, they always retained the marks in their human form; but she had never heard that any witch had been bitten to death. When the devil appointed any general meeting of the witches, the custom was that they should proceed through the air mounted on broomsticks, or on corn or bean-straws, pronouncing as they went:

> "Horse and pattock, horse and go,
> Horse and pellats, ho! ho! ho!"

They generally left behind them a broom or a three-legged stool, which, when placed in their beds and duly charmed, assumed the human shape till their return. This was done that the neighbours might not know when they were absent.

She added that the devil furnished his favourite witches with servant imps to attend upon them. These imps were called, "The Roaring Lion," "Thief of Hell," "Wait-upon-Herself," "Ranting Roarer," "Care-for-Naught," &c., and were known by their liveries, which were generally yellow, sad-dun, sea-green, pea-green, or grass-green. Satan never called the witches by the names they had received at baptism; neither were they allowed, in his presence, so to designate each other. Such a breach of the infernal etiquette assuredly drew down his most severe displeasure. But as some designation was necessary, he re-baptised them in their own blood by the names of "Able-and-Stout," "Over-the-dike-with-it," "Raise-the-wind," "Pickle-nearest-the-wind," "Batter-them-down-Maggy," "Blow-Kale," and such like. The devil himself was not very particular what name they called him, so that it was not "Black John." If any witch was unthinking enough to utter these words, he would rush out upon her and beat and buffet her unmercifully, or tear her flesh with a wool-card. Other names he did not care about; and once gave instructions to a noted warlock that whenever he wanted his aid, he was to strike the ground three times and exclaim, "Rise up, foul thief!"

Sir G. Mackenzie.

Upon this confession many persons were executed. So strong was the popular feeling, that no one once accused of witchcraft was acquitted; at least acquittals did not average one in a hundred trials. Witch-finding, or witch-pricking, became a trade, and a set of mercenary vagabonds roamed about the country provided with long pins to run into the flesh of supposed criminals. It was no unusual thing then, nor is it now, that in aged persons there should be some spot on the body totally devoid of feeling. It was the object of the witch-pricker to discover this spot, and the unhappy wight who did not bleed when pricked upon it was doomed to the death. If not immediately cast into prison, her life was rendered miserable by the persecution of her neighbours. It is recorded of many poor women, that the annoyances they endured in this way were so excessive, that they preferred death. Sir George Mackenzie, the Lord Advocate, at the time when witch trials were so frequent, and himself a devout believer in the crime, relates, in his *Criminal Law*, first published in 1678, some remarkable instances of it. He says, "I went, when I was a justice-depute, to examine some women who had confessed judicially; and one of them, who was a silly creature, told me, under secrecy, that she had not confessed because she was guilty, but being a poor creature, who wrought for her meat, and being defamed for a witch, she knew she should starve, for no person thereafter would either give her meat or lodging, and that all men would beat her and set dogs at her, and that, therefore, she desired to be out of the world; whereupon she wept most bitterly, and upon her knees called God to witness to what she said." Sir George, though not wholly elevated above the prejudices of his age upon this subject, was clear-sighted enough to see the danger to society of the undue encouragement given to the witch prosecutions. He was convinced that three-fourths of them were unjust and unfounded. He says, in the work already quoted, that the persons who were in general accused of this crime were poor ignorant men and women who did not understand the nature of the accusation, and who mistook their own superstitious fears for witchcraft. One poor wretch, a weaver, confessed that he was a warlock, and, being asked why, he replied, because "he had seen the devil dancing, like a fly, about the candle!" A simple woman, who, because she was called a witch, believed that she was, asked the judge upon the bench whether a person might be a witch and not know it? Sir George adds, that all the supposed criminals were subjected to severe torture in prison from their gaolers, who thought they did God good service by vexing and tormenting them; "and I know," says this humane and enlightened magistrate, "that this usage was the ground of all their confession; and albeit, the poor miscreants cannot prove this usage, the actors in it being the only witnesses; yet the judge should be jealous of it, as that which did at first elicit the confession, and for fear of which they dare not retract it." Another author,[31] also a firm believer in witchcraft, gives a still more lamentable instance of a woman who preferred execution as a witch to live on under the imputation. This woman, who knew that three others were to be strangled and burned on an early day, sent for the minister of the parish, and confessed that she had sold her soul to Satan. "Whereupon being called before the judges, she was condemned to die with the rest. Being carried forth to the place of execution, she remained silent during the first, second, and third prayer, and then, perceiving that there remained no more but to rise and go to the stake, she lifted up her body, and, with a loud voice, cried out, 'Now all you that see me this day, know that I am now to die as a witch, by my own confession; and I free all men, especially the ministers and magistrates, of the guilt of my blood. I take it wholly upon myself. My blood be upon my own head. And, as I must make answer to the God of heaven presently, I declare I am as free of witchcraft as any child. But, being delated by a malicious woman, and put in prison under the name of a witch, disowned by my husband and friends, and seeing no ground of hope of ever coming out again, I made up that confession to destroy my own life, being weary of it, and choosing rather to die than to live.'" As a proof of the singular obstinacy and blindness of the believers in witches, it may be stated that the minister who relates this story only saw in the dying speech of the unhappy woman an additional proof that she was a witch. True, indeed is it, that "none are so blind as those who will not see."

It is time, however, to return to James VI., who is fairly entitled to share with Pope Innocent, Sprenger, Bodinus, and Matthew Hopkins the glory or the odium of being at the same time a chief enemy and chief encourager of witchcraft. Towards the close of the sixteenth century, many learned men, both on the continent and in the isles of Britain, had endeavoured to disabuse the public mind on this subject. The most celebrated were Wierus, in Germany; Pietro d'Apone, in Italy; and Reginald Scot, in England. Their works excited the attention of the zealous James, who, mindful of the involuntary compliment which his merits had extorted from the devil, was ambitious to deserve it by still continuing "his greatest enemie." In the year 1597, he published in Edinburgh his famous treatise on Demonology. Its design may be gathered from the following passage in the introduction: "The fearful abounding," says the king, "at this time and in this country of these detestable slaves of the devil, the witches or enchanters, hath moved me, beloved reader, to despatch in post this following treatise of mine, not in any wise, as I protest, to serve for a show of mine own learning and ingene [ingenuity], but only (moved of conscience) to press thereby, so far as I can, to resolve the doubting hearts of many, both that such assaults of Satan are most certainly practised, and that the instrument thereof merits most severely to be punished, against the damnable opinions of two, principally in our age; whereof the one called Scot, an Englishman, is not ashamed in public print to deny that there can be such thing as witchcraft, and so maintains the old error of the Sadducees in denying of spirits. The other, called Wierus, a German physician, sets out a public apology for all these crafts-folks, whereby procuring for them impunity, he plainly betrays himself to have been one of that profession." In other parts of this treatise, which the author had put into the form of a dialogue, to "make it more pleasant and facile," he says: "Witches ought to be put to death, according to the law of God, the civil and imperial law, and the municipal law of all Christian nations: yea, to spare the life, and not strike whom God bids strike and so severely punish in so odious a treason against God, is not only unlawful, but doubtless as great a sin in the magistrate as was Saul's sparing Agag." He says also that the crime is so abominable, that it may be proved by evidence which would not be received against any other offenders,—young children, who knew not the nature of an oath, and persons of an infamous character, being sufficient witnesses against them; but lest the innocent should be accused of a crime so difficult to be acquitted of, he recommends that in all cases the ordeal should be resorted to. He says, "Two good helps may be used: the one is the finding of their mark, and the trying the insensibleness thereof; the other is their floating on the water,—for, as in a secret murther, if the dead carcass be at any time thereafter handled by the murtherer, it will gush out of blood, as if the blood were crying to Heaven for revenge of the murtherer (God having appointed that secret supernatural sign for trial of that secret unnatural crime), so that it appears that God hath appointed (for a supernatural sign of the monstrous impiety of witches) that the water shall refuse to receive them in her bosom that have shaken off them the sacred water of baptism, and wilfully refused the benefit thereof; — no, not so much as their eyes are able to shed tears (threaten and torture them as you please), while first they repent (God not permitting them to dissemble their obstinacy in so horrible a crime); albeit, the womenkind especially, be able otherwise to shed tears at every light occasion when they will, yea, although it were dissembling like the crocodiles."

Pietro d'Apone.

When such doctrines as these were openly promulgated by the highest authority in the realm, and who, in promulgating them, flattered, but did not force the public opinion, it is not surprising that the sad delusion should have increased and multiplied until the race of wizards and witches replenished the earth. The reputation which he lost by being afraid of a naked sword, he more than regained by his courage in combating the devil. The Kirk shewed itself a most zealous coadjutor, especially during those halcyon days when it was not at issue with the king upon other matters of doctrine and prerogative.

On his accession to the throne of England in 1603, James came amongst a people who had heard with admiration of his glorious deeds against the witches. He himself left no part of his ancient prejudices behind him; and his advent was the signal for the persecution to burst forth in England with a fury equal to that in Scotland. It had languished a little during the latter years of the reign of Elizabeth; but the very first parliament of King James brought forward the subject. James was flattered by their promptitude, and the act passed in 1604. On the second reading in the House of Lords, the bill passed into a committee, in which were twelve bishops. By it was enacted, "That if any person shall use, practise, or exercise any conjuration of any wicked or evil spirit, or shall consult, covenant with, or feed any such spirit, the first offence to be imprisonment for a year, and standing in the pillory once a quarter; the second offence to be death."

The minor punishment seems but rarely to have been inflicted. Every record that has been preserved mentions that the witches were hanged and burned, or burned, without the previous strangling, "alive and quick." During the whole of James's reign, amid the civil wars of his successor, the sway of the Long Parliament, the usurpation of Cromwell, and the reign of Charles II., there was no abatement of the persecution. If at any time it raged with less virulence, it was when Cromwell and the Independents were masters. Dr. Zachary Grey, the editor of an edition of "Hudibras," informs us, in a note to that work, that he himself perused a list of three thousand witches who were executed in the time of the Long Parliament alone. During the first eighty years of the seventeenth century, the number executed has been estimated at five hundred annually, making the frightful total of forty thousand. Some of these cases deserve to be cited. The great majority resemble closely those already mentioned; but two or three of them let in a new light upon the popular superstition.

Every one has heard of the "Lancashire witches," a phrase now used to compliment the ladies of that county for their bewitching beauty; but it is not every one who has heard the story in which it originated. A villanous boy, named Robinson, was the chief actor in the tragedy. He confessed many years afterwards that he had been suborned by his father and other persons to give false evidence against the unhappy witches whom he brought to the stake. The time of this famous trial was about the year 1634. This boy Robinson, whose father was a wood-cutter, residing on the borders of Pendle Forest, in Lancashire, spread abroad many rumours against one Mother Dickenson, whom he accused of being a witch. These rumours coming to the ears of the local magistracy, the boy was sent for and strictly examined. He told the following extraordinary story without hesitation or prevarication, and apparently in so open and honest a manner, that no one who heard him doubted the truth of it. He said, that as he was roaming about in one of the glades of the forest, amusing himself by gathering blackberries, he saw two greyhounds before him, which he thought at the time belonged to some gentleman of the neighbourhood. Being fond of sport, he proposed to have a course; and a hare being started, he incited the hounds to run. Neither of them would stir. Angry at the beasts, he seized hold of a switch, with which he was about to punish them, when one of them suddenly started up in the form of a woman, and the other of a little boy. He at once recognised the woman to be the witch Mother Dickenson. She offered him some money to induce him to sell his soul to the devil; but he refused. Upon this she took a bridle out of her pocket, and shaking it over the head of the other little boy, he was instantly turned into a horse. Mother Dickenson then seized him in her arms, sprang upon the horse, and placing him before her, rode with the swiftness of the wind over forests, fields, bogs, and rivers, until they came to a large barn. The witch alighted at the door, and, taking him by the hand, led him inside. There he saw seven old women pulling at seven halters which hung from the roof. As they pulled, large pieces of meat, lumps of butter, loaves of bread, basins of milk, hot puddings, black puddings, and other rural dainties, fell from the halters on to the floor. While engaged in this charm, they made such ugly faces, and looked so fiendish, that he was quite frightened. After they had pulled in this manner enough for an ample feast, they set-to, and shewed, whatever might be said of the way in which their supper was procured, that their epicurism was a little more refined than that of the Scottish witches, who, according to Gellie Duncan's confession, feasted upon dead men's flesh in the old kirk of Berwick. The boy added, that as soon as supper was ready, many other witches came to partake of it, several of whom he named.

In consequence of this story, many persons were arrested, and the boy Robinson was led about from church to church, in order that he might point out to the officers by whom he was accompanied the hags he had seen in the barn. Altogether, about twenty persons were thrown into prison; eight of them were condemned to die, including Mother Dickenson, upon this evidence alone, and executed accordingly. Among the wretches who concocted this notable story, not one was ever brought to justice for his perjury; and Robinson, the father, gained considerable sums by threatening persons who were rich enough to buy off exposure.

Among the ill-weeds which flourished amid the long dissensions of the civil war, Matthew Hopkins, the witch-finder, stands eminent in his sphere. This vulgar fellow resided, in the year 1644, at the town of Manningtree, in Essex, and made himself very conspicuous in discovering the devil's marks upon several unhappy witches. The credit he gained by his skill in this instance seems to have inspired him to renewed exertions. In the course of a very short time, whenever a witch was spoken of in Essex, Matthew Hopkins was sure to be present, aiding the judges with his knowledge of "such cattle," as he called them. As his reputation increased, he assumed the title of "Witch-finder General," and travelled through the counties of Norfolk, Essex, Huntingdon, and Sussex, for the sole purpose of finding out witches. In one year he brought sixty poor creatures to the stake. The test he commonly adopted was that of swimming, so highly recommended by King James in his *Demonologie*. The hands and feet of the suspected persons were tied together crosswise, the thumb of the right hand to the toe of the left foot, and *vice versa*. They were then wrapped up in a large sheet or blanket, and laid upon their backs in a pond or river. If they sank, their friends and relatives had the poor consolation of knowing they were innocent; but there was an end of them: if they floated, which, when laid carefully on the water, was generally the case, there was also an end of them; for they were deemed guilty of witch-craft, and burned accordingly.

Another test was to make them repeat the Lord's prayer and creed. It was affirmed that no witch could do so correctly. If she missed a word, or even pronounced one incoherently, which in her trepidation it was most probable she would, she was accounted guilty. It was thought that witches could not weep more than three tears, and those only from the left eye. Thus the conscious innocence of many persons, which gave them fortitude to bear unmerited torture without flinching, was construed by their unmerciful tormentors into proofs of guilt. In some districts the test resorted to was to weigh the culprit against the church Bible. If the suspected witch proved heavier than the Bible, she was set at liberty. This mode was far too humane for the witch-finders by profession. Hopkins always maintained that the most legitimate modes were pricking and swimming.

Hopkins used to travel through his counties like a man of consideration, attended by his two assistants, always putting up at the chief inn of the place, and always at the cost of the authorities. His charges were twenty shillings a town, his expenses of living while there, and his carriage thither and back. This he claimed whether he found witches or not. If he found any, he claimed twenty shillings a head in addition when they were brought to execution. For about three years he carried on this infamous trade, success making him so insolent and rapacious that high and low became his enemies. The Rev. Mr. Gaul, a clergyman of Houghton, in Huntingdonshire, wrote a pamphlet impugning his pretensions, and accusing him of being a common nuisance. Hopkins replied in an angry letter to the functionaries of Houghton, stating his intention to visit their town; but desiring to know whether it afforded many such sticklers for witchcraft as Mr. Gaul, and whether they were willing to receive and entertain him with the customary hospitality, if he so far honoured them. He added, by way of threat, that in case he did not receive a satisfactory reply, "he would waive their shire altogether, and betake himself to such places where he might do and punish, not only without control, but with thanks and recompense." The authorities of Houghton were not much alarmed at this awful threat of letting them alone. They very wisely took no notice either of him or his letter.

Mr. Gaul describes in his pamphlet one of the modes employed by Hopkins, which was sure to swell his revenues very considerably. It was a proof even more atrocious than the swimming. He says, that the "Witch-finder General" used to take the suspected witch and place her in the middle of a room, upon a stool or table, cross-legged, or in some other uneasy posture. If she refused to sit in this manner, she was bound with strong cords. Hopkins then placed persons to watch her for four-and-twenty hours, during which time she was to be kept without meat or drink. It was supposed that one of her imps would come during that interval and suck her blood. As the imp might come in the shape of a wasp, a moth, a fly, or other insect, a hole was made in the door or window to let it enter. The watchers were ordered to keep a sharp look out, and endeavour to kill any insect that appeared in the room. If any fly escaped, and they could not kill it, the woman was guilty; the fly was her imp, and she was sentenced to be burned, and twenty shillings went into the pockets of Master Hopkins. In this manner he made one old woman confess, because four flies had appeared in the room, that she was attended by four imps, named "Ilemazar," "Pye-wackett," "Peck-in-the-crown," and "Grizel-Greedigut."

Matthew Hopkins.[32]

It is consoling to think that this impostor perished in his own snare. Mr. Gaul's exposure and his own rapacity weakened his influence among the magistrates; and the populace, who began to find that not even the most virtuous and innocent were secure from his persecution, looked upon him with undisguised aversion. He was beset by a mob at a village in Suffolk, and accused of being himself a wizard. An old reproach was brought against him, that he had, by means of sorcery, cheated the devil out of a certain memorandum-book, in which he, Satan, had entered the names of all the witches in England. "Thus," said the populace, "you find out witches, not by God's aid, but by the devil's." In vain he denied his guilt. The populace longed to put him to his own test. He was speedily stripped, and his thumbs and toes tied together. He was then placed in a blanket, and cast into a pond. Some say that he floated, and that he was taken out, tried, and executed upon no other proof of his guilt. Others assert that he was drowned. This much is positive, that there was an end of him. As no judicial entry of his trial and execution is to be found in any register, it appears most probable that he expired by the hands of the mob. Butler has immortalised this scamp in the following lines of his *Hudibras*:

> "Hath not this present Parliament
> A lieger to the devil sent,
> Fully empower'd to treat about
> Finding revolted witches out?
> And has he not within a year
> Hang'd threescore of them in one shire?
> Some only for not being drown'd,
> And some for sitting above ground
> Whole days and nights upon their breeches,
> And feeling pain, were hang'd for witches;
> And some for putting knavish tricks
> Upon green geese or turkey chicks;
> Or pigs that suddenly deceased
> Of griefs unnatural, as he guessed;
> Who proved himself at length a witch,
> And made a rod for his own breech."

In Scotland also witch-finding became a trade. They were known under the designation of "common prickers," and, like Hopkins, received a fee for each witch they discovered. At the trial of Janet Peaston, in 1646, the magistrates of Dalkeith "caused John Kincaid of Tranent, the common pricker, to exercise his craft upon her. He found two marks of the devil's making; for she could not feel the pin when it was put into either of the said marks, nor did the marks bleed when the pin was taken out again. When she was asked where she thought the pins were put in her, she pointed to a part of her body distant from the real place. They were pins of three inches in length."[33]

These common prickers became at last so numerous that they were considered nuisances. The judges refused to take their evidence; and in 1678 the privy council of Scotland condescended to hear the complaint of an honest woman who had been indecently exposed by one of them, and expressed their opinion that common prickers were common cheats.

But such an opinion was not formed in high places before hundreds of innocent persons had fallen victims. The parliaments had encouraged the delusion both in England and Scotland; and by arming these fellows with a sort of authority, had in a manner forced the magistrates and ministers to receive their evidence. The fate of one poor old gentleman, who fell a victim to the arts of Hopkins in 1646, deserves to be recorded. Mr. Louis, a venerable clergyman, upwards of seventy years of age, and who had been rector of Framlingham, in Suffolk, for fifty years, excited suspicion that he was a wizard. Being a violent royalist, he was likely to meet with no sympathy at that time; and even his own parishioners, whom he had served so long and so faithfully, turned their backs upon him as soon as he was accused. Placed under the hands of Hopkins, who knew so well how to bring the refractory to confession, the old man, the light of whose intellect had become somewhat dimmed from age, confessed that he was a wizard. He said he had two imps that continually excited him to do evil; and that one day, when he was walking on the sea-coast, one of them prompted him to express a wish that a ship, whose sails were just visible in the distance, might sink. He consented, and saw the vessel sink before his eyes. He was, upon this confession, tried and condemned. On his trial, the flame of reason burned up as brightly as ever. He denied all that had been alleged against him, and cross-examined Hopkins with great tact and severity. After his condemnation, he begged that the funeral service of the Church might be read for him. The request was refused, and he repeated it for himself from memory as he was led to the scaffold.

A poor woman in Scotland was executed upon evidence even less strong than this. John Bain, a common pricker, swore that, as he passed her door, he heard her talking to the devil. She said, in defence, that it was a foolish practice she had of talking to herself, and several of her neighbours corroborated her statement; but the evidence of the pricker was received. He swore that none ever talked to themselves who were not witches. The devil's mark being found upon her, the additional testimony of her guilt was deemed conclusive, and she was "convict and brynt."

From the year 1652 to 1682, these trials diminished annually in number, and acquittals were by no means so rare as they had been. To doubt in witchcraft was no longer dangerous. Before country justices, condemnations on the most absurd evidence still continued; but when the judges of the land had to charge the jury, they took a more humane and philosophical view. By degrees, the educated classes (comprised in those days within very narrow limits) openly expressed their unbelief of modern witchcraft, although they were not bold enough to deny its existence altogether. Between them and the believers in the old doctrine fierce arguments ensued, and the sceptics were designated Sadducees. To convince them, the learned and Reverend Joseph Glanvil wrote his well-known work, *Sadducismus Triumphatus*, and *The Collection of Relations*; the first part intended as a philosophical inquiry into witchcraft, and the power of the devil "to assume a mortal shape:" the latter containing what he considered a multitude of well-authenticated modern instances.

Sir Matthew Hale.

But though progress was made, it was slow. In 1664, the venerable Sir Matthew Hale condemned two women, named Amy Duny and Rose Cullender, to the stake at St. Edmondsbury, upon evidence the most ridiculous. These two old women, whose ugliness gave their neighbours the first idea that they were witches, went to a shop to purchase herrings, and were refused.

Indignant at the prejudice against them, they were not sparing of their abuse. Shortly afterward, the daughter of the herring-dealer fell sick, and a cry was raised that she was bewitched by the old women who had been refused the herrings. This girl was subject to epileptic fits. To discover the guilt of Amy Duny and Rose Cullender, the girl's eyes were blinded closely with a shawl, and the witches were commanded to touch her. They did so, and she was immediately seized with a fit. Upon this evidence they were sent to prison. The girl was afterwards touched by an indifferent person, and the force of her imagination was so great, that, thinking it was again the witches, she fell down in a violent fit as before. This, however, was not received in favour of the accused. The following extract, from the published reports of the trial, will shew the sort of evidence which was received:

"Samuel Pacey, of Leystoff (a good, sober man), being sworn, said that, on Thursday the 10th of October last, his younger daughter, Deborah, about nine years old, was suddenly taken so lame that she could not stand on her legs, and so continued till the 17th of the same month, when the child desired to be carried to a bank on the east side of the house, looking towards the sea; and, while she was sitting there, Amy Duny came to this examinant's house to buy some herrings, but was denied. Then she came twice more, but, being as often denied, she went away discontented and grumbling. At this instant of time, the child was taken with terrible fits, complaining of a pain in her stomach, as if she was pricked with pins, shrieking out with a voice like a whelp, and thus continued till the 30th of the same month. This examinant further saith, that Amy Duny, having long had the reputation of a witch, and his child having, in the intervals of her fits, constantly cried out on her as the cause of her disorder, saying, that the said Amy did appear to her and fright her; he himself did suspect the said Amy to be a witch, and charged her with being the cause of his child's illness, and set her in the stocks. Two days after, his daughter Elizabeth was taken with such strange fits, that they could not force open her mouth without a tap; and the younger child being in the same condition, they used to her the same remedy. Both children grievously complained that Amy Duny and another woman, whose habit and looks they described, did appear to them and torment them, and would cry out, 'There stands Amy Duny! There stands Rose Cullender!' the other person who afflicted them. Their fits were not alike. Sometimes they were lame on the right side; sometimes on the left; and sometimes so sore, that they could not bear to be touched. Sometimes they were perfectly well in other respects, but they could not *hear*; at other times they could not *see*. Sometimes they lost their speech for one, two, and once for eight days together. At times they had swooning fits, and, when they could speak, were taken with a fit of coughing, and vomited phlegm and crooked pins; and once a great twopenny nail, with above forty pins; which nail he, the examinant, saw vomited up, with many of the pins. The nail and pins were produced in the court. Thus the children continued for two months, during which time the examinant often made them read in the New Testament, and observed, when they came to the words *Lord Jesus*, or *Christ*, they could not pronounce them, but fell into a fit. When they came to the word *Satan*, or *devil*, they would point, and say, 'This bites, but makes me speak right well.' Finding his children thus tormented without hopes of recovery, he sent them to his sister, Margaret Arnold, at Yarmouth, being willing to try whether change of air would help them.

"Margaret Arnold was the next witness. Being sworn, she said, that about the 30th of November, Elizabeth and Deborah Pacey came to her house, with her brother, who told her what had happened, and that he thought his children bewitched. She, this examinant, did not much regard it, supposing the children had played tricks, and put the pins into their mouths themselves. She therefore took all the pins from their clothes, sewing them with thread instead of pinning them. But, notwithstanding, they raised, at times, at least thirty pins in her presence, and had terrible fits; in which fits they would cry out upon Amy Duny and Rose Cullender, saying, that they saw them and heard them threatening, as before; that they saw things like mice running about the house; and one of them catched one, and threw it into the fire, which made a noise like a rat. Another time the younger child, being out of doors, a thing like a bee would have forced itself into her mouth, at which the child ran screaming into the house, and before this examinant could come at her, fell into a fit, and vomited a twopenny nail, with a broad head. After that, this examinant asked the child how she came by this nail, when she answered, 'The bee brought the nail, and forced it into my mouth.' At other times, the eldest child told this examinant that she saw flies bring her crooked pins. She would then fall into a fit, and vomit such pins. One time the said child said she saw a mouse, and crept under the table to look for it; and afterwards, the child seemed to put something into her apron, saying, 'She had caught it.' She then ran to the fire, and threw it in, on which there did appear to this examinant something like a flash of gunpowder, although she does own she saw nothing in the child's hand. Once the child, being speechless, but otherwise very sensible, ran up and down the house, crying, 'Hush! hush!' as if she had seen poultry; but this examinant saw nothing. At last the child catched at something, and threw it into the fire. Afterwards, when the child could speak, this examinant asked her what she saw at the time? She answered that she saw a duck. Another time the youngest child said, after a fit, that Amy Duny had been with her, and tempted her to drown herself, or cut her throat, or otherwise destroy herself. Another time they both cried out upon Amy Duny and Rose Cullender, saying, 'Why don't you come yourselves? Why do you send your imps to torment us?'"

Sir Thomas Brown.

The celebrated Sir Thomas Brown, the author of *Vulgar Errors*, was also examined as a witness upon the trial. Being desired to give his opinion of the three persons in court, he said he was clearly of opinion that they were bewitched. He said there had lately been a discovery of witches in Denmark, who used the same way of tormenting persons, by conveying crooked pins, needles, and nails into their bodies. That he thought, in such cases, the devil acted upon human bodies by natural means, namely, by exciting and stirring up the superabundant humours; he did afflict them in a more surprising manner by the same diseases their bodies were usually subject to; that these fits might be natural, only raised to a great degree by the subtlety of the devil, co-operating with the malice of these witches.

The evidence being concluded, Sir Matthew Hale addressed the jury. He said, he would waive repeating the evidence, to prevent any mistake, and told the jury there were two things they had to inquire into. First, Whether or not these children were bewitched; secondly, Whether these women did bewitch them. He said, he did not in the least doubt there were witches; first, Because the Scriptures affirmed it; secondly, Because the wisdom of all nations, particularly our own, had provided laws against witchcraft, which implied their belief of such a crime. He desired them strictly to observe the evidence, and begged of God to direct their hearts in the weighty concern they had in hand, since, to condemn the innocent and let the guilty go free are both an abomination to the Lord.

The jury then retired, and in about half an hour returned a verdict of guilty upon all the indictments, being thirteen in number. The next morning the children came with their father to the lodgings of Sir Matthew Hale, very well, and quite restored to their usual health. Mr. Pacey, being asked at what time their health began to improve, replied, that they were quite well in half an hour after the conviction of the prisoners.

Many attempts were made to induce the unfortunate women to confess their guilt; but in vain, and they were both hanged.

Eleven trials were instituted before Chief Justice Holt for witch-craft, between the years 1694 and 1701. The evidence was of the usual character; but Holt appealed so successfully in each case to the common sense of the jury, that they were every one acquitted. A general feeling seemed to pervade the country that blood enough had been shed upon these absurd charges. Now and then, the flame of persecution burnt up in a remote district; but these instances were no longer looked upon as mere matters of course. They appear, on the contrary, to have excited much attention; a sure proof, if no other were to be obtained, that they were becoming unfrequent.

A case of witchcraft was tried in 1711, before Lord Chief Justice Powell; in which, however, the jury persisted in a verdict of guilty, though the evidence was of the usual absurd and contradictory character, and the enlightened judge did all in his power to bring them to a right conclusion. The accused person was one Jane Wenham, better known as the Witch of Walkerne; and the persons who were alleged to have suffered from her witchcraft were two young women, named Thorne and Street. A witness, named Mr. Arthur Chauncy, deposed, that he had seen Ann Thorne in several of her fits, and that she always recovered upon prayers being said, or if Jane Wenham came to her. He related, that he had pricked the prisoner several times in the arms, but could never fetch any blood from her; that he had seen her vomit pins, when there were none in her clothes or within her reach; and that he had preserved several of them, which he was ready to produce. The judge, however, told him that was needless, *as he supposed they were crooked pins.*

Mr. Francis Bragge, another witness, deposed, that strange "cakes" of bewitched feathers having been taken from Ann Thorne's pillow, he was anxious to see them. He went into a room where some of these feathers were, and took two of the cakes, and compared them together. They were both of a circular figure, something larger than a crown piece; and he observed that the small feathers were placed in a nice and curious order, at equal distances from each other, making so many radii of the circle, in the centre of which the quill-ends of the feathers met. He counted the number of these feathers, and found them to be exactly thirty-two in each cake. He afterwards endeavoured to pull off two or three of them, and observed that they were all fastened together by a sort of viscous matter, which would stretch seven or eight times in a thread before it broke. Having taken off several of these feathers, he removed the viscous matter with his fingers, and found under it, in the centre, some short hairs, black and grey, matted together, which he verily believed to be cat's hair. He also said, that Jane Wenham confessed to him that she had bewitched the pillow, and had practised witchcraft for sixteen years.

The judge interrupted the witness at this stage, and said, he should very much like to see an enchanted feather, and seemed to wonder when he was told that none of these strange cakes had been preserved. His lordship asked the witness why he did not keep one or two of them, and was informed that they had all been burnt, in order to relieve the bewitched person of the pains she suffered, which could not be so well effected by any other means.

A man, named Thomas Ireland, deposed, that hearing several times a great noise of cats crying and screaming about his house, he went out and frightened them away, and they all ran towards the cottage of Jane Wenham. One of them he swore positively had a face very like Jane Wenham's. Another man, named Burville, gave similar evidence, and swore that he had often seen a cat with Jane Wenham's face. Upon one occasion he was in Ann Thorne's chamber, when several cats came in, and among them the cat above stated. This witness would have favoured the court with a much longer statement, but was stopped by the judge, who said he had heard quite enough.

The prisoner, in her defence, said nothing, but that "she was a clear woman." The learned judge then summed up, leaving it to the jury to determine whether such evidence as they had heard was sufficient to take away the prisoner's life upon the indictment. After a long deliberation they brought in their verdict, that she was guilty upon the evidence. The judge then asked them whether they found her guilty upon the indictment of conversing with the devil in the shape of a cat? The sapient foreman very gravely answered, "We find her guilty of *that*." The learned judge then very reluctantly proceeded to pass sentence of death; but, by his persevering exertions, a pardon was at last obtained, and the wretched old woman was set at liberty.

In the year 1716, a woman and her daughter – the latter only nine years of age – were hanged at Huntingdon for selling their souls to the devil, and raising a storm by pulling off their stockings and making a lather of soap. This appears to have been the last judicial execution in England. From that time to the year 1736, the populace raised at intervals the old cry, and more than once endangered the lives of poor women by dragging them through ponds on suspicion; but the philosophy of those who, from their position, sooner or later give the tone to the opinions and morals of the poor, was silently working a cure for the evil. The fear of witches ceased to be epidemic, and became individual, lingering only in minds fettered by inveterate prejudice or brutalising superstition. In the year 1736, the penal statute of James I. was finally blotted from the statute-book, and suffered no longer to disgrace the advancing intelligence of the country. Pretenders to witchcraft, fortune-tellers, conjurors, and all their train, were liable only to the common punishment of rogues and impostors – imprisonment and the pillory.

In Scotland, the delusion also assumed the same phases, and was gradually extinguished in the light of civilisation. As in England, the progress of improvement was slow. Up to the year 1665, little or no diminution of the mania was perceptible. In 1643, the General Assembly recommended that the privy council should institute a standing commission, composed of any "understanding gentlemen or magistrates," to try the witches, who were stated to have increased enormously of late years. In 1649, an act was passed, confirmatory of the original statute of Queen Mary, explaining some points of the latter which were doubtful, and enacting severe penalties, not only against witches themselves, but against all who covenanted with them, or sought by their means to pry into the secrets of futurity, or cause any evil to the life, lands, or limbs of their neighbours. For the next ten years, the popular madness upon this subject was perhaps more furious than ever; upwards of four thousand persons suffered for the crime during that interval. This was the consequence of the act of parliament and the unparalleled severity of the magistrates; the latter frequently complained that for two witches they burned one day, there were ten to burn the next: they never thought that they themselves were the cause of the increase. In a single circuit, held at Glasgow, Ayr, and Stirling, in 1659, seventeen unhappy creatures were burned by judicial sentence for trafficking with Satan. In one day (November 7, 1661), the privy council issued no less than fourteen commissions for trials in the provinces. Next year, the violence of the persecution seems to have abated. From 1662 to 1668, although "the understanding gentlemen and magistrates" already mentioned, continued to try and condemn, the High Court of Justiciary had but one offender of this class to deal with, and she was acquitted. James Welsh, a common pricker, was ordered to be publicly whipped through the streets of Edinburgh for falsely accusing a woman of witchcraft; a fact which alone proves that the superior court sifted the evidence in these cases with much more care and severity than it had done a few years previously. The enlightened Sir George Mackenzie, styled by Dryden "the noble wit of Scotland," laboured hard to introduce this rule into court, that the confessions of the witches should be held of little worth, and that the evidence of the prickers and other interested persons should be received with distrust and jealousy. This was reversing the old practice, and saved many innocent lives. Though a firm believer both in ancient and modern witchcraft, he could not shut his eyes to the atrocities daily committed under the name of justice. In his work on the Criminal Law of Scotland, published in 1678, he says, "From the horridness of this crime, I do conclude that, of all others, it requires the clearest relevancy and most convincing probature; and I condemn, next to the witches themselves, those cruel and too forward judges who burn persons by thousands as guilty of this crime." In the same year, Sir John Clerk plumply refused to serve as a commissioner on trials for witchcraft, alleging, by way of excuse, "that he was not himself good conjuror enough to be duly qualified." The views entertained by Sir George Mackenzie were so favourably received by the Lords of Session, that he was deputed, in 1680, to report to them on the cases of a number of poor women who were then in prison awaiting their trial. Sir George stated that there was no evidence against them whatever but their own confessions, which were absurd and contradictory, and drawn from them by severe torture. They were immediately discharged.

For the next sixteen years the Lords of Session were unoccupied with trials for witchcraft. Not one is entered upon the record. But in 1697 a case occurred which equalled in absurdity any of those that signalised the dark reign of King James. A girl named Christiana Shaw, eleven years of age, the daughter of John Shaw of Bargarran, was subject to fits; and being of a spiteful temper, she accused her maid-servant, with whom she had frequent quarrels, of bewitching her. Her story unfortunately was believed. Encouraged to tell all the persecutions of the devil which the maid had sent to torment her, she in the end concocted a romance that involved twenty-one persons. There was no other evidence against them but the fancies of this lying child, and the confessions which pain had extorted from them; but upon this no less than five women were condemned before Lord Blantyre and the rest of the commissioners, appointed specially by the privy council to try this case. They were burned on the Green at Paisley. The warlock of the party, one John Reed, who was also condemned, hanged himself in prison. It was the general belief in Paisley that the devil had strangled him lest he should have revealed in his last moments too many of the unholy secrets of witchcraft. This trial excited considerable disgust in Scotland. The Rev. Mr. Bell, a contemporary writer, observed that, in this business, "persons of more goodness and esteem than most of their calumniators were defamed for witches." He adds, that the persons chiefly to blame were "certain ministers of too much forwardness and absurd credulity, and some topping professors in and about Glasgow."[34]

After this trial, there again occurs a lapse of seven years, when the subject was painfully forced upon public attention by the brutal cruelty of the mob at Pittenween. Two women were accused of having bewitched a strolling beggar who was subject to fits, or who pretended to be so, for the purpose of exciting commiseration. They were cast into prison, and tortured until they confessed. One of them, named Janet Cornfoot, contrived to escape, but was brought back to Pittenween next day by a party of soldiers. On her approach to the town she was unfortunately met by a furious mob, composed principally of fishermen and their wives, who seized upon her with the intention of swimming her. They forced her away to the sea-shore, and tying a rope around her body, secured the end of it to the mast of a fishing-boat lying alongside. In this manner they ducked her several times. When she was half dead, a sailor in the boat cut away the rope, and the mob dragged her through the sea to the beach. Here, as she lay quite insensible, a brawny ruffian took down the door of his hut, close by, and placed it on her back. The mob gathered large stones from the beach and piled them upon her till the wretched woman was pressed to death. No magistrate made the slightest attempt to interfere; and the soldiers looked on, delighted spectators. A great outcry was raised against this culpable remissness, but no judicial inquiry was set on foot. This happened in 1704.

The next case we hear of is that of Elspeth Rule, found guilty of witchcraft before Lord Anstruther, at the Dumfries circuit, in 1708. She was sentenced to be marked in the cheek with a red-hot iron, and banished the realm of Scotland for life.

Again there is a long interval. In 1718, the remote county of Caithness, where the delusion remained in all its pristine vigour for years after it had ceased elsewhere, was startled from its propriety by the cry of witchcraft. A silly fellow, named William Montgomery, a carpenter, had a mortal antipathy to cats; and somehow or other these animals generally chose his back-yard as the scene of their catterwaulings. He puzzled his brains for a long time to know why he, above all his neighbours, should be so pestered. At last he came to the sage conclusion that his tormentors were no cats, but witches. In this opinion he was supported by his maid-servant, who swore a round oath that she had often heard the aforesaid cats talking together in human voices. The next time the unlucky tabbies assembled in his back-yard, the valiant carpenter was on the alert. Arming himself with an axe, a dirk, and a broadsword, he rushed out among them. One of them he wounded in the back, a second in the hip, and the leg of a third he maimed with his axe; but he could not capture any of them. A few days afterwards, two old women of the parish died; and it was said, that when their bodies were laid out, there appeared upon the back of one the mark as of a recent wound, and a similar scar upon the hip of the other. The carpenter and his maid were convinced that they were the very cats, and the whole county repeated the same story. Every one was upon the look-out for proofs corroborative; a very remarkable one was soon discovered. Nanny Gilbert, a wretched old creature of upwards of seventy years of age, was found in bed with her leg broken. As she was ugly enough for a witch, it was asserted that she also was one of the cats that had fared so ill at the hands of the carpenter. The latter, when informed of the popular suspicion, asserted that he distinctly remembered to have struck one of the cats a blow with the back of his broadsword, which ought to have broken her leg. Nanny was immediately dragged from her bed and thrown into prison. Before she was put to the torture, she explained in a very natural and intelligible manner how she had broken her limb; but this account did not give satisfaction. The professional persuasions of the torturer made her tell a different tale, and she confessed that she was indeed a witch, and had been wounded by Montgomery on the night stated; that the two old women recently deceased were witches also, besides about a score of others whom she named. The poor creature suffered so much by the removal from her own home, and the tortures inflicted upon her, that she died the next day in prison. Happily for the persons she had named in her confession, Dundas of Arniston, at that time the king's advocate-general, wrote to the sheriff-depute, one Captain Ross of Littledean, cautioning him not to proceed to trial, the "thing being of too great difficulty, and beyond the jurisdiction of an inferior court." Dundas himself examined the precognition with great care, and was so convinced of the utter folly of the whole case, that he quashed all further proceedings.

We find this same sheriff-depute of Caithness very active four years afterwards in another trial for witchcraft. In spite of the warning he had received that all such cases were to be tried in future by the superior courts, he condemned to death an old woman at Dornoch, upon the charge of bewitching the cows and pigs of her neighbours. This poor creature was insane, and actually laughed and clapped her hands at sight of "the bonnie fire" that was to consume her. She had a daughter who was lame both of her hands and feet, and one of the charges brought against her was, that she had used this daughter as a pony in her excursions to join the devil's sabbath, and that the devil himself had shod her, and produced lameness.

This was the last execution that took place in Scotland for witchcraft. The penal statutes were repealed in 1736; and, as in England, whipping, the pillory, or imprisonment, were declared the future punishments of all pretenders to magic or witchcraft. Still for many years after this the superstition lingered both in England and Scotland, and in some districts is far from being extinct even at this day. But before we proceed to trace it any further than to its legal extinction, we have yet to see the frightful havoc it made in continental Europe from the commencement of the seventeenth to the middle of the eighteenth century. France, Germany, and Switzerland were the countries which suffered most from the epidemic. The number of victims in these countries during the sixteenth century has already been mentioned; but at the early part of the seventeenth, the numbers are so great, especially in Germany, that were they not to be found in the official records of the tribunals, it would be almost impossible to believe that mankind could ever have been so maddened and deluded. To use the words of the learned and indefatigable Horst,[35] "the world seemed to be like a large madhouse for witches and devils to play their antics in." Satan was believed to be at every body's call to raise the whirlwind, draw down the lightning, blight the productions of the earth, or destroy the health and paralyse the limbs of man. This belief, so insulting to the majesty and beneficence of the Creator, was shared by the most pious ministers of religion. Those who in their morning and evening prayers acknowledged the one true God, and praised him for the blessings of the seed-time and the harvest, were convinced that frail humanity could enter into a compact with the spirits of hell to subvert his laws and thwart all his merciful intentions. Successive popes, from Innocent VIII. downwards, promulgated this degrading doctrine, which spread so rapidly, that society seemed to be divided into two great factions, the bewitching and the bewitched.

The commissioners named by Innocent VIII. to prosecute the witch-trials in Germany were, Jacob Sprenger, so notorious for his work on demonology, entitled the *Malleus Maleficarum, or Hammer to knock down Witches*; Henry Institor, a learned jurisconsult; and the Bishop of Strasburgh. Bamberg, Trèves, Cologne, Paderborn, and Würzburg, were the chief seats of the commissioners, who, during their lives alone, condemned to the stake, on a very moderate calculation, upwards of three thousand victims. The number of witches so increased, that new commissioners were continually appointed in Germany, France, and Switzerland. In Spain and Portugal the Inquisition alone took cognisance of the crime. It is impossible to search the records of those dark, but now happily non-existing tribunals; but the mind recoils with affright even to form a guess of the multitudes who perished.

The mode of trial in the other countries is more easily ascertained. Sprenger in Germany, and Bodinus and Delrio in France, have left but too ample a record of the atrocities committed in the much-abused names of justice and religion. Bodinus, of great repute and authority in the seventeenth century, says, "The trial of this offence must not be conducted like other crimes. Whoever adheres to the ordinary course of justice perverts the spirit of the law, both divine and human. He who is accused of sorcery should never be acquitted, unless the malice of the prosecutor be clearer than the sun; for it is so difficult to bring full proof of this secret crime, that out of a million of witches not one would be convicted if the usual course were followed!" Henri Boguet, a witch-finder, who styled himself "The Grand Judge of Witches for the Territory of St. Claude," drew up a code for the guidance of all persons engaged in the witch-trials, consisting of seventy articles, quite as cruel as the code of Bodinus. In this document he affirms, that a mere suspicion of witchcraft justifies the immediate arrest and torture of the suspected person. If the prisoner muttered, looked on the ground, and did not shed any tears, all these were proofs positive of guilt! In all cases of witchcraft, the evidence of the child ought to be taken against its parent; and persons of notoriously bad character, although not to be believed upon their oaths on the ordinary occasions of dispute that might arise between man and man, were to be believed, if they swore that any person had bewitched them! Who, when he hears that this diabolical doctrine was the universally received opinion of the ecclesiastical and civil authorities, can wonder that thousands upon thousands of unhappy persons should be brought to the stake? that Cologne should for many years burn its three hundred witches annually? the district of Bamberg its four hundred? Nuremberg, Geneva, Paris, Toulouse, Lyons, and other cities, their two hundred?

A few of these trials may be cited, taking them in the order of priority, as they occurred in different parts of the Continent. In 1595, an old woman residing in a village near Constance, angry at not being invited to share the sports of the country people on a day of public rejoicing, was heard to mutter something to herself, and was afterwards seen to proceed through the fields towards a hill, where she was lost sight of. A violent thunder-storm arose about two hours afterwards, which wet the dancers to the skin, and did considerable damage to the plantations. This woman, suspected before of witchcraft, was seized and imprisoned, and accused of having raised the storm, by filling a hole with wine, and stirring it about with a stick. She was tortured till she confessed, and was burned alive the next evening.

City of Lyons.

About the same time two sorcerers in Toulouse were accused of having dragged a crucifix about the streets at midnight, stopping at times to spit upon and kick it, and uttering at intervals an exorcism to raise the devil. The next day a hail-storm did considerable damage to the crops; and a girl, the daughter of a shoemaker in the town, remembered to have heard in the night the execrations of the wizards. Her story led to their arrest. The usual means to produce confession were resorted to. The wizards owned that they could raise tempests whenever they pleased, and named several persons who possessed similar powers. They were hanged, and then burned in the market-place, and seven of the persons they had mentioned shared the same fate.

Hoppo and Stadlin, two noted wizards of Germany, were executed in 1599. They implicated twenty or thirty witches, who went about causing women to miscarry, bringing down the lightning of heaven, and making maidens bring forth toads. To this latter fact several girls were found to swear most positively! Stadlin confessed that he had killed seven infants in the womb of one woman.

Bodinus highly praises the exertions of a witch-finder named Nider, in France, who prosecuted so many that he could not calculate them. Some of these witches could, by a single word, cause people to fall down dead; others made women go with child three years instead of nine months; while others, by certain invocations and ceremonies, could turn the faces of their enemies upside down, or twist them round to their backs. Although no witness was ever procured who saw persons in this horrible state, the witches confessed that they had the power and exercised it. Nothing more was wanting to ensure the stake.

At Amsterdam a crazy girl confessed that she could cause sterility in cattle, and bewitch pigs and poultry by merely repeating the magic words *Turius und Shurius Inturius*! She was hanged and burned. Another woman in the same city, named Kornelis van Purmerund, was arrested in consequence of some disclosures the former had made. A witness came forward and swore that she one day looked through the window of her hut, and saw Kornelis sitting before a fire muttering something to the devil. She was sure it was to the devil, because she heard him answer her. Shortly afterwards twelve black cats ascended out of the floor, and danced on their hind legs around the witch for the space of about half an hour. They then vanished with a horrid noise, and leaving a disagreeable smell behind them. She also was hanged and burned.

At Bamberg, in Bavaria, the executions from the year 1610 to 1640 were at the rate of about a hundred annually. One woman, suspected of witchcraft, was seized because, having immoderately praised the beauty of a child, it had shortly afterwards fallen ill and died. She confessed upon the rack that the devil had given her the power to work evil upon those she hated, by speaking words in their praise. If she said with unwonted fervour, "What a strong man!" "What a lovely woman!" "What a sweet child!" the devil understood her, and afflicted them with diseases immediately. It is quite unnecessary to state the end of this poor creature. Many women were executed for causing strange substances to lodge in the bodies of those who offended them. Bits of wood, nails, hair, egg-shells, bits of glass, shreds of linen and woollen cloth, pebbles, and even hot cinders and knives, were the articles generally chosen. These were believed to remain in the body till the witches confessed or were executed, when they were voided from the bowels, or by the mouth, nostrils, or ears. Modern physicians have often had cases of a similar description under their care, where girls have swallowed needles, which have been voided on the arms, legs, and other parts of the body. But the science of that day could not account for these phenomena otherwise than by the power of the devil; and every needle swallowed by a servant-maid cost an old woman her life. Nay, if no more than one suffered in consequence, the district might think itself fortunate. The commissioners seldom stopped short at one victim. The revelations of the rack in most cases implicated half a score.

Bamberg.

Of all the records of the witch-trials preserved for the wonder of succeeding ages, that of Würzburg, from 1627 to 1629, is the most frightful. Hauber, who has preserved this list in his *Acta et Scripta Magica*, says, in a note at the end, that it is far from complete, and that there were a great many other burnings too numerous to specify. This record, which relates to the city only, and not to the province of Würzburg, contains the names of one hundred and fifty-seven persons who were burned in two years in twenty-nine burnings, averaging from five to six at a time. The list comprises three play-actors, four innkeepers, three common councilmen of Würzburg, fourteen vicars of the cathedral, the burgomaster's lady, an apothecary's wife and daughter, two choristers of the cathedral, Göbel Babelin, the prettiest girl in the town, and the wife, the two little sons and the daughter of the councillor Stolzenberg. Rich and poor, young and old, suffered alike. At the seventh of these recorded burnings, the victims are described as a wandering boy, twelve years of age, and four strange men and women found sleeping in the market-place. Thirty-two of the whole number appear to have been vagrants, of both sexes, who, failing to give a satisfactory account of themselves, were accused and found guilty of witchcraft. The number of children on the list is horrible to think upon. The thirteenth and fourteenth burnings comprised four persons, who are stated to have been a little maiden nine years of age, a maiden still less, her sister, their mother, and their aunt, a pretty young woman of twenty-four. At the eighteenth burning the victims were two boys of twelve, and a girl of fifteen; at the nineteenth, the young heir of the noble house of Rotenhahn, aged nine, and two other boys, one aged ten, and the other twelve. Among other entries appear the names of Baunach, the fattest, and Steinacher, the richest burgher in Würzburg. What tended to keep up the delusion in this unhappy city, and, indeed, all over Europe, was the number of hypochondriac and diseased persons who came voluntarily forward and made confession of witchcraft. Several of the victims in the foregoing list had only themselves to blame for their fate. Many again, including the apothecary's wife and daughter already mentioned, pretended to sorcery, and sold poisons, or attempted by means of charms and incantations to raise the devil. But throughout all this fearful period the delusion of the criminals was as great as that of the judges. Depraved persons who in ordinary times would have been thieves or murderers, added the desire of sorcery to their depravity, sometimes with the hope of acquiring power over their fellows, and sometimes with the hope of securing impunity in this world by the protection of Satan. One of the persons executed at the first burning, a prostitute, was heard repeating the exorcism which was supposed to have the power of raising the arch enemy in the form of a goat. This precious specimen of human folly has been preserved by Horst in his *Zauberbibliothek*. It ran as follows, and was to be repeated slowly, with many ceremonies and wavings of the hand:

> "*Lalle, Bachera, Magotte, Baphia, Dajam,*
> *Vagoth Heneche Ammi Nagaz, Adomator*
> *Raphael Immanuel Christus, Tetragrammaton*
> *Agra Jod Loi. König! König!*"

The two last words were uttered quickly, and with a sort of scream, and were supposed to be highly agreeable to Satan, who loved to be called a king. If he did not appear immediately, it was necessary to repeat a further exorcism. The one in greatest repute was as follows, and was to be read backwards, with the exception of the last two words:

> "*Anion, Lalle, Sabolos, Sado, Pater, Aziel*
> *Adonai Sado Vagoth Agra, Jod,*
> *Baphra! Komm! Komm!*"

When the witch wanted to get rid of the devil, who was sometimes in the habit of prolonging his visits to an unconscionable length, she had only to repeat the following, also backwards, when he generally disappeared, leaving behind him a suffocating smell:

> "*Zellianelle Heotti Bonus Vagotha*
> *Plisos sother osech unicus Beelzebub*
> *Dax! Komm! Komm!*"

This nonsensical jargon soon became known to all the idle and foolish boys of Germany. Many an unhappy urchin, who in a youthful frolic had repeated it, paid for his folly the penalty of his life. Three, whose ages varied from ten to fifteen, were burned alive at Würzburg for no other offence. Of course every other boy in the city became still more convinced of the power of the charm. One boy confessed that he would willingly have sold himself to the devil, if he could have raised him, for a good dinner and cakes every day of his life, and a pony to ride upon. This luxurious youngster, instead of being horsewhipped for his folly, was hanged and burned.

The small district of Lindheim was, if possible, even more notorious than Würzburg for the number of its witch-burnings. In the year 1633 a famous witch, named Pomp Anna, who could cause her foes to fall sick by merely looking at them, was discovered and burned, along with three of her companions. Every year in this parish, consisting at most of a thousand persons, the average number of executions was five. Between the years 1660 and 1664, the number consumed was thirty. If the executions all over Germany had been in this frightful proportion, hardly a family could have escaped losing one of its members.

In 1627, a ballad entitled the *Druten Zeitung*, or the *Witches' Gazette*, was very popular in Germany. It detailed, according to the title-page of a copy printed at Smalcald in 1627, "An account of the remarkable events which took place in Franconia, Bamberg, and Würzburg, with those wretches who from avarice or ambition have sold themselves to the devil, and how they had their reward at last: set to music, and to be sung to the tune of Dorothea." The sufferings of the witches at the stake are explained in it with great minuteness, the poet waxing extremely witty when he describes the horrible contortions of pain upon their countenances, and the shrieks that rent the air when any one of more than common guilt was burned alive. A trick resorted to in order to force one witch to confess, is told in this doggrel as an excellent joke. As she obstinately refused to own that she was in league with the powers of evil, the commissioners suggested that the hangman should dress himself in a bear's skin, with the horns, tail, and all the et-ceteras, and in this form penetrate into her dungeon. The woman, in the darkness of her cell, could not detect the imposture, aided as it was by her own superstitious fears. She thought she was actually in the presence of the prince of hell; and when she was told to keep up her courage, and that she should be relieved from the power of her enemies, she fell on her knees before the supposed devil, and swore to dedicate herself hereafter, body and soul, to his service. Germany is, perhaps, the only country in Europe where the delusion was so great as to have made such detestable verses as these the favourites of the people:

> "Man shickt ein Henkersknecht
> Zu ihr in Gefängniss n'unter,
> Den man hat kleidet recht,

> *Mit einer Bärnhaute,*
> *Als wenns der Teufel wär;*
> *Als ihm die Drut anschaute*
> *Meints ihr Buhl kam daher.*
> *Sie sprach zu ihm behende,*
> *Wie lässt du mich so lang*
> *In der Obrigkeit Hände?*
> *Hilf mir aus ihren Zwang,*
> *Wie du mir hast verheissen,*
> *Ich bin ja eben dein,*
> *Thu mich aus der Angst entreissen*
> *O liebster Buhle mein!"*[36]

This rare poet adds, that in making such an appeal to the hangman, the witch never imagined the roast that was to be made of her, and puts in, by way of parenthesis, "was not that fine fun! — *was das war für ein Spiel!*" As feathers thrown into the air shew how the wind blows, so this trumpery ballad serves to shew the current of popular feeling at the time of its composition. All readers of history are familiar with the celebrated trial of the Maréchale d'Ancre, who was executed in Paris in the year 1617. Although witchcraft was one of the accusations brought against her, the real crime for which she suffered was her ascendency over the mind of Mary of Medicis, and the consequent influence she exercised indirectly over the unworthy king, Louis XIII. Her coachman gave evidence that she had sacrificed a cock at midnight in one of the churches, and others swore they had seen her go secretly into the house of a noted witch named Isabella. When asked by what means she had acquired so extraordinary an influence over the mind of the Queen Mother, she replied boldly that she exercised no other power over her than that which a strong mind can always exercise over the weak. She died with great firmness.

In two years afterwards, scenes far more horrible than any that had yet taken place in France were enacted at Labourt, at the foot of the Pyrenees. The parliament of Bourdeaux, scandalised at the number of witches who were said to infest Labourt and its neighbourhood, deputed one of its own members, the noted Pierre de l'Ancre, and its president, Espaignel, to inquire into the matter, with full powers to punish the offenders. They arrived at Labourt in May, 1619. De l'Ancre wrote a book setting forth all his great deeds in this battle against the powers of evil. It is full of obscenity and absurdity, but the facts may be relied on as far as they relate to the number of trials and executions, and the strange confessions which torture forced from the unhappy criminals.

De l'Ancre states as a reason why so many witches were to be found at Labourt, that the country was mountainous and sterile! He discovered many of them from their partiality to smoking tobacco. It may be inferred from this that he was of the opinion of King James, that tobacco was the "devil's weed." When the commission first sat, the number of persons brought to trial was about forty a day. The acquittals did not average so many as five per cent. All the witches confessed that they had been present at the great Domdaniel, or Sabbath. At these saturnalia the devil sat upon a large gilded throne, sometimes in the form of a goat; sometimes as a gentleman, dressed all in black, with boots, spurs, and sword; and very often as a shapeless mass, resembling the trunk of a blasted tree, seen indistinctly amid the darkness. They generally proceeded to the Domdaniel, riding on spits, pitch-forks, or broomsticks, and on their arrival indulged with the fiends in every species of debauchery. Upon one occasion they had had the audacity to celebrate this festival in the very heart of the city of Bourdeaux. The throne of the arch fiend was placed in the middle of the Place de Gallienne, and the whole space was covered with the multitude of witches and wizards who flocked to it from far and near, some arriving even from distant Scotland. After two hundred poor wretches had been hanged and burned, there seemed no diminution in the number of criminals to be tried. Many of the latter were asked upon the rack what Satan had said when he found that the commissioners were proceeding with such severity? The general reply was, that he did not seem to care much about it. Some of them asserted that they had boldly reproached him for suffering the execution of their friends, saying, *"Out upon thee, false fiend! thy promise was that they should not die! Look, how thou hast kept thy word! They have been burned, and are a heap of ashes!"* Upon these occasions he was never offended: he would give orders that the sports of the Domdaniel should cease, and producing illusory fires that did not burn, he encouraged them to walk through, assuring them that the fires lighted by the executioner gave no more pain than those. They would then ask him, where their friends were, since they had not suffered; to which the "Father of Lies" invariably replied, that they were happy in a far country, and could see and hear all that was then passing; and that, if they called by name those they wished to converse with, they might hear their voices in reply. Satan then imitated the voices of the defunct witches so successfully that they were all deceived. Having answered all objections, the orgies recommenced and lasted till the cock crew. De l'Ancre was also very zealous in the trial of unhappy mono-maniacs for the crime of lycanthropy. Several who were arrested confessed, without being tortured, that they were *weir-wolves*, and that at night they rushed out among the flocks and herds killing and devouring. One young man at Besançon, with the full consciousness of the awful fate that awaited him, voluntarily gave himself up to the commissioner Espaignel, and confessed that he was the servant of a strong fiend, who was known by the name of "Lord of the Forests:" by his power he was transformed into the likeness of a wolf. The "Lord of the Forests" assumed the same shape; but was much larger, fiercer, and stronger. They prowled about the pastures together at midnight, strangling the watch-dogs that defended the folds, and killing more sheep than they could devour. He felt, he said, a fierce pleasure in these excursions, and howled in excess of joy as he tore with his fangs the warm flesh of the sheep asunder. This youth was not alone in this horrid confession; many others voluntarily owned that they were *weir-wolves*, and many more were forced by torture to make the same avowal. Such criminals were thought to be too atro-cious to be hanged first and then burned: they were generally sentenced to be burned alive, and their ashes to be scattered to the winds. Grave and learned doctors of divinity openly sus-tained the possibility of these transformations, relying mainly upon the history of Nebuchadnezzar. They could not imagine why, if he had been an ox, modern men could not become wolves by Divine permission and the power of the devil. They also contended that, if men should confess, it was evidence enough, if there had been no other. Delrio mentions that one gentleman accused of lycanthropy was put to the torture no less than twenty times; but still he would not confess. An intoxicating draught was then given him, and under its influence he confessed that he was a *weir-wolf*. Delrio cites this to shew the extreme equity of the commissioners. They never burned any body till he confessed; and if one course of torture would not suffice, their patience was not exhausted, and they tried him again and again, even to the twentieth time! Well may we exclaim, when such atrocities have been committed in the name of religion,

"Quel lion, quel tigre égale en cruauté,
Une injuste fureur qu'arme la piété?"

The trial of the unhappy Urbain Grandier, the curate of Loudun, for bewitching a number of girls in the convent of the Ursulines in that town, was, like that of the Maréchale d'Ancre, an accusation resorted to by his enemies to ruin one against whom no other charge could be brought so readily. This noted affair, which kept France in commotion for months, and the true character of which was known even at that time, merits no more than a passing notice in this place. It did not spring from the epidemic dread of sorcery then so prevalent, but was carried on by wretched intriguers, who had sworn to have the life of their foe. Such a charge could not be refuted in 1634: the accused could not, as Bodinus expresses it, "make the malice of the prosecutors more clear than the sun;" and his own denial, however intelligible, honest, and straightforward, was held as nothing in refutation of the testimony of the crazy women who imagined themselves bewitched. The more absurd and contradictory their assertions, the stronger the argument employed by his enemies that the devil was in them. He was burned alive, under circumstances of great cruelty.[37]

A singular instance of the epidemic fear of witchcraft occurred at Lille, in 1639. A pious but not very sane lady, named Antoinette

Bourignon, founded a school, or *hospice*, in that city. One day, on entering the schoolroom, she imagined that she saw a great number of little black angels flying about the heads of the children. In great alarm she told her pupils of what she had seen, warning them to beware of the devil whose imps were hovering about them. The foolish woman continued daily to repeat the same story, and Satan and his power became the only subject of conversation, not only between the girls themselves, but between them and their instructors. One of them at this time ran away from the school. On being brought back and interrogated, she said she had not run away, but had been carried away by the devil; she was a witch, and had been one since the age of seven. Some other little girls in the school went into fits at this announcement, and, on their recovery, confessed that they also were witches. At last the whole of them, to the number of fifty, worked upon each other's imaginations to such a degree that they also confessed that they were witches — that they attended the Domdaniel, or meeting of the fiends — that they could ride through the air on broom-sticks, feast on infants' flesh, or creep through a key-hole.

The citizens of Lille were astounded at these disclosures. The clergy hastened to investigate the matter; many of them, to their credit, openly expressed their opinion that the whole affair was an imposture — not so the majority; they strenuously insisted that the confessions of the children were valid, and that it was necessary to make an example by burning them all for witches. The poor parents, alarmed for their offspring, implored the examining Capuchins with tears in their eyes to save their young lives, insisting that they were bewitched, and not bewitching. This opinion also gained ground in the town. Antoinette Bourignon, who had put these absurd notions into the heads of the children, was accused of witchcraft, and examined before the council. The circumstances of the case seemed so unfavourable towards her that she would not stay for a second examination. Disguising herself as she best could, she hastened out of Lille and escaped pursuit. If she had remained four hours longer, she would have been burned by judicial sentence as a witch and a heretic. It is to be hoped that, wherever she went, she learned the danger of tampering with youthful minds, and was never again entrusted with the management of children.

The Duke of Brunswick and the Elector of Menz were struck with the great cruelty exercised in the torture of suspected persons, and convinced, at the same time, that no righteous judge would consider a confession extorted by pain, and contradictory in itself, as sufficient evidence to justify the execution of any accused person. It is related of the Duke of Brunswick that he invited two learned Jesuits to his house, who were known to entertain strong opinions upon the subject of witchcraft, with a view of shewing them the cruelty and absurdity of such practices. A woman lay in the dungeon of the city accused of witchcraft, and the duke, having given previous instructions to the officiating torturers, went with the two Jesuits to hear her confession. By a series of artful leading questions the poor creature, in the extremity of her anguish, was induced to confess that she had often attended the sabbath of the fiends upon the Brocken; that she had seen two Jesuits there, who had made themselves notorious, even among witches, for their abominations; that she had seen them assume the form of goats, wolves, and other animals; and that many noted witches had borne them five, six, and seven children at a birth, who had heads like toads, and legs like spiders. Being asked if the Jesuits were far from her, she replied that they were in the room beside her. The Duke of Brunswick led his astounded friends away, and explained the stratagem. This was convincing proof to both of them that thousands of persons had suffered unjustly; they knew their own innocence, and shuddered to think what their fate might have been if an enemy instead of a friend had put such a confession into the mouth of a criminal. One of these Jesuits was Frederick Spee, the author of the *Cautio Criminalis*, published in 1631. This work, exposing the horrors of the witch-trials, had a most salutary effect in Germany: Schonbrunn, Archbishop and Elector of Menz, abolished the torture entirely within his dominions, and his example was imitated by the Duke of Brunswick and other potentates. The number of supposed witches immediately diminished, and the violence of the mania began to subside. The Elector of Brandenburg issued a rescript, in 1654, with respect to the case of Anna of Ellerbrock, a supposed witch, forbidding the use of torture, and stigmatising the swimming of witches as an unjust, cruel, and deceitful test.

This was the beginning of the dawn after the long-protracted darkness. The tribunals no longer condemned witches to execution by hundreds in a year. Würzburg, the grand theatre of the burnings, burned but one where, forty years previously, it had burned three score. From 1660 to 1670 the electoral chambers, in all parts of Germany, constantly commuted the sentence of death passed by the provincial tribunals into imprisonment for life, or burning on the cheek.

Rouen.

A truer philosophy had gradually disabused the public mind. Learned men freed themselves from the trammels of a debasing superstition, and governments, both civil and ecclesiastical, repressed the popular delusion they had so long encouraged. The parliament of Normandy condemned a number of women to death, in the year 1670, on the old charge of riding on broomsticks to the Domdaniel; but Louis XIV. commuted the sentence into banishment for life. The parliament remonstrated, and sent the king the following remarkable request. The reader will perhaps be glad to see this document at length. It is of importance, as the last effort of a legislative assembly to uphold this great error; and the arguments they used and the instances they quoted are in the highest degree curious. It reflects honour upon the memory of Louis XIV. that he was not swayed by it.

"REQUEST OF THE PARLIAMENT OF ROU-
EN TO THE KING, IN 1670.

"Sire, — Emboldened by the authority which your majesty has committed into our hands in the province of Normandy, to try and punish offences, and more particularly those offences of the nature of witchcraft, which tend to the destruction of religion and the ruin of nations, we, your parliament, remonstrate humbly with your majesty upon certain cases of this kind which have been lately brought before us. We cannot permit the letter addressed by your majesty's command to the attorney-general of this district, for the reprieve of certain persons condemned to death for witchcraft, and for the staying of proceedings in several other cases, to remain unnoticed, and without remarking upon the consequences which may ensue. There is also a letter from your secretary of state, declaring your majesty's intention to commute the punishment of these criminals into one of perpetual banishment, and to submit to the opinion of the procureur-general, and of the most learned members of the parliament of Paris, whether, in the matter of witchcraft, the jurisprudence of the parliament of Rouen is to be followed in preference to that of the parliament of Paris, and of the other parliaments of the kingdom which judge differently.

"Although by the ordinances of the kings your predecessors, parliaments have been forbidden to pay any attention to lettres de cachet; we, nevertheless, from the knowledge which we have, in common with the whole kingdom, of the care bestowed by your majesty for the good of your subjects, and from the submission and obedience to your commandments which we have always manifested, have stayed all proceedings, in conformity to your orders; hoping that your majesty, considering the importance of the crime of witchcraft, and the consequences likely to ensue from its impunity, will be graciously pleased to grant us once more your permission to continue the trials, and execute judgment upon those found guilty. And as, since we received the letter of your secretary of state, we have also been made acquainted with the determination of your majesty, not only to commute the sentence of death passed upon these witches into one of perpetual banishment from the

province, but to re-establish them in the possession of their goods and chattels, and of their good fame and character, your parliament have thought it their duty, on occasion of these crimes, the greatest which men can commit, to make you acquainted with the general and uniform feelings of the people of this province with regard to them; it being, moreover, a question in which are concerned the glory of God and the relief of your suffering subjects, who groan under their fears from the threats and menaces of this sort of persons, and who feel the effects of them every day in the mortal and extraordinary maladies which attack them, and the surprising damage and loss of their possessions.

"Your majesty knows well that there is no crime so opposed to the commands of God as witchcraft, which destroys the very foundation of religion, and draws strange abominations after it. It is for this reason, sire, that the Scriptures pronounce the punishment of death against offenders, and that the Church and the holy fathers have fulminated their anathemas, and that canonical decisions have one and all decreed the most severe punishments, to deter from this crime; and that the Church of France, animated by the piety of the kings your predecessors, has expressed so great a horror at it, that, not judging the punishment of perpetual imprisonment, the highest it has the power to inflict, sufficiently severe, it has left such criminals to be dealt with by the secular power.

"It has been the general feeling of all nations that such criminals ought to be condemned to death, and all the ancients were of the same opinion. The law of the 'Twelve Tables,' which was the principal of the Roman laws, ordains the same punishment. All juris-consults agreed in it, as well as the constitutions of the emperors, and more especially those of Constantine and Theodosius, who, enlightened by the Gospel, not only renewed the same punishment, but also deprived, expressly, all persons found guilty of witchcraft of the right of appeal, and declared them to be unworthy of a prince's mercy. And Charles VIII., sire, inspired by the same sentiments, passed that beautiful and severe ordinance (cette belle et sévère ordonnance), which enjoined the judges to punish witches according to the exigencies of the case, under a penalty of being themselves fined or imprisoned, or dismissed from their office; and decreed, at the same time, that all persons who refused to denounce a witch, should be punished as accomplices; and that all, on the contrary, who gave evidence against one should be rewarded.

"From these considerations, sire, and in the execution of so holy an ordinance, your parliaments, by their decrees, proportion their punishments to the guilt of the offenders; and your parliament of Normandy has never, until the present time, found that its practice was different from that of other courts; for all the books which treat upon this matter cite an infinite number of decrees condemning witches to be burnt, or broken on the wheel, or to other punishments. The following are examples: — In the time of Chilperic, as may be seen in Gregory of Tours, b. vi. c. 35 of his History of France; all the decrees of the parliament of Paris passed according to, and in conformity with, this ancient jurisprudence of the kingdom, cited by Imbert, in his Judicial Practice; all those cited by Monstrelet, in 1459, against the witches of Artois; the decrees of the same parliament, of the 13th of October 1573, against Mary Le Fief, native of Saumur; of the 21st of October 1596, against the Sieur de Beaumont, who pleaded, in his defence, that he had only sought the aid of the devil for the purpose of unbewitching the afflicted and of curing diseases; of the 4th of July 1606, against Francis du Bose; of the 20th of July 1582, against Abel de la Rue, native of Coulommiers; of the 2d of October 1593, against Rousseau and his daughter; of 1608, against another Rousseau and one Peley, for witchcraft and adoration of the devil at the Sabbath, under the figure of a he-goat, as confessed by them; the decree of 4th of February 1615, against Leclerc, who appealed from the sentence of the parliament of Orleans, and who was condemned for having attended the Sabbath, and confessed, as well as two of his accomplices, who died in prison, that he had adored the devil, renounced his baptism and his faith in God, danced the witches' dance, and offered up unholy sacrifices; the decrees of the 6th of May 1616, against a man named Leger, on a similar accusation; the pardon granted by Charles IX. to Trois Echelles, upon condition of revealing his accomplices, but afterwards revoked for renewed sorcery on his part; the decree of the parliament of Paris, cited by Mornac in 1595; the judgments passed in consequence of the commission given by Henry IV. to the Sieur de l'Ancre, councillor of the parliament of Bourdeaux; of the 20th of March 1619, against Etienne Audibert; those passed by the chamber of Nerac, on the 26th of June 1620, against several witches; those passed by the parliament of Toulouse in 1577, as cited by Gregory Tolosanus, against four hundred persons accused of this crime, and who were all marked with the sign of

the devil. Besides all these, we might recal to your majesty's recollection the various decrees of the parliament of Provence, especially in the case of Gaufrédy in 1611; the decrees of the parliament of Dijon, and those of the parliament of Rennes, following the example of the condemnation of the Marshal de Rays, who was burned in 1441, for the crime of witchcraft, in presence of the Duke of Brittany; – all these examples, sire, prove that the accusation of witchcraft has always been punished with death by the parliaments of your kingdom, and justify the uniformity of their practice.

"These, sire, are the motives upon which your parliament of Normandy has acted in decreeing the punishment of death against the persons lately brought before it for this crime. If it has happened that, on any occasion, these parliaments, and the parliament of Normandy among the rest, have condemned the guilty to a less punishment than that of death, it was for the reason that their guilt was not of the deepest dye; your majesty, and the kings your predecessors, having left full liberty to the various tribunals to whom they delegated the administration of justice, to decree such punishment as was warranted by the evidence brought before them.

"After so many authorities, and punishments ordained by human and divine laws, we humbly supplicate your majesty to reflect once more upon the extraordinary results which proceed from the malevolence of this sort of people; on the deaths from unknown diseases, which are often the consequences of their menaces, on the loss of the goods and chattels of your subjects, on the proofs of guilt continually afforded by the insensibility of the marks upon the accused, on the sudden transportation of bodies from one place to another, on the sacrifices and nocturnal assemblies, and other facts, corroborated by the testimony of ancient and modern authors, and verified by so many eye-witnesses, composed partly of accomplices, and partly of people who had no interest in the trials beyond the love of truth, and confirmed, moreover, by the confessions of the accused parties themselves; and that, sire, with so much agreement and conformity between the different cases, that the most ignorant persons convicted of this crime have spoken to the same circumstances, and in nearly the same words, as the most celebrated authors who have written about it, all of which may be easily proved to your majesty's satisfaction by the records of various trials before your parliaments.

"These, sire, are truths so intimately bound up with the principles of our religion, that, extraordinary although they be, no person has been able to this time to call them in question. If some have cited, in opposition to these truths, the pretended canon of the Council of Ancyre, and a passage from St. Augustin, in a treatise upon the Spirit and the Soul, it has been without foundation; and it would be easy to convince your majesty that neither the one nor the other ought to be accounted of any authority; and, besides that, the canon, in this sense, would be contrary to the opinion of all succeeding councils of the Church, Cardinal Baronius, and all learned commentators agree that it is not to be found in any old edition. In effect, in those editions wherein it is found, it is in another language, and is in direct contradiction to the twenty-third canon of the same council, which condemns sorcery, according to all preceding constitutions. Even supposing that this canon was really promulgated by the Council of Ancyre, we must observe that it was issued in the second century, when the principal attention of the Church was directed to the destruction of paganism. For this reason, it condemns that class of women who said they could pass through the air, and over immense regions, with Diana and Herodias, and enjoins all preachers to teach the falsehood of such an opinion, in order to deter people from the worship of these false divinities; but it does not question the power of the devil over the human body, which is, in fact, proved by the holy Gospel of Jesus Christ himself. And with regard, sire, to the pretended passage of St. Augustin, everybody knows that it was not written by him, because the writer, whoever he was, cites Bœtius, who died more than eighty years after the time of St. Augustin. Besides, there is still more convincing proof in the fact, that the same father establishes the truth of witchcraft in all his writings, and more particularly in his City of God; and in his first volume, question the 25th, wherein he states that sorcery is a communion between man and the devil, which all good Christians ought to look upon with horror.

"Taking all these things into consideration, sire, the officers of your parliament hope, from the justice of your majesty, that you will be graciously pleased to receive the humble remonstrances they have taken the liberty to make. They are compelled, for the acquittal of their own consciences and in discharge of their duty, to make known to your majesty, that the decrees they passed against the sorcerers and witches brought before them, were passed after a mature deliberation on the part

of all the judges present, and that nothing has been done therein which is not conformable to the universal jurisprudence of the kingdom, and for the general welfare of your majesty's subjects, of whom there is not one who can say that he is secure from the malevolence of such criminals. We therefore supplicate your majesty to suffer us to carry into effect the sentences we passed, and to proceed with the trial of the other persons accused of the same crime; and that the piety of your majesty will not suffer to be introduced during your reign an opinion contrary to the principles of that holy religion for which you have always employed so gloriously both your cares and your arms."

Louis, as we have already mentioned, paid no attention to this appeal. The lives of the old women were spared, and prosecutions for mere witchcraft, unconnected with other offences, were discontinued throughout France. In 1680 an act was passed for the punishment, not of witches, but of pretenders to witchcraft, fortune-tellers, divineresses, and poisoners.

Thus the light broke in upon Germany, France, England, and Scotland about the same time, gradually growing clearer and clearer till the middle of the eighteenth century, when witchcraft was finally reckoned amongst exploded doctrines, and the belief in it confined to the uttermost vulgar. Twice, however, did the madness burst forth again as furious, while it lasted, as ever it had been. The first time in Sweden, in 1669, and the second in Germany so late as 1749. Both these instances merit particular mention. The first is one of the most extraordinary upon record, and for atrocity and absurdity is unsurpassed in the annals of any nation.

Louis XIV.

It having been reported to the king of Sweden that the little village of Mohra, in the province of Dalecarlia, was troubled exceedingly with witches, he appointed a commission of clergy and laymen to trace the rumour to its source, with full powers to punish the guilty. On the 12th of August 1669, the commissioners arrived in the bewitched village, to the great joy of the credulous inhabitants. On the following day the whole population, amounting to three thousand persons, assembled in the church. A sermon was preached, "declaring the miserable case of those people that suffered themselves to be deluded by the devil," and fervent prayer was offered up that God would remove the scourge from among them.

The whole assembly then adjourned to the rector's house, filling all the street before it, when the king's commission was read, charging every person who knew any thing of the witchery, to come forward and declare the truth. A passion of tears seized upon the multitude; men, women, and children began to weep and sob, and all promised to divulge what they had heard or knew. In this frame of mind they were dismissed to their homes. On the following day they were again called together, when the depositions of several persons were taken publicly before them all. The result was that seventy persons, including fifteen children, were taken into custody. Numbers also were arrested in the neighbouring district of Elfdale. Being put to the torture, they all confessed their guilt. They said they used to go to a gravel-pit, that lay hard by the cross-way, where they put a vest upon their heads, and danced "round and round and round about." They then went to the cross-way, and called three times upon the devil; the first time in a low still voice; the second, somewhat louder; and the third, very loudly, with these words, "Antecessor, come, and carry us to Blockula!" This invocation never failed to bring him to their view. He generally appeared as a little old man, in a grey coat, with red and blue stockings, with exceedingly long garters. He had besides a very high-crowned hat, with bands of many-coloured linen enfolded about it, and a long red beard that hung down to his middle.

The first question he put to them was, whether they would serve him soul and body? On their answering in the affirmative, he told them to make ready for the journey to Blockula. It was necessary to procure, in the first place, "some scrapings of altars and filings of church clocks." Antecessor then gave them a horn with some salve in it, wherewith they anointed themselves. These preparations ended, he brought beasts for them to ride upon, — horses, asses, goats, and monkeys; and giving them a saddle, a hammer, and a nail, uttered the word of command, and away they went. Nothing stopped them. They flew over churches, high walls, rocks, and mountains, until they came to the green meadow where Blockula was situated. Upon these occasions they carried as many children with them as they could; for the devil, they said, "did plague and whip them if they did not procure him children, insomuch that they had no peace or quiet for him."

Many parents corroborated a part of this evidence, stating that their children had repeatedly told them that they had been carried away in the night to Blockula, where the devil had beaten them black and blue. They had seen the marks in the morning, but they soon disappeared. One little girl was examined, who swore positively that she was carried through the air by the witches, and when at a great height she uttered the holy name of Jesus. She immediately fell to the ground, and made a great hole in her side. "The devil, however, picked her up, healed her side, and carried her away to Blockula." She added (and her mother confirmed her statement), that she had till that day "an exceeding great pain in her side." This was a clencher, and the nail of conviction was driven home to the hearts of the judges.

The place called Blockula, whither they were carried, was a large house, with a gate to it, "in a delicate meadow, whereof they could see no end." There was a very long table in it, at which the witches sat down; and in other rooms "there were very lovely and delicate beds for them to sleep upon."

After a number of ceremonies had been performed, by which they bound themselves body and soul to the service of Antecessor, they sat down to a feast composed of broth, made of colworts and bacon, oatmeal, bread and butter, milk and cheese. The devil always took the chair, and sometimes played to them on the harp or the fiddle while they were eating. After dinner they danced in a ring, sometimes naked, and sometimes in their clothes, cursing and swearing all the time. Some of the women added particulars too horrible and too obscene for repetition.

Once the devil pretended to be dead, that he might see whether his people regretted him. They instantly set up a loud wail, and wept three tears each for him; at which he was so pleased, that he jumped up among them, and hugged in his arms those who had been most obstreperous in their sorrow.

Such were the principal details given by the children, and corroborated by the confessions of the full-grown witches. Any thing more absurd was never before stated in a court of justice. Many of the accused contradicted themselves most palpably; but the commissioners gave no heed to discrepancies. One of them, the parson of the district, stated in the course of the inquiry, that on a particular night, which he mentioned, he had been afflicted with a headache so agonising, that he could not account for it otherwise than by supposing he was bewitched. In fact, he thought a score of witches must have been dancing on the crown of his head. This announcement excited great horror among the pious dames of the auditory, who loudly expressed their wonder that the devil should have power to hurt so good a man. One poor witch, who lay in the very jaws of death, confessed that she knew too well the cause of the minister's headache. The devil had sent her with a sledge hammer and a large nail to drive into the good man's skull. She had hammered at it for some time, but the skull was so enormously *thick*, that she made no impression upon it. Every hand was held up in astonishment. The pious minister blessed God that his skull was so solid, and he became renowned for his thick head all the days of his life. Whether the witch intended a joke does not appear, but she was looked upon as a criminal more than usually atrocious. Seventy persons were condemned to death on these so awful, yet so ridiculous confessions. Twenty-three of them were burned together in one fire in the village of Mohra, in the presence of thousands of delighted spectators. On the following day fifteen children were murdered in the same manner, offered up in sacrifice to the bloody Moloch of superstition. The remaining thirty-two were executed at the neighbouring town of Fahluna. Besides these, fifty-six children were found guilty of witchcraft in a minor degree, and sentenced to various punishments, such as running the gauntlet, imprisonment, and public whipping once a week for a twelvemonth.

Long after the occurrence of this case, it was cited as one of the most convincing proofs upon record of the prevalence of witchcraft. When men wish to construct or support a theory, how they torture facts into their service! The lying whimsies of a few sick children, encouraged by foolish parents, and drawn out by superstitious neighbours, were sufficient to set a country in a flame. If, instead of commissioners as deeply sunk in the slough of ignorance as the people they were sent amongst, there had been deputed a few men firm in courage and clear in understanding, how different would have been the result! Some of the poor children who were burned would have been sent to an infirmary; others would have been well flogged; the credulity of the parents would have been laughed at; and the lives of seventy persons spared. The belief in witchcraft remains in Sweden to this day; but happily the annals of that country present no more such instances of lamentable aberration of intellect as the one just cited.

In New England, about the same time, the colonists were scared by similar stories of the antics of the devil. All at once a fear seized upon the multitude, and supposed criminals were arrested day after day in such numbers, that the prisons were found too small to contain them. A girl named Goodwin, the daughter of a mason, who was hypochondriac and subject to fits, imagined that an old Irish woman, named Glover, had bewitched her. Her two brothers, in whose constitutions there was apparently a predisposition to similar fits, went off in the same way, crying out that the devil and Dame Glover were tormenting them. At times their joints were so stiff that they could not be moved; while at others, said the neighbours, they were so flexible, that the bones appeared softened into sinews. The supposed witch was seized, and as she could not repeat the Lord's Prayer without making a mistake in it, she was condemned and executed.

But the popular excitement was not allayed. One victim was not enough; the people waited agape for new disclosures. Suddenly two hysteric girls in another family fell into fits daily, and the cry of witchcraft resounded from one end of the colony to the other. The feeling of suffocation in the throat, so common in cases of hysteria, was said by the patients to be caused by the devil himself, who had stuck balls in the windpipe to choke them. They felt the pricking of thorns in every part of the body, and one of them vomited needles. The case of these girls, who were the daughter and niece of a Mr. Parvis, the minister of a Calvinist chapel, excited so much attention, that all the weak women in the colony began to fancy themselves similarly afflicted. The more they brooded on it, the more convinced they became. The contagion of this mental disease was as great as if it had been a pestilence. One after the other the women fainted away, asserting on their recovery that they had seen the spectres of witches. Where there were three or four girls in a family, they so worked each upon the diseased imagination of the other, that they fell into fits five or six times in a day. Some related that the devil himself appeared to them, bearing in his hand a parchment-roll, and promising that if they would sign an agreement, transferring to him their immortal souls, they should be immediately relieved from fits and all the ills of the flesh. Others asserted that they saw witches only, who made them similar promises, threatening that they should never be free from aches and pains till they had agreed to become the devil's. When they refused, the witches pinched, or bit, or pricked them with long pins and needles. More than two hundred persons named by these mischievous visionaries were thrown into prison. They were of all ages and conditions of life, and many of them of exemplary character. No less than nineteen were condemned and executed before reason returned to the minds of the colonists. The most horrible part of this lamentable history is, that among the victims there was a little child only five years old. Some women swore that they had seen it repeatedly in company with the devil, and that it had bitten them often with its little teeth for refusing to sign a compact with the evil one. It can hardly increase our feelings of disgust and abhorrence when we learn that this insane community actually tried and executed a dog for the same offence!

One man, named Cory, stoutly refused to plead to the preposterous indictment against him. As was the practice in such cases, he was pressed to death. It is told of the Sheriff of New England, who superintended the execution, that when this unhappy man thrust out his tongue in his mortal agony, he seized hold of a cane, and crammed it back again into the mouth. If ever there were a fiend in human form, it was this sheriff: a man who, if the truth were known, perhaps plumed himself upon his piety — thought he was doing God good service, and

"Hoped to merit heaven by making earth a hell!"

Arguing still in the firm belief of witchcraft, the bereaved people began to inquire, when they saw their dearest friends snatched away from them by these wide-spreading accusations, whether the whole proceedings were not carried on by the agency of the devil. Might not the great enemy have put false testimony into the mouths of the witnesses, or might not the witnesses be witches themselves? Every man who was in danger of losing his wife, his child, or his sister, embraced this doctrine with avidity. The revulsion was as sudden as the first frenzy. All at once, the colonists were convinced of their error. The judges put a stop to the prosecutions, even of those who had confessed their guilt. The latter were no sooner at liberty than they retracted all they had said, and the greater number hardly remembered the avowals which agony had extorted from them. Eight persons, who had been tried and condemned, were set free; and gradually girls ceased to have fits and to talk of the persecutions of the devil. The judge who had condemned the first criminal executed on this charge, was so smitten with sorrow and humiliation at his folly, that he set apart the anniversary of that day as one of solemn penitence and fasting. He still clung to the belief in witchcraft; no new light had broken in upon him on that subject, but, happily for the community, the delusion had taken a merciful turn. The whole colony shared the feeling; the jurors on the different trials openly expressed their penitence in the churches; and those who had suffered were regarded as the victims, and not as the accomplices of Satan.

It is related that the Indian tribes in New England were sorely puzzled at the infatuation of the settlers, and thought them either a race inferior to, or more sinful than the French colonists in the vicinity, amongst whom, as they remarked, "the Great Spirit sent no witches."

Returning again to the continent of Europe, we find that, after the year 1680, men became still wiser upon this subject. For twenty years the populace were left to their belief, but governments in general gave it no aliment in the shape of executions. The edict of Louis XIV. gave a blow to the superstition, from which it never recovered. The last execution in the Protestant cantons of Switzerland was at Geneva, in 1652. The various potentates of Germany, although they could not stay the trials, invariably commuted the sentence into imprisonment, in all cases where the pretended witch was accused of pure witchcraft, unconnected with any other crime. In the year 1701, Thomasius, the learned professor at the University of Halle, delivered his inaugural thesis, *De Crimine Magiæ* which struck another blow at the falling monster of popular error. But a faith so strong as that in witchcraft was not to be eradicated at once: the arguments of learned men did not penetrate to the villages and hamlets; but still they achieved great things; they rendered the belief an unworking faith, and prevented the supply of victims, on which for so many ages it had battened and grown strong.

Once more the delusion broke out; like a wild beast wounded to the death, it collected all its remaining energies for the final convulsion, which was to shew how mighty it had once been. Germany, which had nursed the frightful error in its cradle, tended it on its death-bed, and Würzburg, the scene of so many murders on the same pretext, was destined to be the scene of the last. That it might lose no portion of its bad renown, the last murder was as atrocious as the first. This case offers a great resemblance to that of the witches of Mohra and New England, except in the number of its victims. It happened so late as the year 1749, to the astonishment and disgust of the rest of Europe.

View in Würzburg.

A number of young women in a convent at Würzburg fancied themselves bewitched; they felt, like all hysteric subjects, a sense of suffocation in the throat. They went into fits repeatedly; and one of them, who had swallowed needles, evacuated them at abscesses, which formed in different parts of the body. The cry of sorcery was raised, and a young woman, named Maria Renata Sänger, was arrested on the charge of having leagued with the devil, to bewitch five of the young ladies. It was sworn on the trial that Maria had been frequently seen to clamber over the convent walls in the shape of a pig — that, proceeding to the cellar, she used to drink the best wine till she was intoxicated; and then start suddenly up in her own form. Other girls asserted that she used to prowl about the roof like a cat, and often penetrate into their chamber, and frighten them by her dreadful howlings. It was also said that she had been seen in the shape of a hare, milking the cows dry in the meadows belonging to the convent; that she used to perform as an actress on the boards of Drury Lane theatre in London, and, on the very same night, return upon a broomstick to Würzburg, and afflict the young ladies with pains in all their limbs. Upon this evidence she was condemned, and burned alive in the market-place of Würzburg. Here ends this frightful catalogue of murder and superstition. Since that day, the belief in witchcraft has fled from the populous abodes of men, and taken refuge in remote villages and districts too wild, rugged, and inhospitable to afford a resting-place for the foot of civilisation. Rude fishers and uneducated labourers still attribute every phenomenon of nature which they cannot account for, to the devil and witches. Catalepsy, that wondrous disease, is still thought by ignorant gossips to be the work of Satan; and hypochondriacs, uninformed by science of the nature of their malady, devoutly believe in the reality of their visions. The reader would hardly credit the extent of the delusion upon this subject in the very heart of England at this day. Many an old woman leads a life of misery from the unfeeling insults of her neighbours, who raise the scornful finger and hooting voice at her, because in her decrepitude she is ugly, spiteful, perhaps insane, and realises in her personal appearance the description preserved by tradition of the witches of yore. Even in the neighbourhood of great towns the taint remains of this once widely-spread contagion. If no victims fall beneath it, the enlightenment of the law is all that prevents a recurrence of scenes as horrid as those of the seventeenth century. Hundreds upon hundreds of witnesses could be found to swear to absurdities as great as those asserted by the infamous Matthew Hopkins. In the *Annual Register* for 1760, an instance of the belief in witchcraft is related, which shews how superstition lingers. A dispute arose in the little village of Glen, in Leicestershire, between two old women, each of whom vehemently accused the other of witchcraft. The quarrel at last ran so high that a challenge ensued, and they both agreed to be tried by the ordeal of swimming. They accordingly stripped to their shifts — procured some men, who tied their thumbs and great toes together, cross-wise, and then, with a cart-rope about their middle, suffered themselves to be thrown into a pool of water. One of them sank immediately, but the other continued struggling a short time upon the surface of the water, which the mob deeming an infallible sign of her guilt, pulled her out, and insisted that she should immediately impeach all her accomplices in the craft. She accordingly told them that, in the neighbouring village of Burton, there were several old women as "much witches as she was." Happily for her, this negative information was deemed suffi-cient, and a student in astrology, or "white-witch," coming up at the time, the mob, by his direction, proceeded forthwith to Burton in search of all the delinquents. After a little consultation on their arrival, they went to the old woman's house on whom they had fixed the strongest suspicion. The poor old creature on their approach locked the outer door, and from the window of an upstairs room asked what they wanted. They informed her that she was charged with being guilty of witchcraft, and that they were come to duck her; remonstrating with her at the same time upon the necessity of submission to the ordeal, that, if she were innocent, all the world might know it. Upon her persisting in a positive refusal to come down, they broke open the door and carried her out by force, to a deep gravel-pit full of water. They tied her thumbs and toes together and threw her into the water, where they kept her for several minutes, drawing her out and in two or three times by the rope round her middle. Not being able to satisfy themselves whether she were a witch or no, they at last let her go, or, more properly speaking, they left her on the bank to walk home by herself, if she ever recovered. Next day, they tried the same experiment upon another woman, and afterwards upon a third; but, fortunately, neither of the victims lost her life from this brutality. Many of the ringleaders in the outrage were apprehended during the week, and tried before the justices at quarter-sessions. Two of them were sentenced to stand in the pillory and to be imprisoned for a month; and as many as twenty more were fined in small sums for the assault, and bound over to keep the peace for a twelvemonth.

"So late as the year 1785," says Arnot, in his collection and abridgment of *Criminal Trials in Scotland*, "it was the custom among the sect of Seceders to read from the pulpit an annual confession of sins, national and personal; amongst the former of which was particularly mentioned the 'Repeal by parliament of the penal statute against witches, contrary to the express laws of God.'"

Lady Hatton's house, Cross Street, Hatton Garden.

Many houses are still to be found in England with the horse-shoe (the grand preservative against witchcraft) nailed against the threshold. If any over-wise philosopher should attempt to remove them, the chances are that he would have more broken bones than thanks for his interference. Let any man walk into Cross Street, Hatton Garden, and from thence into Bleeding-heart Yard, and learn the tales still told and believed of one house in that neighbourhood, and he will ask himself in astonishment if such things can be in the nineteenth century. The witchcraft of Lady Hatton, the wife of the famous Sir Christopher, so renowned for his elegant dancing in the days of Elizabeth, is as devoutly believed as the Gospels. The room is to be seen where the devil seized her after the expiration of the contract he had made with her, and bore her away bodily to the pit of Tophet: the pump against which he dashed her is still pointed out, and the spot where her heart was found, after he had torn it out of her bosom with his iron claws, has received the name of Bleeding-heart Yard, in confirmation of the story. Whether the horse-shoe still remains upon the door of the haunted house, to keep away other witches, is uncertain. A former inmate relates that, "about twenty years ago, more than one old woman begged for admittance repeatedly, to satisfy themselves that it was in its proper place. One poor creature, apparently insane, and clothed in rags, came to the door with a tremendous double-knock, as loud as that of a fashionable footman, and walked straight along the passage to the horse-shoe. Great was the wonderment of the inmates, especially when the woman spat upon the horse-shoe, and expressed her sorrow that she could do no harm while it remained there. After spitting upon, and kicking it again and again, she coolly turned round and left the house, without saying a word to any body. This poor creature perhaps intended a joke, but the probability is that she imagined herself a witch. In Saffron Hill, where she resided, her ignorant neighbours gave her that character, and looked upon her with no little fear and aversion."

More than one example of the popular belief in witchcraft occurred in the neighbourhood of Hastings so lately as the year 1830. An aged woman, who resided in the Rope-walk of that town, was so repulsive in her appearance, that she was invariably accused of being a witch by all the ignorant people who knew her. She was bent completely double; and though very old, her eye was unusually bright and malignant. She wore a red cloak, and supported herself on a crutch: she was, to all outward appearance, the very *beau ideal* of a witch. So dear is power to the human heart, that this old woman actually encouraged the popular superstition; she took no pains to remove the ill impression, but seemed to delight that she, old and miserable as she was, could keep in awe so many happier and stronger fellow-creatures. Timid girls crouched with fear when they met her, and many would go a mile out of their way to avoid her. Like the witches of the olden time, she was not sparing of her curses against those who offended her. The child of a woman who resided within two doors of her was afflicted with lameness, and the mother constantly asserted that the old woman had bewitched her. All the neighbours credited the tale. It was believed, too, that she could assume the form of a cat. Many a harmless puss has been hunted almost to the death by mobs of men and boys, upon the supposition that the animal would start up before them in the true shape of Mother — —.

In the same town there resided a fisherman, who was the object of unceasing persecution, because it was said that he had sold himself to the devil. It was currently reported that he could creep through a keyhole, and that he had made a witch of his daughter, in order that he might have the more power over his fellows. It was also believed that he could sit on the points of pins and needles and feel no pain. His brother fishermen put him to this test whenever they had an opportunity. In the alehouses which he frequented, they often placed long needles in the cushions of the chairs in such a manner that he could not fail to pierce himself when he sat down. The result of these experiments tended to confirm their faith in his supernatural powers. It was asserted that he never flinched. Such was the popular feeling in the fashionable town of Hastings a few years ago; very probably it is the same now.

In the north of England, the superstition lingers to an almost inconceivable extent. Lancashire abounds with witch-doctors, a set of quacks who pretend to cure diseases inflicted by the devil. The practices of these worthies may be judged of by the following case, reported in the *Hertford Reformer* of the 23d of June 1838. The witch-doctor alluded to is better known by the name of the *cunning man*, and has a large practice in the counties of Lincoln and Nottingham. According to the writer in the *Reformer*, the dupe, whose name is not mentioned, had been for about two years afflicted with a painful abscess, and had been prescribed for without relief by more than one medical gentleman. He was urged by some of his friends, not only in his own village but in neighbouring ones, to consult the witch-doctor, as they were convinced he was under some evil influence. He agreed, and sent his wife to the *cunning man*, who lived in New St. Swithin's, in Lincoln. She was informed by this ignorant impostor that her husband's disorder was an infliction of the devil, occasioned by his next-door neighbours, who had made use of certain charms for that purpose. From the description he gave of the process, it appears to be the same as that employed by Dr. Fian and Gellie Duncan to work woe upon King James. He stated that the neighbours, instigated by a witch, whom he pointed out, took some wax and moulded it before the fire into the form of her husband, as near as they could represent him; they then pierced the image with pins on all sides, repeated the Lord's Prayer backwards, and offered prayers to the devil that he would fix his stings into the person whom that figure represented, in like manner as they pierced *it* with pins. To counteract the effects of this diabolical process, the witch-doctor prescribed a certain medicine, and a charm to be worn next the body, on that part where the disease principally lay. The patient was to repeat the 109th and 119th Psalms every day, or the cure would not be effectual. The fee which he claimed for this advice was a guinea. So efficacious is faith in the cure of any malady, that the patient actually felt much better after a three weeks' course of this prescription. The notable charm which the quack had given was afterwards opened, and found to be a piece of parchment covered with some cabalistic characters and signs of the planets. The next-door neighbours were in great alarm that the witch-doctor would, on the solicitation of the recovering patient, employ some means to punish them for their pretended witch-craft. To escape the infliction, they feed another cunning man, in Nottinghamshire, who told them of a similar charm, which would preserve them from all the malice of their enemies. The writer concludes by saying, that "the doctor, not long after he had been thus consulted, wrote to say, that he had discovered that his patient was not afflicted by Satan, as he had imagined, but by God, and would continue more or less in the same state till his life's end."

An impostor carried on a similar trade in the neighbourhood of Tunbridge Wells about the year 1830. He had been in practice for several years, and charged enormous fees for his advice. This fellow pretended to be the seventh son of a seventh son, and to be endowed in consequence with miraculous powers for the cure of all diseases, but especially of those resulting from witchcraft. It was not only the poor who employed him, but ladies who rode in their carriages. He was often sent for from a distance of sixty or seventy miles by these people, who paid all his expenses to and fro, besides rewarding him handsomely. He was about eighty years of age, and his extremely venerable appearance aided his imposition in no slight degree. His name was Okey or Oakley.

In France, the superstition at this day is even more prevalent than it is in England. Garinet, in his history of Magic and Sorcery in that country, cites upwards of twenty instances which occurred between the years 1805 and 1818. In the latter year no less than three tribunals were occupied with trials originating in this humiliating belief: we shall cite only one of them. Julian Desbourdes, aged fifty-three, a mason, and inhabitant of the village of Thilouze, near Bourdeaux, was taken suddenly ill, in the month of January 1818. As he did not know how to account for his malady, he suspected at last that he was bewitched. He communicated this suspicion to his son-in-law Bridier, and they both went to consult a sort of idiot, named Baudouin, who passed for a conjuror or *white-witch*. This man told them that Desbourdes was certainly bewitched, and offered to accompany them to the house of an old man named Renard, who, he said, was undoubtedly the criminal. On the night of the 23d of January all three proceeded stealthily to the dwelling of Renard, and accused him of afflicting persons with diseases by the aid of the devil. Desbourdes fell on his knees and earnestly entreated to be restored to his former health, promising that he would take no measures against him for the evil he had done. The old man denied in the strongest terms that he was a wizard; and when Desbourdes still pressed him to remove the spell from him, he said he knew nothing about the spell, and refused to remove it. The idiot Baudouin, the *white-witch*, now interfered, and told his companions that no relief for the malady could ever be procured until the old man confessed his guilt. To force him to confession they lighted some sticks of sulphur which they had brought with them for the purpose, and placed them under the old man's nose.

In a few moments he fell down suffocated and apparently lifeless. They were all greatly alarmed; and thinking that they had killed the man, they carried him out and threw him into a neighbouring pond, hoping to make it appear that he had fallen in accidentally. The pond, however, was not very deep, and the coolness of the water reviving the old man, he opened his eyes and sat up. Desbourdes and Bridier, who were still waiting on the bank, were now more alarmed than before, lest he should recover and inform against them. They therefore waded into the pond, seized their victim by the hair of the head, beat him severely, and then held him under water till he was drowned.

They were all three apprehended on the charge of murder a few days afterwards. Desbourdes and Bridier were found guilty of aggravated manslaughter only, and sentenced to be burnt on the back, and to work in the galleys for life. The *white-witch* Baudouin was acquitted on the ground of insanity.

M. Garinet further informs us that France, at the time he wrote (1818), was overrun by a race of fellows who made a trade of casting out devils and finding out witches. He adds also, that many of the priests in the rural districts encouraged the superstition of their parishioners by resorting frequently to exorcisms whenever any foolish persons took it into their heads that a spell had been thrown over them. He recommended, as a remedy for the evil, that all these exorcists, whether lay or clerical, should be sent to the galleys, and felt assured that the number of witches would then very sensibly diminish.

Many other instances of this lingering belief might be cited both in France and Great Britain, and indeed in every other country in Europe. So deeply rooted are some errors, that ages cannot remove them. The poisonous tree that once overshadowed the land may be cut down by the sturdy efforts of sages and philosophers; the sun may shine clearly upon spots where venomous things once nestled in security and shade; but still the entangled roots are stretched beneath the surface, and may be found by those who dig. Another king like James I. might make them vegetate again; and, more mischievous still, another pope like Innocent VIII. might raise the decaying roots to strength and verdure. Still it is consoling to think that the delirium has passed away; that the raging madness has given place to a milder folly; and that we may now count by units the votaries of a superstition which in former ages numbered its victims by tens of thousands, and its votaries by millions.

Floating a witch.

Chapter 3.

The Slow Poisoners.

Place de Greve.

Pescara. The like was never read of.
Stephano. In my judgment,
To all that shall but hear it, 'twill appear
A most impossible fable.
Pescara. Troth, I'll tell you,
And briefly as I can, by what degrees
They fell into this madness.

Duke of Milan.

The atrocious system of poisoning by poisons so slow in their operation as to make the victim appear, to ordinary observers, as if dying from a gradual decay of nature, has been practised in all ages. Those who are curious in the matter may refer to Beckmann on secret poisons, in his *History of Inventions*, in which he has collected several instances of it from the Greek and Roman writers. Early in the sixteenth century the crime seems to have gradually increased, till in the seventeenth it spread over Europe like a pestilence. It was often exercised by pretended witches and sorcerers, and finally became a branch of education amongst all who laid any claim to magical and supernatural arts. In the twenty-first year of Henry VIII. an act was passed rendering it high treason. Those found guilty of it were to be boiled to death. One of the first in point of date, and hardly second to any in point of atrocity, is the murder by this means of Sir Thomas Overbury; which disgraced the court of James I. in the year 1613. A slight sketch of it will be a fitting introduction to the history of the poisoning mania, which was so prevalent in France and Italy fifty years later.

Robert Kerr, a Scottish youth, was early taken notice of by James I., and loaded with honours, for no other reason that the world could ever discover than the beauty of his person. James, even in his own day, was suspected of being addicted to the most abominable of all offences; and the more we examine his history now, the stronger the suspicion becomes. However that may be, the handsome Kerr, lending his smooth cheek even in public to the disgusting kisses of his royal master, rose rapidly in favour. In the year 1613, he was made Lord High Treasurer of Scotland, and created an English peer by the style and title of Viscount Rochester. Still further honours were in store for him.

In this rapid promotion he had not been without a friend. Sir Thomas Overbury, the king's secretary—who appears, from some threats in his own letters, to have been no better than a pander to the vices of the king, and privy to his dangerous secrets—exerted all his backstair influence to forward the promotion of Kerr, by whom he was doubtless repaid in some way or other. Overbury did not confine his friendship to this—if friendship ever could exist between two such men—but acted the part of an *entremetteur*, and assisted Rochester to carry on an adulterous intrigue with the Lady Frances Howard, the wife of the Earl of Essex. This woman was a person of violent passions, and lost to all sense of shame. Her husband was in her way, and to be freed from him she instituted proceedings for a divorce, on grounds which a woman of any modesty or delicacy of feeling would die rather than avow. Her scandalous suit was successful, and was no sooner decided than preparations on a scale of the greatest magnificence were made for her marriage with Lord Rochester.

Sir Thomas Overbury, who had willingly assisted his patron to intrigue with the Countess of Essex, seems to have imagined that his marriage with so vile a woman might retard his advancement. He accordingly employed all his influence to dissuade him from it; but Rochester was bent on the match, and his passions were as violent as those of the countess. On one occasion, when Overbury and the viscount were walking in the gallery of Whitehall, Overbury was overheard to say, "Well, my lord, if you do marry that base woman, you will utterly ruin your honour and yourself. You shall never do it with my advice or consent; and if you do, you had best look to stand fast." Rochester flung from him in a rage, exclaiming with an oath, "I will be even with you for this." These words were the death-warrant of the unfortunate Overbury. He had mortally wounded the pride of Rochester in insinuating that by his (Overbury's) means he might be lowered in the king's favour; and he had endeavoured to curb the burning passions of a heartless, dissolute, and reckless man.

Overbury's imprudent remonstrances were reported to the countess; and from that moment she also vowed the most deadly vengeance against him. With a fiendish hypocrisy, however, they both concealed their intentions; and Overbury, at the solicitation of Rochester, was appointed ambassador to the court of Russia. This apparent favour was but the first step in a deep and deadly plot. Rochester, pretending to be warmly attached to the interests of Overbury, advised him to refuse the embassy, which he said was but a trick to get him out of the way. He promised, at the same time, to stand between him and any evil consequences which might result from his refusal. Overbury fell into the snare, and declined the embassy. James, offended, immediately ordered his committal to the Tower.

He was now in safe custody, and his enemies had opportunity to commence the work of vengeance. The first thing Rochester did was to procure, by his influence at court, the dismissal of the Lieutenant of the Tower, and the appointment of Sir Jervis Elwes, one of his creatures, to the vacant post. This man was but one instrument; and another being necessary, was found in Richard

Weston, a fellow who had formerly been shopman to a druggist. He was installed in the office of under-keeper, and as such had the direct custody of Overbury. So far all was favourable to the designs of the conspirators.

In the mean time the insidious Rochester wrote the most friendly letters to Overbury, requesting him to bear his ill-fortune patiently, and promising that his imprisonment should not be of long duration; for that his friends were exerting themselves to soften the king's displeasure. Still pretending the extreme of sympathy for him, he followed up the letters by presents of pastry and other delicacies, which could not be procured in the Tower. These articles were all poisoned. Occasionally, presents of a similar description were sent to Sir Jervis Elwes, with the understanding that these articles were not poisoned, when they were unaccompanied by letters: of these the unfortunate prisoner never tasted. A woman named Turner, who had formerly kept a house of ill-fame, and who had more than once lent it to further the guilty intercourse of Rochester and Lady Essex, was the agent employed to procure the poisons. They were prepared by Dr. Forman, a pretended fortune-teller of Lambeth, assisted by an apothecary named Franklin. Both these persons knew for what purposes the poisons were needed, and employed their skill in mixing them in the pastry and other edibles, in such small quantities as gradually to wear out the constitution of their victim. Mrs. Turner regularly furnished the poisoned articles to the under-keeper, who placed them before Overbury. Not only his food but his drink was poisoned. Arsenic was mixed with the salt he ate, and cantharides with the pepper. All this time his health declined sensibly. Daily he grew weaker and weaker; and with a sickly appetite craved for sweets and jellies. Rochester continued to condole with him, and anticipated all his wants in this respect, sending him abundance of pastry, and occasionally partridges and other game, and young pigs. With the sauce for the game, Mrs. Turner mixed a quantity of cantharides, and poisoned the pork with lunar-caustic. As stated on the trial, Overbury took in this manner poison enough to have poisoned twenty men; but his constitution was strong, and he still lingered. Franklin, the apothecary, confessed that he prepared with Dr. Forman seven different sorts of poisons, viz. aquafortis, arsenic, mercury, powder of diamonds, lunar caustic, great spiders, and cantharides. Overbury held out so long that Rochester became impatient, and in a letter to Lady Essex, expressed his wonder that things were not sooner despatched. Orders were immediately sent by Lady Essex to the keeper to finish with the victim at once. Overbury had not been all this time without suspicion of treachery, although he appears to have had no idea of poison. He merely suspected that it was intended to confine him for life, and to set the king still more bitterly against him. In one of his letters he threatened Rochester that unless he were speedily liberated, he would expose his villany to the world. He says, "You and I, ere it be long, will come to a public trial of another nature." * * * "Drive me not to extremities, lest I should say something that both you and I should repent." * * * "Whether I live or die, your shame shall never die, but ever remain to the world, to make you the most odious man living." * * * "I wonder much you should neglect him to whom such secrets of all kinds have passed." * * * "Be these the fruits of common secrets, common dangers?"

Sir Thomas Overbury.

All these remonstrances, and hints as to the dangerous secrets in his keeping, were ill calculated to serve him with a man so reckless as Lord Rochester: they were more likely to cause him to be sacrificed than to be saved. Rochester appears to have acted as if he thought so. He doubtless employed the murderer's reasoning, that "dead men tell no tales," when, after receiving letters of this description, he complained to his paramour of the delay. Weston was spurred on to consummate the atrocity; and the patience of all parties being exhausted, a dose of corrosive sublimate was administered to him in October 1613, which put an end to his sufferings, after he had been for six months in their hands. On the very day of his death, and before his body was cold, he was wrapped up carelessly in a sheet, and buried without any funeral ceremony in a pit within the precincts of the Tower.

Sir Anthony Weldon, in his *Court and Character of James I.*, gives a somewhat different account of the closing scene of this tragedy. He says, "Franklin and Weston came into Overbury's chamber, and found him in infinite torment, with contention between the strength of nature and the working of the poison; and it being very like that nature had gotten the better in this contention, by the thrusting out of boils, blotches, and blains, they, fearing it might come to light by the judgment of physicians, the foul play that had been offered him, consented to stifle him with the bedclothes, which accordingly was performed; and so ended his miserable life, with the assurance of the conspirators that he died by the poison; none thinking otherwise than these two murderers."

The sudden death, the indecent haste of the funeral, and the non-holding of an inquest upon the body, strengthened the suspicions that were afloat. Rumour, instead of whispering, began to speak out; and the relatives of the deceased openly expressed their belief that their kinsman had been murdered. But Rochester was still all powerful at court, and no one dared to utter a word to his discredit. Shortly afterwards, his marriage with the Countess of Essex was celebrated with the utmost splendour, the king himself being present at the ceremony.

It would seem that Overbury's knowledge of James's character was deeper than Rochester had given him credit for, and that he had been a true prophet when he predicted that his marriage would eventually estrange James from his minion. At this time, however, Rochester stood higher than ever in the royal favour; but it did not last long — conscience, that busy monitor, was at work. The tongue of rumour was never still; and Rochester, who had long been a guilty, became at last a wretched man. His cheeks lost their colour — his eyes grew dim; and he became moody, careless, and melancholy. The king, seeing him thus, took at length no pleasure in his society, and began to look about for another favourite. George Villiers, Duke of Buckingham, was the man to his mind: quick-witted, handsome, and unscrupulous. The two latter qualities alone were sufficient to recommend him to James I. In proportion as the influence of Rochester declined, that of Buckingham increased. A falling favourite has no friends; and rumour wagged her tongue against Rochester louder and more pertinaciously than ever. A new favourite, too, generally endeavours to hasten by a kick the fall of the old one; and Buckingham, anxious to work the complete ruin of his forerunner in the king's good graces, encouraged the relatives of Sir Thomas Overbury to prosecute their inquiries into the strange death of their kinsman.

James was rigorous enough in the punishment of offences when he was not himself involved. He piqued himself, moreover, on his dexterity in unravelling mysteries. The affair of Sir Thomas Overbury found him congenial occupation. He set to work by ordering the arrest of Sir Jervis Elwes. James, at this early stage of the proceedings, does not seem to have been aware that Rochester was so deeply implicated. Struck with horror at the atrocious system of slow poisoning, the king sent for all the judges. According to Sir Anthony Weldon, he knelt down in the midst of them, and said, "My lords the judges, it is lately come to my hearing that you have now in examination a business of poisoning. Lord! in what a miserable condition shall this kingdom be (the only famous nation for hospitality in the world) if our tables should become such a snare, as that none could eat without danger of life, and that Italian custom should be introduced among us! Therefore, my lords, I charge you, as you will answer it at that great and dreadful day of judgment, that you examine it strictly, without favour, affection, or partiality. And if you shall spare any guilty of this crime, God's curse light on you and your posterity! and if I spare any that are guilty, God's curse light on me and my posterity for ever!"

Duke of Buckingham.

The imprecation fell but too surely upon the devoted house of Stuart. The solemn oath was broken, and God's curse *did* light upon him and his posterity!

The next person arrested after Sir Jervis Elwes, was Weston, the under-keeper; then Franklin and Mrs. Turner; and lastly, the Earl and Countess of Somerset, to which dignity Rochester had been advanced since the death of Overbury.

Weston was first brought to trial. Public curiosity was on the stretch. Nothing else was talked of, and the court on the day of trial was crowded to suffocation. The *State Trials* report, that Lord Chief Justice Coke "laid open to the jury the baseness and cowardliness of poisoners, who attempt that secretly against which there is no means of preservation or defence for a man's life; and how rare it was to hear of any poisoning in England, so detestable it was to our nation. But the devil had taught divers to be cunning in it, so that they can poison in what distance of space they please, by consuming the *nativum calidum*, or *humidum radicale*, in one month, two or three, or more, as they list, which they four manner of ways do execute, viz. *haustu, gustu, odore,* and *contactu.*"

Lord Coke.

When the indictment was read over, Weston made no other reply than "Lord have mercy upon me! Lord have mercy upon me!" On being asked how he would be tried, he refused to throw himself upon a jury of his country, and declared that he would be tried by God alone. In this he persisted for some time. The fear of the dreadful punishment for contumacy[38] induced him at length to plead "Not guilty," and take his trial in due course of law.

All the circumstances against him were fully proved, and he was found guilty and executed at Tyburn. Mrs. Turner, Franklin, and Sir Jervis Elwes were also brought to trial, found guilty, and executed between the 19th of October and the 4th of December 1615; but the grand trial of the Earl and Countess of Somerset did not take place till the month of May following.

On the trial of Sir Jervis Elwes, circumstances had transpired, shewing a guilty knowledge of the poisoning on the part of the Earl of Northampton, the uncle of Lady Somerset, and the chief falconer Sir Thomas Monson. The former was dead; but Sir Thomas Monson was arrested and brought to trial. It appeared, however, that he was too dangerous a man to be brought to the scaffold. He knew too many of the odious secrets of James I., and his dying speech might contain disclosures which would compromise the king. To conceal old guilt it was necessary to incur new: the trial of Sir Thomas Monson was brought to an abrupt conclusion, and himself set at liberty.

The Earl of Somerset.

Already James had broken his oath. He now began to fear that he had been rash in engaging so zealously to bring the poisoners to punishment. That Somerset would be declared guilty there was no doubt, and that he looked for pardon and impunity was equally evident to the king. Somerset, while in the Tower, asserted confidently that James would not *dare* to bring him to trial. In this he was mistaken; but James was in an agony. What the secret was between them will now never be known with certainty; but it may be surmised. Some have imagined it to be the vice to which the king was addicted; while others have asserted that it related to the death of Prince Henry, a virtuous young man, who had held Somerset in especial abhorrence. This prince died early, unlamented by his father, and, as public opinion whispered at the time, poisoned by Somerset. Probably some crime or other lay heavy upon the soul of the king; and Somerset, his accomplice, could not be brought to public execution with safety. Hence the dreadful tortures of James when he discovered that his favourite was so deeply implicated in the murder of Overbury. Every means was taken by the agonised king to bring the prisoner into what was called a safe frame of mind. He was secretly advised to plead guilty, and trust to the clemency of the king. The same advice was conveyed to the countess. Bacon was instructed by the king to draw up a paper of all the points of "mercy and favour" to Somerset which might result from the evidence; and Somerset was again recommended to plead guilty, and promised that no evil should ensue to him. The countess was first tried. She trembled and shed tears during the reading of the indictment, and, in a low voice, pleaded guilty. On being asked why sentence of death should not be passed against her, she replied meekly, "I can much aggravate, but nothing extenuate my fault. I desire mercy, and that the lords will intercede for me with the king." Sentence of death was passed upon her.

Next day the earl was brought to trial. He appears to have mistrusted the promises of James, and he pleaded not guilty. With a self-possession and confidence which he felt, probably, from his knowledge of the king's character, he rigorously cross-examined the witnesses, and made a stubborn defence. After a trial which lasted eleven hours he was found guilty, and condemned to the felon's death.

The Countess of Somerset.

Whatever may have been the secrets between the criminal and the king, the latter, notwithstanding his terrific oath, was afraid to sign the death-warrant. It might, perchance, have been his own. The earl and countess were committed to the Tower, where they remained for nearly five years. At the end of this period, to the surprise and scandal of the community, and the disgrace of its chief magistrate, they both received the royal pardon, but were ordered to reside at a distance from the court. Having been found guilty of felony, the estates of the earl had become forfeited; but James granted him out of their revenues an income of 4000l. per annum! Shamelessness could go no further.

Of the after-life of these criminals nothing is known, except that the love they had formerly borne each other was changed into aversion, and that they lived under the same roof for months together without the interchange of a word.

The exposure of their atrocities did not put a stop to the practice of poisoning. On the contrary, as we shall see hereafter, it engendered that insane imitation which is so strange a feature of the human character. James himself is supposed, with great probability, to have fallen a victim to it. In the notes to Harris's *Life and Writings of James I.*, there is a good deal of information on the subject. The guilt of Buckingham, although not fully established, rests upon circumstances of suspicion stronger than have been sufficient to lead hundreds to the scaffold. His motives for committing the crime are stated to have been a desire of revenge for the coldness with which the king, in the latter years of his reign, began to regard him; his fear that James intended to degrade him; and his hope that the great influence he possessed over the mind of the heir-apparent would last through a new reign, if the old one were brought to a close.

In the second volume of the *Harleian Miscellany*, there is a tract, entitled the *Forerunner of Revenge*, written by George Eglisham, doctor of medicine, and one of the physicians to King James. Harris, in quoting it, says that it is full of rancour and prejudice. It is evidently exaggerated, but forms nevertheless a link in the chain of evidence. Eglisham says, "The king being sick of an ague, the duke took this opportunity, when all the king's doctors of physic were at dinner, and offered to him a white powder to take, the which he a long time refused; but, overcome with his flattering importunity, he took it in wine, and immediately became worse and worse, falling into many swoonings and pains, and violent fluxes of the belly, so tormented, that his majesty cried out aloud of this white powder, 'Would to God I had never taken it!'" He then tells us "of the Countess of Buckingham (the duke's mother) applying the plaister to the king's heart and breast, whereupon he grew faint and short-breathed, and in agony; that the physicians exclaimed that the king was poisoned; that Buckingham commanded them out of the room, and committed one of them close prisoner to his own chamber, and another to be removed from court; and that, after his majesty's death, his body and head swelled above measure; his hair, with the skin of his head, stuck to his pillow, and his nails became loose on his fingers and toes." Clarendon, who, by the way, was a partisan of the duke's, gives a totally different account of James's death. He says, "It was occasioned by an ague (after a short indisposition by the gout), which, meeting many humours in a fat unwieldy body of fifty-eight years old, in four or five fits carried him out of the world, — after whose death many scandalous and libellous discourses were raised, without the least colour or ground, as appeared upon the strictest and most malicious examination that could be made, long after, in a time of license, when nobody was afraid of offending majesty, and when prosecuting the highest reproaches and contumelies against the royal family was held very meritorious." Notwithstanding this confident declaration, the world will hardly be persuaded that there was not some truth in the rumours that were abroad. The inquiries which were instituted were not strict, as he asserts, and all the unconstitutional influence of the powerful favourite was exerted to defeat them. In the celebrated accusations brought against Buckingham by the Earl of Bristol, the poisoning of King James was placed last on the list; and the pages of history bear evidence of the summary mode in which they were, for the time, got rid of.

The man from whom Buckingham is said to have procured his poisons was one Dr. Lamb, a conjuror and empiric, who, besides dealing in poisons, pretended to be a fortune-teller. The popular fury, which broke with comparative harmlessness against his patron, was directed against this man, until he could not appear with safety in the streets of London. His fate was melancholy. Walking one day in Cheapside, disguised, as he thought, from all observers, he was recognised by some idle boys, who began to hoot and pelt him with stones, calling out, "The poisoner! the poisoner! Down with the wizard! down with him!" A mob very soon collected, and the doctor took to his heels and ran for his life. He was pursued and seized in Wood Street, and from thence dragged by the hair through the mire to St. Paul's Cross; the mob beating him with sticks and stones, and calling out, "Kill the wizard! kill the poisoner!"

Paul's Cross; Seventeenth Century.

Charles I., on hearing of the riot, rode from Whitehall to quell it; but he arrived too late to save the victim. Every bone in his body was broken, and he was quite dead. Charles was excessively indignant, and fined the city six hundred pounds for its inability to deliver up the ring-leaders to justice.

But it was in Italy that poisoning was most prevalent. From a very early period, it seems to have been looked upon in that country as a perfectly justifiable means of getting rid of an enemy. The Italians of the sixteenth and seventeenth centuries poisoned their opponents with as little compunction as an Englishman of the present day brings an action at law against any one who has done him an injury. The writings of contemporary authors inform us that, when La Spara and La Tophania carried on their infernal trade, ladies put poison-bottles on their dressing-tables as openly, and used them with as little scruple upon others, as modern dames use *Eau de Cologne* or lavender-water upon themselves. So powerful is the influence of fashion, it can even cause murder to be regarded as a venial peccadillo.

In the memoirs of the last Duke of Guise, who made a Quixotic attempt, in 1648, to seize upon the government of Naples, we find some curious particulars relative to the popular feeling with regard to poisoning. A man named Gennaro Annese, who, after the short and extraordinary career of Masaniello the fisherman, had established himself as a sort of captain-general of the populace, rendered himself so obnoxious to the Duke of Guise, that the adherents of the latter determined to murder him. The captain of the guard, as the duke himself very coolly informs us, was requested to undertake this office. It was suggested to him that the *poniard* would be the most effectual instrument, but the man turned up his eyes with pious horror at the proposition. He was ready to *poison* Gennaro Annese whenever he might be called upon to do so; but to poniard him, he said, would be disgraceful, and unbecoming an officer of the guards! At last, poison was agreed upon, and Augustino Molla, an attorney in the duke's confidence, brought the bottle containing the liquid to shew it to his master. The following is the Duke's own account: *"Augustino came to me at night, and told me: 'I have brought you something which will free you from Gennaro. He deserves death, and it is no great matter after what fashion justice is done upon him. Look at this vial, full of clear and beautiful water: in four days' time, it will punish all his treasons. The captain of the guard has undertaken to give it him; and as it has no taste at all, Gennaro will suspect nothing.'"*

The duke further informs us that the dose was duly administered; but that Gennaro, fortunately for himself, ate nothing for dinner that day but cabbage dressed with oil, which acting as an antidote, caused him to vomit profusely, and saved his life. He was exceedingly ill for five days, but never suspected that he had been poisoned.

In process of time, poison-vending became a profitable trade. Eleven years after this period, it was carried on at Rome to such an extent, that the sluggish government was roused to interference. Beckmann, in his *History of Inventions*, and Lebret, in his *Magazin zum Gebrauche der Staaten Kirche Geschichte*, or *Magazine of Materials for a History of a State Church*, relates that, in the year 1659, it was made known to Pope Alexander VII. that great numbers of young women had avowed in the confessional that they had poisoned their husbands with slow poisons. The Catholic clergy, who in general hold the secrets of the confessional so sacred, were shocked and alarmed at the extraordinary prevalence of the crime. Although they refrained from revealing the names of the penitents, they conceived themselves bound to apprise the head of the Church of the enormities that were practised. It was also the subject of general conversation in Rome that young widows were unusually abundant. It was remarked, too, that if any couple lived unhappily together, the husband soon took ill and died. The papal authorities, when once they began to inquire, soon learned that a society of young wives had been formed, and met nightly, for some mysterious purpose, at the house of an old woman named Hieronyma Spara. This hag was a reputed witch and fortune-teller, and acted as president of the young viragos, several of whom, it was afterwards ascertained, belonged to the first families of Rome.

In order to have positive evidence of the practices of this female conclave, a lady was employed by the government to seek an interview with them. She dressed herself out in the most magnificent style; and having been amply provided with money, she found but little difficulty, when she had stated her object, of procuring an audience of La Spara and her sisterhood. She pretended to be in extreme distress of mind on account of the infidelities and ill-treatment of her husband, and implored La Spara to furnish her with a few drops of the wonderful elixir, the efficacy of which in sending cruel husbands to "their last long sleep" was so much vaunted by the ladies of Rome. La Spara fell into the snare, and sold her some of her "drops" at a price commensurate with the supposed wealth of the purchaser.

The liquor thus obtained was subjected to an analysis, and found to be, as was suspected, a slow poison; clear, tasteless, and limpid, like that spoken of by the Duke of Guise. Upon this evidence, the house was surrounded by the police, and La Spara and her companions taken into custody. La Spara, who is described as having been a little ugly old woman, was put to the torture, but obstinately refused to confess her guilt. Another of the women, named La Gratiosa, had less firmness, and laid bare all the secrets of the infernal sisterhood. Taking a confession extorted by anguish on the rack at its true value (nothing at all), there is still sufficient evidence to warrant posterity in the belief of their guilt. They were found guilty, and condemned, according to their degrees of culpability, to various punishments. La Spara, Gratiosa, and three young women, who had poisoned their husbands, were hanged together at Rome. Upwards of thirty women were whipped publicly through the streets; and several, whose high rank screened them from more degrading punishment, were banished from the country, and mulcted in heavy fines. In a few months afterwards, nine women more were hanged for poisoning; and another bevy, including many young and beautiful girls, were whipped half naked through the streets of Rome.

This severity did not put a stop to the practice, and jealous women and avaricious men, anxious to step into the inheritance of fathers, uncles, or brothers, resorted to poison. As it was quite free from taste, colour, and smell, it was administered without exciting suspicion. The skilful vendors compounded it of different degrees of strength, so that the poisoners had only to say whether they wanted their victims to die in a week, a month, or six months, and they were suited with corresponding doses. The vendors were chiefly women, of whom the most celebrated was a hag named Tophania, who was in this way accessory to the death of upwards of six hundred persons. This woman appears to have been a dealer in poisons from her girlhood, and resided first at Palermo and then at Naples. That entertaining traveller, Father Lebat, has given, in his letters from Italy, many curious particulars relating to her. When he was at Civita Vecchia, in 1719, the Viceroy of Naples discovered that poison was extensively sold in the latter city, and that it went by the name of *aqueta*, or little-water. On making further inquiry, he ascertained that Tophania (who was by this time near seventy years of age, and who seems to have begun her evil courses very soon after the execution of La Spara,) sent large quantities of it to all parts of Italy in small vials, with the inscription, "Manna of St. Nicholas of Barri."

The tomb of St. Nicholas of Barri was celebrated throughout Italy. A miraculous oil was said to ooze from it, which cured nearly all the maladies that flesh is heir to, provided the recipient made use of it with the due degree of *faith*. La Tophania artfully gave this name to her poison to elude the vigilance of the custom-house officers, who, in common with every body else, had a pious respect for St. Nicholas de Barri and his wonderful oil.

The poison was similar to that manufactured by La Spara. Hahnemann the physician, and father of the homœopathic doctrine, writing upon this subject, says it was compounded of arsenical neutral salts, occasioning in the victim a gradual loss of appetite, faintness, gnawing pains in the stomach, loss of strength, and wasting of the lungs. The Abbé Gagliardi says, that a few drops of it were generally poured into tea, chocolate, or soup, and its effects were slow, and almost imperceptible. Garelli, physician to the Emperor of Austria, in a letter to Hoffmann, says it was crystallised arsenic, dissolved in a large quantity of water by decoction, with the addition (for some unexplained purpose) of the herb *cymbalaria*. The Neapolitans called it *Aqua Toffnina*; and it became notorious all over Europe under the name of *Aqua Tophania*.

Although this woman carried on her infamous traffic so extensively, it was extremely difficult to meet with her. She lived in continual dread of discovery. She constantly changed her name and residence; and pretending to be a person of great godliness, resided in monasteries for months together. Whenever she was more than usually apprehensive of detection she sought ecclesiastical protection. She was soon apprised of the search made for her by the Viceroy of Naples, and, according to her practice, took refuge in a monastery. Either the search after her was not very rigid, or her measures were exceedingly well taken; for she contrived to elude the vigilance of the authorities for several years. What is still more extraordinary, as shewing the ramifications of her system, her trade was still carried on to as great an extent as before. Lebat informs us that she had so great a sympathy for poor wives who hated their husbands and wanted to get rid of them, but could not afford to buy her wonderful *aqua*, that she made them presents of it.

She was not allowed, however, to play at this game for ever; she was at length discovered in a nunnery, and her retreat cut off. The viceroy made several representations to the superior to deliver her up, but without effect. The abbess, supported by the archbishop of the diocese, constantly refused. The public curiosity was in consequence so much excited at the additional importance thus thrust upon the criminal, that thousands of persons visited the nunnery in order to catch a glimpse of her.

The patience of the viceroy appears to have been exhausted by these delays. Being a man of sense, and not a very zealous Catholic, he determined that even the Church should not shield a criminal so atrocious. Setting the privileges of the nunnery at defiance, he sent a troop of soldiers, who broke over the walls, and carried her away *vi et armis*. The archbishop, Cardinal Pignatelli, was highly indignant, and threatened to excommunicate and lay the whole city under interdict. All the inferior clergy, animated by the *esprit du corps*, took up the question, and so worked upon the superstitious and bigoted people, that they were ready to rise in a mass to storm the palace of the viceroy and rescue the prisoner.

These were serious difficulties; but the viceroy was not a man to be daunted. Indeed, he seems to have acted throughout with a rare union of astuteness, coolness, and energy. To avoid the evil consequences of the threatened excommunication, he placed a guard round the palace of the archbishop, judging that the latter would not be so foolish as to launch out an anathema which would cause the city to be starved, and himself in it. The market-people would not have dared to come to the city with provisions so long as it remained under the ban. There would have been too much inconvenience to himself and his ghostly brethren in such a measure; and, as the viceroy anticipated, the good cardinal reserved his thunders for some other occasion.

Still there was the populace. To quiet their clamour and avert the impending insurrection, the agents of the government adroitly mingled with the people, and spread abroad a report that Tophania had poisoned all the wells and fountains of the city. This was enough. The popular feeling was turned against her immediately. Those who, but a moment before, had looked upon her as a saint, now reviled her as a devil, and were as eager for her punishment as they had before been for her escape. Tophania was then put to the torture. She confessed the long catalogue of her crimes, and named all the persons who had employed her. She was shortly afterwards strangled, and her corpse thrown over the wall into the garden of the convent from whence she had been taken. This appears to have been done to conciliate the clergy, by allowing them, at least, the burial of one who had taken refuge within their precincts.

After her death the mania for poisoning seems to have abated; but we have yet to see what hold it took upon the French people at a somewhat earlier period. So rooted had it become in France between the years 1670 and 1680, that Madame de Sevigné, in one of her letters, expresses her fear that Frenchman and poisoner would become synonymous terms.

As in Italy, the first notice the government received of the prevalence of this crime was given by the clergy, to whom females of high rank, and some among the middle and lower classes, had avowed in the confessional that they had poisoned their husbands. In consequence of these disclosures, two Italians, named Exili and Glaser, were arrested, and thrown into the Bastille, on the charge of compounding and selling the drugs used for these murders. Glaser died in prison, but Exili remained without trial for several months; and there, shortly afterwards, he made the acquaintance of another prisoner, named Sainte Croix, by whose example the crime was still further disseminated among the French people.

The most notorious of the poisoners that derived their pernicious knowledge from this man was Madame de Brinvilliers, a young woman connected both by birth and marriage with some of the noblest families of France. She seems, from her very earliest years, to have been heartless and depraved; and, if we may believe her own confession, was steeped in wickedness ere she had well entered her teens. She was, however, beautiful and accomplished; and, in the eye of the world, seemed exemplary and kind. Guyot de Pitaval, in the *Causes Célèbres*, and Madame de Sevigné, in her letters, represent her as mild and agreeable in her manners, and offering no traces on her countenance of the evil soul within. She was married in 1651 to the Marquis de Brinvilliers, with whom she lived unhappily for some years. He was a loose, dissipated character, and was the means of introducing Sainte Croix to his wife, a man who cast a blight upon her life, and dragged her on from crime to crime, till her offences became so great that the mind shudders to dwell upon them. For this man she conceived a guilty passion, to gratify which she plunged at once into the gulf of sin. She was drawn to its most loathsome depths ere retribution overtook her.

She had as yet shewn a fair outside to the world, and found but little difficulty in effecting a legal separation from her husband, who had not the art to conceal his vices. The proceeding gave great offence to her family. She appears, after this, to have thrown off the mask completely, and carried on her intrigues so openly with her lover, Sainte Croix, that her father, M. D'Aubray, scandalised at her conduct, procured a *lettre de cachet*, and had him imprisoned in the Bastille for a twelvemonth.

The Bastille.

Sainte Croix, who had been in Italy, was a dabbler in poisons. He knew something of the secrets of the detestable La Spara, and improved himself in them from the instructions of Exili, with whom he speedily contracted a sort of friendship. By him he was shewn how to prepare, not only the liquid poisons employed in Italy, but that known as *succession powder*, which afterwards became so celebrated in France. Like his mistress, he appeared amiable, witty, and intelligent, and shewed no signs to the world of the two fierce passions, revenge and avarice, which were gnawing at his heart. Both these passions were to be sated on the unfortunate family of D'Aubray; his revenge, because they had imprisoned him; and his avarice, because they were rich. Reckless and extravagant, he was always in want of money, and he had no one to supply him but Madame de Brinvilliers, whose own portion was far from sufficient to satisfy his need. Groaning to think that any impediment should stand between him and wealth, he conceived the horrid idea of poisoning M. D'Aubray her father, and her two brothers, that she might inherit the property. Three murders were nothing to such a villain. He communicated his plan to Madame de Brinvilliers; and she, without the slightest scruple, agreed to aid him: he undertook to compound the poisons, and she to administer them. The zeal and alacrity with which she set to work seem hardly credible. Sainte Croix found her an apt scholar; and she soon became as expert as himself in the manufacture of poisons. To try the strength of the first doses, she used to administer them to dogs, rabbits, and pigeons. Afterwards, wishing to be more certain of their effects, she went round to the hospitals, and administered them to the sick poor in the soups which she brought in apparent charity.[39] None of the poisons were intended to kill at the first dose; so that she could try them once upon an individual without fear of murder. She tried the same atrocious experiment upon the guests at her father's table, by poisoning a pigeon-pie! To be more certain still, she next poisoned herself! When convinced by this desperate essay of the potency of the draught, she procured an antidote from Sainte Croix, and all doubts being removed, commenced operations upon her grey-headed father. She administered the first dose with her own hands, in his chocolate. The poison worked well. The old man was taken ill, and his daughter, apparently full of tenderness and anxiety, watched by his bedside. The next day she gave him some broth, which she recommended as highly nourishing. This also was poisoned. In this manner she gradually wore out his frame, and in less than ten days he was a corpse! His death seemed so much the result of disease, that no suspicions were excited.

When the two brothers arrived from the provinces to render the last sad duties to their sire, they found their sister as grieved, to all outward appearance, as even filial affection could desire: but the young men only came to perish. They stood between Sainte Croix and the already half-clutched gold, and their doom was sealed. A man, named La Chaussée, was hired by Sainte Croix to aid in administering the poisons; and, in less than six weeks time, they had both gone to their long home.

Suspicion was now excited; but so cautiously had all been done, that it found no one upon whom to attach itself. The marquise had a sister, and she was entitled, by the death of her relatives, to half the property. Less than the whole would not satisfy Sainte Croix, and he determined that she should die the same death as her father and brothers. She was too distrustful, however; and, by quitting Paris, she escaped the destruction that was lurking for her.

The marquise had undertaken these murders to please her lover. She was now anxious to perpetrate another on her own account. She wished to marry Sainte Croix; but, though separated from her husband, she was not divorced. She thought it would be easier to poison him than to apply to the tribunals for a divorce, which might, perhaps, be refused. But Sainte Croix had no longer any love for his guilty instrument. Bad men do not admire others who are as bad as themselves. Though a villain himself, he had no desire to marry one, and was not at all anxious for the death of the marquis. He seemed, however, to enter into the plot, and supplied her with poison for her husband; but he took care to provide a remedy. La Brinvilliers poisoned him one day, and Sainte Croix gave him an antidote the next. In this manner he was buffeted about between them for some time, and finally escaped, with a ruined constitution and a broken heart.

But the day of retribution was at hand, and a terrible mischance brought the murders to light. The nature of the poisons compounded by Sainte Croix was so deadly, that, when working in his laboratory, he was obliged to wear a mask, to preserve himself from suffocation. One day, the mask slipped off, and the miserable wretch perished in his crimes. His corpse was found, on the following morning, in the obscure lodging where he had fitted up his laboratory. As he appeared to be without friends or relatives, the police took possession of his effects. Among other things, was found a small box, to which was affixed the following singular document:

"I humbly beg, that those into whose hands this box may fall, will do me the favour to deliver it into the hands only of the Marchioness de Brinvilliers, who resides in the Rue Neuve St. Paul, as every thing it contains concerns her, and belongs to her alone; and as, besides, there is nothing in it that can be of use to any person but her. In case she shall be dead before me, it is my wish that it be burned, with every thing it contains, without opening or altering any thing. In order that no one may plead ignorance, I swear by the God that I adore, and by all that is held most sacred, that I assert nothing but the truth: and if my intentions, just and reasonable as they are, be thwarted in this point by any persons, I charge their consciences with it, both in this world and that which is to come, in order that I may unload mine. I protest that this is my last will. Done at Paris, May 25, 1672. (Signed) Sainte Croix."

This earnest solicitation, instead of insuring respect, as was intended, excited curiosity. The box was opened, and found to contain some papers, and several vials and powders. The latter were handed to a chemist for analysis, and the documents were retained by the police, and opened. Among them was found a promissory note of the Marchioness de Brinvilliers, for thirty thousand francs, to the order of Sainte Croix. The other papers were of greater importance, as they implicated both her and her servant, La Chaussée, in the recent murders. As soon as she was informed of the death of Sainte Croix, she made an attempt to gain possession of his papers and the box; but, being refused, she saw that there was no time to be lost, and immediately quitted. Next morning the police were on her trail; but she succeeded in escaping to England. La Chaussée was not so fortunate. Altogether ignorant of the fatal mischance which had brought his villanies to light, he did not dream of danger. He was arrested and brought to trial: being put to the torture, he confessed that he had administered poison to the Messieurs d'Aubray, and that he had received a hundred pistoles, and the promise of an annuity for life, from Sainte Croix and Madame de Brinvilliers, for the job. He was condemned to be broken alive on the wheel, and the marchioness was, by default, sentenced to be beheaded. He was executed accordingly, in March 1673, on the Place de Grève, in Paris.

La Brinvilliers appears to have resided for nearly three years in England. Early in 1676, thinking that the rigour of pursuit was over, and that she might venture to return to the Continent, she proceeded secretly to Liège. Notwithstanding her care, the French authorities were soon apprised of her return; and arrangements were promptly made with the municipality of that city to permit the agents of the French police to arrest her within the limits of their jurisdiction. Desgrais, an officer of the *maréchaussée*, accordingly left Paris for that purpose. On his arrival in Liège, he found that she had sought shelter within the walls of a convent. Here the arm of the law, long as it is said to be, could not reach her: but Desgrais was not a man to be baffled, and he resorted to stratagem to accomplish what force could not. Having disguised himself as a priest, he sought admission to the convent, and obtained an interview with La Brinvilliers. He said, that being a Frenchman, and passing through Liège, he could not leave that city without paying a visit to a lady whose beauty and misfortunes were so celebrated. Her vanity was flattered by the compliment. Desgrais saw, to use a vulgar but forcible expression, "that he had got on the blind side of her;" and he adroitly continued to pour out the language of love and admiration till the deluded marchioness was thrown completely off her guard. She agreed, without much solicitation, to meet him outside the walls of the convent, where their amorous intrigue might be carried on more conveniently than within. Faithful to her appointment with her supposed new lover, she came, and found herself, not in the embrace of a gallant, but in the custody of a policeman.

Her trial was not long delayed. The proofs against her were abundant. The dying declaration of La Chaussée would have been alone enough to convict her; but besides that, there were the mysterious document attached to the box of St. Croix, her flight from France, and, stronger and more damning proof than all, a paper, in her own handwriting, found among the effects of St. Croix, in which she detailed to him the misdeeds of her life, and spoke of the murder of her father and brothers in terms that left no doubt of her guilt. During the trial, all Paris was in commotion. La Brinvilliers was the only subject of conversation. All the details of her crimes were published, and greedily devoured; and the idea of secret poisoning first put into the heads of hundreds, who afterwards became guilty of it.

On the 16th of July, 1676, the Superior Criminal Court of Paris pronounced a verdict of guilty against her, for the murder of her father and brothers, and the attempt upon the life of her sister. She was condemned to be drawn on a hurdle, with her feet bare, a rope about her neck, and a burning torch in her hand, to the great entrance of the cathedral of Notre Dame, where she was to make the *amende honorable* in sight of all the people; to be taken from thence to the Place de Grève, and there to be beheaded. Her body was afterwards to be burned, and her ashes scattered to the winds.

After her sentence, she made a full confession of her guilt. She seems to have looked upon death without fear; but it was recklessness, not courage, that supported her. Madame de Sevigné says, that when on the hurdle, on her way to the scaffold, she entreated her confessor to exert his influence with the executioner to place himself next to her, that his body might hide from her view "that scoundrel Desgrais, who had entrapped her." She also asked the ladies, who had been drawn to their windows to witness the procession, what they were looking at? adding, "a pretty sight you have come to see, truly!" She laughed when on the scaffold, dying as she had lived, impenitent and heartless. On the morrow, the populace came in crowds to collect her ashes to preserve them as relics. She was regarded as a martyred saint, and her ashes were supposed to be endowed, by divine grace, with the power of curing all diseases. Popular folly has often canonised persons whose pretensions to sanctity were extremely equivocal; but the disgusting folly of the multitude, in this instance, has never been surpassed.

Before her death, proceedings were instituted against M. de Penautier, treasurer of the province of Languedoc, and receiver-general for the clergy, who was accused by a lady, named St. Laurent, of having poisoned her husband, the late receiver-general, in order to obtain his appointment. The circumstances of this case were never divulged, and the greatest influence was exerted to prevent it from going to trial. He was known to have been intimate with Sainte Croix and Madame de Brinvilliers, and was thought to have procured his poisons from them. The latter, however, refused to say any thing which might implicate him. The inquiry was eventually stifled, after Penautier had been several months in the Bastille.

The Cardinal de Bonzy was accused by the gossips of the day of being an accomplice of Penautier. The cardinal's estates were burdened with the payment of several heavy annuities; but, about the time that poisoning became so fashionable, all the annuitants died off, one after the other. The cardinal, in talking of these annuitants, afterwards used to say, "Thanks to my star, I have outlived them all!" A wit, seeing him and Penautier riding in the same carriage, cried out, in allusion to this expression, *"There go the Cardinal de Bonzy and his star!"*

It was now that the mania for poisoning began to take hold of the popular mind. From this time until the year 1682, the prisons of France teemed with persons accused of this crime; and it is very singular that other offences decreased in a similar proportion. We have already seen the extent to which it was carried in Italy. It was, if possible, surpassed in France. The diabolical ease with which these murders could be effected, by means of these scentless and tasteless poisons, enticed the evil-minded. Jealousy, revenge, avarice, even petty spite, alike resorted to them. Those who would have been deterred, by fear of detection, from using the pistol or the dagger, or even strong doses of poison, which kill at once, employed slow poisons without dread. The corrupt government of the day, although it could wink at the atrocities of a wealthy and influential courtier like Penautier, was scandalised to see the crime spreading among the people. Disgrace was, in fact, entailed, in the eyes of Europe, upon the name of Frenchman. Louis XIV., to put a stop to the evil, instituted what was called the Chambre Ardente, or Burning Chamber, with extensive powers for the trial and punishment of the prisoners.

Two women, especially, made themselves notorious at this time, and were instrumental to the deaths of hundreds of individuals. They both resided in Paris, and were named Lavoisin and Lavigoreux. Like Spara and Tophania, of whom they were imitators, they chiefly sold their poisons to women who wanted to get rid of their husbands; and, in some few instances, to husbands who wanted to get rid of their wives. Their ostensible occupation was that of midwives. They also pretended to be fortune-tellers, and were visited by persons of every class of society. The rich and poor thronged alike to their *mansardes* to learn the secrets of the future. Their prophecies were principally of death. They foretold to women the approaching dissolution of husbands, and to needy heirs the end of rich relatives, who had made them, as Byron expresses it, "wait too, too long already." They generally took care to be instrumental in fulfilling their own predictions. They used to tell their wretched employers that some sign of the approaching death would take place in the house, such as the breaking of glass or china; and they paid servants considerable fees to cause a breakage, as if by accident, exactly at the appointed time. Their occupation as midwives made them acquainted with the secrets of many families, which they afterwards turned to dreadful account.

It is not known how long they had carried on this awful trade before they were discovered. Detection finally overtook them at the close of the year 1679. They were both tried, found guilty, and burned alive on the Place de Grève, on the 22d of February, 1680, after their hands had been bored through with a red-hot iron, and then cut off. Their numerous accomplices in Paris and in the provinces were also discovered and brought to trial. According to some authors, thirty, and to others, fifty of them, chiefly women, were hanged in the principal cities.

Lavoisin kept a list of the visitors who came to her house to purchase poisons. This paper was seized by the police on her arrest, and examined by the tribunals. Among the names were found those of the Marshal de Luxembourg, the Countess de Soissons, and the Duchess de Bouillon. The marshal seems only to have been guilty of a piece of discreditable folly in visiting a woman of this description, but the popular voice at the time imputed to him something more than folly. The author of the *Memoirs of the Affairs of Europe since the Peace of Utrecht*, says, "The miserable gang who dealt in poison and prophecy alleged that he had sold himself to the devil, and that a young girl of the name of Dupin had been poisoned by his means. Among other stories, they said he had made a contract with the devil, in order to marry his son to the daughter of the Marquis of Louvois. To this atrocious and absurd accusation the marshal, who had surrendered himself at the Bastille on the first accusation against him, replied with the mingled sentiment of pride and innocence, 'When Mathieu de Montmorenci, my ancestor, married the widow of Louis le Gros, he did not have recourse to the devil, but to the states-general, in order to obtain for the minor king the support of the house of Montmorenci.' This brave man was imprisoned in a cell six feet and a half long, and his trial, which was interrupted for several weeks, lasted altogether fourteen months. No judgment was pronounced upon him."

The Countess of Soissons fled to Brussels, rather than undergo the risk of a trial; and was never able to clear herself from the stigma that attached to her, of having made an attempt to poison the Queen of Spain by doses of succession-powder. The Duchess of Bouillon was arrested, and tried by the Chambre Ardente. It would appear, however, that she had nothing to do with the slow poisons, but had merely endeavoured to pry into the secrets of futurity, and gratify her curiosity with a sight of the devil. One of the presidents of the Chambre, La Reynie, an ugly little old man, very seriously asked her whether she had really seen the devil; to which the lady replied, looking him full in the face, "Oh, yes! I see him now. He is in the form of a little ugly old man, exceedingly illnatured, and is dressed in the robes of a Counsellor of State." M. la Reynie prudently refrained from asking any more questions of a lady with so sharp and ready a tongue. The duchess was imprisoned for several months in the Bastille; and nothing being proved against her, she was released at the intercession of her powerful friends. The severe punishment of criminals of this note might have helped to abate the fever of imitation among the vulgar; — their comparative impunity had a contrary tendency. The escape of Penautier, and the wealthy Cardinal de Bonzy his employer, had the most pernicious effect. For two years longer the crime continued to rage, and was not finally suppressed till the stake had blazed, or the noose dangled, for upwards of a hundred individuals.[40]

Chapter 4.

Haunted Houses

Palace of Woodstock.

Here's a knocking indeed!... Knock! knock! knock!... Who's there, i'
the name o' Beelzebub?... Who's there, i' the devil's name? Knock!
knock! knock! — Never at quiet?

Macbeth.

Who has not either seen or heard of some house, shut up and
uninhabitable, fallen into decay, and looking dusty and dreary,
from which, at midnight, strange sounds have been heard to
issue — aerial knockings — the rattling of chains, and the groaning
of perturbed spirits? — a house that people have thought it unsafe
to pass after dark, and which has remained for years without a
tenant, and which no tenant would occupy, even were he paid to
do so? There are hundreds of such houses in England at the
present day; hundreds in France, Germany, and almost every
country of Europe, which are marked with the mark of fear —
places for the timid to avoid, and the pious to bless themselves
at, and ask protection from, as they pass — the abodes of ghosts
and evil spirits. There are many such houses in London; and if
any vain boaster of the march of intellect would but take the
trouble to find them out and count them, he would be convinced

that intellect must yet make some enormous strides before such old superstitions can be eradicated.

The idea that such houses exist is a remnant of the witch creed, which merits separate notice from its comparative harmlessness, and from its being not so much a madness as a folly of the people. Unlike other notions that sprang from the belief in witchcraft, and which we have already dwelt upon at sufficient length, it has sent no wretches to the stake or the gibbet, and but a few to the pillory only.

Many houses have been condemned as haunted, and avoided by the weak and credulous, from circumstances the most trifling in themselves, and which only wanted a vigorous mind to clear up, at once, and dissipate all alarm. A house in Aix-la-Chapelle, a large desolate-looking building, remained uninhabited for five years, on account of the mysterious knockings that there were heard within it at all hours of the day and night. Nobody could account for the noises; and the fear became at last so excessive, that the persons who inhabited the houses on either side relinquished their tenancy, and went to reside in other quarters of the town, where there was less chance of interruption from evil spirits. From being so long without an inhabitant, the house at last grew so ruinous, so dingy, and so miserable in its outward appearance, and so like the place that ghosts might be supposed to haunt, that few persons cared to go past it after sunset. The knocking that was heard in one of the upper rooms was not very loud, but it was very regular. The gossips of the neighbourhood asserted that they often heard groans from the cellars, and saw lights moved about from one window to another immediately after the midnight bell had tolled. Spectres in white habiliments were reported to have gibed and chattered from the windows; but all these stories could bear no investigation. The knocking, however, was a fact which no one could dispute, and several ineffectual attempts were made by the proprietor to discover the cause. The rooms were sprinkled with holy water; the evil spirits were commanded in due form, by a priest, to depart thence to the Red Sea; but the knockings still continued, in spite of all that could be done in that way. Accident at last discovered the cause, and restored tranquillity to the neighbourhood. The proprietor, who suffered not only in his mind but in his pocket, had sold the building at a ruinously small price, to get rid of all future annoyance. The new proprietor was standing in a room on the first floor when he heard the door driven to at the bottom with a considerable noise, and then fly open immediately, about two inches and no more. He stood still a minute and watched, and the same thing occurred a second and a third time. He examined the door attentively, and all the mystery was unravelled. The latch of the door was broken, so that it could not be fastened, and it swung chiefly upon the bottom hinge. Immediately opposite was a window, in which one pane of glass was broken; and when the wind was in a certain quarter, the draught of air was so strong that it blew the door to with some violence. There being no latch, it swung open again; and when there was a fresh gust, was again blown to. The new proprietor lost no time in sending for a glazier, and the mysterious noises ceased for ever. The house was replastered and repainted, and once more regained its lost good name. It was not before two or three years, however, that it was thoroughly established in popular favour; and many persons, even then, would always avoid passing it, if they could reach their destination by any other street.

A similar story is narrated by Sir Walter Scott, in his *Letters on Demonology and Witchcraft*, the hero of which was a gentleman of birth and distinction, well known in the political world. Shortly after he succeeded to his title and estates, there was a rumour among the servants concerning a strange noise that used to be heard at night in the family mansion, and the cause of which no one could ascertain. The gentleman resolved to discover it himself, and to watch for that purpose with a domestic who had grown old in the family, and who, like the rest, had whispered strange things about the knocking having begun immediately upon the death of his old master. These two watched until the noise was heard, and at last traced it to a small store-room, used as a place for keeping provisions of various kinds for the family, and of which the old butler had the key. They entered this place, and remained for some time without hearing the noises which they had traced thither. At length the sound was heard, but much lower than it seemed to be while they were farther off, and their imaginations were more excited. They then discovered the cause without difficulty. A rat, caught in an old-fashioned trap, had occasioned the noise by its efforts to escape, in which it was able to raise the trap-door of its prison to a certain height, but was then obliged to drop it. The noise of the fall resounding through the house had occasioned the mysterious rumours, which, but for the investigation of the proprietor, would, in all probability, have acquired so bad a name for the dwelling that no servants would have inhabited it. The circumstance was told to Sir Walter Scott by the gentleman to whom it happened.

Saint Louis.

But, in general, houses that have acquired this character have been more indebted for it to the roguery of living men than to accidents like these. Six monks played off a clever trick of the kind upon that worthy king, Louis, whose piety has procured him in the annals of his own country the designation of "the Saint." Having heard his confessor speak in terms of warm eulogy of the goodness and learning of the monks of the order of St. Bruno, he expressed his wish to establish a community of them near Paris. Bernard de la Tour, the superior, sent six of the brethren, and the king gave them a handsome house to live in in the village of Chantilly. It so happened that from their windows they had a very fine view of the ancient palace of Vauvert, which had been built for a royal residence by King Robert, but deserted for many years. The worthy monks thought the palace would just suit them; but their modesty was so excessive that they were ashamed to ask the king for a grant of it in due form. This difficulty was not to be overcome, and the monks set their ingenuity to work to discover another plan. The palace of Vauvert had never laboured under any imputation upon its character until they became its neighbours; but, somehow or other, it almost immediately afterwards began to acquire a bad name. Frightful shrieks were heard to proceed from it at night; blue, red, and green lights were suddenly seen to glimmer from the windows, and as suddenly to disappear; the clanking of chains was heard, and the howling as of persons in great pain. These disturbances continued for several months, to the great terror of all the country round, and even of the pious King Louis, to whom, at Paris, all the rumours were regularly carried with whole heaps of additions that accumulated on the way. At last a great spectre, clothed all in pea-green, with a long white beard and a serpent's tail, took his station regularly at midnight in the principal window of the palace, and howled fearfully, and shook his fists at the passengers. The six monks at Chantilly, to whom all these things were duly narrated, were exceedingly wrath that the devil should play such antics right opposite their dwelling, and hinted to the commissioners sent down by Saint Louis to investigate the matter, that if they were allowed to inhabit the palace, they would very soon make a clearance of the evil spirits. The king was quite charmed with their piety, and expressed to them how grateful he felt for their disinterestedness. A deed was forthwith drawn up, the royal sign-manual was affixed to it, and the palace of Vauvert became the property of the monks of St. Bruno. The deed is dated 1259. The disturbances ceased immediately, the lights disappeared, and the green ghost (so said the monks) was laid at rest for ever under the waves of the Red Sea.[41]

In the year 1580, one Gilles Blacre had taken the lease of a house in the suburbs of Tours, but repenting him of his bargain with the landlord, Peter Piquet, he endeavoured to prevail upon him to cancel the agreement. Peter, however, was satisfied with his tenant and his terms, and would listen to no compromise. Very shortly afterwards, the rumour was spread all over Tours that the house of Gilles Blacre was haunted. Gilles himself asserted that he verily believed his house to be the general rendezvous of all the witches and evil spirits of France. The noise they made was awful, and quite prevented him from sleeping. They knocked against the wall, howled in the chimneys, broke his window-glass, scattered his pots and pans all over his kitchen, and set his chairs and tables a dancing the whole night through. Crowds of persons assembled round the house to hear the mysterious noises: and the bricks were observed to detach themselves from the wall, and fall into the streets upon the heads of those who had not said their paternoster before coming out in the morning. These things having continued for some time, Gilles Blacre made his complaint to the Civil Court of Tours, and Peter Piquet was summoned to shew cause why the lease should not be annulled. Poor Peter could make no defence, and the court unanimously agreed that no lease could hold good under such circumstances, and annulled it accordingly, condemning the unlucky owner to all the expenses of the suit. Peter appealed to the parliament of Paris; and after a long examination, the parliament confirmed the lease. "Not," said the judge, "because it has not been fully and satisfactorily proved that the house is troubled by evil spirits, but that there was an informality in the proceedings before the Civil Court of Tours, that rendered its decision null and of no effect."

A similar cause was tried before the Parliament of Bourdeaux, in the year 1595, relative to a house in that city which was sorely troubled by evil spirits. The parliament appointed certain ecclesiastics to examine and report to them, and on their report in the affirmative that the house was haunted, the lease was annulled, and the tenant absolved from all payment of rent and taxes.[42]

One of the best stories of a haunted house is that of the royal palace of Woodstock, in the year 1649, when the commissioners sent from London by the Long Parliament to take possession of it, and efface all the emblems of royalty about it, were fairly driven out by their fear of the devil, and the annoyances they suffered from a roguish cavalier, who played the imp to admiration. The commissioners, dreading at that time no devil, arrived at Woodstock on the 13th of October, 1649. They took up their lodgings in the late king's apartments — turned the beautiful bedrooms and withdrawing-rooms into kitchens and sculleries — the council-hall into a brew-house, and made the dining-room a place to keep firewood in. They pulled down all the insignia of royal state, and treated with the utmost indignity every thing that recalled to their memory the name or the majesty of Charles Stuart. One Giles Sharp accompanied them in the capacity of clerk, and seconded their efforts, apparently with the greatest zeal. He aided them to uproot a noble old tree, merely because it was called the *King's* Oak, and tossed the fragments into the dining-room to make cheerful fires for the commissioners. During the first two days, they heard some strange noises about the house, but they paid no great attention to them. On the third, however, they began to suspect they had got into bad company; for they heard, as they thought, a supernatural dog under their bed, which gnawed their bed-clothes. On the next day, the chairs and tables began to dance, apparently of their own accord. On the fifth day, something came into the bedchamber and walked up and down; and fetching the warming-pan out of the withdrawing-room, made so much noise with it that they thought five church-bells were ringing in their ears. On the sixth day, the plates and dishes were thrown up and down the dining-room. On the seventh, they penetrated into the bedroom in company with several logs of wood, and usurped the soft pillows intended for the commissioners. On the eighth and ninth nights, there was a cessation of hostilities; but on the tenth, the bricks in the chimneys became locomotive, and rattled and danced about the floors, and round the heads of the commissioners, all the night long. On the eleventh, the demon ran away with their breeches; and on the twelfth filled their beds so full of pewter platters that they could not get into them. On the thirteenth night, the glass became unaccountably seized with a fit of cracking, and fell into shivers in all parts of the house. On the fourteenth, there was a noise as if forty pieces of artillery had been fired off, and a shower of pebble-stones, which so alarmed the commissioners that, "struck with great horror, they cried out to one another for help."

They first of all tried the efficacy of prayers to drive away the evil spirits; but these proving unavailing, they began seriously to reflect whether it would not be much better to leave the place altogether to the devils that inhabited it. They ultimately resolved, however, to try it a little longer; and having craved forgiveness of all their sins, betook themselves to bed. That night they slept in tolerable comfort, but it was merely a trick of their tormentor to lull them into false security. When, on the succeeding night, they heard no noises, they began to flatter themselves that the devil was driven out, and prepared accordingly to take up their quarters for the whole winter in the palace. These symptoms on their part became the signal for renewed uproar among the fiends. On the 1st of November, they heard something walking with a slow and solemn pace up and down the withdrawing-room, and immediately afterwards a shower of stones, bricks, mortar, and broken glass pelted about their ears. On the 2d the steps were again heard in the withdrawing-room, sounding to their fancy very much like the treading of an enormous bear, which continued for about a quarter of an hour. This noise having ceased, a large warming-pan was thrown violently upon the table, followed by a number of stones and the jawbone of a horse. Some of the boldest walked valiantly into the withdrawing-room, armed with swords and pistols; but could discover nothing. They were afraid that night to go to sleep, and sat up, making fires in every room, and burning candles and lamps in great abundance; thinking that, as the fiends loved darkness, they would not disturb a company surrounded with so much light. They were deceived, however: buckets of water came down the chimneys and extinguished the fires; and the candles were blown out, they knew not how. Some of the servants who had betaken themselves to bed were drenched with putrid ditch-water as they lay, and arose in great fright, muttering incoherent prayers, and exposing to the wondering eyes of the commission-ers their linen all dripping with green moisture, and their knuckles red with the blows they had at the same time received from some invisible tormentors. While they were still speaking, there was a noise like the loudest thunder, or the firing of a whole park of artillery, upon which they all fell down upon their knees and implored the protection of the Almighty. One of the commissioners then arose, the others still kneeling, and asked in a courageous voice, and in the name of God, who was there, and what they had done that they should be troubled in that manner. No answer was returned, and the noises ceased for a while. At length, however, as the commissioners said, "the devil came again, and brought with it seven devils worse than itself." Being again in darkness, they lighted a candle and placed it in the doorway, that it might throw a light upon the two chambers at once; but it was suddenly blown out, and one commissioner said that he had "seen the similitude of a horse's hoof striking the candle and candlestick into the middle of the chamber, and afterwards making three scrapes on the snuff to put it out." Upon this, the same person was so bold as to draw his sword; but he asserted positively that he had hardly withdrawn it from the scabbard before an invisible hand seized hold of it and tugged with him for it, and prevailing, struck him so violent a blow with the pommel that he was quite stunned. Then the noises began again; upon which, with one accord, they all retired into the presence-chamber, where they passed the night, praying and singing psalms.

They were by this time convinced that it was useless to struggle any longer with the powers of evil that seemed determined to make Woodstock their own. These things happened on the Saturday night; and being repeated on the Sunday, they deter-mined to leave the place immediately, and return to London. By

Tuesday morning early, all their preparations were completed; and, shaking the dust off their feet, and devoting Woodstock and all its inhabitants to the infernal gods, they finally took their departure.[43]

Many years elapsed before the true cause of these disturbances was discovered. It was ascertained at the Restoration, that the whole was the work of Giles Sharp, the trusty clerk of the commissioners. This man, whose real name was Joseph Collins, was a concealed royalist, and had passed his early life within the bowers of Woodstock; so that he knew every hole and corner of the place, and the numerous trap-doors and secret passages that abounded in the building. The commissioners, never suspecting the true state of his opinions, but believing him to be revolution-ary to the back-bone, placed the utmost reliance upon him; a confidence which he abused in the manner above detailed, to his own great amusement and that of the few cavaliers whom he let into the secret.

Quite as extraordinary and as cleverly managed was the trick played off at Tedworth, in 1661, at the house of Mr. Mompesson, and which is so circumstantially narrated by the Rev. Joseph Glanvil, under the title of *The Demon of Tedworth*, and appended, among other proofs of witchcraft, to his noted work called *Sadducismus Triumphatus*. About the middle of April, in the year above mentioned, Mr. Mompesson, having returned to his house at Tedworth from a journey he had taken to London, was informed by his wife, that during his absence they had been troubled with the most extraordinary noises. Three nights afterwards he heard the noise himself; and it appeared to him to be that of "a great knocking at his doors, and on the outside of his walls." He immediately arose, dressed himself, took down a pair of pistols, and walked valiantly forth to discover the disturber, under the impression that it must be a robber; but, as he went, the noise seemed to travel before or behind him; and when he arrived at the door from which he thought it proceeded, he saw nothing, but still heard "a strange hollow sound." He puzzled his brains for a long time, and searched every corner of the house; but discovering nothing, he went to bed again. He was no sooner snug under the clothes than the noise began again more furiously than ever, sounding very much like a "thumping and drumming on the top of his house, and then by degrees going off into the air."

These things continued for several nights, when it came to the recollection of Mr. Mompesson that some time before he had given orders for the arrest and imprisonment of a wandering drummer, who went about the country with a large drum, disturbing quiet people and soliciting alms, and that he had detained the man's drum, and that probably the drummer was a wizard, and had sent evil spirits to haunt his house to be revenged of him. He became strengthened in his opinion every day, especially when the noises assumed, to his fancy, a resemblance to the beating of a drum, "like that at the breaking up of a guard." Mrs. Mompesson being brought to bed, the devil, or the drummer, very kindly and considerately refrained from making the usual riot; but, as soon as she recovered strength, began again "in a ruder manner than before, following and vexing the young children, and beating their bedsteads with so much violence that every one expected they would fall in pieces." For an hour together, as the worthy Mr. Mompesson repeated to his wondering neighbours, this infernal drummer "would beat 'Roundheads and Cuckolds,' the 'Tat-too,' and several other points of war, as cleverly as any soldier." When this had lasted long enough, he changed his tactics, and scratched with his iron talons under the children's bed. "On the 5th of November," says the Rev. Joseph Glanvil, "it made a mighty noise; and a servant observing two boards in the children's room seeming to move, he bid it give him one of them. Upon which the board came (nothing moving it that he saw) within a yard of him. The man added, 'Nay, let me have it in my hand;' upon which the spirit, devil, or drummer pushed it towards him so close that he might touch it." "This," continues Glanvil, "was in the day-time, and was seen by a whole room full of people. That morning it left a sulphureous smell behind it, which was very offensive. At night the minister, one Mr. Cragg, and several of the neighbours came to the house on a visit. Mr. Cragg went to prayers with them, kneeling at the children's bedside, where it then became very troublesome and loud. During prayer-time, the spirit withdrew into the cock-loft, but returned as soon as prayers were done; and then, in sight of the company, the chairs walked about the room of themselves, the children's shoes were hurled over their heads, and every loose thing moved about the chamber. At the same time, a bed-staff was thrown at the minister, which hit him on the leg, but so favourably, that a lock of wool could not have fallen more softly." On another occasion, the blacksmith of the village, a fellow who cared neither for ghost nor devil, slept with John the footman, that he also might hear the disturbances and be cured of his incredulity, when there "came a noise in the room as if one had been shoeing a horse, and somewhat came, as it were, with a pair of pincers," snipping and snapping at the poor blacksmith's nose the greater part of the night. Next day it came panting like a dog out of breath; upon which some woman present took a bed-staff to knock at it, "which was caught suddenly out of her hand and thrown away; and company coming up, the room was presently filled with a *bloomy noisome smell*, and was very hot, though without fire, in a very sharp and severe winter. It continued in the bed, panting and scratching for an hour and a half, and then went into the next room, where it knocked a little, and seemed to rattle a chain."

The rumour of these wonderful occurrences soon spread all over the country, and people from far and near flocked to the haunted house of Tedworth, to believe or doubt as their natures led them, but all filled with intense curiosity. It appears, too, that the fame of these events reached the royal ear, and that some gentlemen were sent by the king to investigate the circumstances, and draw up a report of what they saw or heard. Whether the royal commissioners were more sensible men than the neighbours of Mr. Mompesson, and required more clear and positive evidence than they, or whether the powers with which they were armed to punish any body who might be found carrying on this deception frightened the evil-doers, is not certain; but Glanvil himself reluctantly confesses that all the time they were in the house the noises ceased, and nothing was heard or seen. "However," says he, "as to the quiet of the house when the courtiers were there, the intermission may have been accidental, or perhaps the demon was not willing to give so public a testimony of those transactions which might possibly convince those who he had rather should continue in unbelief of his existence."

As soon as the royal commissioners took their departure, the infernal drummer recommenced his antics, and hundreds of persons were daily present to hear and wonder. Mr. Mompesson's servant was so fortunate as not only to hear, but to see this pertinacious demon, for it came and stood at the foot of his bed. "The exact shape and proportion of it he could not discover; but he saw a great body, with two red and glaring eyes, which, for some time, were fixed steadily on him, and at length disappeared." Innumerable were the antics it played. Once it purred like a cat; beat the children's legs black and blue; put a long spike into Mr. Mompesson's bed, and a knife into his mother's; filled the porringers with ashes; hid a Bible under the grate; and turned the money black in people's pockets. "One night," said Mr. Mompesson, in a letter to Mr. Glanvil, "there were seven or eight of these devils in the shape of men, who, as soon as a gun was fired, would shuffle away into an arbour;" a circumstance which might have convinced Mr. Mompesson of the mortal nature of his persecutors, if he had not been of the number of those worse than blind, who shut their eyes and refuse to see.

In the mean time the drummer, the supposed cause of all the mischief, passed his time in Gloucester gaol, whither he had been committed as a rogue and a vagabond. Being visited one day by some person from the neighbourhood of Tedworth, he asked what was the news in Wiltshire, and whether people did not talk a great deal about a drumming in a gentleman's house there? The visitor replied that he heard of nothing else; upon which the drummer observed, "I have done it; I have thus plagued him; and he shall never be quiet until he hath made me satisfaction for taking away my drum." No doubt the fellow, who seems to have been a gipsy, spoke the truth, and that the gang of which he was a member knew more about the noises at Mr. Mompesson's house than any body else. Upon these words, however, he was brought to trial at Salisbury for witchcraft; and, being found guilty, was sentenced to transportation; a sentence which, for its leniency, excited no little wonder in that age, when such an accusation, whether proved or not, generally insured the stake or the gibbet. Glanvil says that the noises ceased immediately the drummer was sent beyond the seas; but that, somehow or other, he managed to return from transportation; "by raising storms and affrighting the seamen, it was said;" when the disturbances were forthwith renewed, and continued at intervals for several years. Certainly, if the confederates of this roving gipsy were so pertinacious in tormenting poor weak Mr. Mompesson, their pertinacity is a most extraordinary instance of what revenge is capable of. It was believed by many, at the time, that Mr. Mompesson himself was privy to the whole matter, and permitted and encouraged these tricks in his house for the sake of notoriety; but it seems more probable that the gipsies were the real delinquents, and that Mr. Mompesson was as much alarmed and bewildered as his credulous neighbours, whose excited imaginations conjured up no small portion of these stories,

"Which rolled, and as they rolled grew larger visibly."

Many instances of a similar kind, during the seventeenth century, might be gleaned from Glanvil and other writers of that period; but they do not differ sufficiently from these to justify a detail of them. The most famous of all haunted houses acquired its notoriety much nearer our own time; and the circumstances connected with it are so curious, and afford so fair a specimen of the easy credulity even of well-informed and sensible people, as to merit a little notice in this chapter. The Cock-Lane Ghost, as it was called, kept London in commotion for a considerable time, and was the theme of conversation among the learned and the illiterate, and in every circle, from that of the prince to that of the peasant.

The haunted house in Cock Lane.

At the commencement of the year 1760, there resided in Cock Lane, near West Smithfield, in the house of one Parsons, the parish clerk of St. Sepulchre's, a stockbroker, named Kent. The wife of this gentleman had died in child-bed during the previous year, and his sister-in-law, Miss Fanny, had arrived from Norfolk to keep his house for him. They soon conceived a mutual affection, and each of them made a will in the other's favour. They lived some months in the house of Parsons, who, being a needy man, borrowed money of his lodger. Some difference arose betwixt them, and Mr. Kent left the house, and instituted legal proceedings against the parish-clerk for the recovery of his money.

While this matter was yet pending, Miss Fanny was suddenly taken ill of the small-pox; and, notwithstanding every care and attention, she died in a few days, and was buried in a vault under Clerkenwell church. Parsons now began to hint that the poor lady had come unfairly by her death, and that Mr. Kent was accessory to it, from his too great eagerness to enter into possession of the property she had bequeathed him. Nothing further was said for nearly two years; but it would appear that Parsons was of so revengeful a character, that he had never forgotten or forgiven his differences with Mr. Kent, and the indignity of having been sued for the borrowed money. The strong passions of pride and avarice were silently at work during all that interval, hatching schemes of revenge, but dismissing them one after the other as impracticable, until, at last, a notable one suggested itself. About the beginning of the year 1762, the alarm was spread over all the neighbourhood of Cock Lane, that the house of Parsons was haunted by the ghost of poor Fanny, and that the daughter of Parsons, a girl about twelve years of age, had several times seen and conversed with the spirit, who had, moreover, informed her, that she had not died of the small-pox, as was currently reported, but of poison, administered by Mr. Kent. Parsons, who originated, took good care to countenance these reports; and, in answer to numerous inquiries, said his house was every night, and had been for two years, in fact, ever since the death of Fanny, troubled by a loud knocking at the doors and in the walls. Having thus prepared the ignorant and credulous neighbours to believe or exaggerate for themselves what he had told them, he sent for a gentleman of a higher class in life, to come and witness these extraordinary occurrences. The gentleman came accordingly, and found the daughter of Parsons, to whom the spirit alone appeared, and whom alone it answered, in bed, trembling violently, having just seen the ghost, and been again informed that she had died from poison. A loud knocking was also heard from every part of the chamber, which so mystified the not very clear understanding of the visitor, that he departed, afraid to doubt and ashamed to believe, but with a promise to bring the clergyman of the parish and several other gentlemen on the following day, to report upon the mystery.

On the following night he returned, bringing with him three clergymen, and about twenty other persons, including two negroes, when, upon a consultation with Parsons, they resolved to sit up the whole night, and await the ghost's arrival. It was then explained by Parsons, that although the ghost would never render itself visible to any body but his daughter, it had no objection to answer the questions that might be put to it, by any person present, and that it expressed an affirmation by one knock, a negative by two, and its displeasure by a kind of scratching. The child was then put into bed along with her sister, and the clergymen examined the bed and bed-clothes to satisfy themselves that no trick was played, by knocking upon any substance concealed among the clothes. As on the previous night, the bed was observed to shake violently.

Room in the haunted house in Cock Lane.[44]

After some hours, during which they all waited with exemplary patience, the mysterious knocking was heard in the wall, and the child declared that she saw the ghost of poor Fanny. The following questions were then gravely put by the clergyman, through the medium of one Mary Frazer, the servant of Parsons, and to whom it was said the deceased lady had been much attached. The answers were in the usual fashion, by a knock or knocks:

"Do you make this disturbance on account of the ill-usage you received from Mr. Kent?" – "Yes."

"Were you brought to an untimely end by poison?" – "Yes."

"How was the poison administered, in beer or purl?" – "In purl."

"How long was that before your death?" – "About three hours."

"Can your former servant, Carrots, give any information about the poison?" – "Yes."

"Are you Kent's wife's sister?" – "Yes."

"Were you married to Kent after your sister's death?" – "No."

"Was any body else, besides Kent, concerned in your murder?" – "No."

"Can you, if you like, appear visibly to any one?" – "Yes."

"Will you do so?" – "Yes."

"Can you go out of this house?" – "Yes."

"Is it your intention to follow this child about every where?" – "Yes."

"Are you pleased in being asked these questions?" – "Yes."

"Does it ease your troubled soul?" – "Yes."

[Here there was heard a mysterious noise, which some wiseacre present compared to the fluttering of wings.]

"How long before your death did you tell your servant, Carrots, that you were poisoned? An hour?" – "Yes."

[Carrots, who was present, was appealed to; but she stated positively that such was not the fact, as the deceased was quite speechless an hour before her death. This shook the faith of some of the spectators, but the examination was allowed to continue.]

"How long did Carrots live with you?" – "Three or four days."

[Carrots was again appealed to, and said that this was true.]

"If Mr. Kent is arrested for this murder, will he confess?" – "Yes."

"Would your soul be at rest if he were hanged for it?" – "Yes."

"Will he be hanged for it?" – "Yes."

"How long a time first?" – "Three years."

"How many clergymen are there in this room?" – "Three."

"How many negroes?" – "Two."

"Is this watch (held up by one of the clergymen) white?" – "No."

"Is it yellow?" – "No."

"Is it blue?" – "No."

"Is it black?" – "Yes."

[The watch was in a black shagreen case.]

"At what time this morning will you take your departure?"

The answer to this question was four knocks, very distinctly heard by every person present; and accordingly, at four o'clock precisely the ghost took its departure to the Wheatsheaf public-house close by, where it frightened mine host and his lady almost out of their wits, by knocking in the ceiling right above their bed.

The rumour of these occurrences very soon spread over London, and every day Cock Lane was rendered impassable by the crowds of people who assembled around the house of the parish clerk, in expectation of either seeing the ghost or of hearing the mysterious knocks. It was at last found necessary, so clamorous were they for admission within the haunted precincts, to admit those only who would pay a certain fee, an arrangement which was very convenient to the needy and money-loving Mr. Parsons. Indeed, things had taken a turn greatly to his satisfaction; he not only had his revenge, but he made a profit out of it. The ghost, in consequence, played its antics every night, to the great amusement of many hundreds of people and the great perplexity of a still greater number.

Unhappily, however, for the parish clerk, the ghost was induced to make some promises which were the means of utterly destroying its reputation. It promised, in answer to the questions of the Rev. Mr. Aldritch of Clerkenwell, that it would not only follow the little Miss Parsons wherever she went, but would also attend him, or any other gentleman, into the vault under St. John's Church, where the body of the murdered woman was deposited, and would there give notice of its presence by a distinct knock upon the coffin. As a preliminary, the girl was conveyed to the house of Mr. Aldritch near the church, where a large party of ladies and gentlemen, eminent for their acquirements, their rank, or their wealth, had assembled. About ten o'clock on the night of the first of February, the girl having been brought from Cock Lane in a coach, was put to bed by several ladies in the house of Mr. Aldritch; a strict examination having been previously made that nothing was hidden in the bed-clothes. While the gentlemen in an adjoining chamber were deliberating whether they should proceed in a body to the vault, they were summoned into the bedroom by the ladies, who affirmed, in great alarm, that the ghost was come, and that they heard the knocks and scratches. The gentlemen entered accordingly, with a determination to suffer no deception. The little girl, on being asked whether she saw the ghost, replied, "No; but she felt it on her back like a mouse." She was then required to put her hands out of bed, and they being held by some of the ladies, the spirit was summoned in the usual manner to answer, if it were in the room. The question was several times put with great solemnity; but the customary knock was not heard in reply in the walls, neither was there any scratching. The ghost was then asked to render itself visible, but it did not choose to grant the request. It was next solicited to give some token of its presence by a sound of any sort, or by touching the hand or cheek of any lady or gentleman in the room; but even with this request the ghost would not comply.

There was now a considerable pause, and one of the clergymen went down stairs to interrogate the father of the girl, who was waiting the result of the experiment. He positively denied that there was any deception, and even went so far as to say that he himself, upon one occasion, had seen and conversed with the awful ghost. This having been communicated to the company, it was unanimously resolved to give the ghost another trial; and the clergyman called out in a loud voice to the supposed spirit, that the gentleman to whom it had promised to appear in the vault was about to repair to that place, where he claimed the fulfilment of its promise. At one hour after midnight they all proceeded to the church, and the gentleman in question, with another, entered the vault alone, and took up their position alongside of the coffin of poor Fanny. The ghost was then summoned to appear, but it appeared not; it was summoned to knock, but it knocked not; it was summoned to scratch, but it scratched not; and the two retired from the vault, with a firm belief that the whole business was a deception practised by Parsons and his daughter. There were others, however, who did not wish to jump so hastily to a conclusion, and who suggested that they were perhaps trifling with this awful and supernatural being, which, being offended with them for their presumption, would not condescend to answer them. Again, after serious consultation, it was agreed on all hands that if the ghost answered any body at all, it would answer Mr. Kent, the supposed murderer; and he was accordingly requested to go down into the vault. He went with several others, and summoned the ghost to answer whether he had indeed poisoned her. There being no answer, the question was put by Mr. Aldritch, who conjured it, if it were indeed a spirit, to end their doubts, make a sign of its presence, and point out the guilty person. There being still no answer for the space of half an hour, during which time all these boobies waited with the most praiseworthy perseverance, they returned to the house of Mr. Aldritch, and ordered the girl to get up and dress herself. She was strictly examined, but persisted in her statement that she used no deception, and that the ghost had really appeared to her.

So many persons had, by their openly expressed belief of the reality of the visitation, identified themselves with it, that Parsons and his family were far from being the only persons interested in the continuance of the delusion. The result of the experiment convinced most people; but these were not to be convinced by any evidence, however positive, and they therefore spread abroad the rumour, that the ghost had not appeared in the vault because Mr. Kent had taken care beforehand to have the coffin removed. That gentleman, whose position was a very painful one, immediately procured competent witnesses, in whose presence the vault was entered, and the coffin of poor Fanny opened. Their depositions were then published; and Mr. Kent indicted Parsons and his wife, his daughter, Mary Frazer the servant, the Rev. Mr. Moor, and a tradesman, two of the most prominent patrons of the deception, for a conspiracy. The trial came on in the Court of King's Bench, on the 10th of July, before Lord Chief-Justice Mansfield, when, after an investigation which lasted twelve hours, the whole of the conspirators were found guilty. The Rev. Mr. Moor and his friend were severely reprimanded in open court, and recommended to make some pecuniary compensation to the prosecutor for the aspersions they had been instrumental in throwing upon his character. Parsons was sentenced to stand three times in the pillory, and to be imprisoned for two years; his wife to one year's, and his servant to six months' imprisonment in the Bridewell. A printer, who had been employed by them to publish an account of the proceedings for their profit, was also fined fifty pounds, and discharged.

The precise manner in which the deception was carried on has never been explained. The knocking in the wall appears to have been the work of Parsons' wife, while the scratching part of the business was left to the little girl. That any contrivance so clumsy could have deceived any body cannot fail to excite our wonder. But thus it always is. If two or three persons can only be found to take the lead in any absurdity, however great, there is sure to be plenty of imitators. Like sheep in a field, if one clears the stile, the rest will follow.

About ten years afterwards, London was again alarmed by the story of a haunted house. Stockwell, near Vauxhall, the scene of the antics of this new ghost, became almost as celebrated in the annals of superstition as Cock Lane. Mrs. Golding, an elderly lady, who resided alone with her servant, Anne Robinson, was sorely surprised on the evening of Twelfth-Day, 1772, to observe a most extraordinary commotion among her crockery. Cups and saucers rattled down the chimney — pots and pans were whirled down stairs, or through the windows; and hams, cheeses, and loaves of bread disported themselves upon the floor as if the devil were in them. This, at least, was the conclusion that Mrs. Golding came to; and being greatly alarmed, she invited some of her neighbours to stay with her, and protect her from the evil one. Their presence, however, did not put a stop to the insurrection of china, and every room in the house was in a short time strewed with the fragments. The chairs and tables joined, at last, in the tumult, and things looked altogether so serious and inexplicable, that the neighbours, dreading that the house itself would next be seized with a fit of motion, and tumble about their ears, left poor Mrs. Golding to bear the brunt of it by herself. The ghost in this case was solemnly remonstrated with, and urged to take its departure; but the demolition continuing as great as before, Mrs. Golding finally made up her mind to quit the house altogether. She took refuge with Anne Robinson in the house of a neighbour; but his glass and crockery being immediately subjected to the same persecution, he was reluctantly compelled to give her notice to quit. The old lady thus forced back to her own house, endured the disturbance for some days longer, when suspecting that Anne Robinson was the cause of all the mischief, she dismissed her from her service. The extraordinary appearances immediately ceased, and were never afterwards renewed; a fact which is of itself sufficient to point out the real disturber. A long time afterwards, Anne Robinson confessed the whole matter to the Reverend Mr. Brayfield. This gentleman confided the story to Mr. Hone, who has published an explanation of the mystery. Anne, it appears, was anxious to have a clear house, to carry on an intrigue with her lover, and resorted to this trick to effect her purpose. She placed the china on the shelves in such a manner that it fell on the slightest motion, and attached horse-hairs to other articles, so that she could jerk them down from an adjoining room without being perceived by any one. She was exceedingly dexterous at this sort of work, and would have proved a formidable rival to many a juggler by profession. A full explanation of the whole affair may be found in the *Every-day Book*.

The latest instance of the popular panic occasioned by a house supposed to be haunted, occurred in Scotland, in the winter of the year 1838. On the 5th of December, the inmates of the farm-house of Baldarroch, in the district of Banchory, Aberdeenshire, were alarmed by observing a great number of sticks, pebble-stones, and clods of earth flying about their yard and premises. They endeavoured, but in vain, to discover who was the delin-quent; and the shower of stones continuing for five days in succession, they came at last to the conclusion that the devil and his imps were alone the cause of it. The rumour soon spread over all that part of the country, and hundreds of persons came from far and near to witness the antics of the devils of Baldarroch. After the fifth day, the shower of clods and stones ceased on the outside of the premises, and the scene shifted to the interior. Spoons, knives, plates, mustard-pots, rolling-pins, and flat-irons appeared suddenly endued with the power of self-motion, and were whirled from room to room, and rattled down the chim-neys in a manner which nobody could account for. The lid of a mustard-pot was put into a cupboard by the servant-girl in the presence of scores of people, and in a few minutes afterwards came bouncing down the chimney, to the consternation of every body. There was also a tremendous knocking at the doors and on the roof, and pieces of stick and pebble-stones rattled against the windows and broke them. The whole neighbourhood was a scene of alarm; and not only the vulgar, but persons of educa-tion, respectable farmers, within a circle of twenty miles, ex-pressed their belief in the supernatural character of these events, and offered up devout prayers to be preserved from the machi-nations of the Evil One. The note of fear being once sounded, the visitors, as is generally the case in all tales of wonder, strove with each other who should witness the most extraordinary occurrences; and within a week, it was generally believed in the parishes of Banchory-Ternan, Drumoak, Durris, Kincardine-O'Neil, and all the circumjacent districts of Mearns and Aberdeenshire, that the devil had been seen in the act of hammering upon the house-top of Baldarroch. One old man asserted positively that, one night, after having been to see the strange gambols of the knives and mustard-pots, he met the phantom of a great black man, "who wheeled round his head with a whizzing noise, making a wind about his ears that almost blew his bonnet off," and that he was haunted by him in this manner for three miles. It was also affirmed and believed, that all horses and dogs that approached this enchanted ground were immediately affected; that a gentleman, slow of faith, had been cured of his incredulity by meeting the butter-churn jumping in at the door as he himself was going out; that the roofs of houses had been torn off, and that several ricks in the corn-yard had danced a quadrille together, to the sound of the devil's bagpipes re-echoing from the mountain-tops. The women in the family of the persecuted farmer of Baldarroch also kept their tongues in perpetual motion; swelling with their strange stories the tide of popular wonder. The goodwife herself, and all her servants, said that, whenever they went to bed, they were attacked with stones and other missiles, some of which came below the blankets and gently tapped their toes. One evening, a shoe suddenly darted across a garret where some labourers were sitting, and one of the men, who attempted to catch it, swore positively that it was so hot and heavy he was unable to hold it. It was also said that the bearbeater (a sort of mortar used to bruise barley in) — an object of such weight that it requires several men to move it — spontaneously left the barn and flew over the house-top, alighting at the feet of one of the servant-maids, and hitting her, but without hurting her in the least, or even causing her any alarm; it being a fact well known to her, that all objects thus thrown about by the devil lost their specific gravity, and could harm nobody, even though they fell upon a person's head.

Among the persons drawn to Baldarroch by these occurrences were the heritor, the minister, and all the elders of the Kirk, under whose superintendence an investigation was immediately commenced. Their proceedings were not promulgated for some days; and, in the mean time, rumour continued to travel through all the Highlands, magnifying each mysterious incident the farther it got from home. It was said, that when the goodwife put her potato-pot on the fire, each potato, as the water boiled, changed into a demon, and grinned horribly at her as she lifted the lid; that not only chairs and tables, but carrots and turnips, skipped along the floor in the merriest manner imaginable; that shoes and boots went through all the evolutions of the Highland fling without any visible wearers directing their motions; and that a piece of meat detached itself from the hook on which it hung in the pantry, and placed itself before the fire, whence all the efforts of the people of the house were unable to remove it until it was thoroughly roasted; and that it then flew up the chimney with a tremendous bang. At Baldarroch itself the belief was not quite so extravagant; but the farmer was so convinced that the devil and his imps were alone the cause of all the disturbance, that he travelled a distance of forty miles to an old conjuror, named Willie Foreman, to induce him, for a handsome fee, to remove the enchantment from his property. There were, of course, some sensible and educated people, who, after stripping the stories circulated of their exaggeration, attributed all the rest to one or other of two causes; first, that some gipsies, or strolling mendicants, hidden in the neighbouring plantation, were amusing themselves by working on the credulity of the country people; or, secondly, that the inmates of Baldarroch carried on this deception themselves, for some reason or other, which was not very clear to any body. The last opinion gained but few believers, as the farmer and his family were much respected; and so many persons had, in the most open manner, expressed their belief in the supernatural agency, that they did not like to stultify themselves by confessing that they had been deceived.

At last, after a fortnight's continuance of the noises, the whole trick was discovered. The two servant lasses were strictly examined, and then committed to prison. It appeared that they were alone at the bottom of the whole affair, and that the extraordinary alarm and credulity of their master and mistress, in the first instance, and of the neighbours and country people afterwards, made their task comparatively easy. A little common dexterity was all they had used; and, being themselves unsuspected, they swelled the alarm by the wonderful stories they invented. It was they who loosened the bricks in the chimneys, and placed the dishes in such a manner on the shelves, that they fell on the slightest motion. In short, they played the same tricks as those used by the servant girl at Stockwell, with the same results, and for the same purpose — the gratification of a love of mischief. They were no sooner secured in the county gaol than the noises ceased, and most people were convinced that human agency alone had worked all the wonder. Some few of the most devoutly superstitious still held out in their first belief, and refused to listen to any explanation.

These tales of haunted houses, especially those of the last and present century, however they may make us blush for popular folly, are yet gratifying in their results; for they shew that society has made a vast improvement. Had Parsons and his wife, and the other contrivers of the Cock Lane deception, lived two hundred years earlier, they would not perhaps have found a greater number of dupes, but they would have been hanged as witches, instead of being imprisoned as vagabonds. The ingenious Anne Robinson and the sly lasses of Baldarroch would doubtless have met a similar fate. Thus it is pleasant to reflect, that though there may be as much folly and credulity in the world as ever in one class of society, there is more wisdom and mercy in another than ever were known before. Lawgivers, by blotting from the statute-book the absurd or sanguinary enactments of their predecessors, have made one step towards teaching the people. It is to be hoped that the day is not far distant when lawgivers will teach the people by some more direct means, and prevent the recurrence of delusions like these, and many worse, which might be cited, by securing to every child born within their dominions an education in accordance with the advancing state of civilisation. If ghosts and witches are not yet altogether exploded, it is the fault, not so much of the ignorant people, as of the law and the government that have neglected to enlighten them.

Chapter 5.

Popular Follies of Great Cities.

La faridondaine – la faridondon,
Vive la faridondaine!

— *Beranger.*

The popular humours of a great city are a never-failing source of amusement to the man whose sympathies are hospitable enough to embrace all his kind, and who, refined though he may be himself, will not sneer at the humble wit or grotesque peculiarities of the boozing mechanic, the squalid beggar, the vicious urchin, and all the motley group of the idle, the reckless, and the imitative that swarm in the alleys and broadways of a metropolis. He who walks through a great city to find subjects for weeping, may find plenty at every corner to wring his heart; but let such a man walk on his course, and enjoy his grief alone – we are not of those who would accompany him. The miseries of us poor earth-dwellers gain no alleviation from the sympathy of those who merely hunt them out to be pathetic over them. The weeping philosopher too often impairs his eyesight by his woe, and becomes unable from his tears to see the remedies for the evils which he deplores. Thus it will often be found that the man of no tears is the truest philanthropist, as he is the best physician who wears a cheerful face, even in the worst of cases.

So many pens have been employed to point out the miseries, and so many to condemn the crimes and vices, and more serious follies of the multitude, that ours shall not increase the number, at least in this chapter. Our present task shall be less ungracious, and wandering through the busy haunts of great cities, we shall seek only for amusement, and note as we pass a few of the harmless follies and whimsies of the poor.

And, first of all, walk where we will, we cannot help hearing from every side a phrase repeated with delight, and received with laughter, by men with hard hands and dirty faces, by saucy butcher lads and errand-boys, by loose women, by hackney coachmen, cabriolet-drivers, and idle fellows who loiter at the corners of streets. Not one utters this phrase without producing a laugh from all within hearing. It seems applicable to every circumstance, and is the universal answer to every question; in short, it is the favourite slang phrase of the day, a phrase that, while its brief season of popularity lasts, throws a dash of fun and frolicsomeness over the existence of squalid poverty and ill-requited labour, and gives them reason to laugh as well as their more fortunate fellows in a higher stage of society.

London is peculiarly fertile in this sort of phrases, which spring up suddenly, no one knows exactly in what spot, and pervade the whole population in a few hours, no one knows how. Many years ago the favourite phrase (for, though but a monosyllable, it was a phrase in itself) was Quoz. This odd word took the fancy of the multitude in an extraordinary degree, and very soon acquired an almost boundless meaning. When vulgar wit wished to mark its incredulity, and raise a laugh at the same time, there was no resource so sure as this popular piece of slang. When a man was asked a favour which he did not choose to grant, he marked his sense of the suitor's unparalleled presumption by exclaiming *Quoz!* When a mischievous urchin wished to annoy a passenger, and create mirth for his comrades, he looked him in the face, and cried out *Quoz!* and the exclamation never failed in its object. When a disputant was desirous of throwing a doubt upon the veracity of his opponent, and getting summarily rid of an argument which he could not overturn, he uttered the word *Quoz*, with a contemptuous curl of his lip, and an impatient shrug of his shoulders. The universal monosyllable conveyed all his meaning, and not only told his opponent that he lied, but that he erred egregiously if he thought that any one was such a nincompoop as to believe him. Every alehouse resounded with *Quoz*; every street-corner was noisy with it, and every wall for miles around was chalked with it.

But, like all other earthly things, *Quoz* had its season, and passed away as suddenly as it arose, never again to be the pet and the idol of the populace. A new claimant drove it from its place, and held undisputed sway till, in its turn, it was hurled from its pre-eminence, and a successor appointed in its stead.

"What a shocking bad hat!" was the phrase that was next in vogue. No sooner had it become universal, than thousands of idle but sharp eyes were on the watch for the passenger whose hat shewed any signs, however slight, of ancient service. Immediately the cry arose, and, like the war-whoop of the Indians, was repeated by a hundred discordant throats. He was a wise man who, finding himself under these circumstances "the observed of all observers," bore his honours meekly. He who shewed symptoms of ill-feeling at the imputations cast upon his hat, only brought upon himself redoubled notice. The mob soon perceive whether a man is irritable, and, if of their own class, they love to make sport of him. When such a man, and with such a hat, passed in those days through a crowded neighbourhood, he might think himself fortunate if his annoyances were confined to the shouts and cries of the populace. The obnoxious hat was often snatched from his head and thrown into the gutter by some practical joker, and then raised, covered with mud, upon the end of a stick, for the admiration of the spectators, who held their sides with laughter, and exclaimed, in the pauses of their mirth, *"Oh, what a shocking bad hat!"* *"What a shocking bad hat!"* Many a nervous poor man, whose purse could but ill spare the outlay, doubtless purchased a new hat before the time, in order to avoid exposure in this manner.

The origin of this singular saying, which made fun for the metropolis for months, is not involved in the same obscurity as that which shrouds the origin of *Quoz* and some others. There had been a hotly contested election for the borough of Southwark, and one of the candidates was an eminent hatter. This gentleman, in canvassing the electors, adopted a somewhat professional mode of conciliating their good-will, and of bribing them without letting them perceive that they were bribed. Whenever he called upon or met a voter whose hat was not of the best material, or, being so, had seen its best days, he invariably said, *"What a shocking bad hat you have got; call at my warehouse, and you shall have a new one!"* Upon the day of election this circumstance was remembered, and his opponents made the most of it, by inciting the crowd to keep up an incessant cry of

"What a shocking bad hat!" all the time the honourable candidate was addressing them. From Southwark the phrase spread over all London, and reigned for a time the supreme slang of the season.

Hookey Walker, derived from the chorus of a popular ballad, was also high in favour at one time, and served, like its predecessor *Quoz*, to answer all questions. In the course of time, the latter word alone became the favourite, and was uttered with a peculiar drawl upon the first syllable, and a sharp turn upon the last. If a lively servant girl was importuned for a kiss by a fellow she did not care about, she cocked her little nose, and cried *"Walker!"* If a dustman asked his friend for the loan of a shilling, and his friend was either unable or unwilling to accommodate him, the probable answer he would receive was, *"Walker!"* If a drunken man was reeling about the streets, and a boy pulled his coat-tails, or a man knocked his hat over his eyes to make fun of him, the joke was always accompanied by the same exclamation. This lasted for two or three months, and *"Walker!"* walked off the stage, never more to be revived for the entertainment of that or any future generation.

The next phrase was a most preposterous one. Who invented it, how it arose, or where it was first heard, are alike unknown. Nothing about it is certain, but that for months it was *the* slang *par excellence* of the Londoners, and afforded them a vast gratification. *"There he goes with his eye out!"* or *"There she goes with her eye out!"* as the sex of the party alluded to might be, was in the mouth of every body who knew the town. The sober part of the community were as much puzzled by this unaccountable saying as the vulgar were delighted with it. The wise thought it very foolish, but the many thought it very funny, and the idle amused themselves by chalking it upon walls, or scribbling it upon monuments. But "all that's bright must fade," even in slang. The people grew tired of their hobby, and *"There he goes with his eye out!"* was heard no more in its accustomed haunts.

Another very odd phrase came into repute in a brief space afterwards, in the form of the impertinent and not universally apposite query, *"Has your mother sold her mangle?"* But its popularity was not of that boisterous and cordial kind which ensures a long continuance of favour. What tended to impede its progress was, that it could not be well applied to the older portions of society. It consequently ran but a brief career, and then sank into oblivion. Its successor enjoyed a more extended fame, and laid its foundations so deep, that years and changing fashions have not sufficed to eradicate it. This phrase was *"Flare up!"* and it is, even now, a colloquialism in common use. It took its rise in the time of the Reform riots, when Bristol was nearly half burned by the infuriated populace. The flames were said to have *flared up* in the devoted city. Whether there was any thing peculiarly captivating in the sound, or in the idea of these words, is hard to say; but whatever was the reason, it tickled the mob-fancy mightily, and drove all other slang out of the field before it. Nothing was to be heard all over London but *"flare up!"* It answered all questions, settled all disputes, was applied to all persons, all things, and all circumstances, and became suddenly the most comprehensive phrase in the English language. The man who had overstepped the bounds of decorum in his speech was said to have *flared up*; he who had paid visits too repeated to the gin-shop, and got damaged in consequence, had *flared up*. To put one's self into a passion; to stroll out on a nocturnal frolic, and alarm a neighbourhood, or to create a disturbance in any shape, was to *flare up*. A lovers' quarrel was a *flare up*; so was a boxing-match between two blackguards in the streets; and the preachers of sedition and revolution recommended the English nation to *flare up*, like the French. So great a favourite was the word, that people loved to repeat it for its very sound. They delighted apparently in hearing their own organs articulate it; and labouring men, when none who could respond to the call were within hearing, would often startle the aristocratic echoes of the West by the well-known slang phrase of the East. Even in the dead hours of the night, the ears of those who watched late, or who could not sleep, were saluted with the same sound. The drunkard reeling home shewed that he was still a man and a citizen, by calling *"flare up!"* in the pauses of his hiccough. Drink had deprived him of the power of arranging all other ideas; his intellect was sunk to the level of the brute's; but he clung to humanity by the one last link of the popular cry. While he could vociferate that sound, he had rights as an Englishman, and would not sleep in a gutter, like a dog! Onwards he went, disturbing quiet streets and comfortable people by his whoop, till exhausted nature could support him no more, and he rolled powerless into the road. When, in due time afterwards, the policeman stumbled upon him as he lay, that guardian of the peace turned the full light of his lantern on his face, and exclaimed, "Here's a poor devil who has been *flaring up!*" Then came the stretcher, on which the victim of deep potations was carried to the watch-house, and pitched into a dirty cell, among a score of wretches about as far gone as himself, who saluted their new comrade by a loud, long shout of *flare up!*

So universal was this phrase, and so enduring seemed its popularity, that a speculator, who knew not the evanescence of slang, established a weekly newspaper under its name. But he was like the man who built his house upon the sand; his foundation gave way under him, and the phrase and the newspaper were washed into the mighty sea of the things that were. The people grew at last weary of the monotony, and "*flare up*" became vulgar even among them. Gradually it was left to little boys who did not know the world, and in process of time sank altogether into neglect. It is now heard no more as a piece of popular slang; but the words are still used to signify any sudden outburst either of fire, disturbance, or ill-nature.

The next phrase that enjoyed the favour of the million was less concise, and seems to have been originally aimed against precocious youths who gave themselves the airs of manhood before their time. "*Does your mother know you're out?*" was the provoking query addressed to young men of more than reasonable swagger, who smoked cigars in the streets, and wore false whiskers to look irresistible. We have seen many a conceited fellow who could not suffer a woman to pass him without staring her out of countenance, reduced at once into his natural insignificance by the mere utterance of this phrase. Apprentice lads and shopmen in their Sunday clothes held the words in abhorrence, and looked fierce when they were applied to them. Altogether the phrase had a very salutary effect, and in a thousand instances shewed young Vanity that it was not half so pretty and engaging as it thought itself. What rendered it so provoking was the doubt it implied as to the capability of self-guidance possessed by the individual to whom it was addressed. "*Does your mother know you're out?*" was a query of mock concern and solicitude, implying regret and concern that one so young and inexperienced in the ways of a great city should be allowed to wander abroad without the guidance of a parent. Hence the great wrath of those who verged on manhood, but had not reached it, whenever they were made the subject of it. Even older heads did not like it; and the heir of a ducal house, and inheritor of a warrior's name, to whom they were applied by a cabriolet-driver who was ignorant of his rank, was so indignant at the affront, that he summoned the offender before the magisterial bench. The fellow had wished to impose upon his lordship by asking double the fare he was entitled to; and when his lordship resisted the demand, he was insultingly asked "if his mother knew he was out?" All the drivers on the stand joined in the query, and his lordship was fain to escape their laughter by walking away with as much haste as his dignity would allow. The man pleaded ignorance that his customer was a lord, but offended justice fined him for his mistake.

When this phrase had numbered its appointed days, it died away like its predecessors, and "*Who are you?*" reigned in its stead. This new favourite, like a mushroom, seems to have sprung up in a night, or, like a frog in Cheapside, to have come down in a sudden shower. One day it was unheard, unknown, uninvented; the next it pervaded London. Every alley resounded with it; every highway was musical with it,

"*And street to street, and lane to lane flung back*
The one unvarying cry."

The phrase was uttered quickly, and with a sharp sound upon the first and last words, leaving the middle one little more than an aspiration. Like all its compeers which had been extensively popular, it was applicable to almost every variety of circumstance. The lovers of a plain answer to a plain question did not like it at all. Insolence made use of it to give offence; ignorance to avoid exposing itself; and waggery to create laughter. Every new comer into an alehouse tap-room was asked unceremoniously, "*Who are you?*" and if he looked foolish, scratched his head, and did not know what to reply, shouts of boisterous merriment resounded on every side. An authoritative disputant was not unfrequently put down, and presumption of every kind checked by the same query. When its popularity was at its height, a gentleman, feeling the hand of a thief in his pocket, turned suddenly round and caught him in the act, exclaiming, "*Who are you?*" The mob which gathered round applauded to the very echo, and thought it the most capital joke they had ever heard, the very acmé of wit, the very essence of humour. Another circumstance of a similar kind gave an additional fillip to the phrase, and infused new life and vigour into it just as it was dying away. The scene occurred in the chief criminal court of the kingdom. A prisoner stood at the bar; the offence with which he had been charged was clearly proved against him; his counsel had been heard, not in his defence, but in extenuation, insisting upon his previous good life and character as reasons for the lenity of the court. "And where are your witnesses?" inquired the learned judge who presided. "Please you, my lord, I knows the prisoner at the bar, and a more honester feller never breathed," said a rough voice in the gallery. The officers of the court looked aghast, and the strangers tittered with ill-suppressed laughter. "*Who are you?*" said the judge, looking suddenly up, but with imperturbable gravity. The court was convulsed; the titter broke out into a laugh; and it was several minutes before silence and decorum could be restored. When the ushers recovered their self-possession, they made diligent search for the profane transgressor; but he was not to be found. Nobody knew him; nobody had seen him. After a while the business of the court again proceeded. The next prisoner brought up for trial augured favourably of his prospects when he learned that the solemn lips of the representative of justice had uttered the popular phrase as if he felt and appreciated it. There was no fear that such a judge would use undue severity. His heart was with the people; he understood their language and their manners, and would make allowances for the temptations which drove them into crime. So thought many of the prisoners, if we may infer it from the fact that the learned judge suddenly acquired an immense increase of popularity. The praise of his wit was in every mouth, and "*Who are you?*" renewed its lease, and remained in possession of public favour for another term in consequence.

But it must not be supposed that there were no interregna between the dominion of one slang phrase and another. They did not arise in one long line of unbroken succession, but shared with song the possession of popular favour. Thus, when the people were in the mood for music, slang advanced its claims to no purpose; and when they were inclined for slang, the sweet voice of music wooed them in vain. About thirty years ago London resounded with one chorus, with the love of which every body seemed to be smitten. Girls and boys, young men and old, maidens and wives and widows, were all alike musical. There was an absolute mania for singing; and the worst of it was, that, like good Father Philip in the romance of *The Monastery*, they seemed utterly unable to change their tune. "Cherry ripe!" "Cherry ripe!" was the universal cry of all the idle in the town. Every unmelodious voice gave utterance to it; every crazy fiddle, every cracked flute, every wheezy pipe, every street-organ was heard in the same strain, until studious and quiet men stopped their ears in desperation, or fled miles away into the fields or woodlands to be at peace. This plague lasted for a twelvemonth, until the very name of cherries became an abomination in the land. At last the excitement wore itself away, and the tide of favour set in a new direction. Whether it was another song or a slang phrase is difficult to determine at this distance of time; but certain it is, that very shortly afterwards people went mad upon a dramatic subject, and nothing was to be heard of but "*Tommy and Jerry.*" Verbal wit had amused the multitude long enough, and they became more practical in their recreation. Every youth on the town was seized with the fierce desire of distinguishing himself by knocking down the "*charlies*," being locked up all night in a watch-house, or kicking up a row among loose women and blackguard men in the low dens of St. Giles's. Imitative boys vied with their elders in similar exploits, until this unworthy passion (for such it was) had lasted, like other follies, its appointed time, and the town became merry after another fashion. It was next thought the height of vulgar wit to answer all questions by placing the point of the thumb upon the tip of the nose, and twirling the fingers in the air. If one man wished to insult or annoy another, he had only to make use of this cabalistic sign in his face, and his object was accomplished. At every street-corner where a group was assembled, the spectator who was curious enough to observe their movements would be sure to see the fingers of some of them at their noses, either as a mark of incredulity, surprise, refusal, or mockery, before he had watched two minutes. There is some remnant of this absurd custom to be seen to this day; but it is thought low even among the vulgar.

About sixteen years ago, London became again most preposterously musical. The *vox populi* wore itself hoarse by singing the praises of "The Sea, the Sea!" If a stranger (and a philosopher) had walked through London, and listened to the universal chorus, he might have constructed a very pretty theory upon the love of the English for the sea-service, and our acknowledged superiority over all other nations upon that element. "No wonder," he might have said, "that this people is invincible upon the ocean. The love of it mixes with their daily thoughts; they celebrate it even in the market-place; their street-minstrels excite charity by it; and high and low, young and old, male and female, chant *lo pæans* in its praise. Love is not honoured in the national songs of this warlike race—Bacchus is no god to them; they are men of sterner mould, and think only of 'the Sea, the Sea!' and the means of conquering upon it."

Such would, doubtless, have been his impression if he had taken the evidence only of his ears. Alas, in those days for the refined ears that *were* musical! great was their torture when discord, with its thousand diversities of tone, struck up this appalling anthem — there was no escape from it. The migratory minstrels of Savoy caught the strain, and pealed it down the long vistas of quiet streets, till their innermost and snuggest apartments re-echoed with the sound. Men were obliged to endure this crying evil for full six months, wearied to desperation, and made *sea*-sick on the dry land.

Several other songs sprang up in due succession, afterwards, but none of them, with the exception of one, entitled "All round my Hat," enjoyed any extraordinary share of favour, until an American actor introduced a vile song called "Jim Crow." The singer sang his verses in appropriate costume, with grotesque gesticulations, and a sudden whirl of his body at the close of each verse. It took the taste of the town immediately, and for months the ears of orderly people were stunned by the senseless chorus —

> *"Turn about and wheel about,*
> *And do just so —*
> *Turn about and wheel about,*
> *And jump, Jim Crow!"*

Street-minstrels blackened their faces in order to give proper effect to the verses; and fatherless urchins, who had to choose between thieving and singing for their livelihood, took the latter course, as likely to be the more profitable, as long as the public taste remained in that direction. The uncouth dance, its accompaniment, might be seen in its full perfection on market nights in any great thoroughfare; and the words of the song might be heard, piercing above all the din and buzz of the ever-moving multitude. He, the calm observer, who during the hey-day popularity of this doggrel,

> *"Sate beside the public way,*
> *Thick strewn with summer dust, and saw the stream*
> *Of people there was hurrying to and fro,*
> *Numerous as gnats upon the evening gleam,"*
> might have exclaimed with Shelley, that
> *"The million, with fierce song and maniac dance,*
> *Did rage around."*

The philosophic theorist we have already supposed soliloquising upon the English character, and forming his opinion of it from their exceeding love for a sea-song, might, if he had again dropped suddenly into London, have formed another very plausible theory to account for our unremitting efforts for the abolition of the slave-trade. "Benevolent people!" he might have said, "how unbounded are your sympathies! Your unhappy brethren of Africa, differing from you only in the colour of their skins, are so dear to you, and you begrudge so little the twenty millions you have paid on their behalf, that you love to have a memento of them continually in your sight. Jim Crow is the representative of that injured race, and as such is the idol of your populace! See how they all sing his praises! how they imitate his peculiarities! how they repeat his name in their moments of leisure and relaxation! They even carve images of him to adorn their hearths, that his cause and his sufferings may never be forgotten! Oh, philanthropic England! oh, vanguard of civilisation!"

Such are a few of the peculiarities of the London multitude, when no riot, no execution, no murder, no balloon, disturbs the even current of their thoughts. These are the whimsies of the mass — the harmless follies by which they unconsciously endeavour to lighten the load of care which presses upon their existence. The wise man, even though he smile at them, will not altogether withhold his sympathy, and will say, "Let them enjoy their slang phrases and their choruses if they will; and if they cannot be happy, at least let them be merry." To the Englishman, as well as to the Frenchman of whom Beranger sings, there may be some comfort in so small a thing as a song, and we may own with him that

> "Au peuple attristé
> Ce qui rendra la gaîté,
> C'est la GAUDRIOLE!
> O gué!
> C'est la GAUDRIOLE!"

Chapter 6.

Popular Admiration of Great Thieves..

Sherwood Forest.

Jack. Where shall we find such another set of practical philosophers,
who, to a man, are above the fear of death!
Wat. Sound men and true!
Robin. Of tried courage and indefatigable industry!
Ned. Who is there here that would not die for his friend?
Harry. Who is there here that would betray him for his interest?
Mat. Shew me a gang of courtiers that could say as much!
Dialogue of Thieves in the Beggar's Opera.

Whether it be that the multitude, feeling the pangs of poverty,
sympathise with the daring and ingenious depredators who take
away the rich man's superfluity, or whether it be the interest that
mankind in general feel for the records of perilous adventure, it
is certain that the populace of all countries look with admiration
upon great and successful thieves. Perhaps both these causes
combine to invest their career with charms in the popular eye.
Almost every country in Europe has its traditional thief, whose
exploits are recorded with all the graces of poetry, and whose
trespasses

"Are cited up in rhymes,
And sung by children in succeeding tunes."[45]

Those travellers who have made national manners and character-
istics their peculiar study, have often observed and remarked
upon this feeling. The learned Abbé le Blanc, who resided for
some time in England at the commencement of the eighteenth
century, says, in his amusing letters on the English and French
nations, that he continually met with Englishmen who were not
less vain in boasting of the success of their highwaymen than of
the bravery of their troops. Tales of their address, their cunning,
or their generosity, were in the mouths of every body, and a
noted thief was a kind of hero in high repute. He adds that the
mob, in all countries, being easily moved, look in general with
concern upon criminals going to the gallows; but an English mob
looked upon such scenes with extraordinary interest: they
delighted to see them go through their last trials with resolution,
and applauded those who were insensible enough to die as they
had lived, braving the justice both of God and men: such, he
might have added, as the noted robber Macpherson, of whom
the old ballad says:

> *"Sae rantingly, sae wantonly,*
> *Sae dauntingly gaed he:*
> *He played a spring, and danced it round*
> *Beneath the gallows tree."*

Among these traditional thieves the most noted in England, or
perhaps in any country, is Robin Hood, a name which popular
affection has encircled with a peculiar halo. "He robbed the rich
to give to the poor;" and his reward has been an immortality of
fame, a tithe of which would be thought more than sufficient to
recompense a benefactor of his species. Romance and poetry
have been emulous to make him all their own; and the forest of
Sherwood, in which he roamed with his merry men, armed with
their long bows, and clad in Lincoln green, has become the resort
of pilgrims, and a classic spot sacred to his memory. The few
virtues he had, which would have ensured him no praise if he
had been an honest man, have been blazoned forth by popular
renown during seven successive centuries, and will never be

forgotten while the English tongue endures. His charity to the poor, and his gallantry and respect for women, have made him the pre-eminent thief of all the world.

Among English thieves of a later date, who has not heard of Claude Duval, Dick Turpin, Jonathan Wild, and Jack Sheppard, those knights of the road and of the town, whose peculiar chivalry formed at once the dread and the delight of England during the eighteenth century? Turpin's fame is unknown to no portion of the male population of England after they have attained the age of ten. His wondrous ride from London to York has endeared him to the imagination of millions; his cruelty in placing an old woman upon a fire, to force her to tell him where she had hidden her money, is regarded as a good joke; and his proud bearing upon the scaffold is looked upon as a virtuous action. The Abbé le Blanc, writing in 1737, says he was continually entertained with stories of Turpin—how, when he robbed gentlemen, he would generously leave them enough to continue their journey, and exact a pledge from them never to inform against him, and how scrupulous such gentlemen were in keeping their word. He was one day told a story with which the relator was in the highest degree delighted. Turpin, or some other noted robber, stopped a man whom he knew to be very rich, with the usual salutation—"Your money or your life!" but not finding more than five or six guineas about him, he took the liberty of entreating him, in the most affable manner, never to come out so ill provided; adding that, if he fell in with him, and he had no more than such a paltry sum, he would give him a good licking. Another story, told by one of Turpin's admirers, was of a robbery he had committed upon a Mr. C. near Cambridge. He took from this gentleman his watch, his snuff-box, and all his money but two shillings, and, before he left him, required his word of honour that he would not cause him to be pursued or brought before a justice. The promise being given, they both parted very courteously. They afterwards met at Newmarket, and renewed their acquaintance. Mr. C. kept his word religiously; he not only refrained from giving Turpin into custody, but made a boast that he had fairly won some of his money back again in an honest way. Turpin offered to bet with him on some favourite horse, and Mr. C. accepted the wager with as good a grace as he could have done from the best gentleman in England. Turpin lost his bet and paid it immediately, and was so smitten with the generous behaviour of Mr. C., that he told him how deeply he regretted that the trifling affair which had happened between them did not permit them to drink together. The narrator of this anecdote was quite proud that England was the birthplace of such a highwayman.[46]

Not less familiar to the people of England is the career of Jack Sheppard, as brutal a ruffian as ever disgraced his country, but who has claims upon the popular admiration which are very generally acknowledged. He did not, like Robin Hood, plunder the rich to relieve the poor, nor rob with an uncouth sort of courtesy, like Turpin; but he escaped from Newgate with the fetters on his limbs. This achievement, more than once repeated, has encircled his felon brow with the wreath of immortality, and made him quite a pattern thief among the populace. He was no more than twenty-three years of age at the time of his execution, and he died much pitied by the crowd. His adventures were the sole topics of conversation for months; the print-shops were filled with his effigies, and a fine painting of him was made by Sir Richard Thornhill. The following complimentary verses to the artist appeared in the *British Journal* of November 28th, 1724:

> "Thornhill! 'tis thine to gild with fame
> Th' obscure, and raise the humble name;
> To make the form elude the grave,
> And Sheppard from oblivion save!
> Apelles Alexander drew –
> Cæsar is to Aurelius due;
> Cromwell in Lilly's works doth shine,
> And Sheppard, Thornhill, lives in thine!"

This was a very equivocal sort of compliment, and might have meant, that if Apelles were worthy to paint a monarch, Thornhill was worthy to paint a thief. But the artist did not view it in that light, nor did the public; for they considered the verses to be very neat, pointed, and flattering. So high was Jack's fame, that he was thought a very fit subject for the stage; and a pantomime entertainment, called "*Harlequin Jack Sheppard*," was devised by one Thurmond, and brought out with considerable success at Drury Lane Theatre. All the scenes were painted from nature, including the public-house that the robber frequented in Clare Market, and the condemned cell from which he had made his escape in Newgate.[47]

The Rev. Mr. Villette, the editor of the *Annals of Newgate*, published in 1754, relates a curious sermon, which he says a friend of his heard delivered by a street-preacher about the time of Jack's execution. The orator, after animadverting on the great care men took of their bodies, and the little care they bestowed upon their souls, continued as follows, by way of exemplifying the position: — "We have a remarkable instance of this in a notorious malefactor, well known by the name of Jack Sheppard. What amazing difficulties has he overcome! what astonishing things has he performed! and all for the sake of a stinking, miserable carcass, hardly worth the hanging! How dexterously did he pick the chain of his padlock with a crooked nail! how manfully he burst his fetters asunder, climb up the chimney, wrench out an iron bar, break his way through a stone wall, make the strong door of a dark entry fly before him, till he got upon the leads of the prison, then, fixing a blanket to the wall with a spike, he stole out of the chapel! How intrepidly did he descend to the top of the turner's house! how cautiously pass down the stair, and make his escape to the street-door!

"Oh, that ye were all like Jack Sheppard! Mistake me not, my brethren — I don't mean in a carnal, but in a spiritual sense; for I propose to spiritualise these things. What a shame it would be if we should not think it worth our while to take as much pains, and employ as many deep thoughts to save our souls as he has done to preserve his body!

"Let me exhort ye, then, to open the locks of your hearts with the nail of repentance! Burst asunder the fetters of your beloved lusts, mount the chimney of hope, take from thence the bar of good resolution, break through the stone wall of despair, and all the strongholds in the dark entry of the valley of the shadow of death! Raise yourselves to the leads of divine meditation, fix the blanket of faith with the spike of the Church, let yourselves down to the turner's house of resignation, and

descend the stairs of humility! So shall you come to the door of deliverance from the prison of iniquity, and escape the clutches of that old executioner the devil!"

Jonathan Wild, whose name has been immortalised by Fielding, was no favourite with the people. He had none of the virtues which, combined with crimes, make up the character of the great thief. He was a pitiful fellow, who informed against his comrades, and was afraid of death. This meanness was not to be forgiven by the crowd; and they pelted him with dirt and stones on his way to Tyburn, and expressed their contempt by every possible means. How different was their conduct to Turpin and Jack Sheppard, who died in their neatest attire, with nosegays in their button-holes, and with the courage that a crowd expects. It was anticipated that the body of Turpin would have been delivered up to the surgeons for dissection; and the people seeing some men very busily employed in removing it, suddenly set upon them, rescued the body, bore it about the town in triumph, and then buried it in a very deep grave, filled with quicklime, to hasten the progress of decomposition. They would not suffer the corpse of their hero — of the man who had ridden from London to York in four-and-twenty hours — to be mangled by the rude hands of unmannerly surgeons.

The death of Claude Duval would appear to have been no less triumphant. Claude was a gentlemanly thief. According to Butler, in the famous ode to his memory, he

"Taught the wild Arabs of the road
To rob in a more gentle mode;
Take prizes more obligingly than those
Who never had been bred filous;
And how to hang in a more graceful fashion
Than e'er was known before to the dull English nation."

In fact, he was the pink of politeness, and his gallantry to the fair sex was proverbial. When he was caught at last, pent in "stone walls and chains and iron grates," their grief was in proportion to his rare merits and his great fame. Butler says, that to his dungeon

"Came ladies from all parts,

To offer up close prisoners their hearts.
Which he received as tribute due –
* * * *

Never did bold knight to relieve
Distressed dames, such dreadful feats achieve,
As feeble damsels for his sake
Would have been proud to undertake,
And, bravely ambitious to redeem
The world's loss and their own,
Strove who should have the honour to lay down,
And change a life with him."

Among the noted thieves of France, there is none to compare with the famous Aimerigot Têtenoire, who flourished in the reign of Charles VI. This fellow was at the head of four or five hundred men, and possessed two very strong castles in Limousin and Auvergne. There was a good deal of the feudal baron about him, although he possessed no revenues but such as the road afforded him. At his death he left a singular will. "I give and bequeath," said the robber, "one thousand five hundred francs to St. George's Chapel, for such repairs as it may need; to my sweet girl, who so loyally loved me, I give two thousand five hundred; and the surplus I give to my companions. I hope they will all live as brothers, and divide it amicably among them. If they cannot agree, and the devil of contention gets among them, it is no fault of mine; and I advise them to get a good strong sharp axe, and break open my strong box. Let them scramble for what it contains, and the devil seize the hindmost." The people of Auvergne still recount with admiration the daring feats of this brigand.

Of later years, the French thieves have been such unmitigated scoundrels as to have left but little room for popular admiration. The famous Cartouche, whose name has become synonymous with ruffian in their language, had none of the generosity, courtesy, and devoted bravery which are so requisite to make a robber-hero. He was born at Paris, towards the end of the seventeenth century, and broken alive on the wheel in November 1727. He was, however, sufficiently popular to have been pitied at his death, and afterwards to have formed the subject of a much-admired drama, which bore his name, and was played with great success in all the theatres of France during the years 1734, 5, and 6. In our own day the French have been more fortunate in a robber; Vidocq bids fair to rival the fame of Turpin and Jack Sheppard. Already he has become the hero of many an apocryphal tale — already his compatriots boast of his manifold achievements, and express their doubts whether any other country in Europe could produce a thief so clever, so accomplished, so gentlemanly, as Vidocq.

Germany has its Schinderhannes, Hungary its Schubry, and Italy and Spain a whole host of brigands, whose names and exploits are familiar as household words in the mouths of the children and populace of those countries.

The Italian banditti are renowned over the world; and many of them are not only very religious (after a fashion) but very charitable. Charity from such a source is so unexpected, that the people doat upon them for it. One of them, when he fell into the hands of the police, exclaimed, as they led him away, "Ho fatto più carità!" — "I have given away more in charity than any three convents in these provinces." And the fellow spoke truth.

In Lombardy, the people cherish the memory of two notorious robbers, who flourished about two centuries ago under the Spanish government. Their story, according to Macfarlane, is contained in a little book well known to all the children of the province, and read by them with much more gusto than their Bibles.

Schinderhannes, the robber of the Rhine, is a great favourite on the banks of the river which he so long kept in awe. Many amusing stories are related by the peasantry[48] of the scurvy tricks he played off upon rich Jews, or too-presuming officers of justice — of his princely generosity, and undaunted courage. In short, they are proud of him, and would no more consent to have the memory of his achievements dissociated from their river than they would have the rock of Ehrenbreitstein blown to atoms by gunpowder.

There is another robber-hero, of whose character and exploits the people of Germany speak admiringly. Mausch Nadel was captain of a considerable band that infested the Rhine, Switzerland, Alsatia, and Lorraine, during the years 1824, 5, and 6. Like Jack Sheppard, he endeared himself to the populace by his most hazardous escape from prison. Being confined at Bremen, in a dungeon on the third story of the prison of that town, he contrived to let himself down without exciting the vigilance of the sentinels, and to swim across the Weser, though heavily laden with irons. When about half-way over, he was espied by a sentinel, who fired at him, and shot him in the calf of the leg: but the undaunted robber struck out manfully, reached the shore, and was out of sight before the officers of justice could get ready their boats to follow him. He was captured again in 1826, tried at Mayence, and sentenced to death. He was a tall, strong, handsome man, and his fate, villain as he was, excited much sympathy all over Germany. The ladies especially were loud in their regret that nothing could be done to save a hero so good-looking, and of adventures so romantic, from the knife of the headsman. Mr. Charles Macfarlane, in speaking of Italian banditti, remarks, that the abuses of the Catholic religion, with its confessions and absolutions, have tended to promote crime of this description. But he adds more truly, that priests and monks have not done half the mischief which has been perpetrated by ballad-mongers and story-tellers. If he had said playwrights also, the list would have been complete. In fact, the theatre, which can only expect to prosper, in a pecuniary sense, by pandering to the tastes of the people, continually recurs to the annals of thieves and banditti for its most favourite heroes. These theatrical robbers, with their picturesque attire, wild haunts, jolly, reckless, devil-may-care manners, take a wonderful hold upon the imagination, and whatever their advocates may say to the contrary, exercise a very pernicious influence upon public morals. In the Memoirs of the Duke of Guise upon the Revolution of Naples in 1647 and 1648, it is stated, that the manners, dress, and mode of life of the Neapolitan banditti were rendered so captivating upon the stage, that the authorities found it absolutely necessary to forbid the representation of dramas in which they figured, and even to prohibit their costume at the masquerades. So numerous were the banditti at this time, that the duke found no difficulty in raising an army of them, to aid him in his endeavours to seize on the throne of Naples. He thus describes them:[49] "They were three thousand five hundred men, of whom the oldest came short of five-and-forty years, and the youngest was above twenty. They were all tall and well made, with long black hair, for the most part curled; coats of black Spanish leather, with sleeves of velvet, or cloth of gold; cloth breeches with gold lace, most of them scarlet; girdles of velvet, laced with gold, with two pistols on each side; a cutlass hanging at a belt, suitably trimmed, three fingers broad and two feet long; a hawking-bag at their girdle, and a powder-flask hung about their neck with a great silk riband. Some of them carried firelocks, and others blunderbusses; they had all good shoes, with silk stockings, and every one a cap of cloth of gold, or cloth of silver, of different colours, on his head, which was very delightful to the eye."

The Beggar's Opera, in our own country, is another instance of the admiration that thieves excite upon the stage. Of the extraordinary success of this piece, when first produced, the following account is given in the notes to *The Dunciad*, and quoted by Johnson in his *Lives of the Poets*: "This piece was received with greater applause than was ever known. Besides being acted in London sixty-three days without interruption, and renewed the next season with equal applause, it spread into all the great towns of England; was played in many places to the thirtieth and fortieth time; at Bath and Bristol, &c. fifty. It made its progress into Wales, Scotland, and Ireland, where it was performed twenty-four days successively. The ladies carried about with them the favourite songs of it in fans, and houses were furnished with it in screens. The fame of it was not confined to the author only. The person who acted Polly, till then obscure, became all at once the favourite of the town;[50] her pictures were engraved and sold in great numbers; her life written, books of letters and verses to her published, and pamphlets made even of her sayings and jests. Furthermore, it drove out of England, for that season, the

Italian Opera, which had carried all before it for ten years." Dr. Johnson, in his life of the author, says, that Herring, afterwards Archbishop of Canterbury, censured the opera, as giving encouragement, not only to vice, but to crimes, by making the highwayman the hero, and dismissing him at last unpunished; and adds, that it was even said, that after the exhibition the gangs of robbers were evidently multiplied. The Doctor doubts the assertion, giving as his reason that highwaymen and house-breakers seldom frequent the playhouse, and that it was not possible for any one to imagine that he might rob with safety, because he saw Macheath reprieved upon the stage. But if Johnson had wished to be convinced, he might very easily have discovered that highwaymen and housebreakers did frequent the theatre, and that nothing was more probable than that a laughable representation of successful villany should induce the young and the already vicious to imitate it. Besides, there is the weighty authority of Sir John Fielding, the chief magistrate of Bow Street, who asserted positively, and proved his assertion by the records of his office, that the number of thieves was greatly increased at the time when that opera was so popular.

We have another instance of the same result much nearer our own times. Schiller's *Räuber*, that wonderful play, written by a green youth, perverted the taste and imagination of all the young men in Germany. An accomplished critic of our own country (Hazlitt), speaking of this play, says it was the first he ever read, and such was the effect it produced on him, that "it stunned him, like a blow." After the lapse of five-and-twenty years, he could not forget it; it was still, to use his own words, "an old dweller in the chambers of his brain," and he had not even then recovered enough from it to describe how it was. The high-minded, metaphysical thief, its hero, was so warmly admired, that several raw students, longing to imitate a character they thought so noble, actually abandoned their homes and their colleges, and betook themselves to the forests and the wilds to levy contributions upon travellers. They thought they would, like Moor, plunder the rich, and deliver eloquent soliloquies to the setting sun or the rising moon; relieve the poor when they met them, and drink flasks of Rhenish with their free companions in rugged mountain passes, or in tents in the thicknesses of the forests. But a little experience wonderfully cooled their courage; they found that real, everyday robbers were very unlike the conventional banditti of the stage, and that three months in prison, with bread and water for their fare, and damp straw to lie upon, was very well to read about by their own firesides, but not very agreeable to undergo in their own proper persons.

Lord Byron, with his soliloquising, high-souled thieves, has, in a slight degree, perverted the taste of the juvenile rhymers of his country. As yet, however, they have shewn more good sense than their fellows of Germany, and have not taken to the woods or the highways. Much as they admire Conrad the Corsair, they will not go to sea, and hoist the black flag for him. By words only, and not by deeds, they testify their admiration, and deluge the periodicals and music-shops of the land with verses describing pirates' and bandits' brides, and robber adventures of every kind.

But it is the playwright who does most harm; and Byron has fewer sins of this nature to answer for than Gay or Schiller. With the aid of scenery, fine dresses and music, and the very false notions they convey, they vitiate the public taste, not knowing,

"Vulgaires rimeurs!
Quelle force ont les arts pour demolir les mœurs."

In the penny theatres that abound in the poor and populous districts of London, and which are chiefly frequented by striplings of idle and dissolute habits, tales of thieves and murderers are more admired, and draw more crowded audiences, than any other species of representation. There the footpad, the burglar, and the highwayman are portrayed in their natural colours, and give pleasant lessons in crime to their delighted listeners. There the deepest tragedy and the broadest farce are represented in the career of the murderer and the thief, and are applauded in proportion to their depth and their breadth. There, whenever a crime of unusual atrocity is committed, it is brought out afresh, with all its disgusting incidents copied from the life, for the amusement of those who will one day become its imitators.

With the mere reader the case is widely different; and most people have a partiality for knowing the adventures of noted rogues. Even in fiction they are delightful: witness the eventful story of Gil Blas de Santillane, and of that great rascal Don Guzman d'Alfarache. Here there is no fear of imitation. Poets, too, without doing mischief, may sing of such heroes when they please, wakening our sympathies for the sad fate of Jemmy Dawson, or Gilderoy, or Macpherson the Dauntless; or celebrating in undying verse the wrongs and the revenge of the great thief of Scotland, Rob Roy. If, by the music of their sweet rhymes, they can convince the world that such heroes are but mistaken philosophers, born a few ages too late, and having both a theoretical and practical love for

> *"The good old rule, the simple plan,*
> *That they should take who have the power,*
> *That they should keep who can;"*

the world may perhaps become wiser, and consent to some better distribution of its good things, by means of which thieves may become reconciled to the age, and the age to them. The probability, however, seems to be, that the charmers will charm in vain, charm they ever so wisely.

Chapter 7.

Duels and Ordeals.

Fight between Du Guesclin and Troussel.

There was an ancient sage philosopher,
Who swore the world, as he could prove,
Was mad of fighting.

— *Hudibras.*

Most writers, in accounting for the origin of duelling, derive it from the warlike habits of those barbarous nations who overran Europe in the early centuries of the Christian era, and who knew no mode so effectual for settling their differences as the point of the sword. In fact, duelling, taken in its primitive and broadest sense, means nothing more than combating, and is the universal resort of all wild animals, including man, to gain or defend their possessions, or avenge their insults. Two dogs who tear each other for a bone, or two bantams fighting on a dunghill for the love of some beautiful hen, or two fools on Wimbledon Common, shooting at each other to satisfy the laws of offended honour, stand on the same footing in this respect, and are each and all mere duellists. As civilisation advanced, the best-informed men naturally grew ashamed of such a mode of adjusting disputes, and the promulgation of some sort of laws for obtaining redress for injuries was the consequence. Still there were many cases in which the allegations of an accuser could not be rebutted by any positive proof on the part of the accused; and in all these, which must have been exceedingly numerous in the early stages of European society, the combat was resorted to. From its decision there was no appeal. God was supposed to nerve the arm of the combatant whose cause was just, and to grant him the victory over his opponent. As Montesquieu well remarks,[51] this belief was not unnatural among a people just emerging from barbarism. Their manners being wholly warlike, the man deficient in courage, the prime virtue of his fellows, was not unreasonably suspected of other vices besides cowardice, which is generally found to be co-existent with treachery. He, therefore, who shewed himself most valiant in the encounter was absolved by public opinion from any crime with which he might be charged. As a necessary consequence, society would have been reduced to its original elements, if the men of thought, as distinguished from the men of action, had not devised some means for taming the unruly passions of their fellows. With this view, governments commenced by restricting within the narrowest possible limits the cases in which it was lawful to prove or deny guilt by the single combat. By the law of Gondebaldus king of the Burgundians, passed in the year 501, the proof by combat was allowed in all legal proceedings in lieu of swearing. In the time of Charlemagne, the Burgundian practice had spread over the empire of the Francs, and not only the suitors for justice, but the witnesses, and even the judges, were obliged to defend their cause, their evidence, or their decision at the point of the sword. Louis the Debonnaire, his successor, endeavoured to remedy the growing evil by permitting the duel only in appeals of felony, in civil cases, or issue joined in a writ of right, and in cases of the court of chivalry, or attacks upon a man's knighthood. None were exempt from these trials but women, the sick and the maimed, and persons under fifteen or above sixty years of age. Ecclesiastics were allowed to produce champions in their stead. This practice in the course of time extended to all trials of civil and criminal cases, which had to be decided by battle.

The clergy, whose dominion was an intellectual one, never approved of a system of jurisprudence which tended so much to bring all things under the rule of the strongest arm. From the first they set their faces against duelling, and endeavoured, as far as the prejudices of their age would allow them, to curb the warlike spirit, so alien from the principles of religion. In the Council of Valentia, and afterwards in the Council of Trent, they excommunicated all persons engaged in duelling; and not only them, but even the assistants and spectators, declaring the custom to be hellish and detestable, and introduced by the devil for the destruction both of body and soul. They added also, that princes who connived at duels should be deprived of all temporal power, jurisdiction, and dominion over the places where they had permitted them to be fought. It will be seen hereafter that this clause only encouraged the practice which it was intended to prevent.

But it was the blasphemous error of these early ages to expect that the Almighty, whenever he was called upon, would work a miracle in favour of a person unjustly accused. The priesthood, in condemning the duel, did not condemn the principle on which it was founded. They still encouraged the popular belief of divine interference in all the disputes or differences that might arise among nations or individuals. It was the very same principle that regulated the ordeals, which with all their influence they supported against the duel. By the former, the power of deciding the guilt or innocence was vested wholly in their hands; while by the latter they enjoyed no power or privilege at all. It is not to be wondered at that, for this reason, if for no other, they should have endeavoured to settle all differences by the peaceful mode. While that prevailed, they were, as they wished to be, the first party in the state; but while the strong arm of individual prowess was allowed to be the judge in all doubtful cases, their power and influence became secondary to those of the nobility.

Thus it was not the mere hatred of bloodshed which induced them to launch the thunderbolts of excommunication against the combatants: it was a desire to retain the power, which, to do them justice, they were in those times the persons best qualified to wield. The germs of knowledge and civilisation lay within the bounds of their order; for they were the representatives of the intellectual, as the nobility were of the physical power of man. To centralise this power in the Church, and make it the judge of the last resort in all appeals, both in civil and criminal cases, they instituted five modes of trial, the management of which lay wholly in their hands. These were, the oath upon the evangelists; the ordeal of the cross and the fire ordeal, for persons in the higher ranks; the water ordeal, for the humbler classes; and, lastly, the *corsned*, or bread and cheese ordeal, for members of their own body.

The oath upon the evangelists was taken in the following manner. The accused who was received to this proof, says Paul Hay, Count du Chastelet, in his *Memoirs of Bertrand du Guesclin*, swore upon a copy of the New Testament, and on the relics of the holy martyrs, or on their tombs, that he was innocent of the crime imputed to him. He was also obliged to find twelve persons of acknowledged probity who should take oath at the same time that they believed him innocent. This mode of trial led to very great abuses, especially in cases of disputed inheritance, where the hardest swearer was certain of the victory. This abuse was one of the principal causes which led to the preference given to the trial by battle. It is not at all surprising that a feudal baron, or captain of the early ages, should have preferred the chances of a fair fight with his opponent to a mode by which firm perjury would always be successful.

The trial by, or judgment of, the cross, which Charlemagne begged his sons to have recourse to, in case of disputes arising between them, was performed thus: — When a person accused of any crime had declared his innocence upon oath, and appealed to the cross for its judgment in his favour, he was brought into the church, before the altar. The priests previously prepared two sticks exactly like one another, upon one of which was carved a figure of the cross. They were both wrapped up with great care and many ceremonies, in a quantity of fine wool, and laid upon the altar, or on the relics of the saints. A solemn prayer was then offered up to God, that he would be pleased to discover, by the judgment of his holy cross, whether the accused person were innocent or guilty. A priest then approached the altar, and took up one of the sticks, and the assistants unswathed it reverently. If it was marked with the cross, the accused person was innocent; if unmarked, he was guilty. It would be unjust to assert, that the judgments thus delivered were, in all cases, erroneous; and it would be absurd to believe that they were left altogether to chance. Many true judgments were doubtless given, and, in all probability, most conscientiously; for we cannot but believe that the priests endeavoured beforehand to convince themselves by secret inquiry and a strict examination of the circumstances, whether the appellant were innocent or guilty, and that they took up the crossed or uncrossed stick accordingly. Although, to all other observers, the sticks, as enfolded in the wool, might appear exactly similar, those who enwrapped them could, without any difficulty, distinguish the one from the other.

By the fire-ordeal the power of deciding was just as unequivocally left in their hands. It was generally believed that fire would not burn the innocent, and the clergy, of course, took care that the innocent, or such as it was their pleasure or interest to declare so, should be so warned before undergoing the ordeal, as to preserve themselves without any difficulty from the fire. One mode of ordeal was to place red-hot ploughshares on the ground at certain distances, and then, blindfolding the accused person, make him walk barefooted over them. If he stepped regularly in the vacant spaces, avoiding the fire, he was adjudged innocent; if he burned himself, he was declared guilty. As none but the clergy interfered with the arrangement of the ploughshares, they could always calculate beforehand the result of the ordeal. To find a person guilty, they had only to place them at irregular distances, and the accused was sure to tread upon one of them. When Emma, the wife of King Ethelred, and mother of Edward the Confessor, was accused of a guilty familiarity with Alwyn Bishop of Winchester, she cleared her character in this manner. The reputation, not only of their order, but of a queen, being at stake, a verdict of guilty was not to be apprehended from any ploughshares which priests had the heating of. This ordeal was called the *Judicium Dei*, and sometimes the *Vulgaris Purgatio*, and might also be tried by several other methods. One was to hold in the hand, unhurt, a piece of red-hot iron, of the weight of one, two, or three pounds. When we read not only that men with hard hands, but women of softer and more delicate skin, could do this with impunity, we must be convinced that the hands were previously rubbed with some preservative, or that the apparently hot iron was merely cold iron painted red. Another mode was to plunge the naked arm into a caldron of boiling water. The priests then enveloped it in several folds of linen and flannel, and kept the patient confined within the church, and under their exclusive care, for three days. If, at the end of that time, the arm appeared without a scar, the innocence of the accused person was firmly established.[52]

As regards the water-ordeal, the same trouble was not taken. It was a trial only for the poor and humble, and, whether they sank or swam, was thought of very little consequence. Like the witches of more modern times, the accused were thrown into a pond or river; if they sank, and were drowned, their surviving friends had the consolation of knowing that they were innocent; if they swam, they were guilty. In either case society was rid of them.

But of all the ordeals, that which the clergy reserved for themselves was the one least likely to cause any member of their corps to be declared guilty. The most culpable monster in existence came off clear when tried by this method. It was called the *Corsned*, and was thus performed. A piece of barley bread and a piece of cheese were laid upon the altar, and the accused priest, in his full canonicals, and surrounded by all the pompous adjuncts of Roman ceremony, pronounced certain conjurations, and prayed with great fervency for several minutes. The burden of the prayer was, that if he were guilty of the crime laid to his charge, God would send his angel Gabriel to stop his throat, that he might not be able to swallow the bread and cheese. There is no instance upon record of a priest having been choked in this manner.[53]

When, under Pope Gregory VII., it was debated whether the Gregorian chant should be introduced into Castile, instead of the Musarabic, given by St. Isidore of Seville to the churches of that kingdom, very much ill feeling was excited. The churches refused to receive the novelty, and it was proposed that the affair should be decided by a battle between two champions, one chosen from each side. The clergy would not consent to a mode of settlement which they considered impious, but had no objection to try the merits of each chant by the fire-ordeal. A great fire was accordingly made, and a book of the Gregorian and one of the Musarabic chant were thrown into it, that the flames might decide which was most agreeable to God by refusing to burn it. Cardinal Baronius, who says he was an eye-witness of the miracle, relates, that the book of the Gregorian chant was no sooner laid upon the fire, than it leaped out uninjured, visibly, and with a great noise. Every one present thought that the saints had decided in favour of Pope Gregory. After a slight interval, the fire was extinguished; but, wonderful to relate! the other book of St. Isidore was found covered with ashes, but not injured in the slightest degree. The flames had not even warmed it. Upon this it was resolved, that both were alike agreeable to God, and that they should be used by turns in all the churches of Seville.[54]

If the ordeals had been confined to questions like this, the laity would have had little or no objection to them; but when they were introduced as decisive in all the disputes that might arise between man and man, the opposition of all those whose prime virtue was personal bravery, was necessarily excited. In fact, the nobility, from a very early period, began to look with jealous eyes upon them. They were not slow to perceive their true purport, which was no other than to make the Church the last court of appeal in all cases, both civil and criminal: and not only did the nobility prefer the ancient mode of single combat from this cause, in itself a sufficient one, but they clung to it because an acquittal gained by those displays of courage and address which the battle afforded, was more creditable in the eyes of their compeers, than one which it required but little or none of either to accomplish. To these causes may be added another, which was perhaps more potent than either in raising the credit of the judicial combat at the expense of the ordeal. The noble institution of chivalry was beginning to take root, and, notwithstanding the clamours of the clergy, war was made the sole business of life, and the only elegant pursuit of the aristocracy. The fine spirit of honour was introduced, any attack upon which was only to be avenged in the lists, within sight of applauding crowds, whose verdict of approbation was far more gratifying than the cold and formal acquittal of the ordeal. Lothaire, the son of Louis I., abolished that by fire and the trial of the cross within his dominions; but in England they were allowed so late as the time of Henry III., in the early part of whose reign they were prohibited by an order of council. In the mean time, the Crusades had brought the institution of chivalry to the full height of perfection. The chivalric spirit soon achieved the downfall of the ordeal system, and established the judicial combat on a basis too firm to be shaken. It is true that with the fall of chivalry, as an institution, fell the tournament and the encounter in the lists; but the duel, their offspring, has survived to this day, defying the efforts of sages and philosophers to eradicate it. Among all the errors bequeathed to us by a barbarous age, it has proved the most pertinacious. It has put variance between men's reason and their honour; put the man of sense on a level with the fool, and made thousands who condemn it submit to it or practise it.

Those who are curious to see the manner in which these combats were regulated, may consult the learned Montesquieu, where they will find a copious summary of the code of ancient duelling.[55] Truly does he remark, in speaking of the clearness and excellence of the arrangements, that, as there were many wise matters which were conducted in a very foolish manner, so there were many foolish matters conducted very wisely. No greater exemplification of it could be given than the wise and religious rules of the absurd and blasphemous trial by battle.

In the ages that intervened between the Crusades and the new era that was opened out by the invention of gunpowder and printing, a more rational system of legislation took root. The inhabitants of cities, engaged in the pursuits of trade and industry, were content to acquiesce in the decisions of their judges and magistrates whenever any differences arose among them. Unlike the class above them, their habits and manners did not lead them to seek the battle-field on every slight occasion. A dispute as to the price of a sack of corn, a bale of broad-cloth, or a cow, could be more satisfactorily adjusted before the mayor or bailiff of their district. Even the martial knights and nobles, quarrelsome as they were, began to see that the trial by battle would lose its dignity and splendour if too frequently resorted to. Governments also shared this opinion, and on several occasions restricted the cases in which it was legal to proceed to this extremity. In France, before the time of Louis IX., duels were permitted only in cases of *lèse majesté*, *rape*, *incendiarism*, *assassination*, and *burglary*. Louis IX., by taking off all restriction, made them legal in civil cases. This was not found to work well, and, in 1303, Philip the Fair judged it necessary to confine them, in criminal matters, to state offences, rape, and incendiarism; and in civil cases, to questions of disputed inheritance. Knighthood was allowed to be the best judge of its own honour, and might defend or avenge it as often as occasion arose.

Among the earliest duels upon record, is a very singular one that took place in the reign of Louis II. (A. D. 878). Ingelgerius count of Gastinois was one morning discovered by his countess dead in bed at her side. Gontran, a relation of the count, accused the countess of having murdered her husband, to whom, he asserted, she had long been unfaithful, and challenged her to produce a champion to do battle in her behalf, that he might establish her guilt by killing him.[56] All the friends and relatives of the countess believed in her innocence; but Gontran was so stout and bold and renowned a warrior that no one dared to meet him, for which, as Brantôme quaintly says, "mauvais et poltrons parens estaient." The unhappy countess began to despair, when a champion suddenly appeared in the person of Ingelgerius count of Anjou, a boy of sixteen years of age, who had been held by the countess on the baptismal font, and received her husband's name. He tenderly loved his godmother, and offered to do battle in her cause against any and every opponent. The king endeavoured to persuade the generous boy from his enterprise, urging the great strength, tried skill, and invincible courage of the challenger; but he persisted in his resolution, to the great sorrow of all the court, who said it was a cruel thing to permit so brave and beautiful a child to rush to such butchery and death.

Duel between Ingelgerius and Gontran.

When the lists were prepared, the countess duly acknowledged her champion, and the combatants commenced the onset. Gontran rode so fiercely at his antagonist, and hit him on the shield with such impetuosity, that he lost his own balance and rolled to the ground. The young count, as Gontran fell, passed his lance through his body, and then dismounting, cut off his head, which, Brantôme says, "he presented to the king, who received it most graciously, and was very joyful, as much so as if any one had made him a present of a city." The innocence of the countess was then proclaimed with great rejoicings; and she kissed her godson, and wept over his neck with joy, in the presence of all the assembly.

When the Earl of Essex was accused, by Robert de Montfort, before King Henry II., in 1162, of having traitorously suffered the royal standard of England to fall from his hands in a skirmish with the Welsh at Coleshill, five years previously, the latter offered to prove the truth of the charge by single combat. The Earl of Essex accepted the challenge, and the lists were prepared near Reading. An immense concourse of persons assembled to witness the battle. Essex at first fought stoutly, but, losing his temper and self-command, he gave an advantage to his opponent which soon decided the struggle. He was unhorsed, and so severely wounded, that all present thought he was dead. At the solicitation of his relatives, the monks of the Abbey of Reading were allowed to remove the body for interment, and Montfort was declared the victor. Essex, however, was not dead, but stunned only, and, under the care of the monks, recovered in a few weeks from his bodily injuries. The wounds of his mind were not so easily healed. Though a loyal and brave subject, the whole realm believed him a traitor and a coward because he had been vanquished. He could not brook to return to the world deprived of the good opinion of his fellows; he therefore made himself a monk, and passed the remainder of his days within the walls of the abbey.

Du Chastelet relates a singular duel that was proposed in Spain.[57] A Christian gentleman of Seville sent a challenge to a Moorish cavalier, offering to prove against him, with whatever weapons he might choose, that the religion of Jesus Christ was holy and divine, and that of Mahomet impious and damnable. The Spanish prelates did not choose that Christianity should be compromised within their jurisdiction by the result of any such combat; the Moorish cavalier might, perchance, have proved to be the stronger, and they commanded the knight, under pain of excommunication, to withdraw the challenge.

The same author relates that, under Otho I., a question arose among jurisconsults, viz. whether grandchildren, who had lost their father, should share equally with their uncles in the property of their grandfather, at the death of the latter. The difficulty of this question was found so insurmountable, that none of the lawyers of that day could resolve it. It was at last decreed that it should be decided by single combat. Two champions were accordingly chosen; one for, and the other against, the claims of the little ones. After a long struggle, the champion of the uncles was unhorsed and slain; and it was therefore decided that the right of the grandchildren was established, and that they should enjoy the same portion of their grandfather's possessions that their father would have done had he been alive.

Upon pretexts just as strange, and often more frivolous that these, duels continued to be fought in most of the countries of Europe during the whole of the fourteenth and fifteenth centuries. A memorable instance of the slightness of the pretext on which a man could be forced to fight a duel to the death, occurs in the Memoirs of the brave Constable, Du Guesclin. The advantage he had obtained, in a skirmish before Rennes, against William Brembre, an English captain, so preyed on the spirits of William Troussel, the chosen friend and companion of the latter, that nothing would satisfy him but a mortal combat with the Constable. The Duke of Lancaster, to whom Troussel applied for permission to fight the great Frenchman, forbade the battle, as not warranted by the circumstances. Troussel nevertheless burned with a fierce desire to cross his weapon with Du Guesclin, and sought every occasion to pick a quarrel with him. Having so good a will for it, of course he found a way. A relative of his had been taken prisoner by the Constable, in whose hands he remained till he was able to pay his ransom. Troussel resolved to make a quarrel out of this, and despatched a messenger to Du Guesclin, demanding the release of his prisoner, and offering a bond, at a distant date, for the payment of the ransom. Du Guesclin, who had received intimation of the hostile purposes of the Englishman, sent back word that he would not accept his bond, neither would he release his prisoner until the full amount of his ransom was paid. As soon as this answer was received, Troussel sent a challenge to the Constable, demanding reparation for the injury he had done his honour, by refusing his bond, and offering a mortal combat, to be fought three strokes with the lance, three with the sword, and three with the dagger. Du Guesclin, although ill in bed with the ague, accepted the challenge, and gave notice to the Marshal d'Andreghem, the king's lieutenant-general in Lower Normandy, that he might fix the day and the place of combat. The marshal made all necessary arrangements, upon condition that he who was beaten should pay a hundred florins of gold to feast the nobles and gentlemen who were witnesses of the encounter.

The Duke of Lancaster was very angry with his captain, and told him that it would be a shame to his knighthood and his nation if he forced on a combat with the brave Du Guesclin at a time when he was enfeebled by disease and stretched on the couch of suffering. Upon these representations, Troussel, ashamed of himself, sent notice to Du Guesclin that he was willing to postpone the duel until such time as he should be perfectly recovered. Du Guesclin replied, that he could not think of postponing the combat after all the nobility had received notice of it; that he had sufficient strength left not only to meet, but to conquer such an opponent as he was; and that if he did not make his appearance in the lists at the time appointed, he would publish him every where as a man unworthy to be called a knight, or to wear an honourable sword by his side. Troussel carried this haughty message to the Duke of Lancaster, who immediately gave permission for the battle.

On the day appointed, the two combatants appeared in the lists, in the presence of several thousand spectators. Du Guesclin was attended by the flower of the French nobility, including the Marshal de Beaumanoir, Olivier de Mauny, Bertrand de Saint Pern, and the Viscount de la Bellière; while the Englishman appeared with no more than the customary retinue of two seconds, two squires, two coutilliers or daggermen, and two trumpeters. The first onset was unfavourable to the Constable. He received so heavy a blow on his shield-arm, that he fell forward to the left upon his horse's neck; and being weakened by his fever, was nearly thrown to the ground. All his friends thought he could never recover himself, and began to deplore his ill fortune; but Du Guesclin collected his energies for a decisive effort, and at the second charge aimed a blow at the shoulder of his enemy, which felled him to the earth, mortally wounded. He then sprang from his horse, sword in hand, with the intention of cutting off the head of his fallen foe, when the Marshal d'Andreghem threw a golden wand into the arena as a signal that hostilities should cease. Du Guesclin was proclaimed the victor amid the joyous acclamations of the crowd, and retiring, left the field to the meaner combatants, who were afterwards to make sport for the people. Four English and as many French squires fought for some time with pointless lances, when the French gaining the advantage, the sports were declared at an end.

In the time of Charles VI., about the beginning of the fifteenth century, a famous duel was ordered by the parliament of Paris. The Sieur de Carrouges being absent in the Holy Land, his lady was violated by the Sieur Legris. Carrouges, on his return, challenged Legris to mortal combat for the twofold crime of violation and slander, inasmuch as he had denied his guilt by asserting that the lady was a willing party. The lady's asseverations of innocence were held to be no evidence by the parliament, and the duel was commanded, with all the ceremonies. "On the day appointed," says Brantôme,[58] "the lady came to witness the spectacle in her chariot; but the king made her descend, judging her unworthy, because she was criminal in his eyes till her innocence was proved, and caused her to stand upon a scaffold to await the mercy of God and this judgment by the battle. After a short struggle, the Sieur de Carrouges overthrew his enemy, and made him confess both the rape and the slander. He was then taken to the gallows and hanged in the presence of the multitude; while the innocence of the lady was proclaimed by the heralds, and recognised by her husband, the king, and all the spectators."

Numerous battles of a similar description constantly took place, until the unfortunate issue of one encounter of the kind led the French king, Henry II., to declare solemnly that he would never again permit any such encounter, whether it related to a civil or criminal case, or the honour of a gentleman.

This memorable combat was fought in the year 1547. François de Vivonne, lord of La Chataigneraie, and Guy de Chabot, lord of Jarnac, had been friends from their early youth, and were noted at the court of Francis I. for the gallantry of their bearing and the magnificence of their retinue. Chataigneraie, who knew that his friend's means were not very ample, asked him one day in confidence how it was that he contrived to be so well provided? Jarnac replied, that his father had married a young and beautiful woman, who, loving the son far better than the sire, supplied him with as much money as he desired. La Chataigneraie betrayed the base secret to the dauphin, the dauphin to the king, the king to his courtiers, and the courtiers to all their acquaintance. In a short time it reached the ears of the old Lord de Jarnac, who immediately sent for his son, and demanded to know in what manner the report had originated, and whether he had been vile enough not only to carry on such a connexion, but to boast of it? De Jarnac indignantly denied that he had ever said so, or given reason to the world to say so, and requested his father to accompany him to court and confront him with his accuser, that he might see the manner in which he would confound him. They went accordingly; and the younger De Jarnac, entering a room where the dauphin, La Chataigneraie, and several courtiers were present, exclaimed aloud, "That whoever had asserted that he maintained a criminal connexion with his mother-in-law was a liar and a coward!" Every eye was turned to the dauphin and La Chataigneraie, when the latter stood forward and asserted, that De Jarnac had himself avowed that such was the fact, and he would extort from his lips another confession of it. A case like this could not be met or rebutted by any legal proof, and the royal council ordered that it should be decided by single combat. The king, however, set his face against the duel,[59] and forbade them both, under pain of his high displeasure, to proceed any further in the matter. But Francis died in the following year, and the dauphin, now Henry II., who was himself compromised, resolved that the combat should take place.

The lists were prepared in the court-yard of the chateau of St. Germain-en-Laye, and the 10th of July, 1547, was appointed for the encounter. The cartels of the combatants, which are preserved in the *Mémoires de Castelnau*, were as follow:

"Cartel of François de Vivonne, lord of la Chataigneraie.

"Sire,

"Having learned that Guy Chabot de Jarnac, being lately at Compiegne, asserted that whoever had said that he boasted of having criminal intercourse with his mother-in-law was wicked and a wretch, I, sire, with your good will and pleasure, do answer that he has wickedly lied, and will lie as many times as he denies having said that which I affirm he did say; for I repeat, that he told me several times, and boasted of it, that he had slept with his mother-in-law.

"François de Vivonne."

To this cartel De Jarnac replied:

"Sire,

"With your good will and permission, I say, that François de Vivonne has lied in the imputation which he has cast upon me, and of which I spoke to you at Compiegne. I therefore entreat you, sire, most humbly, that you be pleased to grant us a fair field, that we may fight this battle to the death.

"Guy Chabot."

The preparations were conducted on a scale of the greatest magnificence, the king having intimated his intention of being present. La Chataigneraie made sure of the victory, and invited the king and a hundred and fifty of the principal personages of the court to sup with him in the evening, after the battle, in a splendid tent which he had prepared at the extremity of the lists. De Jarnac was not so confident, though perhaps more desperate. At noon, on the day appointed, the combatants met, and each took the customary oath that he bore no charms or amulets about him, or made use of any magic, to aid him against his antagonist. They then attacked each other, sword in hand. La Chataigneraie was a strong robust man, and over confident; De Jarnac was nimble, supple, and prepared for the worst. The combat lasted for some time doubtful, until De Jarnac, overpowered by the heavy blows of his opponent, covered his head with his shield, and, stooping down, endeavoured to make amends by his agility for his deficiency of strength. In this crouching posture he aimed two blows at the left thigh of La Chataigneraie, who had left it uncovered, that the motion of his leg might not be impeded. Each blow was successful, and, amid the astonishment of all the spectators, and to the great regret of the king, La Chataigneraie rolled over upon the sand. He seized his dagger, and made a last effort to strike De Jarnac: but he was unable to support himself, and fell powerless into the arms of the assistants. The officers now interfered, and De Jarnac being declared the victor, fell down upon his knees, uncovered his head, and, clasping his hands together, exclaimed: "*O Domine, non sum dignus!*" La Chataigneraie was so mortified by the result of the encounter, that he resolutely refused to have his wounds dressed. He tore off the bandages which the surgeons applied, and expired two days afterwards. Ever since that time, any sly and unforeseen attack has been called by the French a *coup de Jarnac*. Henry was so grieved at the loss of his favourite, that he made the solemn oath already alluded to, that he would never again, so long as he lived, permit a duel. Some writers have asserted, and among others, Mezerai, that he issued a royal edict forbidding them. This has been doubted by others, and as there appears no registry of the edict in any of the courts, it seems most probable that it was never issued. This opinion is strengthened by the fact, that, two years afterwards, the council ordered another duel to be fought with similar forms, but with less magnificence, on account of the inferior rank of the combatants. It is not anywhere stated that Henry interfered to prevent it, notwithstanding his solemn oath; but that, on the contrary, he encouraged it, and appointed the Marshal de la Marque to see that it was conducted according to the rules of chivalry. The disputants were Fendille and D'Aguerre, two gentlemen of the household, who, quarrelling in the king's chamber, had proceeded from words to blows. The council, being informed of the matter, decreed that it could only be decided in the lists. Marshal de la Marque, with the king's permission, appointed the city of Sedan as the place of combat. Fendille, who was a bad swordsman, was anxious to avoid an encounter with D'Aguerre, who was one of the most expert men of the age; but the council authoritatively command-ed that he should fight, or be degraded from all his honours. D'Aguerre appeared in the field attended by François de Ven-dôme, Count de Chartres, while Fendille was accompanied by the Duke of Nevers. Fendille appears to have been not only an inexpert swordsman, but a thorough coward; one who, like Cowley, might have heaped curses on the man,

> "(Death's factor sure), who brought
> Dire swords into this peaceful world."

On the very first encounter he was thrown from his horse, and, confessing on the ground all that his victor required of him, slunk away ignominiously from the arena.

One is tempted to look upon the death of Henry II. as a judgment upon him for his perjury in the matter of duelling. In a grand tournament instituted on the occasion of the marriage of his daughter, he broke several lances in encounters with some of the bravest knights of the time. Ambitious of still further renown, he would not rest satisfied until he had also engaged the young Count de Montgommeri. He received a wound in the eye from the lance of his antagonist, and died from its effects shortly afterwards, in the forty-first year of his age.

In the succeeding reigns of Francis II., Charles IX., and Henry III., the practice of duelling increased to an alarming extent. Duels were not rare in the other countries of Europe at the same period; but in France they were so frequent, that historians, in speaking of that age, designate it as "l'époque de la fureur des duels." The parliament of Paris endeavoured, as far as in its power lay, to discourage the practice. By a decree dated the 26th of June 1559, it declared all persons who should be present at duels, or aiding and abetting in them, to be rebels to the king, transgressors of the law, and disturbers of the public peace.

When Henry III. was assassinated at St. Cloud in 1589, a young gentleman, named L'Isle-Marivaut, who had been much beloved by him, took his death so much to heart, that he resolved not to survive him. Not thinking suicide an honourable death, and wishing, as he said, to die gloriously in revenging his king and master, he publicly expressed his readiness to fight any body to the death, who should assert that Henry's assassination was not a great misfortune to the community. Another youth, of a fiery temper and tried courage, named Marolles, took him at his word, and the day and place of the combat were forthwith appointed. When the hour had come, and all were ready, Marolles turned to his second, and asked whether his opponent had a casque or helmet only, or whether he wore a *sallade*, or headpiece. Being answered a helmet only, he said gaily, "So much the better; for, sir my second, you shall repute me the wickedest man in all the world, if I do not thrust my lance right through the middle of his head and kill him." Truth to say, he did so at the very first onset, and the unhappy L'Isle-Marivaut expired without a groan. Brantôme, who relates this story, adds, that the victor might have done as he pleased with the body, cut off the head, dragged it out of the camp, or exposed it upon an ass; but that being a wise and very courteous gentleman, he left it to the relatives of the deceased to be honourably buried, contenting himself with the glory of his triumph, by which he gained no little renown and honour among the ladies of Paris.

Henry IV.

On the accession of Henry IV. that monarch determined to set his face against duelling; but such was the influence of early education and the prejudices of society upon him, that he never could find it in his heart to punish a man for this offence. He thought it tended to foster a warlike spirit among his people. When the chivalrous Créqui demanded his permission to fight Don Philippe de Savoire, he is reported to have said, "Go, and if I were not a king, I would be your second." It is no wonder that when such was known to be the king's disposition, his edicts attracted but small attention. A calculation was made by M. de Lomenie, in the year 1607, that since the accession of Henry, in 1589, no less than four thousand French gentlemen had lost their lives in these conflicts; which, for the eighteen years, would have been at the rate of four or five in a week, or eighteen per month! Sully, who reports this fact in his Memoirs, does not throw the slightest doubt upon its exactness; and adds, that it was chiefly owing to the facility and ill-advised good-nature of his royal master that the bad example had so empoisoned the court, the city, and the whole country. This wise minister devoted much of his time and attention to the subject; for the rage, he says, was such as to cause him a thousand pangs, and the king also. There was hardly a man moving in what was called good society, who had not been engaged in a duel either as principal or second; and if there were such a man, his chief desire was to free himself from the imputation of non-duelling, by picking a quarrel with somebody. Sully constantly wrote letters to the king, in which he prayed him to renew the edicts against this barbarous custom, to aggravate the punishment against offenders, and never, in any instance, to grant a pardon, even to a person who had wounded another in a duel, much less to any one who had taken away life. He also advised, that some sort of tribunal, or court of honour, should be established, to take cognisance of injurious and slanderous language, and of all such matters as usually led to duels; and that the justice to be administered by this court should be sufficiently prompt and severe to appease the complainant, and make the offender repent of his aggression.

Gallery at Fontainebleau.

Henry, being so warmly pressed by his friend and minister, called together an extraordinary council in the gallery of the palace of Fontainebleau, to take the matter into consideration. When all the members were assembled, his majesty requested that some person conversant with the subject would make a report to him on the origin, progress, and different forms of the duel. Sully complacently remarks, that none of the councillors gave the king any great reason to felicitate them on their erudition. In fact, they all remained silent. Sully held his peace with the rest; but he looked so knowing, that the king turned towards him, and said: — "Great master! by your face I conjecture that you know more of this matter than you would have us believe. I pray you, and indeed I command, that you tell us what you think and what you know." The coy minister refused, as he says, out of mere politeness to his more ignorant colleagues; but, being again pressed by the king, he entered into a history of duelling both in ancient and modern times. He has not preserved this history in his Memoirs; and, as none of the ministers or councillors present thought proper to do so, the world is deprived of a discourse which was, no doubt, a learned and remarkable one. The result was, that a royal edict was issued, which Sully lost no time in transmitting to the most distant provinces, with a distinct notification to all parties concerned that the king was in earnest, and would exert the full rigour of the law in punishment of the offenders. Sully himself does not inform us what were the provisions of the new law; but Father Matthias has been more explicit, and from him we learn, that the marshals of France were created judges of a court of chivalry, for the hearing of all causes wherein the honour of a noble or gentleman was concerned, and that such as resorted to duelling should be punished by death and confiscation of property, and that the seconds and assistants should lose their rank, dignity, or offices, and be banished from the court of their sovereign.[60]

But so strong a hold had the education and prejudice of his age upon the mind of the king, that though his reason condemned, his sympathies approved the duel. Notwithstanding this threatened severity, the number of duels did not diminish, and the wise Sully had still to lament the prevalence of an evil which menaced society with utter disorganisation. In the succeeding reign the practice prevailed, if possible, to a still greater extent, until the Cardinal de Richelieu, better able to grapple with it than Sully had been, made some severe examples in the very highest classes. Lord Herbert, the English ambassador at the court of Louis XIII., repeats, in his letters, an observation that had been previously made in the reign of Henry IV., that it was rare to find a Frenchman moving in good society who had not killed his man in a duel. The Abbé Millot says of this period, that the duel madness made the most terrible ravages. Men had actually a frenzy for combating. Caprice and vanity, as well as the excitement of passion, imposed the necessity of fighting. Friends were obliged to enter into the quarrels of their friends, or be themselves called out for their refusal, and revenge became hereditary in many families. It was reckoned that in twenty years eight thousand letters of pardon had been issued to persons who had killed others in single combat.[61]

Other writers confirm this statement. Amelot de Houssaye, in his Memoirs, says, upon this subject, that duels were so common in the first years of the reign of Louis XIII., that the ordinary conversation of persons when they met in the morning was, "*Do you know who fought yesterday?*" and after dinner, "*Do you know who fought this morning?*" The most infamous duellist at that period was De Bouteville. It was not at all necessary to quarrel with this assassin, to be forced to fight a duel with him. When he heard that any one was very brave, he would go to him, and say, *"People tell me that you are brave; you and I must fight together!"* Every morning the most notorious bravos and duellists used to assemble at his house, to take a breakfast of bread and wine, and practise fencing. M. de Valençay, who was afterwards elevated to the rank of a cardinal, stood very high in the estimation of De Bouteville and his gang. Hardly a day passed but what he was engaged in some duel or other, either as principal or second; and he once challenged De Bouteville himself, his best friend, because De Bouteville had fought a duel without inviting him to become his second. This quarrel was only appeased on the promise of De Bouteville that, in his next encounter, he would not fail to avail himself of his services. For that purpose he went out the same day, and picked a quarrel with the Marquis des Portes. M. de Valençay, according to agreement, had the pleasure of serving as his second, and of running through the body M. de Cavois, the second of the Marquis des Portes, a man who had never done him any injury, and whom he afterwards acknowledged he had never seen before.

Cardinal Richelieu devoted much attention to this lamentable state of public morals, and seems to have concurred with his great predecessor Sully, that nothing but the most rigorous severity could put a stop to the evil. The subject indeed was painfully forced upon him by his enemies. The Marquis de Themines, to whom Richelieu, then Bishop of Luçon, had given offence by some representations he had made to Mary of Medicis, determined, since he could not challenge an ecclesiastic, to challenge his brother. An opportunity was soon found. Themines, accosting the Marquis de Richelieu, complained, in an insulting tone, that the Bishop of Luçon had broken his faith. The Marquis resented both the manner and matter of his speech, and readily accepted a challenge. They met in the Rue d'Angoulême, and the unfortunate Richelieu was stabbed to the heart, and instantly expired. From that moment the bishop became the steady foe of the practice of duelling. Reason and the impulse of brotherly love alike combined to make him detest it, and when his power in France was firmly established, he set vigorously about repressing it. In his *Testament Politique*, he has collected his thoughts upon the subject, in the chapter entitled "Des moyens d'arrêter les Duels." In spite of the edicts that he published, the members of the nobility persisted in fighting upon the most trivial and absurd pretences. At last Richelieu made a terrible example. The infamous De Bouteville challenged and fought the Marquis de Beuvron; and although the duel itself was not fatal to either, its consequences were fatal to both. High as they were, Richelieu resolved that the law should reach them both, and they were both tried, found guilty, and beheaded. Thus did society get rid of one of the most bloodthirsty scoundrels that ever polluted it.

Sully.

In 1632 two noblemen fought a duel in which they were both killed. The officers of justice had notice of the breach of the law, and arrived at the scene of combat before the friends of the parties had time to remove the bodies. In conformity with the cardinal's severe code upon the subject, the bodies were igno-miniously stripped and hanged upon a gallows with their heads downwards, for several hours, within sight of all the peo-ple.[62] This severity sobered the frenzy of the nation for a time; but it was soon forgotten. Men's minds were too deeply imbued with a false notion of honour to be brought to a right way of thinking: by such examples, however striking, Richelieu was unable to persuade them to walk in the right path, though he could punish them for choosing the wrong one. He had with all his acuteness, miscalculated the spirit of duelling. It was not death that a duellist feared; it was shame, and the contempt of his fellows. As Addison remarked more than eighty years afterwards, "Death was not sufficient to deter men who made it their glory to despise it; but if every one who fought a duel were to stand in the pillory, it would quickly diminish the number of those imaginary men of honour, and put an end to so absurd a practice." Richelieu never thought of this.

Sully says, that in his time the Germans were also much addicted to duelling. There were three places where it was legal to fight; Witzburg in Franconia, and Uspach and Halle in Swabia. Thither of course, vast numbers repaired, and murdered each other under sanction of the law. At an earlier period in Germany, it was held highly disgraceful to refuse to fight. Any one who surrendered to his adversary for a simple wound that did not disable him, was reputed infamous, and could neither cut his beard, bear arms, mount on horseback, or hold any office in the state. He who fell in a duel was buried with great pomp and splendour.

In the year 1652, just after Louis XIV. had attained his majority, a desperate duel was fought between the Dukes de Beaufort and De Nemours, each attended by four gentlemen. Although brothers-in-law, they had long been enemies, and their constant dissensions had introduced much disorganisation among the troops which they severally commanded. Each had long sought an opportunity for combat, which at last arose on a misunderstanding relative to the places they were to occupy at the councilboard. They fought with pistols, and, at the first discharge, the Duke de Nemours was shot through the body, and almost instantly expired. Upon this the Marquis de Villars, who seconded Nemours, challenged Héricourt, the second of the Duke de Beaufort, a man whom he had never before seen; and the challenge being accepted, they fought even more desperately than their principals. This combat, being with swords, lasted longer than the first, and was more exciting to the six remaining gentlemen who stayed to witness it. The result was fatal to Héricourt, who fell pierced to the heart by the sword of De Villars. Any thing more savage than this can hardly be imagined. Voltaire says such duels were frequent, and the compiler of the *Dictionnaire d'Anecdotes* informs us that the number of seconds was not fixed. As many as ten, or twelve, or twenty, were not unfrequent, and they often fought together after their principals were disabled. The highest mark of friendship one man could manifest towards another, was to choose him for his second; and many gentlemen were so desirous of serving in this capacity, that they endeavoured to raise every slight misunderstanding into a quarrel, that they might have the pleasure of being engaged in it. The Count de Bussy-Rabutin relates an instance of this in his Memoirs. He says, that as he was one evening coming out of the theatre, a gentleman named Bruc, whom he had not before known, stopped him very politely, and, drawing him aside, asked him if it was true that the Count de Thianges had called him (Bruc) a drunkard? Bussy replied that he really did not know, for he saw the count very seldom. "Oh, he is your uncle!" replied Bruc; "and, as I cannot have satisfaction from him, because he lives so far off in the country, I apply to you." "I see what you are at," replied Bussy, "and, since you wish to put me in my uncle's place, I answer, that whoever asserted that he called you a drunkard, told a lie!" "My brother said so," replied Bruc, "and he is a child." "Horsewhip him, then, for his falsehood," returned De Bussy. "I will not have my brother called, a liar," returned Bruc, determined to quarrel with him; "so draw, and defend yourself!" They both drew their swords in the public street, but were separated by the spectators. They agreed, however, to fight on a future occasion, and with all the regular forms of the duello. A few days afterwards, a gentleman, whom De Bussy had never before seen, and whom he did not know even by name, called upon him and asked if he might have the privilege of serving as his second. He added, that he neither knew him nor Bruc, except by reputation, but having made up his mind to be second of one of them, he had decided upon accompanying De Bussy as the braver man of the two. De Bussy thanked him very sincerely for his politeness, but begged to be excused, as he had already engaged four seconds to accompany him, and he was afraid that if he took any more the affair would become a battle instead of a duel.

When such quarrels as these were looked upon as mere matters of course, the state of society must have been indeed awful. Louis XIV. very early saw the evil, and as early determined to remedy it. It was not, however, till the year 1679, when he instituted the "Chambre Ardente," for the trial of the slow poisoners and pretenders to sorcery, that he published any edict against duelling. In that year his famous edict was promulgated, in which he reiterated and confirmed the severe enactments of his predecessors Henry IV. and Louis XIII., and expressed his determination never to pardon any offender. By this celebrated ordinance a supreme court of honour was established, composed of the marshals of France. They were bound, on taking the office, to give to every one who brought a well-founded complaint before them, such reparation as would satisfy the justice of the case. Should any gentleman against whom complaint was made refuse to obey the mandate of the court of honour, he might be punished by fine and imprisonment; and when that was not possible, by reason of his absenting himself from the kingdom, his estates might be confiscated till his return.

Every man who sent a challenge, be the cause of offence what it might, was deprived of all redress from the court of honour — suspended three years from the exercise of any office in the state — was further imprisoned for two years, and sentenced to pay a fine of half his yearly income.

He who accepted a challenge was subject to the same punishment. Any servant or other person, who knowingly became the bearer of a challenge, was, if found guilty, sentenced to stand in the pillory and be publicly whipped for the first offence; and for the second, sent for three years to the galleys.

Any person who actually fought, was to be held guilty of murder, even though death did not ensue, and was to be punished accordingly. Persons in the higher ranks of life were to be beheaded, and those of the middle class hanged upon a gallows, and their bodies refused Christian burial.

At the same time that Louis published this severe edict, he exacted a promise from his principal nobility that they would never engage in a duel on any pretence whatever. He never swerved from his resolution to pursue all duellists with the utmost rigour, and many were executed in various parts of the country. A slight abatement of the evil was the consequence, and in the course of a few years one duel was not fought where twelve had been fought previously. A medal was struck to commemorate the circumstance, by the express command of the king. So much had he this object at heart, that, in his will, he particularly recommended to his successor the care of his edict against duelling, and warned him against any ill-judged lenity to those who disobeyed it.

A singular law formerly existed in Malta with regard to duelling. By this law it was permitted, but only upon condition that the parties should fight in one particular street. If they presumed to settle their quarrel elsewhere, they were held guilty of murder, and punished accordingly. What was also very singular, they were bound, under heavy penalties, to put up their swords when requested to do so by a priest, a knight, or a woman. It does not appear, however, that the ladies or the knights exercised this mild and beneficent privilege to any great extent; the former were too often themselves the cause of duels, and the latter sympathised too much in the wounded honour of the combatants to attempt to separate them. The priests alone were the great peacemakers. Brydone says, that a cross was always painted on the wall opposite to the spot where a knight had been killed, and that in the "street of duels" he counted about twenty of them.[63]

In England the private duel was also practised to a scandalous extent, towards the end of the sixteenth and beginning of the seventeenth centuries. The judicial combat now began to be more rare, but several instances of it are mentioned in history. One was instituted in the reign of Elizabeth, and another so late as the time of Charles I. Sir Henry Spelman gives an account of that which took place in Elizabeth's reign, which is curious, perhaps the more so when we consider that it was perfectly legal, and that similar combats remained so till the year 1819. A proceeding having been instituted in the Court of Common Pleas for the recovery of certain manorial rights in the county of Kent, the defendant offered to prove by single combat his right to retain possession. The plaintiff accepted the challenge, and the Court having no power to stay the proceedings, agreed to the champions who were to fight in lieu of the principals. The queen commanded the parties to compromise; but it being represented to her majesty that they were justified by law in the course they were pursuing, she allowed them to proceed. On the day appointed, the justices of the Common Pleas, and all the counsel engaged in the cause, appeared as umpires of the combat, at a place in Tothill-fields, where the lists had been prepared. The champions were ready for the encounter, and the plaintiff and defendant were publicly called to come forward and acknowledge them. The defendant answered to his name, and recognised his champion with the due formalities, but the plaintiff did not appear. Without his presence and authority the combat could not take place; and his absence being considered an abandonment of his claim, he was declared to be non-suited, and barred for ever from renewing his suit before any other tribunal whatever.

Lord Bacon.

The queen appears to have disapproved personally of this mode of settling a disputed claim, but her judges and legal advisers made no attempt to alter the barbarous law. The practice of private duelling excited more indignation, from its being of every-day occurrence. In the time of James I. the English were so infected with the French madness, that Bacon, when he was attorney-general, lent the aid of his powerful eloquence to effect a reformation of the evil. Informations were exhibited in the Star Chamber against two persons, named Priest and Wright, for being engaged, as principal and second, in a duel, on which occasion he delivered a charge that was so highly approved of by the Lords of the Council, that they ordered it to be printed and circulated over the country, as a thing *"very meet and worthy to be remembered and made known unto the world."* He began by considering the nature and greatness of the mischief of duelling. *"It troubleth peace – it disfurnisheth war – it bringeth calamity upon private men, peril upon the state, and contempt upon the law. Touching the cause of it,"* he observed, *"that the first motive of it, no doubt, is a false and erroneous imagination of honour and credit; but then, the seed of this mischief being such, it is nourished by vain discourses and green and unripe conceits. Hereunto may be added, that men have almost lost the true notion and understanding of fortitude and valour. For fortitude distinguisheth of the grounds of quarrel whether they be just; and not only so, but whether they be worthy, and setteth a better price upon men's lives than to bestow them idly. Nay, it is weakness and disesteem of a man's self to put a man's life upon such liedger performances. A man's life is not to be trifled with; it is to be offered up and sacrificed to honourable services, public merits, good causes, and noble adventures. It is in expense of blood as it is in expense of money. It is no liberality to make a profusion of money upon every vain occasion, neither is it fortitude to make effusion of blood, except the cause of it be worth."*[64]

The most remarkable event connected with duelling in this reign was that between Lord Sanquir, a Scotch nobleman, and one Turner, a fencing-master. In a trial of skill between them, his lordship's eye was accidentally thrust out by the point of Turner's sword. Turner expressed great regret at the circumstance, and Lord Sanquir bore his loss with as much philosophy as he was master of, and forgave his antagonist. Three years afterwards, Lord Sanquir was at Paris, where he was a constant visitor at the court of Henry IV. One day, in the course of conversation, the affable monarch inquired how he had lost his eye. Sanquir, who prided himself on being the most expert swordsman of the age, blushed as he replied that it was inflicted by the sword of a fencing-master. Henry, forgetting his assumed character of an anti-duellist, carelessly, and as a mere matter of course, inquired whether the man lived? Nothing more was said; but the query sank deep into the proud heart of the Scotch baron, who returned shortly afterwards to England, burning for revenge. His first intent was to challenge the fencing-master to single combat; but, on further consideration, he deemed it inconsistent with his dignity to meet him as an equal in fair and open fight. He therefore hired two bravos, who set upon the fencing-master, and murdered him in his own house at White-friars. The assassins were taken and executed, and a reward of one thousand pounds offered for the apprehension of their employer. Lord Sanquir concealed himself for several days, and then surrendered to take his trial, in the hope (happily false) that Justice would belie her name, and be lenient to a murderer because he was a nobleman, who on a false point of honour had thought fit to take revenge into his own hands. The most power-ful intercessions were employed in his favour, but James, to his credit, was deaf to them all. Bacon, in his character of attorney-general, prosecuted the prisoner to conviction; and he died the felon's death on the 29th of June, 1612, on a gibbet erected in front of the gate of Westminster Hall.

With regard to the public duel, or trial by battle, demanded under the sanction of the law, to terminate a quarrel which the ordinary course of justice could with difficulty decide, Bacon was equally opposed to it, and thought that in no case should it be granted. He suggested that there should be declared a constant and settled resolution in the state to abolish it altogether; that care should be taken that the evil be no more cockered, nor the humour of it fed, but that all persons found guilty should be rigorously punished by the Star Chamber, and those of eminent quality banished from the court.

In the succeeding reign, when Donald Mackay, the first Lord Reay, accused David Ramsay of treason, in being concerned with the Marquis of Hamilton in a design upon the crown of Scotland, he was challenged by the latter to make good his assertion by single combat.[65] It had been at first the intention of the govern-ment to try the case by the common law, but Ramsay thought he would stand a better chance of escape by recurring to the old and almost exploded custom, but which was still the right of every man in appeals of treason. Lord Reay readily accepted the challenge, and both were confined in the Tower until they found security that they would appear on a certain day appointed by the court to determine the question. The management of the affair was delegated to the Marischal Court of Westminster, and the Earl of Lindsay was created Lord Constable of England for the purpose. Shortly before the day appointed, Ramsay confessed in substance all that Lord Reay had laid to his charge, upon which Charles I. put a stop to the proceedings.

But in England, about this period, sterner disputes arose among men than those mere individual matters which generate duels. The men of the Commonwealth encouraged no practice of the kind, and the subdued aristocracy carried their habits and prejudices elsewhere, and fought their duels at foreign courts. Cromwell's parliament, however — although the evil at that time was not so crying — published an order in 1654 for the prevention of duels, and the punishment of all concerned in them. Charles II., on his restoration, also issued a proclamation upon the subject. In his reign an infamous duel was fought — infamous not only from its own circumstances, but from the lenity that was shewn to the principal offenders.

The worthless Duke of Buckingham, having debauched the Countess of Shrewsbury, was challenged by her husband to mortal combat in January 1668. Charles II. endeavoured to prevent the duel, not from any regard to public morality, but from fear for the life of his favourite. He gave commands to the Duke of Albemarle to confine Buckingham to his house, or take some other measures to prevent him from fighting. Albemarle neglected the order, thinking that the king himself might prevent the combat by some surer means. The meeting took place at Barn Elms; the injured Shrewsbury being attended by Sir John Talbot, his relative, and Lord Bernard Howard, son of the Earl of Arundel. Buckingham was accompanied by two of his dependents, Captain Holmes and Sir John Jenkins. According to the barbarous custom of the age, not only the principals, but the seconds engaged each other. Jenkins was pierced to the heart, and left dead upon the field, and Sir John Talbot severely wounded in both arms. Buckingham himself escaping with slight wounds, ran his unfortunate antagonist through the body, and then left the field with the wretched woman, the cause of all the mischief, who, in the dress of a page, awaited the issue of the conflict in a neighbouring wood, holding her paramour's horse to avoid suspicion. Great influence was exerted to save the guilty parties from punishment, and the master, as base as the favourite, made little difficulty in granting a free pardon to all concerned. In a royal proclamation issued shortly afterwards, Charles II. formally pardoned the murderers, but declared his intention never to extend in future any mercy to such offenders. It would be hard, after this, to say who was the most infamous, the king, the favourite, or the courtesan.

In the reign of Queen Anne, repeated complaints were made of the prevalence of duelling. Addison, Swift, Steele, and other writers employed their powerful pens in reprobation of it. Steele especially, in the *Tatler* and *Guardian*, exposed its impiety and absurdity, and endeavoured both by argument and by ridicule to bring his countrymen to a right way of thinking.[66] His comedy of *The Conscious Lovers* contains an admirable exposure of the abuse of the word *honour*, which led men into an error so lamentable. Swift, writing upon the subject, remarked that he could see no harm in rogues and fools shooting each other. Addison and Steele took higher ground; and the latter, in the *Guardian*, summed up nearly all that could be said upon the subject in the following impressive words: — "A Christian and a gentleman are made inconsistent appellations of the same person. You are not to expect eternal life if you do not forgive injuries, and your mortal life is rendered uncomfortable if you are not ready to commit a murder in resentment of an affront; for good sense, as well as religion, is so utterly banished the world, that men glory in their very passions, and pursue trifles with the utmost vengeance, so little do they know that to forgive is the most arduous pitch human nature can arrive at. A coward has often fought, a coward has often conquered; but a coward never forgave." Steele also published a pamphlet, in which he gave a detailed account of the edict of Louis XIV., and the measures taken by that monarch to cure his subjects of their murderous folly.

On the 8th of May, 1711, Sir Cholmely Deering, M.P. for the county of Kent, was slain in a duel by Mr. Richard Thornhill, also a member of the House of Commons. Three days afterwards, Sir Peter King brought the subject under the notice of the legislature; and after dwelling at considerable length on the alarming increase of the practice, obtained leave to bring in a bill for the prevention and punishment of duelling. It was read a first time that day, and ordered for a second reading in the ensuing week. About the same time, the attention of the Upper House of Parliament was also drawn to the subject in the most painful manner. Two of its most noted members would have fought had it not been that Queen Anne received notice of their intention, and exacted a pledge that they would desist; while a few months afterwards two other of its members lost their lives in one of the most remarkable duels upon record. The first affair, which happily terminated without a meeting, was between the Duke of Marlborough and the Earl Pawlet; the latter and fatal encounter was between the Duke of Hamilton and Lord Mohun.

The first arose out of a debate in the Lords upon the conduct of the Duke of Ormond in refusing to hazard a general engagement with the enemy, in which Earl Pawlet remarked that nobody could doubt the courage of the Duke of Ormond. "He was not like a certain general, who led troops to the slaughter, to cause great numbers of officers to be knocked on the head in a battle, or against stone walls, in order to fill his pockets by disposing of their commissions." Every one felt that the remark was aimed at the Duke of Marlborough, but he remained silent, though evidently suffering in mind. Soon after the House broke up, the Earl Pawlet received a visit from Lord Mohun, who told him that the Duke of Marlborough was anxious to come to an explanation with him relative to some expressions he had made use of in that day's debate, and therefore prayed him to "go and take a little air in the country." Earl Pawlet did not affect to misunderstand the hint, but asked him in plain terms whether he brought a challenge from the duke. Lord Mohun said his message needed no explanation, and that he [Lord Mohun] would accompany the Duke of Marlborough. He then took his leave, and Earl Pawlet returned home and told his lady that he was going out to fight a duel with the Duke of Marlborough. His lady, alarmed for her lord's safety, gave notice of his intention to the Earl of Dartmouth, who immediately, in the queen's name, sent to the Duke of Marlborough, and commanded him not to stir abroad. He also caused Earl Pawlet's house to be guarded by two sentinels; and having taken these precautions, informed the queen of the whole affair. Her Majesty sent at once for the duke, expressed her abhorrence of the custom of duelling, and required his word of honour that he would proceed no further. The duke pledged his word accordingly, and the affair terminated.

The lamentable duel between the Duke of Hamilton and Lord Mohun took place in November 1712, and sprang from the following circumstances. A lawsuit had been pending for eleven years between these two noblemen, and they looked upon each other in consequence with a certain degree of coldness. They met together on the 13th of November in the chambers of Mr. Orlebar, a master in Chancery, when, in the course of conversation, the Duke of Hamilton reflected upon the conduct of one of the witnesses in the cause, saying that he was a person who had neither truth nor justice in him. Lord Mohun, somewhat nettled at this remark applied to a witness favourable to his side, made answer hastily, that Mr. Whiteworth, the person alluded to, had quite as much truth and justice in him as the Duke of Hamilton. The duke made no reply, and no one present imagined that he took offence at what was said; and when he went out of the room he made a low and courteous salute to the Lord Mohun. In the evening, General Macartney called twice upon the duke with a challenge from Lord Mohun, and failing in seeing him, sought him a third time at a tavern, where he found him, and delivered his message. The duke accepted the challenge, and the day after the morrow, which was Sunday, the 15th of November, at seven in the morning, was appointed for the meeting.

At that hour they assembled in Hyde Park, the duke being attended by his relative Colonel Hamilton, and the Lord Mohun by General Macartney. They jumped over a ditch into a place called the Nursery, and prepared for the combat. The Duke of

Hamilton, turning to General Macartney, said, "*Sir, you are the cause of this, let the event be what it will.*" Lord Mohun did not wish that the seconds should engage, but the duke insisted that "*Macartney should have a share in the dance.*" All being ready, the two principals took up their positions, and fought with swords so desperately, that after a short time they both fell down mortally wounded. The Lord Mohun expired upon the spot, and the Duke of Hamilton in the arms of his servants as they were carrying him to his coach.

This unhappy termination caused the greatest excitement not only in the metropolis, but all over the country. The Tories, grieved at the loss of the Duke of Hamilton, charged the fatal combat on the Whig party, whose leader, the Duke of Marlborough, had so recently set the example of political duels. They called Lord Mohun the bully of the Whig faction (he had already killed three men in duels, and been twice tried for murder), and asserted openly that the quarrel was concocted between him and General Macartney to rob the country of the services of the Duke of Hamilton by murdering him. It was also asserted that the wound of which the duke died was not inflicted by Lord Mohun, but by Macartney; and every means was used to propagate this belief. Colonel Hamilton, against whom and Macartney the coroner's jury had returned a verdict of wilful murder, surrendered a few days afterwards, and was examined before a privy council sitting at the house of Lord Dartmouth. He then deposed, that seeing Lord Mohun fall, and the duke upon him, he ran to the duke's assistance; and that he might with the more ease help him, he flung down both their swords, and as he was raising the duke up, *he saw Macartney make a push at him.* Upon this deposition, a royal proclamation was immediately issued, offering a reward of 500l. for the apprehension of Macartney, to which the Duchess of Hamilton afterwards added a reward of 300l.

Upon the further examination of Colonel Hamilton, it was found that reliance could not be placed on all his statements, and that he contradicted himself in several important particulars. He was arraigned at the old Bailey for the murder of Lord Mohun, the whole political circles of London being in a fever of excitement for the result. All the Tory party prayed for his acquittal, and a Tory mob surrounded the doors and all the avenues leading to the court of justice for many hours before the trial began. The examination of witnesses lasted seven hours. The criminal still persisted in accusing General Macartney of the murder of the Duke of Hamilton, but in other respects, say the newspapers of the day, prevaricated foully. He was found guilty of manslaughter. This favourable verdict was received with universal applause, "not only from the court and all the gentlemen present, but the common people shewed a mighty satisfaction, which they testified by loud and repeated huzzas."[67]

As the popular delirium subsided, and men began to reason coolly upon the subject, they disbelieved the assertions of Colonel Hamilton that Macartney had stabbed the duke, although it was universally admitted that he had been much too busy and presuming. Hamilton was shunned by all his former companions, and his life rendered so irksome to him, that he sold out of the Guards and retired to private life, in which he died heart-broken four years afterwards.

General Macartney surrendered about the same time, and was tried for murder in the Court of King's Bench. He was, however, found guilty of manslaughter only.

At the opening of the session of Parliament of 1713, the queen made pointed allusion in her speech to the frequency of duelling, and recommended to the legislature to devise some speedy and effectual remedy for it. A bill to that effect was brought forward, but thrown out on the second reading, to the very great regret of all the sensible portion of the community.

A famous duel was fought in 1765 between Lord Byron and Mr. Chaworth. The dispute arose at a club-dinner, and was relative to which of the two had the largest quantity of game on his estates. Infuriated by wine and passion, they retired instantly into an adjoining room, and fought with swords across a table, by the feeble glimmer of a tallow candle. Mr. Chaworth, who was the more expert swordsman of the two, received a mortal wound, and shortly afterwards expired. Lord Byron was brought to trial for the murder before the House of Lords; and it appearing clearly that the duel was not premeditated, but fought at once, and in the heat of passion, he was found guilty of manslaughter only, and ordered to be discharged upon payment of his fees. This was a very bad example for the country, and duelling of course fell into no disrepute after such a verdict.

In France more severity was exercised. In the year 1769, the Parliament of Grenoble took cognisance of the delinquency of the Sieur Duchelas, one of its members, who challenged and killed in a duel a captain of the Flemish legion. The servant of Duchelas officiated as second, and was arraigned with his master for the murder of the captain. They were both found guilty. Duchelas was broken alive on the wheel, and the servant condemned to the galleys for life.

A barbarous and fiercely-contested duel was fought in November 1778, between two foreign adventurers, at Bath, named Count Rice and the Vicomte du Barri. Some dispute arose relative to a gambling transaction, in the course of which Du Barri contradicted an assertion of the other, by saying "That is not true!" Count Rice immediately asked him if he knew the very disagreeable meaning of the words he had employed. Du Barri said he was perfectly well aware of their meaning, and that Rice might interpret them just as he pleased. A challenge was immediately given and accepted. Seconds were sent for, who, arriving with but little delay, the whole party, though it was not long after midnight, proceeded to a place called Claverton Down, where they remained with a surgeon until daylight. They then prepared for the encounter, each being armed with two pistols and a sword. The ground having been marked out by the seconds, Du Barri fired first, and wounded his opponent in the thigh. Count Rice then levelled his pistol, and shot Du Barri mortally in the breast. So angry were the combatants, that they refused to desist; both stepped back a few paces, and then rushing forward, discharged their second pistols at each other. Neither shot took effect, and both throwing away their pistols, prepared to finish the sanguinary struggle by the sword. They took their places, and were advancing towards each other, when the Vicomte du Barri suddenly staggered, grew pale, and, falling on the ground, exclaimed, "*Je vous demande ma vie.*" His opponent had but just time to answer, that he granted it, when the unfortunate Du Barri turned upon the grass, and expired with a heavy groan. The survivor of this savage conflict was then removed to his lodgings, where he lay for some weeks in a dangerous state. The coroner's jury, in the mean while, sat upon the body of Du Barri, and disgraced themselves by returning a verdict of manslaughter only. Count Rice, upon his recovery, was indicted for the murder notwithstanding this verdict. On his trial he entered into a long defence of his conduct, pleading the fairness of the duel, and its unpremeditated nature; and, at the same time, expressing his deep regret for the unfortunate death of Du Barri, with whom for many years he had been bound in ties of the strictest friendship. These considerations appear to have weighed with the jury, and this fierce duellist was again found guilty of manslaughter only, and escaped with a merely nominal punishment.

A duel, less remarkable from its circumstances, but more so from the rank of the parties, took place in 1789. The combatants on this occasion were the Duke of York and Colonel Lenox, the nephew and heir of the Duke of Richmond. The cause of offence was given by the Duke of York, who had said in presence of several officers of the Guards, that words had been used to Colonel Lenox at Daubigny's to which no gentleman ought to have submitted. Colonel Lenox went up to the duke on parade, and asked him publicly whether he had made such an assertion. The Duke of York, without answering his question, coldly ordered him to his post. When parade was over, he took an opportunity of saying publicly in the orderly-room before Colonel Lenox, that he desired no protection from his rank as a prince and his station as commanding officer; adding that, when he was off duty he wore a plain brown coat like a private gentleman, and was ready as such to give satisfaction. Colonel Lenox desired nothing better than satisfaction; that is to say, to run the chance of shooting the duke through the body, or being himself shot. He accordingly challenged his Royal Highness, and they met on Wimbledon Common. Colonel Lenox fired first, and the ball whizzed past the head of his opponent, so near to it as to graze his projecting curl. The duke refused to return the fire, and the seconds interfering, the affair terminated.

Colonel Lenox was very shortly afterwards engaged in another duel arising out of this. A Mr. Swift wrote a pamphlet in reference to the dispute between him and the Duke of York, at some expressions in which he took so much offence, as to imagine that nothing but a shot at the writer could atone for them. They met on the Uxbridge Road, but no damage was done to either party.

The Irish were for a long time renowned for their love of duelling. The slightest offence which it is possible to imagine that one man could offer to another was sufficient to provoke a challenge. Sir Jonah Barrington relates, in his *Memoirs*, that, previous to the Union, during the time of a disputed election in Dublin, it was no unusual thing for three-and-twenty duels to be fought in a day. Even in times of less excitement, they were so common as to be deemed unworthy of note by the regular chroniclers of events, except in cases where one or both of the combatants were killed. In those days, in Ireland, it was not only the man of the military, but of every profession, who had to work his way to eminence with the sword or the pistol. Each political party had its regular corps of bullies, or fire-eaters, as they were called, who qualified themselves for being the pests of society by spending all their spare time in firing at targets. They boasted that they could hit an opponent in any part of his body they pleased, and made up their minds before the encounter began whether they should kill him, disable, or disfigure him for life—lay him on a bed of suffering for a twelvemonth, or merely graze a limb.

The evil had reached an alarming height, when, in the year 1808, an opportunity was offered to King George III. of shewing in a striking manner his detestation of the practice, and of setting an example to the Irish that such murders were not to be committed with impunity. A dispute arose, in the month of June 1807, between Major Campbell and Captain Boyd, officers of the 21st regiment, stationed in Ireland, about the proper manner of giving the word of command on parade. Hot words ensued on this slight occasion, and the result was a challenge from Campbell to Boyd. They retired into the mess-room shortly afterwards, and each stationed himself at a corner, the distance obliquely being but seven paces. Here, without friends or seconds being present, they fired at each other, and Captain Boyd fell mortally wounded between the fourth and fifth ribs. A surgeon, who came in shortly, found him sitting in a chair, vomiting and suffering great agony. He was led into another room, Major Campbell following, in great distress and perturbation of mind. Boyd survived but eighteen hours, and just before his death, said, in reply to a question from his opponent, that the duel was not fair, and added, "You hurried me, Campbell – you're a bad man." – "Good God!" replied Campbell, "will you mention before these gentlemen, was not every thing fair? Did you not say that you were ready?" Boyd answered faintly, "Oh, no! you know I wanted you to wait and have friends." On being again asked whether all was fair, the dying man faintly murmured, "Yes:" but in a minute after, he said, "You're a bad man!" Campbell was now in great agitation, and ringing his hands convulsively, he exclaimed, "Oh, Boyd! you are the happiest man of the two! Do you forgive me?" Boyd replied, "I forgive you – I feel for you, as I know you do for me." He shortly afterwards expired, and Major Campbell made his escape from Ireland, and lived for some months with his family under an assumed name, in the neighbourhood of Chelsea. He was, however, apprehended, and brought to trial at Armagh, in August 1808. He said while in prison, that, if found guilty of murder, he should suffer as an example to duellists in Ireland; but he endeavoured to buoy himself up with the hope that the jury would only convict him of manslaughter. It was proved in evidence upon the trial, that the duel was not fought immediately after the offence was given, but that Major Campbell went home and drank tea with his family before he sought Boyd for the fatal encounter. The jury returned a verdict of wilful murder against him, but recommended him to mercy on the ground that the duel had been a fair one. He was condemned to die on the Monday following, but was afterwards respited for a few days longer. In the mean time the greatest exertions were made in his behalf. His unfortunate wife went upon her knees before the Prince of Wales, to move him to use his influence with the king in favour of her unhappy husband. Every thing a fond wife and a courageous woman could do she tried, to gain the royal clemency; but George III. was inflexible, in consequence of the representations of the Irish viceroy that an example was necessary. The law was therefore allowed to take its course, and the victim of a false spirit of honour died the death of a felon.

The most inveterate duellists of the present day are the students in the Universities of Germany. They fight on the most frivolous pretences, and settle with swords and pistols the schoolboy disputes which in other countries are arranged by the more harmless medium of the fisticuffs. It was at one time the custom among these savage youths to prefer the sword-combat, for the facility it gave them of cutting off the noses of their opponents. To disfigure them in this manner was an object of ambition, and the German duellists reckoned the number of these disgusting trophies which they had borne away, with as much satisfaction as a successful general the provinces he had reduced or the cities he had taken.

But it would be wearisome to enter into the minute detail of all the duels of modern times. If an examination were made into the general causes which produced them, it would be found that in every case they had been either of the most trivial or the most unworthy nature. Parliamentary duels were at one time very common, and amongst the names of those who have soiled a great reputation by conforming to the practice, may be mentioned those of Warren Hastings, Sir Philip Francis, Wilkes, Pitt, Fox, Grattan, Curran, Tierney, and Canning. So difficult is it even for the superior mind to free itself from the trammels with which foolish opinion has enswathed it—not one of these celebrated persons who did not in his secret soul condemn the folly to which he lent himself. The bonds of reason, though iron-strong, are easily burst through; but those of folly, though lithe and frail as the rushes by a stream, defy the stoutest heart to snap them asunder. Colonel Thomas, an officer in the Guards, who was killed in a duel, added the following clause to his will the night before he died: — "In the first place, I commit my soul to Almighty God, in hope of his mercy and pardon for the irreligious step I now (in compliance with the unwarrantable customs of this wicked world) put myself under the necessity of taking." How many have been in the same state of mind as this wise, foolish man! He knew his error, and abhorred it, but could not resist it for fear of the opinion of the prejudiced and unthinking. No other could have blamed him for refusing to fight a duel.

The list of duels that have sprung from the most degrading causes might be stretched out to an almost indefinite extent. Sterne's father fought a duel about a goose; and the great Raleigh about a tavern-bill.[68] Scores of duels (many of them fatal) have been fought from disputes at cards, or a place at a theatre; while hundreds of challenges, given and accepted over-night, in a fit of drunkenness, have been fought out the next morning to the death of one or both of the antagonists.

Two of the most notorious duels of modern times had their origin in causes no more worthy than the quarrel of a dog and the favour of a prostitute: that between Macnamara and Montgomery arising from the former; and that between Best and Lord Camelford from the latter. The dog of Montgomery attacked a dog belonging to Macnamara, and each master interfering in behalf of his own animal, high words ensued. The result was the giving and accepting a challenge to mortal combat. The parties met on the following day, when Montgomery was shot dead, and his antagonist severely wounded. The affair created a great sensation at the time, and Heaviside, the surgeon who attended at the fatal field to render his assistance if necessary, was arrested as an accessory to the murder, and committed to Newgate.

In the duel between Best and Lord Camelford, two pistols were used which were considered to be the best in England. One of them was thought slightly superior to the other, and it was agreed that the belligerents should toss up a piece of money to decide the choice of weapons. Best gained it, and at the first discharge, Lord Camelford fell mortally wounded. But little sympathy was expressed for his fate; he was a confirmed duellist, had been engaged in many meetings of the kind, and the blood of more than one fellow-creature lay at his door. As he had sowed, so did he reap; and the violent man met an appropriate death.

It now only remains to notice the means that have been taken to stay the prevalence of this madness of false honour in the various countries of the civilised world. The efforts of the governments of France and England have already been mentioned, and their want of success is but too well known. The same efforts have been attended with the same results elsewhere. In despotic countries, where the will of the monarch has been strongly expressed and vigorously supported, a diminution of the evil has for a time resulted, but only to be increased again, when death relaxed the iron grasp, and a successor appeared of less decided opinions on the subject. This was the case in Prussia, under the great Frederick, of whose aversion to duelling a popular anecdote is recorded. It is stated of him that he permitted duelling in his army, but only upon the condition that the combatants should fight in presence of a whole battalion of infantry, drawn up on purpose to see fair play. The latter received strict orders, when one of the belligerents fell, to shoot the other immediately. It is added, that the known determination of the king effectually put a stop to the practice.

The Emperor Joseph II. of Austria was as firm as Frederick, although the measures he adopted were not so singular. The following letter explains his views on the subject:

*"To General * * * * *

"My General,

"You will immediately arrest the Count of K. and Captain W. The count is young, passionate, and influenced by wrong notions of birth and a false spirit of honour. Captain W. is an old soldier, who will adjust every dispute with the sword and pistol, and who has received the challenge of the young count with unbecoming warmth.

"I will suffer no duelling in my army. I despise the principles of those who attempt to justify the practice, and who would run each other through the body in cold blood.

"When I have officers who bravely expose themselves to every danger in facing the enemy — who at all times exhibit courage, valour, and resolution in attack and defence, I esteem them highly. The coolness

with which they meet death on such occasions is serviceable to their country, and at the same time redounds to their own honour; but should there be men amongst them who are ready to sacrifice every thing to their vengeance and hatred, I despise them. I consider such a man as no better than a Roman gladiator.

"Order a court-martial to try the two officers. Investigate the subject of their dispute with that impartiality which I demand from every judge; and he that is guilty, let him be a sacrifice to his fate and the laws.

"Such a barbarous custom, which suits the age of the Tamerlanes and Bajazets, and which has often had such melancholy effects on single families, I will have suppressed and punished, even if it should deprive me of one half of my officers. There are still men who know how to unite the character of a hero with that of a good subject; and he only can be so who respects the laws.

"August, 1771. Joseph."[69]

In the United States of America the code varies considerably. In one or two of the still wild and simple states of the far West, where no duel has yet been fought, there is no specific law upon the subject beyond that in the Decalogue, which says, "Thou shalt do no murder;" but duelling every where follows the steps of modern civilisation; and by the time the backwoodsman is transformed into the citizen, he has imbibed the false notions of honour which are prevalent in Europe and around him, and is ready, like his progenitors, to settle his differences with the pistol. In the majority of the States the punishment for challenging, fighting, or acting as second, is solitary imprisonment and hard labour for any period less than a year, and disqualification for serving any public office for twenty years. In Vermont the punishment is total disqualification for office, deprivation of the rights of citizenship, and a fine; in fatal cases, the same punishment as that of murderers. In Rhode Island, the combatant, though death does not ensue, is liable to be carted to the gallows, with a rope about his neck, and to sit in this trim for an hour exposed to the peltings of the mob. He may be further imprisoned for a year, at the option of the magistrate. In Connecticut the punishment is total disqualification for office or employ, and a fine varying from one hundred to a thousand dollars. The laws of Illinois require certain officers of the state to make oath, previous to their instalment, that they have never been, nor ever will be, concerned in a duel.[70]

Amongst the edicts against duelling, promulgated at various times in Europe, may be mentioned that of Augustus King of Poland, in 1712, which decreed the punishment of death against principals and seconds, and minor punishments against the bearers of a challenge. An edict was also published at Munich, in 1773, according to which both principals and seconds, even in duels where no one was either killed or wounded, should be hanged, and their bodies buried at the foot of the gallows.

The king of Naples issued an ordinance against duelling in 1838, in which the punishment of death is decreed against all concerned in a fatal duel. The bodies of those killed, and of those who may be executed in consequence, are to be buried in unconsecrated ground, and without any religious ceremony; nor is any monument to be erected on the spot. The punishment for duels in which either, or both, are wounded, and for those in which no damage whatever is done, varies according to the case, and consists of fine, imprisonment, loss of rank and honours, and incapacity for filling any public situation. Bearers of challenges may also be punished with fine and imprisonment.

It might be imagined that enactments so severe all over the civilised world would finally eradicate a custom, the prevalence of which every wise and good man must deplore. But the frowns of the law never yet have taught, and never will teach, men to desist from this practice, as long as it is felt that the lawgiver sympathises with it in his heart. The stern judge upon the bench may say to the unfortunate wight who has been called a liar by some unmannerly opponent, "If you challenge him, you meditate murder, and are guilty of murder!" but the same judge, divested of his robes of state, and mixing in the world with other men, would say, "If you do not challenge him, if you do not run the risk of making yourself a murderer, you will be looked upon as a mean-spirited wretch, unfit to associate with your fellows, and deserving nothing but their scorn and their contempt!" It is society, and not the duellist, who is to blame. Female influence too, which is so powerful in leading men either to good or to evil, takes in this case the evil part. Mere animal bravery has, unfortunately, such charms in the female eye, that a successful duellist is but too often regarded as a sort of hero; and the man who refuses to fight, though of truer courage, is thought a poltroon, who may be trampled on. Mr. Graves, a member of the American legislature, who, early in 1838, killed a Mr. Cilley in a duel, truly and eloquently said, on the floor of the House of Representatives, when lamenting the unfortunate issue of that encounter, that society was more to blame than he was. "Public opinion," said the repentant orator, "is practically the paramount law of the land. Every other law, both human and divine, ceases to be observed; yea, withers and perishes in contact with it. It was this paramount law of this nation and of this House that forced me, under the penalty of dishonour, to subject myself to the code, which impelled me unwillingly into this tragical affair. Upon the heads of this nation, and at the doors of this House, rests the blood with which my unfortunate hands have been stained!"

As long as society is in this mood; as long as it thinks that the man who refuses to resent an insult, deserved that insult, and should be scouted accordingly; so long, it is to be feared, will duelling exist, however severe the laws may be. Men must have redress for injuries inflicted; and when those injuries are of such a nature that no tribunal will take cognisance of them, the injured will take the law into their own hands, and right themselves in the opinion of their fellows, at the hazard of their lives. Much as the sage may affect to despise the opinion of the world, there are few who would not rather expose their lives a hundred times than be condemned to live on, in society, but not of it — a byword of reproach to all who know their history, and a mark for scorn to point his finger at.

The only practicable means for diminishing the force of a custom which is the disgrace of civilisation, seems to be the establishment of a court of honour, which should take cognisance of all those delicate and almost intangible offences which yet wound so deeply. The court established by Louis XIV. might be taken as a model. No man now fights a duel when a fit apology has been offered; and it should be the duty of this court to weigh dispassionately the complaint of every man injured in his honour, either by word or deed, and to force the offender to make a public apology. If he refused the apology, he would be the breaker of a second law; an offender against a high court, as well as against the man he had injured, and might be punished with fine and imprisonment, the latter to last until he saw the error of his conduct, and made the concession which the court demanded.

If, after the establishment of this tribunal, men should be found of a nature so bloodthirsty as not to be satisfied with its peaceful decisions, and should resort to the old and barbarous mode of an appeal to the pistol, some means might be found of dealing with them. To hang them as murderers would be of no avail; for to such men death would have few terrors. Shame alone would bring them to reason. Transportation, the tread-wheel, or a public whipping, would perhaps be sufficient.

Chapter 8.

Relics.

> *A fouth o' auld knick-knackets,*
> *Rusty airn caps and jinglin' jackets,*
> *Wad hand the Lothians three, in tackets,*
> *A towmond guid;*
> *An' parritch pats, and auld saut backets,*
> *Afore the flood.*

> *- Burns.*

The love for relics is one which will never be eradicated as long as feeling and affection are denizens of the heart. It is a love which is most easily excited in the best and kindliest natures, and which few are callous enough to scoff at. Who would not treasure the lock of hair that once adorned the brow of the faithful wife now cold in death, or that hung down the neck of a beloved infant now sleeping under the sward? Not one! They are home-relics, whose sacred worth is intelligible to all: spoils rescued from the devouring grave, which to the affectionate are beyond all price. How dear to a forlorn survivor the book over whose pages he has pored with one departed! How much greater its value, if that hand, now cold, had written a thought, an opinion, or a name, upon the leaf! Besides these sweet domestic relics, there are others which no one can condemn: relics sanctified by that admiration of greatness and goodness which is akin to love; such as the copy of Montaigne's *Florio*, with the name of Shakspeare upon the leaf, written by the poet of all time himself; the chair preserved at Antwerp, in which Rubens sat when he painted the immortal Descent from the Cross; or the telescope, preserved in the Museum of Florence, which aided Galileo in his sublime discoveries. Who would not look with veneration upon the undoubted arrow of William Tell — the swords of Wallace or of Hampden — or the Bible whose leaves were turned by some stern old father of the faith?

Thus the principle of reliquism is hallowed and enshrined by love. But from this germ of purity how numerous the progeny of errors and superstitions! Men, in their admiration of the great, and of all that appertained to them, have forgotten that goodness is a component part of true greatness, and have made fools of themselves for the jawbone of a saint, the toe-nail of an apostle, the handkerchief a king blew his nose in, or the rope that hanged a criminal. Desiring to rescue some slight token from the graves of their predecessors, they have confounded the famous and the infamous, the renowned and the notorious. Great saints, great sinners; great philosophers, great quacks; great conquerors, great murderers; great ministers, great thieves; each and all have had their admirers, ready to ransack earth, from the equator to either pole, to find a relic of them.

The reliquism of modern times dates its origin from the centuries immediately preceding the Crusades. The first pilgrims to the Holy Land brought back to Europe thousands of apocryphal relics, in the purchase of which they had expended all their store. The greatest favourite was the wood of the true cross, which, like the oil of the widow, never diminished. It is generally asserted, in the traditions of the Romish Church, that the Empress Helen, the mother of Constantine the Great, first discovered the veritable "*true cross*" in her pilgrimage to Jerusalem. The Emperor Theodosius made a present of the greater part of it to St. Ambrose, Bishop of Milan, by whom it was studded with precious stones, and deposited in the principal church of that city. It was carried away by the Huns, by whom it was burnt, after they had extracted the valuable jewels it contained. Fragments, purporting to have been cut from it, were, in the eleventh and twelfth centuries, to be found in almost every church in Europe, and would, if collected together in one place, have been almost sufficient to have built a cathedral. Happy was the sinner who could get a sight of one of them; happier he who possessed one! To obtain them the greatest dangers were cheerfully braved. They were thought to preserve from all evils, and to cure the most inveterate diseases. Annual pilgrimages were made to the shrines that contained them, and considerable revenues collected from the devotees.

Next in renown were those precious relics, the tears of the Saviour. By whom and in what manner they were preserved, the pilgrims did not inquire. Their genuineness was vouched by the Christians of the Holy Land, and that was sufficient. Tears of the

Virgin Mary, and tears of St. Peter, were also to be had, carefully enclosed in little caskets, which the pious might wear in their bosoms. After the tears the next most precious relics were drops of the blood of Jesus and the martyrs, and the milk of the Virgin Mary. Hair and toe-nails were also in great repute, and were sold at extravagant prices. Thousands of pilgrims annually visited Palestine in the eleventh and twelfth centuries, to purchase pretended relics for the home market. The majority of them had no other means of subsistence than the profits thus obtained. Many a nail, cut from the filthy foot of some unscrupulous ecclesiastic, was sold at a diamond's price, within six months after its severance from its parent toe, upon the supposition that it had once belonged to a saint or an apostle. Peter's toes were uncommonly prolific, for there were nails enough in Europe, at the time of the Council of Clermont, to have filled a sack, all of which were devoutly believed to have grown on the sacred feet of that great apostle. Some of them are still shewn in the cathedral of Aix-la-Chapelle. The pious come from a distance of a hundred German miles to feast their eyes upon them.

At Port Royal, in Paris, is kept with great care a thorn, which the priests of that seminary assert to be one of the identical thorns that bound the holy head of the Son of God. How it came there, and by whom it was preserved, has never been explained. This is the famous thorn, celebrated in the long dissensions of the Jansenists and the Molenists, and which worked the miraculous cure upon Mademoiselle Perrier: by merely kissing it she was cured of a disease of the eyes of long standing.[71]

What traveller is unacquainted with the Santa Scala, or Holy Stairs, at Rome? They were brought from Jerusalem along with the true cross, by the Empress Helen, and were taken from the house which, according to popular tradition, was inhabited by Pontius Pilate. They are said to be the steps which Jesus ascended and descended when brought into the presence of the Roman governor. They are held in the greatest veneration at Rome: it is sacrilegious to walk upon them. The knees of the faithful must alone touch them in ascending or descending, and that only after the pilgrims have reverentially kissed them.

Europe still swarms with these religious relics. There is hardly a Roman Catholic church in Spain, Portugal, Italy, France, or Belgium, without one or more of them. Even the poorly endowed churches of the villages boast the possession of miraculous thigh-bones of the innumerable saints of the Romish calendar. Aix-la-Chapelle is proud of the veritable *châsse*, or thigh-bone of Charlemagne, which cures lameness. Halle has a thigh-bone of the Virgin Mary; Spain has seven or eight, all said to be undoubted relics. Brussels at one time preserved, and perhaps does now, the teeth of St. Gudule. The faithful, who suffered from the toothache, had only to pray, look at them, and be cured. Some of these holy bones have been buried in different parts of the Continent. After a certain lapse of time, water is said to ooze from them, which soon forms a spring, and cures all the diseases of the faithful.

It is curious to remark the avidity manifested in all ages, and in all countries, to obtain possession of some relic of any persons who have been much spoken of, even for their crimes. When William Longbeard, leader of the populace of London in the reign of Richard I., was hanged at Smithfield, the utmost eagerness was shewn to obtain a hair from his head, or a shred from his garments. Women came from Essex, Kent, Suffolk, Sussex, and all the surrounding counties, to collect the mould at the foot of his gallows. A hair of his beard was believed to preserve from evil spirits, and a piece of his clothes from aches and pains.

In more modern days, a similar avidity was shewn to obtain a relic of the luckless Masaniello, the fisherman of Naples. After he had been raised by mob favour to a height of power more despotic than monarch ever wielded, he was shot by the same populace in the streets, as if he had been a mad dog. His headless trunk was dragged through the mire for several hours, and cast at night-fall into the city ditch. On the morrow the tide of popular feeling turned once more in his favour. His corpse was sought, arrayed in royal robes, and buried magnificently by torch-light in the cathedral, ten thousand armed men, and as many mourners, attending at the ceremony. The fisherman's dress which he had worn was rent into shreds by the crowd, to be preserved as relics; the door of his hut was pulled off its hinges by a mob of women, and eagerly cut up into small pieces, to be made into images, caskets, and other mementos. The scanty furniture of his poor abode became of more value than the adornments of a palace; the ground he had walked upon was considered sacred, and, being collected in small phials, was sold at its weight in gold, and worn in the bosom as an amulet.

Almost as extraordinary was the frenzy manifested by the populace of Paris on the execution of the atrocious Marchioness de Brinvilliers. There were grounds for the popular wonder in the case of Masaniello, who was unstained with personal crimes. But the career of Madame de Brinvilliers was of a nature to excite no other feelings than disgust and abhorrence. She was convicted of poisoning several persons, and sentenced to be burned in the Place de Grève, and to have her ashes scattered to the winds. On the day of her execution, the populace, struck by her gracefulness and beauty, inveighed against the severity of her sentence. Their pity soon increased to admiration, and, ere evening, she was considered a saint. Her ashes were industriously collected; even the charred wood, which had aided to consume her, was eagerly purchased by the populace. Her ashes were thought to preserve from witchcraft.

In England many persons have a singular love for the relics of thieves and murderers, or other great criminals. The ropes with which they have been hanged are very often bought by collectors at a guinea per foot. Great sums were paid for the rope which hanged Dr. Dodd, and for those more recently which did justice upon Mr. Fauntleroy for forgery, and on Thurtell for the murder of Mr. Weare. The murder of Maria Marten, by Corder, in the year 1828, excited the greatest interest all over the country. People came from Wales and Scotland, and even from Ireland, to visit the barn where the body of the murdered woman was buried. Every one of them was anxious to carry away some memorial of his visit. Pieces of the barn-door, tiles from the roof, and, above all, the clothes of the poor victim, were eagerly sought after. A lock of her hair was sold for two guineas, and the purchaser thought himself fortunate in getting it so cheaply.

So great was the concourse of people to visit the house in Camberwell Lane, where Greenacre murdered Hannah Brown, in 1837, that it was found necessary to station a strong detachment of police on the spot. The crowd was so eager to obtain a relic of the house of this atrocious criminal, that the police were obliged to employ force to prevent the tables and chairs, and even the doors, from being carried away.

In earlier times, a singular superstition was attached to the hand of a criminal who had suffered execution. It was thought that by merely rubbing the dead hand on the body, the patient afflicted with the king's evil would be instantly cured. The executioner at Newgate formerly derived no inconsiderable revenue from this foolish practice. The possession of the hand was thought to be of still greater efficacy in the cure of diseases and the prevention of misfortunes. In the time of Charles II., as much as ten guineas was thought a small price for one of these disgusting relics.

When the maniac, Thom, or Courtenay, was shot, in the spring of 1838, the relic-hunters were immediately in motion to obtain a memento of so extraordinary an individual. His long black beard and hair, which were cut off by the surgeons, fell into the hands of his disciples, by whom they were treasured with the utmost reverence. A lock of his hair commanded a great price, not only amongst his followers, but among the more wealthy inhabitants of Canterbury and its neighbourhood. The tree against which he fell when he was shot, was stripped of all its bark by the curious; while a letter, with his signature to it, was paid for in gold coins; and his favourite horse became as celebrated as its master. Parties of ladies and gentlemen went to Boughton from a distance of a hundred and fifty miles, to visit the scene of that fatal affray, and stroke on the back the horse of the "mad knight of Malta." If a strict watch had not been kept over his grave for months, the body would have been disinterred, and the bones carried away as memorials.

Among the Chinese no relics are more valued than the *boots* which have been worn by an upright magistrate. In Davis's interesting description of the empire of China, we are informed, that whenever a judge of unusual integrity resigns his situation, the people all congregate to do him honour. If he leaves the city where he has presided, the crowd accompany him from his residence to the gates, where his boots are drawn off with great ceremony, to be preserved in the hall of justice. Their place is immediately supplied by a new pair, which, in their turn, are drawn off to make room for others before he has worn them five minutes, it being considered sufficient to consecrate them that he should have merely drawn them on.

Among the most favourite relics of modern times, in Europe, are Shakspeare's mulberry-tree, Napoleon's willow, and the table at Waterloo on which the emperor wrote his despatches. Snuff-boxes of Shakspeare's mulberry-tree are comparatively rare, though there are doubtless more of them in the market than were ever made of the wood planted by the great bard. Many a piece of alien wood passes under this name. The same may be said of Napoleon's table at Waterloo. The original has long since been destroyed, and a round dozen of counterfeits along with it. Many preserve the simple stick of wood; others have them cut into brooches and every variety of ornament; but by far the greater number prefer them as snuff-boxes. In France they are made into *bonbonnières*, and are much esteemed by the many thousands whose cheeks still glow and whose eyes still sparkle at the name of Napoleon.

Bullets from the field of Waterloo, and buttons from the coats of the soldiers who fell in the fight, are still favourite relics in Europe. But the same ingenuity which found new tables after the old one was destroyed, has cast new bullets for the curious. Many a one who thinks himself the possessor of a bullet which aided in giving peace to the world on that memorable day, is the owner of a dump, first extracted from the ore a dozen years afterwards. Let all lovers of genuine relics look well to their money before they part with it to the ciceroni that swarm in the village of Waterloo!

Few travellers stopped at the lonely isle of St. Helena without cutting a twig from the willow that drooped over the grave of Napoleon, prior to the removal of the body by the government of Louis Philippe. Many of them have since been planted in different parts of Europe, and have grown into trees as large as their parent. Relic-hunters, who are unable to procure a twig of the original, are content with one from these. Several of them are growing in the neighbourhood of London.

But in relics, as in every thing else, there is the use and the abuse. The undoubted relics of great men, or great events, will always possess attractions for the thinking and refined. There are few who would not join with Cowley in the extravagant wish introduced in his lines "written while sitting in a chair made of the remains of the ship in which Sir Francis Drake sailed round the world:

> *And I myself, who now love quiet too,*
> *Almost as much, as any chair can do,*
> *Would yet a journey take*
> *An old wheel of that chariot to see,*
> *Which Phaeton so rashly brake.*

Footnotes.

1. Guibert de Nogent.

2. Guibert de Nogent.

3. Guibert de Nogent.

4. M. Wilken's *Geschichte der Kreuzzüge*.

5. Wilken.

6. Fulcher of Chartres; Guibert de Nogent; Vital.

7. William of Tyre; Mills; Wilken, &c.

8. Vide William of Tyre.

9. Guibert de Nogent relates a curious instance of the imitativeness of these juvenile Crusaders. He says that, during the siege of Antioch, the Christian and Saracen boys used to issue forth every evening from the town and camp in great numbers, under the command of captains chosen from among themselves. Armed with sticks instead of swords, and stones instead of arrows, they ranged themselves in battle order, and, shouting each the war-cry of their country, fought with the utmost desperation. Some of them lost their eyes, and many became cripples for life from the injuries they received on these occasions.

10. The sacking of Vitry reflects indelible disgrace upon Louis VII. His predecessors had been long engaged in resistance to the outrageous powers assumed by the Popes, and Louis continued the same policy. The ecclesiastical chapter of Bourges, having elected an archbishop without his consent, he proclaimed the election to be invalid, and took severe and prompt measures against the refractory clergy. Thibault count de Champagne took up arms in defence of the Papal authority, and entrenched himself in the town of Vitry. Louis immediately took the field to chastise the rebel, and he besieged the town with so much vigour that the count was forced to surrender. Upwards of thirteen hundred of the inhabitants, fully one half of whom were women and children, took refuge in the church; and, when the gates of the city were opened, and all resistance had ceased, Louis inhumanly gave orders to set fire to the sacred edifice, and a thousand persons perished in the flames.

11. Philip, Archdeacon of the cathedral of Liege, wrote a detailed account of all the miracles performed by St. Bernard during thirty-four days of his mission. They averaged about ten per day. The disciples of St. Bernard complained bitterly that the people flocked around their master in such numbers, that they could not see half the miracles he performed. But they willingly trusted the eyes of others, as far as faith in the miracles went, and seemed to vie with each other whose credulity should be greatest.

12. James of Vitry; William de Nangis.

13. The desire of comparing two great men has tempted many writers to drown Frederick in the river Cydnus, in which Alexander so imprudently bathed (Q. Curt. lib. iii. c. 4, 5); but, from the march of the emperor, I rather judge that his Saleph is the Calycadnus, a stream of less fame, but of a longer course. — *Gibbon.*

14. Stowe.

15. *Elémens de l'Histoire de France*

16. Strutt's *Sports and Pastimes.*

17. Richard left a high reputation in Palestine. So much terror did his name occasion, that the women of Syria used it to frighten their children for ages afterwards. Every disobedient child became still when told that King Richard was coming. Even men shared the panic that his name created; and a hundred years afterwards, whenever a horse shied at any object in the way, his rider would exclaim, "What! dost thou think King Richard is in the bush?"

18. The following is a list of some of the works of art thus destroyed, from Nicetas, a contemporary Greek author: 1st. A colossal Juno, from the forum of Constantine, the head of which was so large that four horses could scarcely draw it from the place where it stood to the palace. 2d. The statue of Paris, presenting the apple to Venus. 3d. An immense bronze pyramid, crowned by a female figure, which turned with the wind. 4th. The colossal statue of Bellerophon, in bronze, which was broken down and cast into the furnace. Under the inner nail of the horse's hind foot on the left side, was found a seal wrapped in a woollen cloth. 5th. A figure of Hercules, by Lysimachus, of such vast dimensions that the thumb was equal in circumference to the waist of a man. 6th. The Ass and his Driver, cast by order of Augustus after the battle of Actium, in commemoration of his having discovered the position of Anthony through the means of an assdriver. 7th. The Wolf suckling the Twins of Rome. 8th. The gladiator in combat with a lion. 9th. The Hippopotamus. 10th. The Sphinxes. 11th. An Eagle fighting with a Serpent. 12th. A beautiful statue of Helen. 13th. A group, with a monster somewhat resembling a bull, engaged in deadly conflict with a serpent; and many other works of art, too numerous to mention.

19. See Jacob de Voragine and Albericus.

20. *Elémens de l'Histoire de France.*

21. Mills, in his history, gives the name of this chief as "Al Malek al Dhaker Rok neddin Abulfeth Bibars al Ali al Bundokdari al Salehi."

22. The reader will recognise the incident which Sir Walter Scott has introduced into his beautiful romance, *The Talisman*, and which, with the license claimed by poets and romancers, he represents as having befallen King Richard I.

23. See article on "Demonology" in the sixth volume of the *Foreign Quarterly Review*.

24. *Histoire de la Magie en France*. Rois de la seconde race, p. 29.

25. M. Michaud, in his *History of the Crusades*, M. Guinguené, in his *Literary History of Italy*, and some other critics, have objected to Tasso's poem, that he has attributed to the Crusaders a belief in magic, which did not exist at that time. If these critics had referred to the edicts of Charlemagne, they would have seen that Tasso was right, and that a disposition too eager to spy out imperfections in a great work was leading themselves into error.

26. *Entstehungsgeschichte der freistädlischen Bünde im Mittelalter*, von Dr. F. Kortüm. 1827.

27. Bodin, p. 95 Garinet, p. 125; *Anti-demon de Serclier*, p. 346.

28. Tablier. See also Boguet, *Discours sur les Sorciers*; and M. Jules Garinet, *Histoire de la Magie*, p. 150.

29. *Foreign Quarterly Review*, vol. vi. p. 41.

30. *News from Scotland, declaring the Damnable Life of Dr. Fian.*

31. *Satan's Invisible World Discovered*, by the Rev. G. Sinclair.

32. This illustration, representing Matthew Hopkins examining two witches, who are confessing to him the names of their imps and familiars, is copied from Caulfield's *Memoirs of Remarkable Persons*, 1794, where it is taken from an extremely rare print.

33. Pitcairn's *Records of Justiciary*.

34. Preface to *Law's Memorials*, edited by Sharpe.

35. *Zauberbibliothek*, Thiel 5.

36. They sent a hangman's assistant down to her in her prison; they clothed him properly in a bear's skin, as if he were the devil. Him, when the witch saw, she thought he was her familiar. She said to him quickly, "Why hast thou left me so long in the magistrate's hands? Help me out of their power, as thou hast promised, and I will be thine alone. Help me from this anguish, O thou dearest devil [or lover] mine!"

37. A very graphic account of the execution of this unfortunate gentleman is to be found in the excellent romance of M. Alfred de Vigny, entitled *Cinq Mars*; but if the reader wishes for a full and accurate detail of all the circumstances of one of the most extraordinary trials upon record, he is referred to a work published anonymously, at Amsterdam, in 1693, entitled *Histoire des Diables de Loudun, ou de la Possession des Religieuses Ursulines, et de la Condemnation et du Supplice d'Urbain Grandier*.

38. The punishment for the contumacious was expressed by the words *onere, frigore, et fame*. By the first was meant, that the culprit should be extended on his back on the ground, and weights placed over his body, gradually increased, until he expired. Sometimes the punishment was not extended to this length, and the victim being allowed to recover, underwent the second portion, the *frigore*, which consisted in his standing naked in the open air, for a certain space, in the sight of all the people. The third, or *fame*, was more dreadful, the statute saying, "That he was to be preserved with the coarsest bread that could be got, and water out of the next sink, or puddle, to the place of execution; and that day he had water he should have no bread, and that day he had bread he should have no water;" and in this torment he was to linger as long as nature would hold out.

39. This is denied by Voltaire in his *Age of Louis XIV.*; but he does not state for what reason. His words are, "Il est faux qu'elle eut essayé ses poisons dans les hôpitaux, comme le disait le peuple, et comme il est écrit dans les *Causes Célèbres*, ouvrage d'un avocat sans cause et fait pour le peuple."

40. Slow poisoning is a crime which has unhappily been revived in England within the last few years, and which has been carried to an extent sufficient to cast a stain upon the national character. The poisoners have been principally women of the lowest class, and their victims have been their husbands or their children. The motive for the crime has in most instances been the basest that can be imagined, — the desire to obtain from burial-clubs to which they subscribed, the premium, or burial-money. A recent enactment, restricting the sale of arsenic and other poisons, will, it is to be hoped, check, if it do not extirpate this abominable crime. — 1851.

41. Garinet, *Histoire de la Magie en France*, p. 75.

42. Ibid. p. 156.

43. Dr. H. More's *Continuation of Glanvil's Collection of Relations in proof of Witchcraft*.

44. The woman whose ghost was said to manifest itself in Cock Lane was buried in the crypt or cloister of St. John, Clerkenwell. The vault is composed of two aisles, that on the south being much narrower than the other, — it was here she was deposited.

About seven years since, I was sketching a picturesque trefoil-headed door leading into this part of the vault; and the place being at that time in great confusion with coffins, remains of bodies, some of which were dried like mummies, &c., I could find no better seat than one of the coffins. The sexton's boy, who held my light, informed me this was the coffin of *Scratching Fanny*, which recalled the Cock Lane story to my mind. I got off the lid of the coffin, and saw the face of a handsome woman, with an aquiline nose; this feature remaining perfect, an uncommon case, for the cartilage mostly gives way. The remains had become adipocere, and were perfectly preserved. She was said to have been poisoned by deleterious punch, but this was legally disproved; and, if I remember rightly, she was otherwise declared to have died of small-pox; of this disease there was not the least sign; but as some mineral poisons tend to render bodies adipocere, here was some evidence in support of the former allegation. I made particular inquiries at the time of Mr. Bird, churchwarden, a respectable and judicious man; and he gave me good assurance that this coffin had always been looked upon as the one containing the Cock Lane woman. Since that time the vault has been set in order, and the above-mentioned coffin, with others, put away. The niche near the window in the drawing of the Ghost Room is the place where the bed-head was, and where the scratching, knocks, &c. were heard. This is the tradition of the house. Mrs. King, who holds the premises, informs me that her family has had the house about eighty years. —J. W. Archer.

45. Shakspeare's *Rape of Lucretia*.

46. The Abbé, in the second volume, in the letter No. 79, addressed to Monsieur de Buffon, gives the following curious particulars of the robbers of 1737, which are not without interest at this day, if it were only to shew the vast improvement which has taken place since that period. "It is usual in travelling to put ten or a dozen guineas in a separate pocket, as a tribute to the first that comes to demand them the right of passport, which custom has established here in favour of the robbers, who are almost the only highway surveyors in England, has made this necessary; and accordingly the English call these fellows the 'Gentlemen of the Road,' the government letting them exercise their jurisdiction upon travellers without giving them any great molestation. To say the truth, they content themselves with only taking the money of those who obey without disputing; but notwithstanding their boasted humanity, the lives of those who endeavour to get away are not always safe. They are very strict and severe in levying their impost; and if a man has not wherewithal to pay them, he may run the chance of getting himself knocked on the head for his poverty. *"About fifteen years ago, these robbers, with the view of maintaining their rights, fixed up papers at the doors of rich people about London, expressly forbidding all persons, of whatsoever quality or condition, from going out of town without ten guineas and a watch about them, on pain of death. In bad times, when there is little or nothing to be got on the roads, these fellows assemble in gangs, to raise contributions even in London itself, and the watchmen seldom trouble themselves to interfere with them in their vocation."*

47. Since the publication of the first edition of this volume, Jack Sheppard's adventures have been revived. A novel upon the real or fabulous history of the burglar has afforded, by its extraordinary popularity, a further exemplification of the allegations in the text. The *Sixth Report of the Inspector of Prisons for the Northern Districts of England* contains a mass of information upon the pernicious effect of such romances, and of the dramas founded upon them. The Inspector examined several boys attending the prison school in the New Bailey at Manchester, from whose evidence the following passages bearing upon the subject are extracted:

"J. L. (aged 14). The first time I was ever at the theatre was to see *Jack Sheppard*. There were two or three boys near to the house who were going, and they asked me. I took sixpence from the money I used to lay up weekly for clothes. The next time I went, which was the week after, I borrowed the money from a boy; I returned it to him the Saturday after. I then went many times. I took the money from my mother out of her pocket as she was sitting down, and I beside her. There was more than sixpence in her pocket. I got a great love for the theatre, and stole from people often to get there. *I thought this Jack Sheppard was a clever fellow* for making his escape and robbing his master. *If I could get out of gaol, I think I should be as clever as him*: but, after all his exploits, he got done at last. I have had the book out of a library at Dole Field. I had paid two-pence a book for three volumes. I also got *Richard Turpin*, in two volumes, and paid the same. I have seen *Oliver Twist*, and think the Artful Dodger is very like some of the boys here. I am here for picking a pocket of 25l.

"H. C. (aged 15). When we came to Manchester, I went to the play, and saw *Jack Sheppard* the first night it came out. There were pictures of him about the streets on boards and on the walls; one of them was his picking a pocket in the church. I liked *Jack Sheppard* much. I had not been in prison there. I was employed in a warehouse at 6s. 6d. a-week, and was allowed 6d. out of it for myself, and with that I went regularly to the play. I saw *Jack Sheppard* afterwards four times in one week. I got the money out of my money-bag by stealth, and without my master's knowledge. I once borrowed 10s. in my mother's name from Mrs. — —, a shopkeeper, with whom she used to deal; I went to the play with it.

"J. M'D. (aged 15). I have heard of *Jack Sheppard*: a lad whom I know told me of it, who had seen it, and said it was *rare fun* to see him break out of prison.

"J. L. (aged 11). Has been to the play twice, and seen *Jack Sheppard*. Went with his brother the first time, and by himself the second. I took the money to go a second time out of mother's house, off the chimney-piece, where she had left a sixpence. It was the first night *Jack Sheppard* was played. There was great talk about it, and there were nice pictures about it all over the walls. I thought him a very clever fellow; but Blueskin made the most fun. I first went to the markets, and begun by stealing apples. I also knew a lad, — —, who has been transported, and went with him two or three times. The most I ever got was 10s. out of a till."

The Inspector's *Report on Juvenile Delinquency at Liverpool* contains much matter of the same kind; but sufficient has been already quoted to shew the injurious effects of the deification of great thieves by thoughtless novelists.

48. For a full account of this noted robber, and indeed of European thieves and banditti in general, see the very amusing work upon the subject by Mr. Charles Macfarlane.

49. See also *Foreign Quarterly Review*, vol. iv. p. 398.

50. Lavinia Fenton, afterwards Duchess of Bolton.

51. *Esprit des Loix*, liv. xxviii. chap. xvii.

52. Very similar to this is the fire-ordeal of the modern Hindoos, which is thus described in Forbes's *Oriental Memoirs*, vol. i. c. xi.: — "When a man, accused of a capital crime, chooses to undergo the ordeal trial, he is closely confined for several days; his right hand and arm are covered with thick wax-cloth, tied up and sealed, in the presence of proper officers, to prevent deceit. In the English districts the covering was always sealed with the Company's arms, and the prisoner placed under an European guard. At the time fixed for the ordeal, a caldron of oil is placed over a fire; when it boils, a piece of money is dropped into the vessel; the prisoner's arm is unsealed and washed in the presence of his judges and accusers. During this part of the ceremony the attendant Brahmins supplicate the Deity. On receiving their benediction, the accused plunges his hand into the boiling fluid, and takes out the coin. The arm is afterwards again sealed up until the time appointed for a re-examination. The seal is then broken; if no blemish appears, the prisoner is declared innocent; if the contrary, he suffers the punishment due to his crime."… On this trial the accused thus addresses the element before plunging his hand into the boiling oil: — "Thou, O fire! pervadest all things. O cause of purity! who givest evidence of virtue and of sin, declare the truth in this my hand!" If no juggling were practised, the decisions by this ordeal would be all the same way; but as some are by this means declared guilty, and others innocent, it is clear that the Brahmins, like the Christian priests of the middle ages, practise some deception in saving those whom they wish to be thought guiltless.

53. An ordeal very like this is still practised in India. Consecrated rice is the article chosen, instead of bread and cheese. Instances are not rare in which, through the force of imagination, guilty persons are not able to swallow a single grain. Conscious of their crime, and fearful of the punishment of Heaven, they feel a suffocating sensation in their throat when they attempt it, and they fall on their knees, and confess all that is laid to their charge. The same thing, no doubt, would have happened with the bread and cheese of the Roman Church, if it had been applied to any others but ecclesiastics. The latter had too much wisdom to be caught in a trap of their own setting.

54. *Histoire de Messire Bertrand du Guesclin*, par Paul Hay du Chastelet, liv. i. ch. xix.

55. *Esprit des Loix*, liv. xxviii. ch. xxv.

56. *Mémoires de Brantôme touchant les Duels.*

57. *Histoire de Messire Bertrand du Guesclin*, liv. i. ch. xix.

58. *Mémoires de Brantôme touchant les Duels.*

59. Although Francis shewed himself in this case an enemy to duelling, yet in his own case he had not the same objection. Every reader of history must remember his answer to the challenge of the Emperor Charles V. The Emperor wrote that he had failed in his word, and that he would sustain their quarrel single-handed against him. Francis replied, that he lied — *qu'il en avait menti par la gorge,* and that he was ready to meet him in single combat whenever and wherever he pleased.

60. *Le Père Matthias*, tome ii. livre iv.

61. *Elémens de l'Histoire de France*, vol. iii. p. 219.

62. *Mercure de France*, vol. xiii.

63. Brydone's *Tour in Malta*, 1772.

64. See *Life and Character of Lord Bacon*, by Thomas Martin, Barrister-at-Law.

65. See *History of the House and Clan of Mackay*.

66. See *Spectator*, Nos. 84, 97, and 99; and *Tatler*, Nos. 25, 26, 29, 31, 38, and 39; and *Guardian*, No. 20.

67. *Post-Boy*, December 13th, 1712.

68. Raleigh at one period of his life appeared to be an inveterate duellist, and it was said of him that he had been engaged in more encounters of the kind than any man of note among his contemporaries. More than one fellow-creature he had deprived of life; but he lived long enough to be convinced of the sinfulness of his conduct, and made a solemn vow never to fight another duel. The following anecdote of his forbearance is well known, but it will bear repetition:
A dispute arose in a coffee-house between him and a young man on some trivial point, and the latter, losing his temper, impertinently spat in the face of the veteran. Sir Walter, instead of running him through the body, as many would have done, or challenging him to mortal combat, coolly took out his handkerchief, wiped his face, and said, "Young man, if I could as easily wipe from my conscience the stain of killing you, as I can this spittle from my face, you should not live another minute." The young man immediately begged his pardon.

69. Vide the Letters of Joseph II. to distinguished Princes and Statesmen, published for the first time in England in *The Pamphleteer* for 1821. They were originally published in Germany a few years previously, and throw a great light upon the character of that monarch and the events of his reign.

70. *Encyclopedia Americana*, art. Duelling.

71. Voltaire, *Siècle de Louis XIV.*

END OF VOL. II.